W9-BMN-957

INTO
THE HEART OF
JERUSALEM

A TRAVELER'S GUIDE TO
VISITS, CELEBRATIONS,
AND SOJOURNS

Arlynn Nellhaus

John Muir Publications
Santa Fe, New Mexico

John Muir Publications, P.O. Box 613, Santa Fe, New Mexico 87504

Printed in the United States of America
First printing April 1999.

Library of Congress Cataloging in Publication Data

Nellhaus, Arlynn
  Into the heart of Jerusalem : a traveler's guide to visits, celebrations, and
sojourns / by Arlynn Nellhaus.
        p. cm.
  Rev. ed. of: The heart of Jerusalem / by Arlynn Nellhaus. ©1988.
  Includes index.
  ISBN 1-56261-425-8
  1. Jerusalem—Guidebooks. I. Nellhaus, Arlynn. Heart of Jerusalem. II. Title.
DS109. 15.N45 1999
915.694'4204'54—dc21   94-43086
                                                      CIP

Portions of this book were previously published in Heart of Jerusalem,
copyright © 1988 by Arlynn Nellhaus

Editors: Peg Goldstein, Nancy Gillan
Production: Marie J.T. Vigil
Design: Marie J.T. Vigil
Cover design: Rebecca Cook
Maps style development: Laura Perfetti
Maps illustration: Kathleen Sparkes, White Hart Design
Typesetter: Diane Rigoli
Printer: Publishers Press
Front cover: Leo de Wys Inc./D&J Heaton;
              Via Dolorosa, Condemnation Chapel
Back cover: *small*—Leo de Wys Inc./Steve Vidler; bar mitzvah boy
              large—Leo de Wys Inc./D&J Heaton; Old City skyline
Interior photos by Arlynn Nellhaus, except where noted.

Distributed to the book trade by
Publishers Group West
Berkeley, California

Thanks to Shulie Haberfield Mishkin, David Keren, and David Eisenstad, guides par excellence; Uri Ashkenazi, Egged's spokesman; Rabbi Pesach Schindler of Beit Knesset Moreshet Yisrael; Benyamim Tsadaka, Samaritan historian; Shoshana Ben-Dor of the North American Conference on Ethiopian Jewry; Moshe Sharon, professor of the interrelation of religions, Hebrew University; Deborah Millgrim, education authority; Rabbi Jay Karzen; Jerry Barach of Hebrew University's public relations department, Anne Gasner, mystery writer and friend, and especially Nitsan Ilan of the Government Tourist Office, who always came through for me cheerfully and promptly.

Contents

Preface

My adoration of Jerusalem didn't spring from love at first sight. I had visited the city during two trips to Israel. The first was an international convention of women journalists. We spent the first week in Jerusalem. Our hosts made sure we saw the city. I also explored on my own. Five years later, I was in and out of the city to join a group climb of Mount Sinai. On both visits, Jerusalem left me feeling uneasy. A tidal wave of impressions overwhelmed my senses. I couldn't absorb the colorful sights, the cacophony, and the often pungent odors. My mind focused on the city's ugly side: its decrepit buildings, its beggars, its littered sidewalks. I felt more at home in trendy Tel Aviv and sedate Haifa.

Still, when I first saw the Western Wall, that holiest of Jewish places, my emotions surprised me. I felt an unexpected link to that place and to my people. Seeing the wall, I saw four thousand years of Jewish history— my history. At the wall, I knew the thrill of being part of the chain of "stiff-necked people" who say yes to life, no matter what.

Another five years passed. I was granted a leave of absence from my job. Where in the whole world to spend my year? I had already lived in Paris, which I adored, but I wanted to go to someplace new: Rome? Bombay? Rio? I wanted to know them all, but I decided on Israel. For years I had been curious about what it would be like to live there. But where in Israel? On a kibbutz? In Haifa or Tel Aviv, where I had friends?

I mulled over my options and out of them, the one I had considered least of all (at first) emerged as my choice—Jerusalem. As a journalist, I thought I ought to be in the heart of the country. But my real reason was curiosity. Why was it that every person I knew who had visited Jerusalem waxed ecstatic over it and yet I didn't? What had I overlooked during my visits? I seemed to have missed something, and I wanted to find out what. Without knowing anyone in Jerusalem, having only the name of a woman who rented out rooms, I began my trip.

At David Ben-Gurion Airport, after an exhausting flight, I argued with a taxi driver, Aaron, over how much he was going to charge me to drive the 31 miles to Jerusalem. Finally, I decided I was too tired to worry about it. I climbed into his car, taking the seat beside him as he directed me to do. No more than three minutes later, Aaron was carrying on an animated discussion with me. A native Jerusalemite, he talked eloquently of his Yemenite ancestry and his views on democracy, Arabs, the government, peace, and war. I forgot about being tired. About seven minutes later, he invited me to spend Shabbat with his family. Already, I was liking Jerusalem better than I ever had.

Still, as the months passed, I tried to keep Jerusalem from possessing my heart. But bit by bit, love grew. I still saw beggars, dog droppings on the sidewalks, and impoverished neighborhoods. But my eyes also opened to inviting courtyards, the grace of quiet streets, flaming sunsets day after day, and the view from a height of the barren and mysterious Judean Desert scratching away at the city's edges. I smelled the perfumed springtime air that begins with white almond blossoms as January leads into February and culminates with saucer-sized roses in May.

I fell in love with Jerusalem through unexpected peeks into people's lives. One occurred when I was strolling though the Israel Museum, heard entrancing Middle Eastern Jewish music, and followed it to its source. It came from the janitors' radio. The men—vacuum cleaner and brooms beside them—were dancing right there in the exhibit hall. I loved the freedom with which they interrupted their workday and turned the museum into a living, spontaneous repository of culture.

I felt love for Jerusalem when a teenager, standing in front of me in line for a pay phone, overheard me say something to a friend about the telephone tokens we then used. Thinking I had none, she turned and offered me one of hers. It was just one example of the spontaneous generosity between strangers that I encountered over and over.

Many months after I met Aaron—and got to know his wife and five children—he told me, "In Jerusalem, you are never alone." The message was clear: In Jerusalem, you always are with family.

It is a boisterous family from which you can hide little. I once sat on a bench outside a Laundromat doing my Hebrew lesson while I waited for the wash cycle to end. Next to me an attractive young woman also waited for her laundry. As I wrote in my notebook, she leaned closer, waved an index finger, and admonished me, "You made a mistake." She then gave me a mini-Hebrew lesson. Only in a world with a feeling of family, even between strangers, could her act have been not only acceptable but also expected. I needed help; of course she would give it.

This family of Jerusalemites isn't always loving. But the conviction remains that families argue sometimes, so it's no big deal. With family around you, to paraphrase Aaron, how can you be alone in Jerusalem?

Most of all, I fell in love with Jerusalem when, to my surprise, I realized I felt at home. The city embraced me. It made me feel that I belonged. As Elie Wiesel wrote, I hadn't arrived in Jerusalem: I had returned.

Introduction:
This Year in Jerusalem

This book is for people who come to Jerusalem for a few days, six weeks, or a year. It is for those who arrive for the first time or the fifteenth. It is for those who have never been to Jerusalem and those who dream about visiting.

This book describes the sites that give Jerusalem soul and that tourists from all over the world flock to see. But it tells of more than the emotional impact of a visit to the Western Wall or the glowing beauty of the Dome of the Rock. The book also gives a picture of "the Golden City" as a living, modern, urban area.

Jerusalem is known as the Heavenly City, but its earthliness is fascinating, too. So this book is also about Jerusalem's "everydayness" and offers shortcuts on how a person can deal with and enjoy daily life here.

Even in an ancient city of heavenly inspiration, visitors need to know such practicalities as how to find a place to stay, how to remain healthy, and how to shop when bargaining is required. This book answers these kinds of questions.

And there is more to learn in these pages—about the treasures in little-known museums, about the city's living pageantry, about how to chomp on sunflower seeds like a native, about when to go dancing in the streets, and about the plethora of events and occurrences that give Jerusalem heart. After all, as the 115th Psalm said so long ago, "The heavens are the heavens of the Lord and the earth he gave to humans." And heavenly Jerusalem really does exist on earth.

How to Use This Book

This book is divided into 22 chapters. Chapters 1 through 9 are for every traveler to Jerusalem. They contain basic information on how to get there, health considerations, money management, hotels, restaurants, and, of course, the ever-present history and religious beliefs that are the city's internal engine.

Chapter 10 provides seven day-long itineraries for visitors with but one week in Jerusalem. Chapter 11 is for tourists who are lucky enough to have two weeks to spend exploring. Chapters 12 and 13 describe lesser-known sites, including churches and synagogues, for those on a repeat visit or those who have the leisure to stay on as temporary residents. Readers might also choose to substitute some of these sites for those suggested in the one- and two-week itineraries. Chapters 14 and 15 describe the cycle of ceremonies and celebrations you will encounter throughout a Jerusalem year.

Chapters 16 through 22 describe daily life in Jerusalem. The information is intended to guide the long-term visitor in such matters as housing, exercise, heating, and telephones. It fills out the picture of the Golden City for those who feel they have "come home to Jerusalem" and now, indeed, will be staying awhile. This part of the book will also appeal to those who won't be staying on but want to imagine what it would be like to do so.

Names and Terms

Since this is a book to be used in Israel, I figure we should do things the way Israelis do. I use the Hebrew *rehov* for "street" and *kikar* for "square." Addresses appear as they do in Hebrew: street, name, number—as in Rehov Alfassi 23.

Don't be alarmed if the locations of certain places sound a bit vague—that's a local idiosyncrasy. Street numbers and names aren't always to be found, but the place in question is usually in plain sight once you get close. Jerusalem's downtown area simply is called "the center." A shopping mall is known as a *canyon* (cahn-YONE).

Following local practice (and one that has great logic when trying not to offend anyone), dates appear in this book with the designations B.C.E. (before the Common Era) and C.E. (Common Era), instead of B.C. (Before Christ) and A.D. (Anno Domini).

Transliterating Hebrew into English isn't an exact science. But "ch" as in Chanukah and "kh" as in *khan* are pronounced with a guttural "h." And almost all Hebrew words (such as canyon) are accented on the last syllable.

Bruchim HaBa'im: Welcome

Elie Wiesel wrote that one doesn't go to Jerusalem, one returns to Jerusalem. He meant that Jerusalem is, if not a real home, the spiritual home for millions.

In Hebrew, one "goes up" to Jerusalem—reaches a higher spiritual level—figuratively. But the expression is literally true as well. Travel to the city by bus or car from either the east or west, and at a certain point the vehicle must downshift. If you are coming from the west—the airport, perhaps—the highway climbs through rock-ribbed, pine-covered hills. Buses struggle and sound winded. An air of expectancy envelops passengers. After some sharp turns to the right and then the left, a sign made of shrubbery on a low slope to the right of the road announces, "Bruchim HaBa'im": (Blessed Is Your Arrival).

One more left and right and suddenly you have arrived in Jerusalem. Whatever image existed in your dreams, this is the reality.

Jerusalem's beauty, despite its occasional ugliness and dreariness, strikes you the moment you arrive. It is a churning city, driven by a hot-house ambience. Yellow stone buildings top the city's half-mile-high mountain under a blank, blazing blue sky. These buildings, subtly changing from pink to white to golden as the sun rises and sets, give Jerusalem its "Golden City" nickname.

The Lodestar

The spiritual crown of Jerusalem is the walled Old City, home to at least thirty five hundred years of religious history—first of Judaism, more than a thousand years later of Christianity, more than six hundred years after that of Islam. Towering stone walls girdle its four unequal quarters—Armenian, Christian, Jewish, and Moslem. At the foot of the Old City, climbing stepwise up a slope from the Hinnom Valley, is the City of David, the even more ancient Jerusalem that King David built on earlier settlements.

Beyond the Old City's walls and narrow lanes to the west is the modern-yet-seemingly-ages-old, but always Levantine, Jewish section of the city. To the east is its Arab version, more bucolic and graceful.

Maps from the Middle Ages show Jerusalem as "the navel of the world." Today, Jerusalemites are convinced that they truly live in the center of the world and that any other place would be dull. In agreement are Jewish teenage girls in micro-minis, Orthodox Jewish men in wide-brimmed beaver hats and white knee socks, and teenage boys in green army uniforms lugging Uzis. Holding the same opinion are Arab men wearing checkered keffiyehs around their heads and Arab women in long embroidered black dresses. Of the same view are myriad priests, white-robed Dominicans, brown-garbed Franciscans, Greek Orthodox with flat-topped black headdresses and billowing black robes, and Armenians with pointed black headdresses and billowing black robes. They and seemingly endless other varieties of humanity have deep roots in Jerusalem. Jerusalem pulls them like a magnet.

Jews alone have come to the city from more than 70 countries. Jerusalem is their lodestar; they and the city are inextricably entwined. While Jews have been Jerusalem's predominant population since the

3

mid-1800s, they are only one part of the mosaic to which each group's culture, religion, and history add a vital piece.

You wonder why these dissimilar people have gathered in one place. And you wonder even more why they have gathered in this particular rugged, rocky location that, logically, has no justification for existing. No seaport, river, or major commercial crossroads give Jerusalem an easy explanation for being. Instead, what made the city was God—people's faith that God touched this mountain, and that on it they are as close to God as they can be and still keep their feet on the ground. But Jerusalem welcomes believer and nonbeliever alike. It takes no special faith to feel Jerusalem's warmth and electricity.

Although arid and barren, the city has been fought for fiercely. It has been conquered some 37 times and destroyed 18. Yet it manages to rise time and again, through the inexplicable determination on the part of the people who love it. Jerusalem's citizens have often been forced to leave, but they have never abandoned the city.

For Jews, Jerusalem is the eternal capital; its name on their lips daily with their prayers. While Jews believe God is everywhere, God's spiritual home is the Temple Mount. Jews stand before the Western Wall, the remaining structure of the destroyed Second Temple, and feel they are in God's presence. For Christians, Jerusalem is where their Lord was crucified and resurrected. To them, the city means both pain and joy. They share his agony as he fell on the Via Dolorosa and imagine that they walk in his footsteps as he made his way to his crucifixion at Golgotha. They can see his tomb and feel the glory in his resurrection. For Moslems, it is from Jerusalem that Mohammed rode his winged horse on his Night Journey to visit Allah in heaven.

It is these three great religions—Judaism, then Christianity spinning off from Judaism, and Islam spinning off from both of them—that made Jerusalem the Holy City. As a capital, however, it belongs to Judaism. Except for a short, bloody time when Crusaders slaughtered their way into the City of Peace and briefly made it a capital for Christianity, Jerusalem has been a capital only for the Jews. Neither the Arabs, Mamelukes, nor Turks ever made the city their capital, even though it was in their hands for hundreds of years.

Although they established the city's religious foundation and built it as their capital beginning in 1000 B.C.E., Jews could do so more spiritually than physically for the almost two thousand years between their expulsion and the second half of the nineteenth century. During that time, the Jews made a holy temple of all Jerusalem in their hearts and souls. Now they are again the builders.

4

Jerusalem, My Happy Home

On modern maps, the city resembles an amoeba, with wiggly protrusions creeping up hillsides and down valleys. More than 600,000 residents inhabit the city's hills and valleys. For a great city, one that persists in the world's headlines and thoughts, it is quite small. Its center, or downtown area, is little more than a few unpretentious blocks wide.

Six days of the week, the city percolates. Visitors and residents feel a surge of excitement over its history, ancient sites, colorful people, and especially the city's heightened emotions and sense of purpose.

That purpose is hard to define. Perhaps, simply, it is Jerusalem's determination to live. As for these emotions, they are out there like a flag. They are waved, not bunched up and carried close the chest. Jerusalem is about feelings. Jerusalem wears its heart on its sleeve.

After six days of supercharged activity each week comes the seventh day. The Jewish Sabbath (Shabbat) arrives at sunset on Friday. Jerusalem stops running. It is still, reflective, and otherworldly. Now it truly is the Holy City, the City of Peace. Time quietly crawls.

Then, at Shabbat's end, when three stars can be seen in the sky Saturday night, it is as if someone hit a switch and gave the city a jolt. The fervor is back.

You can find a home in Jerusalem—even if you are here for just a short time. If not your physical niche, you can find your spiritual niche. And this spiritual home depends not on a formal religious view but on an attitude. To find your home here, abandon your preconceptions. Drop your defenses. Be like a child. Open your eyes and ears, your mind and heart. And you will find yourself agreeing with the anonymous person who wrote in 1601, "O Jerusalem, my happy home."

1
GETTING TO JERUSALEM

I sraeli Government Tourist Offices in the United States and your own travel agent can offer the most help in arranging your trip to Israel. But do your own browsing though the travel sections of newspapers such as the Sunday *New York Times*. You may find bargain flights.

Most travelers fly to Israel, and this is the simplest way of getting here. But being shoehorned into an airplane seat can make for an abominable experience, and the speed of flight often trivializes cultural differences between countries. In flight, we have no time to repack the cultural baggage we carried with us onto the plane. We have little opportunity to mingle with people from other countries and to allow a bit of them to rub off on us. By the time the plane lands, we still haven't absorbed introductions to the new lifestyle we will face. We tend to think that because we covered great distances in such a short time, differences between backgrounds can be conquered as easily. But it isn't so.

An antidote to jet travel, for anyone with money, time, and a sense of adventure, is to fly to one of several Mediterranean cities in Europe, Cyprus, or Turkey, and then to sail to Haifa. Or you can enter by land or air from Jordan or Egypt, although the lengthy bus ride from Cairo, about 12 hours, can make you feel as if you have been spun in the dryer.

Entering Israel

Holders of valid American and Canadian passports receive a free one-month visa on arrival in Israel. To remain after one month, you must request an extension from the Ministry of the Interior (see page 12). Extensions can continue up to 27 months. To study or work in Israel, you need to obtain a visa from an Israeli embassy or consulate before arriving. The word *before* is important if you want to stay legal.

If you want to travel to an Arab country other than Egypt or Jordan, ask that your passport not be stamped when you go through passport control on arrival—most Arab countries won't allow you to enter on a passport that indicates you were in Israel. (And don't forget to make the same request upon leaving.) You can obtain visas to Egypt and Jordan in Israel, but you'll have to get visas for other Arab countries before entering Israel— or you'll need creative thinking and good luck.

Tip: Check the Government Tourist Office's Web site, www.infotour.co.il, for a variety of information about Israel.

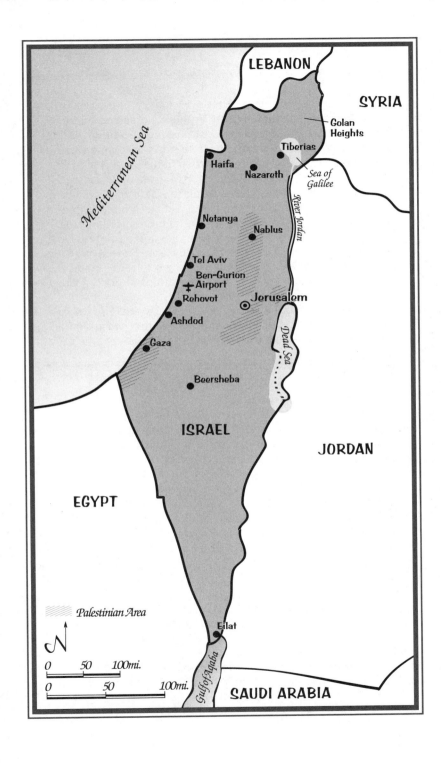

Jerusalem Scene

Rehov Yafo, the main thoroughfare in and out of Jerusalem, roars with cars, trucks, and buses pushing, pushing to get through the congestion. One day, standing on a tiny island dividing traffic lanes, was a bearded young man dressed in the black coat, pants, and high-crowned hat of a Hasidic sect. He wasn't watching for an opening in the traffic so he could make a dash across the busy street. Instead, he calmly stood there reading to himself from a prayer book, as though the cars, trucks, and buses didn't exist.

Traffic bore down on either side of him and passed no more than inches from his elbows and toes. Exhaust fumes fouled the atmosphere. The weight of rumbling, heavy trucks made the ground shake, and the man's side locks, curling in front of either ear, quivered from the rush of air.

But for the man, he wasn't on a traffic island. He was in a world he had created for himself. For him, there wasn't traffic, there wasn't noise, there wasn't even time. There was only God.

Health Requirements

Israel doesn't require special immunizations for entry, but your doctor might recommend one for hepatitis, which is prevalent in the Middle East but not a notable problem in Israel. For additional health-care recommendations, check with the Centers for Disease Control and Prevention in Atlanta: 404/332-4665 or www.cdc.gov.

Exchanging Currency

You may bring any amount of foreign currency into Israel. After passing through passport control at Ben-Gurion Airport, grab a cart for your luggage and hang onto it. While you wait for your luggage to be unloaded, get in line at the bank counter to change cash or traveler's checks for Israeli *shkalim*. Shkalim is the plural of *shekel*, the Israeli unit of money. A shekel is divided into 100 *agarot*.

People staying in Jerusalem for a considerable amount of time will want to read more about financial issues in Chapter 18: "Money Talk."

Getting to the City

To travel from Ben-Gurion Airport to Jerusalem, take Nesher's *sherut*, a shared van that doesn't leave until it is full. To find the van, exit the terminal and look for a prominent sign to your right that says "Jerusalem." The cost, a bargain, is an American $10 bill or the Israeli equivalent.

Unless the driver provides additional services like carrying your luggage upstairs (the custom, even if you're a little old lady, is to leave luggage in the street), there's no tipping. Don't be intimidated if the driver hints strongly for a tip.

As an additional advantage (or disadvantage, depending on your impatience), Nesher might give you a tour of Jerusalem and environs as the van winds its way to passengers' destinations you otherwise might not get to see.

You can also get a sherut to Jerusalem from the Allenby Bridge, across the Jordan River near Jericho, or from Haifa. However, the sherut from Haifa might go only to Tel Aviv, whereupon you will have to take a second sherut to Jerusalem. From Haifa, you can also take a direct bus to Jerusalem.

Bringing the Children

If you are considering bringing your children to Israel, remember that commercial sightseeing trips aren't targeted for young children. The talks, inevitably packed with historical information, could be as dull as oatmeal to them. Consider hiring your own tour guide for the family, if that's

The Silwan neighborhood, opposite the Old City

Picture Perfect

If, instead of print film, you prefer the permanence and color of Kodachrome slides, you should know that Kodachrome can't be processed in Israel. If you can't wait until your return home for processing, arrange to mail your Kodachrome home. Some companies have self-addressed, stamped mailers. Of course, the U.S. stamp isn't good from Israel. If you know trustworthy people who are on their way home, you might consider giving them your film to pop into the mailbox once they arrive. Whatever you do, don't leave film at a hotel desk for pickup—you might lose it forever. To be sure, pay the slight postage and mail it yourself from Israel.

If you use Kodak Ektachrome for slides, it can be processed in Israel. If you want the slides to come back to you in frames, you have to specify that. Otherwise, you'll get strips and framing material for doing your own framing.

financially feasible. Contact the Association of Guides, (03) 751-1132, for more information.

Numerous attractions will strike kids' fancy, however. Some are the Natural History Museum, the Bloomfield Science Museum, the Biblical Zoo, puppet shows (in Hebrew) in the Train Theater in Liberty Bell Park, the Lions Fountain across the street for splashing, the *Monster* sculpture (with its three tongues that are slides) on Rehov Chile in the Kiryat Yovel neighborhood, and the Billy Rose Sculpture Garden and Youth Wing at the Israel Museum. The kids (and you) might also enjoy planting a tree in one of the Keren Kayemet (Jewish National Fund) forests. Call toll free, (177) 022-3484, for more information. Barbara Sofer's book, *Kids Love Israel/Israel Loves Kids*, will offer more ideas.

People planning a lengthy stay in Jerusalem and who wish to enroll their children in school should see the "Youth Has Its Day" section in Chapter 16.

Visa Extensions

For a visa extension beyond the allotted one month, apply in Jerusalem to the Visa Department, Ministry of the Interior, Rehov Shlomzion HaMalka 1. Hours are 8 a.m. to noon Sunday through Thursday and 2 to 3 p.m. Monday and Wednesday (though the snippy young woman at the

What to Bring to Israel

For Short Visits
- Toiletries
- Extra contact lenses or glasses
- Insect repellent
- Medications you normally use and some you might need, such as medicine for diarrhea (especially for trips to Egypt)
- Health insurance forms
- Additional passport photos for visas to other countries
- A Hebrew phrase book
- A camera
- An open mind

For Longer Stays
- Washable clothes; avoid anything that needs dry cleaning
- Home-country postage stamps so friends can mail your letters when they return
- A Hebrew-English dictionary
- Electric-current transformers for Israel's power supply of 220 volts, 50 cycles
- A calculator with metric conversion capabilities
- Binoculars
- Sewing kit
- Flashlight
- Batteries—camera and other kinds
- A backpack for hikes, camping trips, and lugging home groceries
- Warm clothing and rain gear
- A personal computer
- Kitchen supplies
- Bedding

What Not to Bring
- Any electric product that operates only on 60 cycles
- Your cellular phone, unless first verified to be usable in Israel— and be careful about what salespeople tell you
- Preconceived notions

13

information desk told me that those who want to renew visas must be there at 7 a.m.). Be prepared to pay the equivalent of about $34. Have some passport photos with you, just in case.

Climb two flights of stairs or take the elevator in this dingy building and go to the desk, where you'll probably get a number and be directed to wait. At least at that hour of the morning, you'll beat the crowds.

Somehow you will muddle your way to the right desk, where the clerk who stamps your passport is likely to speak English and be surprisingly helpful, despite all appearances to the contrary. If you had planned on a trip to Saudi Arabia, you now can forget it—unless you can figure out a way of getting another passport.

If you don't get your Israeli visa renewed and you overstay your allotted time, you will be subject to a fine when you leave. So plan your travel accordingly.

2
FACTS OF
JERUSALEM LIFE

To deal with Jerusalem knowledgeably, you'll need to digest a few facts beforehand about its traditions, time, places, and—yes—even terrorism. Most importantly, to find your way in Jerusalem you must first become familiar with the people who call the city home.

The Chosen People

Like Israel itself, the people of Jerusalem are vivacious, pushy, loving, and loud. The city would be merely a collection of historic stones without this warm, unruly knot of humanity.

One of the most fascinating aspects of Jerusalemites is their diversity. Even those whose families have lived in Jerusalem for generations retain their ethnic and religious distinctions. Others have more recently come to the City of Peace from all corners of the earth. Pick a place on the globe and you are likely to find Jews with origins there. Jerusalem's Christians have left such homelands as Armenia, Greece, Egypt, Ethiopia, England, the Americas, and the former Soviet Union. Moslems have come from the Mediterranean basin and surrounding countries, especially Syria.

Ethnically, Jews fall into two main groups: Sephardi and Ashkenazi. *Sephardi,* strictly speaking, means Spanish. Originally, the term referred to Spanish Jews and their descendants after the expulsion from Spain in 1492. But the word has come to refer to Jews from Moslem countries as well, many of whom trace their families back to Spain. Another term used to describe these Jews is *Oriental.* A better one might be *Afro-Asian.*

Ashkenazim are Jews with roots in Northern and Eastern Europe. Both the cultural separation and the increasing amalgamation between Ashkenazim and Sephardim are important Israeli dynamics. Centuries of separation have created political and social conflict. Amalgamation is producing understanding, an equalizing of opportunity, and, in the case of "intermarriage," the new Israeli.

Add to these groups the Jews who can't be pigeonholed, like those from India, Ethiopia, Italy, and South America. A Jew from Venezuela has a Hispanic culture, but what if his grandparents came from Russia? How would a census taker classify him?

One Israeli peculiarity is that any Jew whose native language is English is called an *Anglo-Saxon,* even though that person's family might have emigrated to an English-speaking country from Minsk. The designation is astonishing: an Anglo-Saxon is the Queen of England, not Jake Goldberg, even if his native language is English. The designation also grates on those Jews from English-speaking countries who remember that many genuine Anglo-Saxons were the very people who wanted to keep Jews out. Now, by an ironic twist, they are unhappily stuck with that label. Reluctantly, I use that term in this book. The plural is *Anglo-Saxim.*

16

Besides ethnic classifications, Jews fall into religious divisions. These divisions are especially important in Jerusalem, which has a growing population that is highly observant. While neighborhoods often have an ethnic cast, they also have degrees of religious observation.

The range of observance is wide—from Jerusalemites who disparage any form of organized religion to members of a small ultra-Orthodox sect so adherent to the printed word of the Hebrew Bible and their interpretation of it that they don't even recognize the existence of the nation of Israel.

Other religious elements include the Hasidic "courts" of the ultra-Orthodox. Spiritually, Hasids are the descendants of alternative Jewish groups that sprang up in Eastern Europe in the 1700s. There are many Hasidic courts, each formed around its particular spiritual leader and with its own stamp of religiosity and dress. Usually, leadership is passed from father to son, forming a dynasty. Hasids add yet another dimension to Jerusalem's religious interplay.

But for Bureaucracy

The edges of Jerusalem's mosaic become rough now and then and scrape against each other. Sometimes it seems as if differences in the city's population play out most prominently in the realm of bureaucracy.

Female soldiers and a young supporter, Independence Day Parade

17

Descriptions of dealings with Israeli bureaucrats often sound like battle communiques, and on occasion you may feel as if you yourself are facing the guns.

Dealing with bureaucracy is especially difficult for foreigners. Non-Israelis often don't know the language or the way things work here. Added to that is Israel's overlay of Turkish, British, Israeli, and sheer Levantine custom. And procedures don't necessarily go smoothly even for Israelis. After all, a low-level functionary might feel powerful only when he's on the job. He might need to demonstrate that power.

It is best to look on life's occasional hassles in Jerusalem as Near Asian games. Don't sweat them. Consider them quaint local customs. And remember, a smile to the functionary who stands in your way will go further than a shout.

The number system and one-line-for-all are relatively new innovations at post offices, banks, and government offices. These systems have gone far to make business more orderly. But, in any event, keep a newspaper handy to read during the wait. And in case no formal line exists or the numbers are all gone, learn to ask "Mee ha'A-ha-ron?" ("Who's last?") and be prepared to fight to the death anyone who tries to get between you and whoever answered.

Keep your sense of humor. Learn the Arab word *inshallah,* which literally means "God willing" but really means "There's nothing you can do about it, so stop worrying." Also have handy in your Hebrew repertoire *b'vaka-sha* (please), *todah* (thanks), and *slee-cha* (excuse me), even if Israelis don't. Above all, face Jerusalem as if you were embarking on a grand adventure. You are. It might be the greatest of your life.

Telephone Calls

The area code for Jerusalem is 02. When you are making calls in Israel, remember that the country has no flat-rate service. Every call is billed—and by the length of conversation.

Making reservations at certain cosmopolitan restaurants and calling for a taxi or Nesher to and from Ben-Gurion Airport are among the few situations in which Alexander Graham Bell's invention works efficiently in Israel. Calling a business is often pointless, because you will be asked to come in and attend to matters face-to-face. If your call is transferred, you will probably be disconnected.

If the person you're calling isn't at his or her desk, you'll be asked to call back, "Maybe in 10 minutes." You might end up calling again and again with the same response. In this situation, I respond that only the person I'm calling knows when he or she will be back, so I'd like to leave my number for a return phone call. Sometimes this tactic works.

Recommended Reading

- *Carta's Historical Atlas of Jerusalem*, by Dan Bahat.
- *From Time Immemorial*, by Joan Peters. This has become a classic in explaining the sources of the Israeli-Arab conflict
- *Heroes and Hustlers, Hard Hats and Holy Men*, by Ze'ev Chafets. Although not new, it gives an incisive picture of Israeli dynamics and is funny and unsentimental.
- *The History of Israel*, by Howard Sacher
- *Jerusalem Architecture: Periods and Styles*, by David Kroyanker. Architect Kroyanker gives detailed descriptions of several Jerusalem neighborhoods. (Also recommended: any other Jerusalem book you can find by Kroyanker.)
- *Jerusalem Atlas*, by Martin Gilbert
- *Jerusalem in the 20th Century*, by Martin Gilbert
- *Jerusalem, Rebirth of a City*, by Martin Gilbert
- *Kids Love Israel/Israel Loves Kids*, by Barbara Sofer
- *Taste of Israel* by Avi Ganor and Ron Maiber. This is another of Rizzoli's high-quality publications, with rich color photos that will have you dreaming of food.
- *O Jerusalem*, by Larry Collins and Dominique Lapierre. One of the liveliest accounts, if not always accurate, of Jerusalem before and during the War of Independence.
- *The Mandelbaum Gate*, by Muriel Spark. Entertaining fiction set in pre-1967 Jerusalem.
- *A Peace to End All Peace*, by David Fromkin. Tells the frustrating story of the fall of the Ottoman Empire and how the follies of Great Britain and France, especially, created much of the mess of the Middle East.
- *To Live in Jerusalem*, by Rivka Gonen and David Kroyanker. A gorgeous book of Jerusalem lifestyles based on the Israel Museum exhibit of the same name.

For a background on Arabs, read anything by Fuad Ajami or Bernard Lewis. And to read at any time, I can't recommend highly enough *Eretz: The Geographic Magazine from Israel*. It is exquisite. For American subscriptions: 800/681-7727; in Israel: (03) 609-1890. Join the Society for the Protection of Nature in Israel and receive a free subscription.

The Israeli Week

There's good news and bad news about the Israeli week. Bad news first: The weekend lasts only one and a half days. Shabbat, more or less equivalent to Saturday, is the one full day of the weekend. Since stores and businesses close early on Friday afternoon, that is the half day. There's talk of some businesses, such as banks, closing all day Friday, and it might happen. Sunday is business as usual.

Of course, tourists need not be concerned. To you, every day is a weekend. With Jerusalem's stores locked up tight for Shabbat, there is only one day on which you can't spend money on gifts (unless you go to the Arab neighborhoods, where shops are open on Saturday but some are closed on Sunday). Keep in mind that with three major religions in Jerusalem, any day from Friday through Sunday is going to be somebody's day of rest. But other than the Jewish Shabbat, you might not notice too much resting.

The six-day business week can mean good news for people staying in Jerusalem awhile. Since Sunday is a regular business day, it can be a good time to get bureaucratic matters out of the way. But you must plan your shopping and other errands to accommodate various afternoon closings during the week. In addition to everyone in Jewish Jerusalem calling it quits early on Friday afternoon, many neighborhood businesses, including post offices, close at 1 p.m. one day a week.

Standard business hours are 8 a.m. to 1 p.m. and 4 to 7 p.m. Anyone who can takes a nap in the afternoon. So avoid calling people between 1 and 4; you might awaken a snoozer. Major businesses, such as supermarkets, department stores, and shopping malls, and those in the city center and the Talpiot and Givat Shaul industrial areas, forgo the afternoon siesta, although even in the heart of the city, you will still find some businesses closed from 1 to 4.

You will encounter the term "holiday eves" in this book, in sections listing days and hours of operation for museums and other attractions. Since the Jewish day begins at sundown, holidays begin at sundown. "Holiday eve" refers to the afternoon before a Jewish holiday begins.

While all the openings and closings might seem convoluted and Levantine, Israelis are totally practical when it comes to naming days of the week. Except for Saturday, which simply is Shabbat, the rest of the days are numbered. Sunday is "first day" (Yom Rishon), Monday is "second day" (Yom Shini), and so forth. Most shop owners use the English names for days when dealing with tourists. Hours are written international style: for example, 21:30 (for 9:30 p.m.). Dates are written: day.month.year. So October 7, 2003, would be 7.10.03.

20

Finding Your Way

To find your way around Jerusalem, one of your first acquisitions should be a good street map. Some streets, however, don't appear on maps. And even locating a street on a map doesn't solve the problem of finding that street in the real world.

A former *Time* magazine Jerusalem bureau chief used to complain that with all the buildings constructed of Jerusalem stone, every corner looks alike. "The buildings want to be incognito," he insisted.

Making matters worse is that street signs rarely stand on street corners. Instead, they are usually blue-and-white plaques, written in Hebrew, Arabic, and English, found somewhere on the sides of buildings. Often, shrubbery has grown up in front of these plaques. Occasionally, they aren't to be found at all. I lived for many years on a street with no sign whatsoever. I now live on a street where—uh, pardon the expression—Anglo-Saxim, concerned that there was no street sign, installed one in English. No non-English reader can find the street.

You will feel like a detective searching for street signs. With only your map to guide you, you will often have to make an assumption or ask for help from a passerby. Mayor Ehud Olmert's notable contribution to a less-harried Jerusalem life was the installation of lighted street signs at many intersections.

Even with the street located, finding an address can be a mystery. Numbers appear on little squares attached somewhere on a building's facade or gate. Newer buildings have a light with the number. In business areas, one number serves for several establishments.

Safety

Inevitably, whenever I am preparing to fly to Israel and I mention my plan to others, they respond first with silence. Then their eyes get big, and finally they pop the inevitable question: "Aren't you afraid?" My first indignant reaction is to compare Israel with other places in the world. Paris, London, and Tokyo are some of many cities where bombs not infrequently are lobbed. Or I ask if random shootings no longer exist anywhere in the United States. And I especially love to ask, "Can women walk alone at night in your home city?"

Statistics provide perspective. Let's consider the worst possibility: murder. In 1997 there were 211 murders in all of Israel, including deaths caused by terrorists, who happened to be very successful that year. But that total was in a population of some 5.5 million people.

Jerusalem that year had 16 murders in a population of almost 600,000 Arabs and Jews, who often are angry with each other, plus 22 deaths from terrorism. Add to the resident population the hundreds of thousands of tourists, temporary residents, and temporary workers who swell Jerusalem's population but aren't included in a census, and the number of murder victims becomes even smaller statistically.

I compared murder statistics one year with two American cities greatly attractive to tourists and about the same size as Jerusalem. I found Jerusalem had 13 murders, including those from terrorism. Denver had 78 murders, while New Orleans had a whopping 472—more than double all the murders in Israel in 1997. But when have tourists been warned about visiting Denver or New Orleans? In which of these three cities would you be safest?

What is out of proportion are the headlines a terrorist murder in Israel makes worldwide. Over and over I hear from tourists, speaking in a tone of astonishment, "But it's so peaceful here!" For that is what they find—peace, not violence.

But what about a man or woman alone? How safe is that person? Infinitely safer than in the United States. I walk alone at night in western

---

Jerusalem Scene

Uri, a handsome, wiry, and dark-skinned *sabra* (native-born Israeli) of Yemenite descent, has unlimited enthusiasm for Israel. "I was in Europe for three months," says the 25-year-old Jerusalemite. "When I came back, I kissed the ground. There's no place else for me."

He even talks affectionately of his army unit. Serving with it for a month each year is an honor, he says, not a task.

But one year, when he was called for his annual return to his unit, he had a troubling dream a few nights before he was to report for duty. In his dream, he was released from military service because he had no feet. He awoke greatly worried. Was the dream an omen, perhaps?

He told his commanding officer about the dream and asked if he could postpone his return. In another country, Uri would have been laughed at or locked up—probably both. In Israel, his commander reflected a moment and then said, "All right. Come back later."

22

Jerusalem with considerable confidence. Purse snatchers do hang around the hotels, but they don't kill for a purse.

Arab Jerusalem is another story. The moment it gets dark, I feel uncomfortable there. In contrast to Jewish Jerusalem, practically no one is on the streets there after dark. The same is true of the Old City. I try to leave the Moslem Quarter before the shops close. After that, the area seems spooky.

Day or night, it is risky for a woman to go with anyone who presents himself as a guide and offers to take her sightseeing. Rapes have resulted from these offers. Bona fide guides have official credentials, and they don't materialize out of nowhere and solicit employment.

Hitchhiking (called "tremping") is common throughout Israel. (Tremping technique is explained in Chapter 4: "Getting Around Town"). Tremping isn't as safe as it used to be. Female trempers have been raped, and tremping soldiers have been murdered by terrorists. But there are times, such as when buses stop running, when tremping is the only way of reaching your destination. Be smart and save your money for a taxi. But if tremp you must, be cautious. Women should never tremp alone.

Despite these precautions, Israel is basically a safe and peaceful country. As for women, absent is the random violence that has come to haunt their lives in the United States. For that reason, being in Israel can be a glorious, liberating experience for a woman.

Actually, a far, far bigger danger than terrorism is riding in a car on Israeli highways. Parallel with that is the danger to pedestrians crossing streets, especially—ironically—in marked pedestrian crossings. More about that later, but meanwhile remember: do not cross at a signal light unless you see the little green man in the pedestrian signal. Don't pay a moment's attention to signal lights for drivers, only to the little green man.

Jerusalem—The Fashion Center of Nowhere

Rest assured, Jerusalem decidedly isn't the town for fashion mavens. As an American woman from Albuquerque said after a year in which her husband worked at Hadassah Hospital, "You never can be too underdressed in Jerusalem."

And frankly, my dear, it's a relief. What to wear—except to meet a few religious requirements—isn't a question to take up much of anybody's time in Jerusalem.

As for those religious requirements, they are for men: a head covering in synagogues and no shorts in ultra-religious neighborhoods. Women must wear "modest" dress in ultra-Orthodox neighborhoods, which usually means upper arms covered and no slacks. Shorts or micro-minis? Even minis? Don't even dream about them. Pay attention to those signs that warn women about proper dress in certain neighborhoods. The people who put them up mean it—and can get mean about it. In churches, women will be no more welcome—but with fewer spitballs—if they have bare arms or wear shorts. The same for mosques.

Listen carefully to tourist Liz's story about her walk one morning through ultra-Orthodox Mea She'arim, which she enthusiastically reported to her Israeli friend, Batya.

"Everyone was getting ready for Shabbat," Liz related. "Everyone seemed excited. The food stalls had crowds of people around them. Dead chickens were piled on carts. A lot of men in black coats were pushing their children in strollers or carrying their babies in their arms. That was sweet. Some of the men already were dressed for Shabbat. They wore white knee socks. Some had black-and-gold striped robes and wide black beaver hats. The little boys were looking spiffy in their best clothes. When they walked, their side locks bounced like corkscrews. I tell you, it was a colorful scene. I thought I was in a Polish village one hundred years ago."

Batya smiled, "I'm glad you had a good visit. How were you dressed?"

Liz looked at her wide-eyed. "The way I am now."

Startled, Batya stared at Liz's pants and T-shirt a moment and then appeared stricken. "Don't you know you shouldn't go into that neighborhood like that? That you should wear a skirt and have your elbows covered? Something very unpleasant could have happened."

Liz laughed. "That's a lot of nonsense. I had no problem with the way I dressed. The only thing that was unusual was kind of funny. As I walked along, a housewife upstairs dumped her bucket of scrub water onto the street and it landed on me. But nothing bad happened."

"I see," Batya responded, knowingly.

I recommend that women leave their miniskirts and tank tops in their suitcases while in Jerusalem. Not that you don't find Jerusalem women wearing them, but they know where they are walking. And, in general, Jerusalem is a conservative city, which deserves respect.

Still, Israel's basic informality keeps dress casual. Visitors should bring clothes that are simple, sturdy, and washable. (You will have to hock the Mercedes to pay for dry cleaning.)

This isn't to say that Jerusalemites don't have their own style. Among men, influences of country or origin are strong. If he's Israeli and wearing a suit and tie (something of an oddity here), you almost can bet that he comes from a German or English background. You aren't likely to see a young male sabra dressed like that unless he's at his own wedding—and probably not even then.

Tie manufacturers love Israel about as much as bathing-suit makers love Siberia. A man may go anywhere in Israel without a tie. Even ultra-

Orthodox men who wear long black coats whether the temperature is 45 or 95 degrees Fahrenheit don't choke themselves with ties. "Mr. Jerusalem," former-mayor Teddy Kollek, didn't deign to wrap a tie around his bull neck while in Israel, so why should anyone else? True, recent Israeli presidents and prime ministers have been seen in public dressed like members of the international diplomatic fraternity, but they probably adopted the uniform because the foreign press was going to take their picture.

The moment the weather warms, men are in their beloved sandals and short-sleeved shirts. Even businessmen lugging briefcases to the office dress like that. Blue jeans are ubiquitous most of the year, except when the temperature is high.

Women dress with improvised verve. The variety is endless: ankle-length skirts, fluttery dresses of Indian cotton, capes and big colorful scarves draped in various ways around the neck or over the shoulders, and all kinds of hats. The long skirts and wide hats have a graceful and romantic appearance.

Most women are as liberated as the men when warm weather arrives. At the earliest possibility, off come the panty hose—even among the varicose-veins set. Bare legs are socially acceptable in the best (but not the most Orthodox) circles. Women who are strictly observant wear hose, no matter how hot the weather.

Good walking shoes are more important than fancy footwear in Jerusalem. It's easy to get along without the latter, but feet will revolt

Israeli Etiquette

Israelis tell an old joke on themselves: A woman is conducting a survey. She encounters a Russian and says to him, "Excuse me, what is your opinion of the meat shortage?" The Russian answers with his own question, "What is an 'opinion'?"

She approaches a woman, who is an American, and says, "Excuse me, what is your opinion of the meat shortage?" The American asks, "What is a 'shortage'?"

The surveyor approaches another person—an Israeli. "Excuse me," she asks, "what is your opinion of the meat shortage?" The Israeli has his own question, "What is 'excuse me'?"

You get the idea.

without the former. Besides, Jerusalem's stone sidewalks are slippery in dry as well as wet weather. You'll need the surest footing you can get. If you have no rain boots, note that your shoes will become soaked in the rushing rivers that pass for streets in winter.

Weather

Warning: As strange as it might seem, anyone planning to visit Jerusalem in winter should prepare for cold weather. When it rains, it rains icy torrents, and it could rain incessantly from November to April. Snow falls occasionally, turning the Golden City white. And since central heating isn't universal, you may feel the cold deep in your bones.

In winter, arm yourself with a sturdy umbrella (in Jerusalem, real men carry umbrellas), waterproof boots or shoes, a parka or an all-weather coat with a zip-in lining, heavy socks and sweaters, warm pants, gloves, a hat, and, yes, long johns.

Summers are hot and dry. Spring and autumn are glorious. The accompanying chart shows Jerusalem's average monthly temperatures. But remember, averages are deceiving.

Jerusalem Temperatures

MONTH	AVERAGE MIN. F/C	AVERAGE MAX. F/C
January	43/6.1	53/11.4
February	45/7.1	56/13.5
March	48/8.8	62/16.4
April	53/11.7	69/20.4
May	59/15.1	76/14.6
June	63/17.5	81/27.1
July	66/18.7	83/28.1
August	66/18.7	83/28.3
September	64/17.7	81/27.1
October	61/16.2	76/24.5
November	54/12.3	66/18.9
December	46/7.8	56/13.2

Shofar, Bells, and Muezzin Calls

There's no denying it: It's belief in God that made Jerusalem. Despite conflicting views of God, by and large different religions have been able to live peacefully side by side here. The biggest conflicts are within religions—for instance, the struggle over turf among Christians and the resistance to the imposition of an Orthodox lifestyle on non-Orthodox Jews.

It enhances a visit to Israel if you become familiar with not only Jewish and Israeli history but also with the religious views here. Israel was reestablished as a home for the Jewish people in 1948, and Jews make up 80 percent of the population. About 17 percent are Moslems. Less than 3 percent are Christian and other religions, such as Druse.

Keep in mind that despite the many churches and Christian religious sites in Israel, Christians are a small minority in Israel. Of that minority, the most powerful denomination is the Greek Orthodox Church. It got here first and became a big landowner, acquiring almost two-thirds jurisdiction over the Holy Sepulchre and more turf in Bethlehem's Church of the Nativity than any other denomination. The Armenian Orthodox Church is next in local importance. The Roman Catholic Church is a relative Johnny-come-lately, especially any order other than Franciscan. Far behind in significance are the Protestant denominations.

The Druse, included in that 3 percent minority along with Christians, are an important part of Israeli life, despite their small number. Through their participation in military service, they have been heroic in defending Israel. While ethnically Arab, they are religiously separate and distinct from Islam. The faith's main features are its secrecy and its belief in reincarnation. Because the religion is secret—and not every Druse is allowed in on the secrets—there is little more than that to say. It's important to remember that Druse and Moslems aren't the same thing.

Islam

The largest minority religion in Israel is that of the Moslems—Islam. Islam announces its presence in Jerusalem through its *muezzins*, men who call the faithful to prayer five times a day from mosques, usually through a loudspeaker. You can hear the calls most clearly around 4 a.m., when the long, slow nasal sounds wrap themselves around the night air.

Islam, which means "submission to God," has both Jewish and Christian elements but is distinctly separate. The Koran, God's final revelation, canceling all previous revelations, according to Moslems, was received by Mohammed, who began preaching in approximately 613 C.E. The Moslem calendar begins in 622.

Like Judaism, Islam is firmly monotheistic and doesn't have a centralized hierarchy. Jews and Moslems share the ritual of circumcision and both prohibit eating pork. Like Christianity, Islam believes in the physical resurrection of the dead after the Last Judgment and in a heaven and hell. Similar to Christianity, it believes that forgiveness for sin can come only from the grace of God, but through unquestioned obedience and good works there could be mercy.

While Islam accepts the doctrine of Immaculate Conception, it firmly rejects the divinity of Jesus. According to Islamic belief, Jesus was a prophet capable of performing miracles. Islam says that Jesus wasn't crucified—that someone else was crucified in his place.

According to the Koran, God gave Mohammed the correct version of Revelations, negating the Hebrew Bible and the Christian Gospels. Abraham, Adam, Isaac, King David, and other Biblical figures were Moslems, the Koran says.

Judaism

The most important religion in Israel is Judaism. While it is often looked upon as the mother religion to Christianity and Islam, it is far different from both. The single most distinctive difference between Judaism and its daughter religions is that Judaism says each person is born with a pure soul. We don't "sin" as it is understood in Christianity. Judaism believes that we stray from the righteous path into which we were born. Our goal is to get back on that path and only we can do that. No one can do it for us—not even God.

It's not, as some Christians believe, that Jews reject Jesus and the belief that "he died for our sins." It's that the concept of dying for others' sins is simply superfluous to Judaism. To put it a different way: There's no job for Jesus in Judaism. From this belief, that we are born with pure souls, Jews have an entirely different outlook on the world than do Christians and Moslems. There's no fire and brimstone here.

The concept of a messiah was a late development in Judaism. And always, in Judaism the Messiah is a human being who will live and then die. Josef Albo, one of the great rabbis of fifteenth-century Spain, made it plain that belief in a messiah wasn't an integral part of Judaism.

Unlike Christianity and Islam, which are triumphal religions and maintain that terrible things will happen to those who don't believe in them, Judaism says a person doesn't have to be Jewish to be ethical and moral. Non-Jews must only follow the seven laws of Noah, referred to in the Bible and spelled out in the Talmud, that sea of information that summarizes thousands of years of Jewish oral law. Judaism doesn't demand blind belief. In fact, it favors questioning. It hopes for belief after questioning, but the most important thing is people's ethical behavior.

3
THE
JERUSALEM SAGA

History and the Bible are under your feet, in front of your eyes, and even part of your conversation in Jerusalem. You see the slopes of the city King David built, the mount on which King Solomon built the Holy Temple. You walk the route Jesus is said to have walked as he carried the cross to his death. You talk of going to a bar mitzvah at the wall—the last remnant of the Second Temple.

Even the names of streets evoke the mosaic of history. Rehov HaPalmach is named for the attack arm of the Hagana, Israel's pre-independence defense force. Rehov Kaf Tet b'November is named for the date, November 29, 1947, on which the United Nations voted to divide the land into Jewish and Arab states. Other streets are named for great leaders (Rehov Bar Kochba, Shderot Herzl), learned men (Rehov HaRav Kook, Rehov Ibn Gabirol), and important women (Rehov Ruth, Rehov Rahel Immenu).

For three thousand years, since King David's time, Jerusalem has been not only a city but also a spiritual home, first and foremost for Jews. More than a thousand years later, the city acquired meaning for Christians and more than 1,600 years later for Moslems.

The first written mention of Jerusalem ("Rushalimum") appeared on Egyptian pottery almost four thousand years ago. King David conquered the city from the Jebusites, a people of uncertain origin, and bought a threshing floor or simply a field for an altar for the Holy Ark of the Covenant. King David's Jerusalem, the political capital of his kingdom and spiritual center of the Jewish people, already was several hundred years old by the time Rome was founded.

Excavation in the City of David, below the Temple Mount

Israel's location on the path to three continents remains unfortunate to this day. Even an abbreviated account of Jerusalem's history must be lengthy. You will hear the high points referred to repeatedly during your stay. Thus you will need a handy historical reference. The following time line touches on landmark events:

The First Temple Period

960 B.C.E.—After King David set Jerusalem on its path to its future world status, his son, King Solomon, began an ambitious building program with the First Temple.

720 B.C.E.—Sennacherib's invading Assyrian forces sat outside Jerusalem and demanded capitulation. It was in preparation for this siege that King Hezekiah attained immortality with his tunnel, an engineering feat, to bring the waters of the Gihon Spring outside the city to the Pool of Siloam inside the city. The night before Jerusalem was to capitulate, a plague struck the Assyrians, devastating their army and forcing them to abandon their goal.

586 B.C.E.—The Babylonians destroyed not only Jerusalem but also the temple. They carried away most of Jerusalem's inhabitants to captivity in Babylon.

The Second Temple Period

538 B.C.E.—In the rising and sinking of rulers' fortunes, Cyrus of Persia rode the next wave. He conquered Babylon and allowed the Jews to return home and rebuild their temple. It was completed in 515 B.C.E.

332 B.C.E.—The benign Alexander the Great arrived on the scene. Those who succeeded him, Ptolemy of Egypt and Antiochus III of the Hellenist Syrian Seleucid dynasty, were far less tolerant.

170 B.C.E.—Antiochus IV entered Jerusalem. His desecration of the temple and forced pagan ceremonies inspired a revolt led by the Maccabee brothers.

164 B.C.E.—Judah Maccabee took Jerusalem from the Greek rulers, cleansed the temple (an event celebrated by Chanukah), and ushered in a century in which Jews were sovereign again.

63 B.C.E.—Pompey tore down the city's walls and fortifications. With the Roman occupation, Jewish self-rule disappeared for almost two thousand years.

37 B.C.E.—Herod the Great ruled in the name of Rome. A big spender, and wishing to curry favor with the Jews, he rebuilt Jerusalem entirely and turned it into the greatest city of the Middle East. He even refurbished the temple.

With his death, turbulence became more pronounced. Tyranny and cruelty were the hallmarks of Roman rule. The first Jewish rebellion broke out. Among episodes of fierce retribution, two thousand Jewish rebels were crucified at one time. Jews dreamed of and prayed for a hero, a messiah who could lead a successful revolt against the Romans.

33 C.E.—Jesus, who like all Jews was expected to make a pilgrimage three times a year to Jerusalem, came to the city for the Passover pilgrimage in the midst of the political turbulence. It was then that the Roman procurator, Pontius Pilate, had Jesus crucified for reasons debated by historians.

66 c.e.—The Zealots, a determined Jewish group later of Masada fame, began a revolt against Roman rule.

70 c.e.—Titus crushed the revolt, destroyed the Second Temple, exiled Jews from Jerusalem, and carried many to Rome as slaves. Without the temple or kings, Judaism transformed itself through a succession of dynamic rabbis and through efforts to collect and write down two thousand years of oral law.

The Roman Period

132–135 c.e.—Simon Bar-Kochba, pronounced the Messiah by the great Rabbi Akiva, led the second Jewish revolt. He attempted to rid the land of the tyrant Romans in preparation for the Kingdom of God on earth. At first he succeeded, but eventually the Roman emperor Hadrian triumphed. He plowed the city under, turned it into a Roman garrison town, and changed its name to Aelia Capitolina. On the Temple Mount, he erected a temple to Jupiter and a statue to himself. To further obliterate Jewish history, Hadrian renamed the land Syria Palestina, or Palestine. (The name came from the Philistines— a non-indigenous Mediterranean people who had mysteriously disappeared from Israel centuries earlier. The word *Philistine* comes from the Hebrew word for *invader.*)

Hadrian forbade Jews to live in Jerusalem, on penalty of death. For the next two thousand years, Jews alternately were allowed in and banished, according to the whims of foreign rulers. Eventually, Christians were banned from Aelia Capitolina as well.

The Roman conquerors laid out their new Aelia Capitolina like a Roman colonial city, with two main streets at right angles to each other. The Cardo Maximus (north-south street) began at what today is Damascus Gate; the Decumanus (east-west street) at Jaffa Gate. Both can be seen today. Of the Jews' Jerusalem, remnants of the western and southern walls, the retaining walls of the Temple Mount, are among the few remainders.

The Byzantine Period

300 c.e.—After a series of traumas, the Roman Empire split into eastern and western regions. In the early part of the fourth century, Emperor Constantine, ruling in Byzantium (which later became Constantinople), became a Christian.

324 c.e.—Jerusalem had become the focal point of the ever-expanding Christian faith, and Queen Helena, Constantine's mother, traveled to the city. She identified what legend said were holy sites—the place of Jesus' birth, Gethsemane, and the Crucifixion—and ordered churches built over them. Jerusalem became Christianized with the constant building of churches. No building occurred on the Temple Mount, but the area was used as a garbage dump.

614 c.e.—Persia reconquered Jerusalem and destroyed many lives and churches.

629 c.e.—The Byzantines recaptured Jerusalem. But the battles between Byzantium and Persia weakened both and left a vacuum.

The Moslem Period

638 c.e.—Six years after Mohammed's death, Arabs belonging to the new Islamic religion and led by the Caliph Omar invaded Jerusalem and became the newest rulers. Omar made the Christian patriarch Sophronius crawl through the filth on the Temple Mount as punishment for allowing it to be used as a garbage dump.

Over objections of this same Christian patriarch, Omar allowed Jews to return to Jerusalem. Instead of making Jerusalem their capital, the Arabs initially governed from Caesaria.

The Temple Mount became a building site also holy to Moslems. Caliph Abd el-Malik commissioned the Dome of the Rock on the Temple Mount in 697. It commemorates the spot from which, according to the Koran, Prophet Mohammed was carried on his magical horse to "the farthest place," from which he visited Allah in heaven. Legend says that place was Jerusalem.

The Al-Aqsa Mosque, opposite the Dome of the Rock, was built for prayer at the beginning of the eighth century. Both structures were intended to keep Moslems loyal to the Umayyads, based in Damascus, from being lured toward Mecca and falling under the sway of opposing Moslem sects.

During the next four hundred years, Jerusalem went from the jurisdiction of the Damascus-based Umayyad caliphate to the Baghdad-based Abbisids to the Fatimids of Egypt to the Seljuk Turks, who were particularly violent toward non-Moslems. The Christian world was aroused.

The Crusader Period

1099—In the name of Christianity, Europeans rallied to recapture Jerusalem, now held again by the Egyptian Fatimids. They sent military expeditions on a religious crusade to the Middle East. Carrying the standard for Christianity, Godfrey de Bouillon captured Jerusalem, massacred Jews and Moslems alike, and forbade their settlement in the city. The city became the Latin Kingdom of Jerusalem.

1187—Under Sultan Saladin, a Kurd, Moslems recaptured the city and allowed Jews to return.

1228—The Crusaders returned. Through a treaty, Moslems surrendered Jerusalem to Frederick II, who crowned himself King of Jerusalem in the church of the Holy Sepulchre.

1244—Turkish mercenaries of Egypt reduced Jerusalem to rubble.

The Mameluke Period

1250–1517—Jerusalem was ruled by the Mamelukes, soldier-slaves of the Egyptians, who became kings. They were replaced by the Turks of the Ottoman Empire, but left behind distinctive architecture.

The Ottoman Period

1537—Sultan Suleiman, known as "the Magnificent," rebuilt and restored the walls and gates of Jerusalem. They remain today. Except for the years 1832 to 1840, when Mohammed Ali of Egypt ruled, the Ottoman Empire remained in power until 1917. Ali is blamed for denuding the land of trees to build his fleet. It was he who approved of Christian missions, schools, and foreign consulates in Jerusalem.

1860—A wealthy Englishman, Sir Moses Montefiore, administered construction of a windmill and residence, Mishkenot Sha-ananim, the first Jewish settlement outside the Old City, to reduce its oppressive crowding. The settlement didn't succeed. The first successful neighborhood outside the walls was Mahane Yisrael, off Rehov King David. It was built in 1868 for North African immigrants.

A year later, Nahalat Shiva was established near Rehov Yafo, guided by the driving spirit of Yosef Rivlin. This was the first neighborhood outside the walls built for and by Jerusalemites.

In the late 1870s, Arabs also began to move out of the Old City. Not under the same threat as Jews, and with greater financial resources, they built lavish homes, first in Abu Tor, later in then-far-afield Katamon.

1897—Theodor Herzl, a Viennese journalist reacting to the anti-Semitism of the Dreyfus trial in France, established with like-minded Jews the Zionist movement for Jewish independence at a convention in Basel, Switzerland.

The British Mandate Period

1917—On November 2, the British issued what was known as the Balfour Declaration, which supported the establishment of a Jewish homeland in Palestine. The World War I allies later approved it, and the League of Nations incorporated it into the Mandate of Palestine conferred on Britain.

The Ottoman Turks, on the losing German side in the First World War, were replaced by the British. They left behind an impoverished, abused city that shocked Western visitors. British General Edmund Allenby led his triumphant troops into Jerusalem on behalf of his country.

The period of the British Mandate of Palestine began. In 1921, almost three-quarters of the territory was lopped off to form a new country, Transjordan, the future Jordan.

The British brought stability that hadn't existed during the last years of the crumbling Turkish empire, a period made even worse by the terrible hardships of World War I. After 1917, Jewish efforts in farming and commerce also brought prosperity that had been absent from the region for thousands of years.

The combination attracted immigrants—not only Jews but also Arabs. British census figures show that between 1922 and 1931 the city's population grew by more than 20,000 Jews and 21,000 Christian and Moslem Arabs, most coming from abroad.

1931-1939—Jerusalem's population increased by 26,000 Jews, most of them refugees from Germany and Poland, and 15,000 Arabs, primarily from Syria and Jordan.

The influx of Jews sparked a series of Arab riots in 1920, 1929, 1936, 1938, and 1939. While heavier casualties were inflicted elsewhere, Jerusalem didn't escape the violence. Forty-four Jews were killed during the riots, and four thousand were forced to leave their homes in 1929 alone. In 1937 and 1938, Jewish extremists retaliated and killed 25 Arabs.

May 1939—Despite the rise of Hitler and the approach of World War II, the British severely restricted Jewish immigration to a maximum of 75,000 annually and gave the Arabs a veto on all Jewish immigration after 1945.

1946—With World War II and the Holocaust against the Jewish people ended, underground Jewish armies, much of their leadership in Jerusalem, carried out armed resistance to British rule. Britain prevented all but a tiny number of Jewish refugees from entering.

1947—The United Nations voted to partition Palestine into Jewish and Arab sectors and placed Jerusalem under international administration. Jews agreed. Arabs refused and began consistent attacks against Jews.

Independence

1948—The British Mandate ended on May 14, 1948. On May 15 (Iyar 5 in the year 5708 of the Jewish calendar), Jews declared their portion of the partitioned land to be the independent nation of Israel. Immediately, five Arab armies invaded. Under siege, Jewish Jerusalem suffered severe shortages of food, water, and other necessary supplies.

When battles ended, Jerusalem was cut in two. The Old City—the Western Wall—and eastern neighborhoods were occupied illegally by

Jordan. The west and some southern areas went to Israel. Jordan agreed to allow Jews religious access to the Western Wall but never carried out the agreement in practice.

1949—Despite the city's split, Prime Minister David Ben-Gurion declared it Israel's capital. Living in the city during those years was risky. Jordanian soldiers took potshots across the valleys and streets. West Jerusalemites living near the dividing line were in constant danger.

June 1967—The Six-Day War began on June 5 (Iyar 26), after Egypt ordered the buffer UN forces out of Sinai and closed shipping into Eilat. Israel, after bloody battles with Egypt, Jordan, Syria, Iraq, and troops from Saudi Arabia, Kuwait, and Algeria, captured the Old City and the rest of Jerusalem. With peace, a great traffic jam occurred in the city as old-time Jewish West Jerusalemites and old-time Arab East Jerusalemites headed out to visit each other after many years of separation.

The Present and Future

This chronology ends here, for subsequent wars and political decisions haven't altered Jerusalem. Under Israeli rule, Jerusalem's religious sites were opened to all for the first time. Later, the areas previously occupied by Jordan were formally annexed to make one unified city. For the first time since 63 B.C.E., all of Jerusalem was under Jewish jurisdiction.

The city blossomed and grew, with new residents and an unprecedented building boom. It is now Israel's largest city and a major cultural center. Renowned artists from all over the world exhibit and perform here. The city has also developed a viable commercial and industrial base.

Jerusalem may never again resemble the city of Herod with its grandeur and magnificent buildings, but its glory doesn't depend on architecture. Instead, Jerusalem's future depends on its people. If the city's patchwork-quilt population can hang together, the nickname City of Peace will be a reality.

4
GETTING
AROUND TOWN

To get around town—and into and out of town—the bus system, named Egged, works well. But before learning bus routes or schedules, every bus rider in Israel needs to know how to holler, "RAY-guh!" That's the Hebrew equivalent of "Hold it!" or "Wait a second!" Israelis shout "Rayguh" as they run down the street to catch a bus, as they board a bus, as they get off a bus, and probably in their sleep. With rayguh ingrained on your subconscious, you're ready to face Egged.

Bus Basics

For a single cash fare, the driver will give you a little piece of paper. It's a receipt—not a free transfer (in Israel, there is no such thing). You will probably shove the receipt into a pocket to join the stash of bus receipts already there, or maybe use it to wrap your chewing gum. But annoying as it is, hang onto that little piece of paper as long as you are on that bus. Every so often, an inspector boards and asks everyone to produce that shred or their punched bus ticket. If you can't show yours, you might have to pay again. Egged sells monthly passes, tourist passes, and other special tickets that allow people to travel at discounted rates.

In Israel, people still give up their seats to the elderly, and children tend to slide out of theirs for grown-ups. If you are of a venerable age and a child doesn't give up a seat for you, indicate that you want to sit down, and he or she will move without your having to watch your backside afterward.

If you travel during going-to or coming-from school time, you might feel as if you have fallen into the proverbial can of worms when you see the bus packed with wriggling children. The kids, besides being adorable and speaking Hebrew better than you or I, appear to be harmless. In reality, they can be lethal. Strapped to their backs are book bags. When the youngsters turn away from you, guard your eyes or ribs, whichever are closer to their portable People Whammers.

I once thought I was the only person who couldn't figure out how to get off the bus after I got on. I'd hear a ring from somewhere and the bus would come to a halt. Luckily for me, there always was someone else getting off at my stop. One day I discovered the source of those magical rings. In case there was someone else as baffled as I, the first edition of this book carried instructions.

Since that time, I've encountered tourists panicked over how to get the bus to stop. Humph, is my indignant reaction; if they had bought my book, they would know how to do that. The secret, for the price of the book, is the black knobs about two-thirds up the poles. They hold the red push-buttons that ring and turn on the stop sign above the driver.

Egged prints a free route map in English, available at the information booth in the Central Bus Station, hotels, and hostels. The Egged number for Jerusalem route information is (02) 520-4704. For intercity information, call (03) 694-8888.

Remember, Egged buses—interurban, too—stop running close to midnight daily and before Shabbat begins on Friday. They don't resume until 45 minutes after Shabbat ends on Saturday night. Exceptions are lines 8, 25, 31, 32, 36, and 175 to outlying neighborhoods, which have service during the week until 12:30 a.m. and Saturday until 1 a.m. Buses stop at 2 p.m. before Yom Kippur and don't start until two hours after Yom Kippur ends. The eastern Jerusalem Arab bus system runs all week.

Taxis

Taxis in town are plentiful and not exorbitant. You can call a dispatcher or hike to the nearest main street to flag down a taxi. Even with a passenger already in the car, you might get a lift. Taxi (and sherut) drivers aren't tipped, unless the driver performs additional service.

Make sure the driver turns on the meter—it's a legal requirement. If he tells you his meter is broken, either don't board or ask for his name and license number. The meter might miraculously and suddenly work.

Imaginative parking on the streets of Jerusalem

Often, especially at night, a driver might offer a flat rate to your destination without turning on the meter. You can agree to the rate or not. Although this practice isn't legal, it happens a lot. If you take a taxi on an intercity trip, the price is fixed by the Ministry of Transport. The price list should be found in every taxi.

Taxis go into the "Tariff 2" rate schedule from 9 p.m. until 5:29 a.m., when the price is 20 percent more than it is during the day. Tariff 2 pertains also to Shabbat, beginning one hour before the start of Shabbat through 5:29 Sunday morning. Watch for the tariff number that appears on the meter.

If you call and order a taxi, there will be an additional charge equivalent to about 80 cents. If you have luggage, ask for the price of carrying it. Often, the driver will charge whatever he thinks he can get away with. Each bag, unless it is very large, should cost the equivalent of 55 cents. But drivers might ask for up to $3.

It is customary for a single passenger to sit in the seat next to the driver. As Israelis love to tell you, "This is a democracy." But if you are a woman taking a taxi alone at night, you might want to reconsider your own democratic convictions. Up until early evening, I take the front seat. Later, I go by my instincts, as should you.

If you must travel in Jerusalem on Shabbat, even without a car, it isn't impossible. Two taxi companies that operate 24 hours a day every day are Gilo Taxis, (02) 676-5888, and Malha Taxis, (02) 679-4111.

Interurban Transportation

To get to Ben-Gurion Airport during those awful midnight or pre-dawn hours at which travelers often are expected to check in, Nesher, (02) 625-7227, is the company to call. It is the only one approved by the Airports Authority to operate the Jerusalem–Ben-Gurion run. Its fare is $10 or the shekel equivalent one way. A lot of things in Israel don't work efficiently, but Nesher does. To be picked up at your door, call the company or stop by the office at Rehov King George 21 the day before.

Egged's interurban buses are also an excellent way of getting from here to there. They also run frequently to Ben-Gurion Airport. Express Tel Aviv buses leave the Central Bus Station on Rehov Yafo almost continuously. Bus 405 goes to Tel Aviv's nightmare Central Bus Station, in which you might get lost for the next week. (Bring earplugs.) Bus 408 goes to North Tel Aviv's Central Train Station. A Tel Aviv–Jerusalem bus fills up and pulls out, and minutes later another takes its place. Returning to Jerusalem at night, the bus swings down Rehov Yafo, up Rehov Agron, and through Rehavia on Rehov Ramban. If you live near that route, the bus from Tel Aviv could take you almost to your door. Egged's interurban buses, like its city buses in Jerusalem, don't run on Shabbat, but they resume the moment Shabbat ends.

An Egged Isracard is available for 7, 15, or 21 days. The card allows you to travel on any Egged bus anywhere in the country, including on Jerusalem city buses (except Bus 99), as often as you want until your time runs out. Cards are available at any Egged Tlalim office, including the airport, and in Jerusalem at Rehov Shlomzion HaMalka 8, (02) 622-3399 or (02) 624-5526.

Besides buses, you can take a sherut—a taxi shared by seven passengers—between cities. Sheruts run seven days a week. Usually you can find one to your destination—assuming it is relatively major—on Rehov

HaRav Kook, on Rehov Strauss, and at the Central Bus Station. Ask around. A sherut doesn't leave until it is full, then it will travel as if the driver is trying to break the sound barrier. A sherut is a little more expensive than a bus—with no discount for your heart riding in your mouth.

One of the two eastern Jerusalem bus stations is on Sultan Suleiman Street, between Herod and Damascus Gates. From here, buses leave for Hevron, Bethlehem, Mount of Olives, Jericho, Bethany, and other predominantly Arab communities south and west of Jerusalem. The other bus station is on Nablus Road, about a block from the Old City, with service north to such places as Ramallah and the Jerusalem Airport at Atarot (Egged also goes to Atarot).

There is also a train from Jerusalem to Tel Aviv, with a change to Haifa. The train is something of a Toonerville Trolley. The stretch of the trip between Jerusalem and Beit Shemesh, through Nahal Soreq, is especially slow (new equipment may cut the time in half), but spectacular and not to be missed. This is Samson country, where he hid from the Philistines and is said to be buried. It's possible to ride only to Beit Shemesh and then return on the Jerusalem-bound train. The train station is on Derech Hevron at Kikar Remez. Call (02) 673-3794 for schedules.

Tremping

If you absolutely must hitchhike (I admit to doing so during a bus strike), don't raise your thumb. Here, the tremping position is with the right arm down and away from the body at about a 45-degree angle and the index finger extended, as if pointing to the road. Certain marked places on highways are official pickup places for trempers. Women should remember my earlier advice and not tremp alone.

Taxi Companies

- Gilo Taxis, (02) 676-5888
- HaPalmach Taxis, (02) 679-3333
- Malha Taxis, (02) 679-4111
- Rehavia Jerusalem Taxis, (02) 625-4444
- Smadar Taxis, (02) 566-1235
- Talpiot Taxis, (02) 671-1111
- Zion Taxis, (02) 588-6398

Driving

If you are considering driving in Jerusalem, I suggest you crush the thought—that is, unless you love being stuck in an idling car and inhaling exhaust fumes, not being able to find a parking space, driving in an obstacle course with parked cars projecting into traffic and motorcyclists that appear out of nowhere, having to keep an eagle eye out for both innocent pedestrians and those who behave as if they have bumpers on their rear ends, and being honked at by irate drivers because rather than run over a mother pushing a baby stroller you stop your car.

If you still aren't convinced and choose to drive, be aware that the yellow line is on the outside of the highway and the white line is the divider, that stop signs are small and more pink than red, that yellow blinkers at intersections are yellow four ways and everyone approaching thinks he or she has the right of way, that red and yellow lights together mean green is coming up and you should get ready for a getaway, and that the lane in which you're zooming along might suddenly disappear.

Yes, it's all right to park on the wrong side of the street. And, yes, it's all right to park on the sidewalk here and force pedestrians into the street. (Not all right by me, but I can't give traffic tickets.)

At striped pedestrian crossings, you are supposed to stop the moment a pedestrian on the curb moves as if to cross—but only a rare driver does. Nevertheless, that's what I learned in a required traffic rules course I had to take, and pay for, even before I owned a car.

Parking spots are marked by blue-and-white curbs and yellow signs in Hebrew and Arabic. To park in these spots, however, you must display a parking permit in your car window or on the dashboard. Books of permits are available at lottery ticket stands, post offices, and small grocery stores. You can also buy single permits at silver machines, resembling robots and cluttering sidewalks. Keep change handy for the machines; the cost is about $1 an hour. Both the books of permits and the "robots" give instructions in English. You'll need permits from 8 to 6 Sunday through Thursday and until 1:30 p.m. on Friday. No permits are needed on Shabbat or holidays.

Keep a rag in the car to wipe heavy condensation from your windows in the evening. A bottle of window-washing fluid also comes in handy. Gunk in the Jerusalem air keeps windshields perpetually dirty. Electric window washers fight a losing battle.

Driving here is incredibly difficult. It's New York, Boston, and Rome all together, plus a lot of pedestrians wearing black at night. You have to be constantly alert, defensive, and at the same time aggressive, because you won't have much time or space in which to make your move. Still,

I'm frequently impressed at how drivers can cooperate in the middle of a traffic mess to help each other escape.

Remember as you drive to watch the signal light above the arrow that points in the direction you want to go. The red staring at you might not be for you at all.

Footloose

There is one feature of the Golden City about which I can offer little advice: that is, how to walk on a crowded Jerusalem sidewalk. The fact is, it's easier to walk along Fifth Avenue during rush hour. Just getting from one block to another requires complete concentration.

Inevitably, the pedestrian comes to a place in the sidewalk wide enough for just one person. With somebody heading toward you, somebody is going to have to step aside. Invariably, that somebody is me. I have

---

Navigating Elevators

How to get off elevators? That's almost as challenging as getting off the buses. The problem is that the elevator symbol for the entrance level of a building comes in several varieties. The symbol can be a G for ground floor, an L for lobby, what looks like a backward C for the Hebrew word for entrance, a zero, or, most frequently, what looks like an open P, for the word *kar-ku*, which means ground.

Then there are the nightmare places like the Clal Building, with its umpteen levels before you get up to 1; the National Library Building, which has Hebrew letters instead of numbers in the elevators; and the Wolfson Center, where, when you enter from Rehov Diskin, you are on 7 and the top floor. After you shop at the supermarket or see a doctor, you have to remember that to get out, you go up.

To deal with this mental challenge, the moment you get on an elevator, look at the lights that indicate what floor you are on. Then you'll know which button to hit when you want to return. And remember, floors are counted here as in Europe: The first floor is the North American second floor. Often, in smaller buildings, floors get Hebrew letters instead of numbers.

---

found myself leaping out of the way for men, women, children, and dogs. I am the gentleman of Jerusalem—never mind my gender. My backing down causes me plenty of head scratching. Do I blink first?

Something even more baffling occurs on wide sidewalks with enough room for two people to pass comfortably. There, I often find that a pedestrian approaching from the opposite direction shifts his path and heads straight for me—as if I were a target. Jerusalemites walk as if they were heat-guided missiles. Wherever you are, they find you.

Occasionally, I firmly decide not to be the one to give way. Then I walk with my head down, one eye on the sidewalk, the other (because I'm a pessimist) checking the advancing troops. Do you think the sight of me with my head aimed at the pavement is a deterrent to human javelins? Not on your life. I've tried walking with my elbows out like battering rams, but they are as intimidating to Jerusalemites as cooked noodles. All I get out of that are sore elbows.

The only thing I've found to stop a human missile in mid-flight is a large, juicy slice of pizza. As I was eating on the move one day, a human heat-seeking missile in an elegant white suit and hat came heading toward me. Closer and closer he hurtled. Pressed by the rush-hour mob, I couldn't jump out of the way. Suddenly, the man saw my sloppy feast, held high enough and almost close enough to land on his white suit. He halted, laughed—and then moved out of my way.

In the neighborhoods, it's tough to walk on the narrow sidewalks at all, since three-quarters of their width is often taken up by garbage containers and cars. Out of necessity, people walk in the streets, which can be so peaceful that dogs snooze in them.

Let me say it again: On foot, don't cross at an intersection with a signal light until you see the little green man. More pedestrians are hit by cars in pedestrian crossings than any other place. Drivers have so many things to watch for—so many distractions. They aren't trying to hit you, they simply might not see you. You have the right of way, legally. But knowing you're right isn't enough sometimes.

5
A PLACE TO LAY
YOUR HEAD

No one needs a guidebook to find the name of the big Jerusalem hotels. After all, what major city almost anywhere in the world doesn't have a Hilton, a Sheraton, and an imaginatively built Hyatt? But only Jerusalem has the King David Hotel, the romantic American Colony (which you should at least visit even if you don't stay there), and the favored hotel of many American presidents, the Laromme.

Your travel agent can tell you about the next-best hotels—like Prima Kings, Moriah (*mo-ree-AH*), and the Mount Zion with its spectacular views. Good hotels below these include the Windmill, Tirat Batsheva, and Jerusalem Tower. For stays of a week or more, you can nab reduced rates at all hotels before or after the summer and any time other than Christian or Jewish holidays. Most hotels include breakfast in their rates. The high-priced Sheraton Plaza doesn't, which is downright un-Israeli.

Low-Budget Alternatives

Anyone willing to step further afield can practice greater frugality by checking out these less-pricey alternatives to the major hotels:

The **Israel Youth Hostels Association**—phone: (02) 655-8400; e-mail: iyha@netvision.net.il; Web site: www.youth-hostels.org.il.—offers a range of accommodations, from dormitories to private rooms with baths. Breakfast is included everywhere. The Hebrew University Givat Ram campus has a newly upgraded hostel.

Geraniums at Prima Kings Hotel

The **Jerusalem Inn Guest Hotel** at Rehov Horkanos 7 and the **Jerusalem Inn Guest House** at Rehov HaHistadrut 6—phone: (02) 625-2757; fax: (02) 625-1297; e-mail: jerinn@netvision.net.il.— couldn't be more centrally located. Originally hostels, the inns are constantly being upgraded. Now they offer private rooms, including family rooms, and self check-in. The price, about $30 for a single room and $50 for a double, includes breakfast. But owner Moti Belinco warns, "Smokers have to look elsewhere. We're upgrading, not downgrading."

Next up the price scale are **The Ron,** Rehov Yafo 44, phone: (02) 622-3122; fax: (02) 625-0707, and **The Palatin,** Rehov Agrippas 4, (02) 623-3351, both of which are smack in the center of town. The cost at both is approximately $80 a night for a single room, $100 for a double. The Ron has history and a graceful staircase on its side, but The Palatin has better value for the money and offers a 15 percent discount for an e-mail reservation: palatinj@netvision.net.il; www.traveler.net./beds/ohgreviews /e141003.html.

At just about the same price, but somewhat more elegant, is the **Eyal Hotel,** Rehov Shamai 21, phone: (02) 623-4161; fax: (02) 624-4136. It is around the corner from the Ben Yehuda Mall and the restaurants and shops of Nahalat Shiva.

A few dollars more ($105 for a single, up to $150 for a double), spiffier yet, and also close to Ben Yehuda, is the **Jerusalem Tower Hotel** at Rehov Hillel 23, phone (02) 620-9209; fax: (02) 625-2167. An e-mail reservation (jth@isracom.net.il) will bring a price reduction. The manager commented that the best price would come through a reservation made while booking a flight and mentioned El Al specifically. Check to see if the same opportunity exists when you book with other airlines.

Christian hostels are among the least-expensive places to stay in Jerusalem. The **Christian Information Center**, phone: (02) 627-2692; fax: (02) 628-6417, inside Jaffa Gate has a list. Facilities can be spartan, but you can find pristine dormitories and rooms large enough for families.

Ecce Homo Convent, Via Dolorosa 41, Moslem Quarter, Old City, phone: (02) 627-7292, fax (02) 628-8652, has inexpensive dormitories and single, double, and triple rooms. Expect to pay about $30 for a single room, $50 for a double. For atmosphere, Ecce Homo has it—with stone walls in the rooms, rooftop views over the Old City, and a maze of buildings. It also is next to the Lithostrotos, where it is said Jesus was mocked by Roman soldiers. Drawbacks could be the convent's rather tucked-away location and the fact that doors are locked at 11 p.m.

Prices are higher (about $80 for a single room, $100 for a double) at the elegant **Notre Dame of Jerusalem Center** on Paratroopers Street opposite the New Gate, phone: (02) 627-9111, fax: (02) 627-1995. The center frequently offers free concerts.

Arab-owned hotels in eastern Jerusalem are usually less expensive than their western Jerusalem equivalents, but it can be lonely walking to and from them at night. **The Gloria,** just inside Jaffa Gate in the Old City, (02) 628-2431, houses students on the Quaker Peace Studies program, which may or may not be a recommendation in your view. It is a clean, orderly place, and you'll pay about $40 for a single room, $60 for a double. After the initial 13-step climb from the street, grab the elevator up to the reception area.

A few more places to consider are the **YMCA,** (02) 569-2692, at Rehov King David 26, across from the King David Hotel, and **Beit Shmuel** at the World Education Center for Progressive (Reform) Judaism at Hebrew Union College, Rehov Shana 6, (02) 620-3466.

Beit Bernstein, at the Conservative Center at Rehov Agron 4, has been under reconstruction. Its status at this time is unknown. But anyone interested can call the Bernstein office at (02) 625-8286 or the synagogue office at (02) 625-3539.

The **Heritage House**, Rehov Or HaHayim 2 in the Jewish Quarter of the Old City, is a hostel for Jews. It is free, except on Shabbat, when there is a charge of less than $10. Men may reserve space by calling (02) 627-2224, women (02) 628-1220.

With any of these accommodations, try to see for yourself what you will be getting before plunking down your money. Or perhaps trusted friends in Jerusalem can check the places out for you—if you promise not to complain about their decision.

Home Accommodations

Throughout western Jerusalem you can find bed-and-breakfast arrangements and rooms in apartments (flats), usually let by widows. These lodgings often offer the best price and the most personal treatment (possibly more personal than you have in mind—since you could discover the quintessential Jewish mother).

Often, you will hear about these rooms through the grapevine. Plant seeds early by telling everyone you know and meet in Jerusalem that you want to rent a room. It's surprising how many people will give you a lead. Otherwise, contact the **Home Accommodation Association of Jerusalem,** phone: (02) 645-2198, e-mail: hq@bnb.co.il, Web site: www.bnb.co.il or www.virtual.co.il/travel/BnB. The **Israel Holiday Apartment Center,** phone: (02) 623-3459, fax (02) 625-9330, also offers B&B arrangements in flats, rooms with private bathrooms in flats, and private flats—from studios to family-size. Some vacationing Jerusalemites list rooms for rent on the bulletin board at the Association of Americans and Canadians in Israel (AACI), Rehov Mane 9, off Rehov Disraeli. Check the Internet for more listings, especially for bed-and-breakfast establishments.

6
A TASTE OF
JERUSALEM

When most American think of Jewish food they think of Eastern European food. In Israel, however, Jewish food is *Israeli* Jewish food. The difference is as great as that between a matzo ball and a falafel ball.

Israeli cuisine has gotten a bum rap. Tourists often expect gefilte fish and chopped liver, and when they can't find them, they complain bitterly. But the average native knows nothing from corned beef and rye. What Israelis call pastrami resembles bologna. Feh! What do they know? This is the Middle East, not Lublin or Los Angeles.

Israeli cuisine is still evolving. It's like nothing back home, and yet a little bit of the whole world goes into the recipe. It won raves from a gaggle of world-famous chefs who participated in Jerusalem's 3,000th birthday party. Not only did these guest chefs cook, but Jerusalem's best chefs also cooked dinner for them. The stars were surprised, impressed, and effusive with their accolades.

Basically, this is the land of hummus, tahini, pita, falafel, and kebabs; *me'moola'im, shishlik, shwarma,* and *bourekas;* spicy *hareef* peppers; and a seemingly endless variety of olives. These are some of the elements of *mizrachi* (eastern) food indigenous to the Levant and its neighbors. They can be eaten in the local equivalent of a greasy spoon and in some of the finest restaurants.

Food stall in the Mahane Yehuda market

Let's run past these foods again:

- **bourekas**: flaky pastry with cheese or spinach filling
- **falafel**: round balls of deep-fried, ground chickpeas. The name also refers to a serving of falafel and vegetables stuffed into a pita. Add tahini and a touch of *hareef* (hot sauce), and you have an inexpensive meal that can be eaten on the run.
- **hummus**: chickpeas ground into a thick sauce
- **kebabs**: ground, spicy meat shaped like fat sausages and grilled
- **me'moola'im**: vegetables (grape leaves, bell peppers, eggplant, squash, or onions) filled with meat, rice, and myriad spices
- **pita** (a Hebrew word found in the Bible): round, flat bread often stuffed with vegetables and falafel or torn off in chunks and used to "wipe" hummus. (Israeli pita has no relation in taste to the "pita" sold in American supermarkets.) Other items that might be heaped into the pita are onions, pickles, peppers, pickled vegetables, *schug* (a paste of fenugreek, garlic, cumin, dried red or green peppers, coriander, and cardamom), *amba* (a mango sauce), and fried eggplant slices, which are particularly scrumptious.
- **shishlik**: grilled meats
- **shwarma**: thin slices cut from meat grilled on an upright spit (traditionally lamb, but now usually turkey) and eaten in pita
- **tahini**: sesame seed sauce

The stars of Israel's culinary glory shine in those restaurants offering cuisine of the North African and Middle Eastern countries—stretching from Morocco to Iran—from which many Israelis descended.

Moroccan cuisine is usually considered the finest, because the French touch has given it delicacy. In Moroccan restaurants you'll find "cigars"—spiced meat, nuts, raisins, and cinnamon in a thin crust and resembling their namesake (sometimes vegetarian versions are offered)—and *couscous*, a tasty stew of different varieties with a semolina base.

Yemenite cooking includes a four-alarm soup heated by schug, reputed to cure anything that ails you; *cubana*, a special Shabbat cake baked overnight; and a delicacy, ram's penis (not to worry—not frequently found on menus). Kurds and Iraqis vie with each other for the tastiest *kubbeh*—meat encased in bulgur (cracked) wheat and either boiled or fried.

Dining Out

Jerusalem has a choice of restaurants far more extensive than most cities of its size. It seems as if the whole world eventually arrives here and wants to open a restaurant from the old country, wherever that is.

Diners can choose from Indian, Iranian, Indonesian, Japanese,

Chinese, French, Mongolian, Rumanian, Argentinean, and Tex-Mex. Some restaurants specialize in natural foods, vegetarian dishes, soufflés, or various kinds of vegetable pies. The gefilte-fish crowd who pine for the kind of food Bubby used to make—lungs, stuffed spleen (*miltz*), and jellied calf's feet (*pitchas*), not to mention goulash and chopped liver—can find what they're looking for, too, but they will have to look hard.

But it's the Italian restaurants that are most ubiquitous after indigenous mizrachi. It seems like almost every new restaurant that opens is Italian. Some suspect a takeover, although the takeover goes both ways—for it's thought that pizza originated in the Middle East. The elderly owner of a small Yemenite restaurant in my neighborhood that served heavenly *malawah*—a flaky, warm Yemenite bread that soothes the soul—retired. A New Zealander reopened the place as yet another Italian restaurant. I mourn.

American fast food has invaded during the past few years too. You now can find McDonald's, Burger King, Sbarro's, Domino's Pizza (complete with rushing motorcycle delivery), Kentucky Fried Chicken, Dunkin' Donuts, Ben & Jerry's, Nathan's Hot Dogs, and genuine North American–style bagels.

Keeping It Kosher

With the rich local offerings, would you really want to eat at a place that's just like home? Actually, the chains aren't quite like those at home because most are kosher—dairy products and meat aren't served in the same establishment.

The notorious exception is McDonald's. Although bragging that it respects local cultures internationally (serving non-beef hamburgers in India, for instance), McDonald's recently opened a non-kosher restaurant in, of all places, Jerusalem. Many Jerusalemites look on the establishment as a slap in the face. On the other hand, Nathan's Hot Dogs, which aren't kosher in the United States, are kosher here. The thing is, everyone can eat at kosher restaurants; not everyone can eat at non-kosher restaurants.

Because of the laws of *kashrut* (kosher dietary regulations) it takes imagination to prepare internationally known dishes at an Israeli restaurant. Out of this effort emerges a uniquely Israeli flavor. And because of kashrut, vegetarians never had it so good dining out. Israel is paradise for them.

All kosher restaurants and food stands are closed on Shabbat. So what's a hungry visitor to do? If your hotel serves more than breakfast, not to worry. If you aren't a guest at a hotel but you'd like to dine there on Shabbat, check out the possibility of paying for your meal in advance.

Alternatives are the non-kosher restaurants: the King David Street Y restaurant, some places on Rehov Yoel Salomon and Rehov Rivlin in the downtown neighborhood of Nahalat Shiva, and others on Rehov Emek Refaim in the German Colony. Arab restaurants are open in eastern Jerusalem. Then, there's always (dare I say it?) McDonald's.

Splurging

Jerusalem restaurant prices can be high. At least I think $10 for a plate of spaghetti in tomato sauce (with not a single trimming) is high—if you aren't at least surrounded by the upscale atmosphere of the King David Hotel.

But blowing the piggy bank can provide something special. **Mishkenot Sha'ananim** in the Yemin Moshe neighborhood, (02) 625-4424, offers a glorious view of the Old City—try it on a night with a full moon. The view, as well as the (non-kosher) food, could be worth the splurge at least once.

The **Cow on the Roof** in the Sheraton Plaza Hotel, Rehov King George 47, (02) 629-8666, is another renowned Jerusalem restaurant, perhaps even more so in the restaurant trade than Mishkenot Sha'ananim. Here, world-class chef Shalom Kadosh elevates kosher to the sublime. The restaurant lacks a view, for it's located on the hotel's ground floor, despite its name.

Arab bakery in the Jewish Quarter of the Old City

53

Seeds of Israeli Culture

Wherever you go in Israel, there is one food item about which you'll need to be in the know. In 1939, the Ashkenazi writer Ya'acov Rabinowitz complained in *The Wanderings of Amasai* that every Shabbat, Sephardic Jews and Arabs come together "and fill their balconies with nutshells. They crack and crack. It is nauseating."

Rabinowitz was probably referring not to nuts but seeds—especially sunflower seeds. In Hebrew, sunflower seeds are called *garinei chamnia* or usually just plain *garinim*.

Time brings changes, and these days Arabs and Jews aren't getting together on Shabbat as much as they used to—much less to crack nuts. And another change is that you no longer have to be Sephardi to love sunflower seeds. Along with soccer, garinim chomping is a national mania.

While Americans away from home might yearn for a good lean corned beef on rye sandwich, I know a young Israeli who had studied in chilly, orderly Denmark and told me how much he yearned for garinim while he was there. Yuval was going out of his mind missing that reassuring chomp.

Then he made an exciting discovery: pet stores carried sunflower seeds for birds. He rushed to satisfy his yearning, but when he saw the sunflower seeds in the store, he sadly shook his head. "They're so small," he complained to the clerk.

"The birds don't mind," she blithely replied.

Yuval agonized over whether or not to confess his mission, that he wanted larger sunflower seeds not for any bird, but for himself. Finally he did. He was desperate. The Danish woman was astounded to encounter such bizarre tastes.

But even Anglo-Saxim can be imbued with the mania. I know a woman from Philadelphia who sits into the wee hours of the morning chomping sunflower seeds. And, yes, she "cracks and cracks."

Visiting Israel, you might find yourself in an Israeli home with everyone gathered around a bowl that contains, besides sunflower seeds, pumpkin seeds and—if somebody splurged—pistachios, cashews, almonds (a fertility symbol), peanuts, hazelnuts, pecans, and even Brazil nuts.

Everyone will be talking and digging nonstop into the bowl. Another bowl will be close by to catch the shells, but more shells could be on the rug and stuck to clothing than in the bowl.

With everyone lustily reaching for garinim, eventually, you will do the same—and not be able to stop after you've had just one or even a dozen.

But you could be frustrated by the way the veteran garinim crackers around you go about their business. They are fast and efficient. You don't see them pulling shredded shells from their mouths and wondering where the seed went. You don't see them struggling to scrape smashed sunflower shells that stick like Krazy Glue off their wet fingers.

From these experts, you hear a crack or two of the shell between their teeth. Then you see them draw from between their lips a cleanly split shell. Their fingers aren't even damp.

How do they do it? I asked some experts. David, a sabra with Ashkenazi roots, told me his secret one Shabbat. ("That's the only day I have time for this," he confided. And that might be the main difference between Ashkenazim and Sephardim: Sephardim always have time for garinim.)

David's method is to put the narrow end of the sunflower seed between this teeth, crack it gently—just so the shell separates, but not so it breaks into shreds—and then, with his tongue, flip the seed into his mouth.

Shaya, whose grandparents came from Yemen and who can't channel-surf his 28-inch TV without chomping garinim, insists one crack on the shell isn't enough. He advises, "Make two."

Whatever works.

But with the quality of the food (which is expensive), you won't care about a view. The restaurant is open Sunday through Thursday.

Darna, Rehov Horkanos 3, (02) 624-5406, is a Moroccan restaurant with an upscale, exotic ambience and price—but worth the experience. It is called the most beautiful restaurant in Jerusalem.

For Those on a Budget

Now, with the piggy bank broken, what to do? Jerusalem offers ways of eating well and at moderate prices, as well as on the cheap. But give your bill a hard look before you pay; a service fee often is included.

I am loath to name restaurants for fear that naming them will make them disappear. But I'll daringly mention a few that have been around for a long time. As in stock-market prospectuses, let me add that past performance is no guarantee of future performance. (The following restaurants are kosher, unless otherwise noted.)

Mamma Mia and **Pera-e-Mela** are Italian dairy restaurants that happen to be close to each other. Mamma Mia, (02) 624-8080, is at Rehov King George 36 above the parking lot. The entrance is from Rehov Ma'alot. Pera-e-Mela, (02) 625-1975, is at Ma'alot 7. Mamma Mia is big, noisy, and popular. It serves an excellent pesto. I don't know the management ins and outs of Mamma Mia, but Pera-e-Mela is owned and run by Italians, the Ottolenghi family. It is a small, intimate place, where you easily can find yourself in conversation with the people at the next table.

Sima's, Shipudei HaGefen, HaShipudei, and many others on Rehov Agrippas and its side streets in the Mahane Yehuda area all feature grilled meats. So which is best? You often see groups of soldiers having lunch at these places, so I asked them (not at lunchtime). They answered, "They're all good." They should know.

Misadonet, behind Rehov Yoel Salomon 12, (02) 624-8396, is one of several Kurdi restaurants in Jerusalem. It comes as a surprise to some visitors that Jews came from Kurdistan, but they did—and became an important part of Israel. Here you can taste *kubbeh*, the traditional Kurdi dish of meat wrapped in bulgur or cracked wheat, served several ways.

The **Armenian Tavern** (non-kosher), downstairs at Armenian Orthodox Patriarchate Road 79, (02) 627-3854, offers the Armenian version of traditional Middle Eastern food, plus (even here) spaghetti. So-called Armenian Pizza is really a crepe with spicy ground meat wrapped in a thin crust. The *baba ghanoug*—eggplant with tahini—is excellent. The bread basket on the table includes *lavash*, large, floppy bread that's often called Iraqi bread. The Armenian Tavern is open every day of the week.

A moderately priced Moroccan restaurant is **Sahara Tulip** at Rehov Yafo 17, (02) 625-4239. It is both vegetarian and kosher.

The most renowned Arab restaurant is the venerable **Philadelphia** (the town of Amman's Roman name) at al-Zahra Street 9, off Salah ad-Din Street in eastern Jerusalem, (02) 627-6227 or (800) 255-155. It offers a sumptuous *mezze*—tableful of hors d'oeuvres—in addition to stuffed pigeon and various meat and seafood dishes. It's open daily, and there's free shuttle service from hotels.

If you don't feel like sitting in a restaurant, you can buy precooked "take away" food at **Heimishe Essen**, Rehov Keren Kayemet 19, and **Grilled** (that's what the sign says), 42 Rehov HaPalmach 42. If you want food brought to you, there's always Domino's Pizza.

My favorite place for lunch (the only time it's open) is **Ta'ami** on Rehov Shamai 3. This tiny place has long plastic tables, and you sit wherever there is room. Immediately, a harried waiter will plop a basket of warm pita in front of you. Since you didn't ask for it, you will naturally assume the pita is complimentary. Oh, no. It will go on your bill. You'll also get a stained menu. In 30 seconds the waiter will be back, annoyed that you haven't already decided what you want. I adore the stuffed grape leaves. The hummus is about the best. Ta'ami is so typically Israeli with its simplicity, surly waiters, and wonderful food that it's almost a caricature of itself. Its style is kosher-meat.

To track down Indonesian, Mongolian, Eastern European, and other restaurants with tantalizing menus, pick up a free copy of "Your Jerusalem" and "In Jerusalem" in the Friday *Jerusalem Post*. Found in hotels are *This Week in Jerusalem* and *Jerusalem's Best Menus*, which shows menus and prices and often offers discounts.

Israel is a fast-food capital. You can get ready-made sandwiches all over town. Falafel, shwarma, fish cakes, and omelettes are among the filling food you can buy stuffed into a pita or baguette, to be eaten while you walk, should you want to. The additions are what set these fast foods apart—that touch of hot and spicy and the crunch of fresh herbs.

Everybody has a favorite falafel stand. And of course I have mine, which I will share if you promise not to crowd me out of line—and there's almost always a line. My favorite is **Falafel Shalom**, which not too long ago upgraded from a genuine hole in the wall to a storefront across the street at Rehov Bezalel 36.

A last word: Two dishes are named for the city. One is Jerusalem Mixed Grill, consisting of chicken livers, chicken hearts, beef, and onions, available at mizrachi restaurants specializing in grilled meats. The other you are unlikely to find in any restaurant. It is Jerusalem Kugel—a baked noodle pudding made with sugar, eggs, and a lot of pepper and cooked until it's almost black. It is served with a pickle on the side in some synagogues after Saturday morning prayers. I've eaten it at Yeshivat Torah

Chaim on el-Wad in the Moslem Quarter of the Old City, at the Ben Zakkai Synagogue in the Jewish Quarter, and at Rananim Synagogue next to the Great Synagogue. It is also sold at some "take away" stores, including one at Rehov Agrippas 44, where it's available only on Wednesday, Thursday, and Friday. It's worth going to great lengths to taste the dish to which the city has given its name. After all, Proust had his madeleines, you could have your Jerusalem kugel.

Whatever or wherever you eat, as Israelis say before the first bite at a meal, "B'tayavon"—"Good appetite."

7
SHOPPING SPREE

N o word exists in Hebrew equivalent to the English word *shopping*, which connotes a leisurely venture. Israelis go to buy. They don't have time to shop. For them, shopping is a serious business. As well it should be—because of the high prices here for just about everything (except capers) and the fact that once you make a purchase, you're stuck with it.

To meet your shopping and commercial needs in Jerusalem, all you have to remember besides money and/or your credit card is what and when businesses are open. This is the tradition, albeit slipping away:

- Hairdressers and barbers are closed Monday afternoon.
- Small grocery stores, pharmacies, hardware stores, laundries, and dry cleaners are closed Tuesday afternoon.
- Most branch post offices and travel agencies are closed Wednesday afternoon.
- Smaller businesses, except those in the city center and in canyons, tend to close daily between 1 and 4 p.m. and reopen until 7 p.m. Some supermarkets are open straight through until 10 p.m. One supermarket, Super-Sol at Rehov Agron 1, is open from 7 a.m. to midnight Sunday and Monday, and from 7 a.m. Tuesday continuously until 3 p.m. Friday. Needless to say, it has become something of a social center.
- Almost everything in western Jerusalem closes by 1 p.m. at the latest on Friday and stays closed through Shabbat. That includes most restaurants, but they reopen Saturday night.

Got that schedule? In the Old City, the Jewish Quarter follows the same schedule as western Jerusalem. In the Arab section, while Friday and Sunday are Moslem and Christian Sabbaths respectively, stores aren't closed as strictly as those owned by Jews. Often, Arab-owned stores are open seven days a week. The exception is Armenian-owned businesses, which are usually closed on Sunday. With schedules like these, it might seem as if businesses are always closed when you need them. On the other hand, it always is possible to go shopping somewhere.

Wherever you shop, whatever you buy, remember this basic rule: Shop prudently. In my former hometown, Denver, it was often said, "You could return a dead dog." Not in Israel. In general, the local law of return is—after the clerk gives you an astounded, then a sour expression over your audacity to ask—no refunds. The argument is that the value-added tax (see page 66) has already been registered, and it's impossible to unregister it.

If you have the gift of persuasion, you'll find that nothing is impossible. But unless you have that gift, the best you'll be able to do is make an exchange or receive a credit slip, which is just the thing you want to stuff into your wallet before boarding a plane for home.

At the big department store Hamashbir Lazarchan, returns on most items are accepted within 14 days of purchase, but again, you probably won't see your money unless you'll be around for a while. A manager told me that the money has to come from central headquarters, somewhere in the Tel Aviv area (probably in a Brinks van).

But as Israel becomes less socialistic and more capitalistic, the customer is looked on more and more as someone to be courted, not ignored. That definitely is a new concept here. I did once, grudgingly, get money back from a very small hardware store on Agrippas. The best thing, if you're in doubt at all, is to inquire about the return policy before you make the purchase. And if you have a dead dog, it's your problem.

One final warning, as the following apocryphal story clearly shows: What you see is not necessarily what you get.

Hair Care

Women will find stylists as au courant in Jerusalem as in London, Paris, and New York—for a price. And that price is close to what haircuts cost at Fifth Avenue establishments.

About barbers, I really can't say. But if men can't get their ideal haircut in Jerusalem, at least they will be able to hear the best gossip in town in the barber chair.

Hotel hairdressers and barbers are the most expensive and the most likely to speak English. Close in price are establishments in the center of the city. Down the line are the neighborhood beauty salons. Beauty salons on Salah ed-Din Street in eastern Jerusalem are open on Saturday.

The least expensive are the "bootleggers"—hairdressers who work in their homes and out of tax collectors' sight. Needless to say, they don't advertise. It's strictly a word-of-mouth business.

Hairdressing schools are another alternative. The price is right, but the work is slow as the fledgling hairdresser worries his or her way through your hair. In a pinch, an instructor might do some cutting. The results could be excellent—or you might end up wearing a hat for a week or so. One school is Shuki Zikri, upstairs at Rehov Mordechai Ben Hillel 1 (above Kentucky Fried Chicken). No appointment is necessary.

"Ah, just what I was looking for," Gary said to himself when he spotted a tiny shop that had watches and clocks jam-packed in the window.

Gary's watch needed fixing. A visitor from Canada, he was happy to come upon what looked like a watch-repair shop. He entered the shop, which was no bigger than a closet.

"I'd like to have my watch fixed," he told an elderly, bearded man who appeared to be the proprietor.

"I don't fix watches," the man said.

"You don't fix watches?" Gary asked, surprised. "What do you do?"

"I am a *mohel* [one who performs Jewish ritual circumcisions]," the man answered.

Gary chuckled over his mistake. But wait a minute. He asked, "Then why do you have all those watches in the window?"

With a slight smile and a shrug, the man said, "What else should I put in the window?"

Bargaining Daze in the Amazing Maze

By now, you realize that shopping in Jerusalem takes more than money. It takes time. And concentration. And nowhere is this as true as in the Old City, specifically the shopping area known as the *souk* (pronounced "sook"), in the jumbled, dimly lit maze of the Arab section. There, the entire process of shopping and concluding a sale is as labyrinthine as the Old City itself.

Negotiations in the Old City souk

Items in any one store might be so numerous and varied, a novice shopper's natural tendency is simply to gawk at them. Displayed pell-mell inside and outside the shops are Bedouin dresses, sheepskin jackets, camel saddlebags, rugs, brass and copper items, jewelry, Hebron glass, baskets, pottery, T-shirts, Indian scarves, and sheer junk.

And while your eyes lose control, your ears are beset by hawking shopkeepers calling out their standard line: "Come into my shop. I have something wonderful for you. Come into my

62

shop. I can tell you are good luck for me today. Come into my shop. Just to look—nothing else—just to look."

You practically may be pulled inside. Once you are in, the merchant's talk never ends. And for female shoppers, the pinching might begin.

You must have a will of iron to walk out empty-handed. If you happen to be made of such stern stuff, know also that the merchant, no matter what he said to get you into his shop, might shout epithets after you as you leave.

I try to be firm, but it doesn't always work. One Christmas morning, an Arab friend who owns a jewelry store saw me passing by and invited me in to drink tea with him and his red-haired cousin. Or so the invitation went. We compared our experiences in Bethlehem the night before, and the two young men complained of having hangovers. But the red-haired cousin wasn't so hungover he didn't have the presence of mind to show me a board displaying several necklaces and to ask the leading question, "Which do you like?"

I knew I was trapped. Instead of insisting I wasn't buying anything and heading for the door—and risking the cousin's claim that I had wounded his very soul or alienating my friend—I babbled, "Oh, that one's nice—and so's that one—but I don't need another necklace, and I can't afford to buy anything right now, and I don't know anyone in the world I could give ..." Never mind. The red-haired cousin added a pair of matching earrings to the first necklace I pointed to and had them wrapped up and in my lap and his hand out for payment while I still was insisting I wasn't buying anything that morning.

So be tough. Do you think Old City merchants aren't? They share a major characteristic with diamonds (and I don't mean sparkle). No matter how soft these merchants appear to be, no matter how much poetry they may recite to you, nothing scratches them.

I've heard it said, "Don't ask for a price unless you intend to buy." But it's my money, and I must make it stretch as far as possible. If you are looking for a specific item, go comparison shopping. Prices vary from one establishment to the next. I carry pencil and paper to jot down asking prices, and locations so I can find my way back.

And when you determine what you want and where you want to buy it, a new game begins: Middle Eastern bargaining. It's said that the best price in the souk is for Arabs; the worst for American tourists. A variation has it that the worst price is for Israelis. That might be, but Israelis aren't timid about getting that price to where it belongs.

The rule of the game is to never, ever accept the first price that the merchant gives you. Nor the second. Nor even the third, unless it is considerably lower than the first. Your line, in response to the merchant's line, should be, "It's lovely, but I simply can't afford it." Do not insult his merchandise. He might ask, "What can you afford to pay?" or "How much do you want to pay?" You should then come up with a figure well below what you are willing to pay. He will groan and say, "Impossible." You will groan and raise your offer a tiny bit. He will groan and bring his down. Reluctantly moving toward the door to leave usually brings prices down further. Eventually, your prices should meet. Remember, it is a game.

If you shop for Bedouin dresses or jackets, look them over carefully. If they are secondhand, they are desirable because they are old and the needlework, theoretically, is better. But check that color discrepancies from one section of the dress to another are acceptable to you.

Don't let pickpockets ruin your shopping trip. Not all of that jostling and bumping against you in crowded lanes will be accidental.

You may eventually find that you will ask to be led out of the Old City souk blindfolded to avoid squandering any more money. That part of Jerusalem is one concentrated temptation.

If you need a respite from the hard-sell souk, look for the Friendly Falafel at Christian Quarter Road 11. Its owner is one of the few Christians left in the Christian Quarter. In fact, he is a Baptist preacher. Or find an Arab bakery on Khan ez-Zeit Street. The honeyed pastries will soothe your nerves and sweeten your excursion.

The Better Things in Life Aren't Free

The most enjoyable items to shop for, let's face it, are special gifts for yourself and others. And Jerusalem abounds with tempting and unusual gift items. The Jewish Quarter of the Old City has many fine shops, without the hassle of the Arab Quarter. Many of these shops are concentrated along the old Roman road, the Cardo. Western Jerusalem's allures are more spread out than those in the Old City and offer a shopper a chance to catch his breath.

There's always the problem of buying a gift in, say, London only to find it stamped "Made in Thailand." Here are some places that specialize in Israeli-made items:

Kuzari was established in the Bucharan Quarter both to preserve the varied embroidery styles of Jewish communities across the Middle East and to provide income for women in that threadbare neighborhood. Over the years, its offerings have broadened. Besides stunning needlework, high-crowned *kippot*, handbags, challah covers, and T-shirts, you'll find woven *tallitot* in a range of shimmering colors. The prices are right, plus Kuzari sells inexpensive embroidered items useful for remembering friends. The store is at Rehov HaBucharim 10, (02) 582-6632, in what was once the

Davidaieff Mansion but now is home to several community services. Walk around and see what was done architecturally.

Palestinian Pottery (14 Nablus Road, across from the American consulate in eastern Jerusalem) and **Hagop's Pottery** (opposite Zion Gate in the Old City) have long been *the* places to buy Armenian ceramic work. Jerusalem street signs are made of robustly colored Armenian tiles. It is the strong presence of cobalt blue in the design that declares the tiles' ethnic identity. Not only can you buy decorative tiles in a variety of designs but you can also buy dishes, mugs, vases, bowls, and name plates for the door. (Cheap imitations abound, as you know from walking through the souk.) The stores are closed Sunday. Hagop Antreassian's work is the less traditional of the two.

On the HaMashbir Plaza at Rehov King George 20 is a store that goes by initials. In English, they sound like "Gras." Dresses, jackets, ponchos, shoulder bags, and jewelry are some of the items here.

On Rehov Rivlin 12 you'll find **Derech HaKav**, (02) 625-5271, with hand-painted children's dishes and bowls of Biblical and Jerusalem scenes, jewelry, and handmade *gregars* (noisemakers) for Purim. On the same street at number 8 you'll find **Gans**, (02) 625-1159, with a variety of Israeli-made items, including jewelry, wall hangings, platters, and pillow covers.

At Rivlin 18 is the gallery of **Neil Folberg**, an outstanding photographer with splendid books on the Sinai and historic synagogues around the world to his credit. He shows his own and others' work. The gallery is open Sun–Thur 11–7, Fri 10–1, or by appointment, (02) 622-2253.

Opposite the Old City walls, between Jaffa Gate and the base of Yemin Moshe, is Khutzot HaYotzer, a lane of high-quality studios and galleries. Several internationally known artists and craftspeople are based here. Normally, the lane is quite deserted. But at the International Arts and Crafts Fair held here in early August, it's "shop until you drop" time.

Among Old City Jewish Quarter shops, **Colors of Jerusalem** at Rehov Jewish Quarter 43, (02) 628-3493, is outstanding. This is a place to buy collectibles. It has striking silver work, much of it made by store owner Jason Feld. It also sells the work of immigrants from Ethiopia and the former Soviet Union. One irresistible item was a violin decorated with folk art showing the now-lost life of Eastern European Jews. This is a place largely for people not only with money but also with taste.

Also in the Old City, anyone seriously interested in Middle East antiquities will be entranced at **Yaser T. Barakat's** store at Aftemos Square 146–149 in the Moslem Quarter, (02) 628-1139. He has original David Roberts lithographs dating from the 1840s and 1850s, carpets, copper work, Syrian inlaid furniture, and old Palestinian embroidery, of which Barakat humbly said, "You don't see work like this anymore. I have magnificent pieces."

Barbara Shaw has well-designed, colorful aprons, kitchen towels, shoulder bags, and small cases for pencils, makeup, and the like—all with a connection to Jerusalem and Israel. Her products, made with the help of native Israelis and those from other countries, may be purchased at the Association of Americans and Canadians in Israel, at her store at Rehov Harutzim 4, by mail through the Jerusalem Post Book Store or, she magnanimously offers, directly from her. She means it. Call (02) 561-9369 or her mobile phone at 050-694-878.

The **Israel Government Coins and Medals Corp., Ltd.**, (02) 560-0147, is an almost intimidating name for a place that sells gold, silver, and bronze items. You'll find commemorative coins, pendants, kiddush cups, and *chanukiahs* (menorahs). The star is a shimmering silver Seder plate for approximately $460. The sales room is at Rehov Ahad Ha'am 5. And here's a nice touch: The store's brochure notes that "profits are earmarked for the preservation of nature and improvement of the landscape in Israel."

And here is a gift you probably never would think to buy in Israel—chocolate. **Max Brenner Chocolates** at Rehov Emek Refaim 27 in the German Colony are handmade, come in a zillion varieties (it seems), and are produced with the best techniques learned in Switzerland. It's hard even to walk past the store, for hunks of chocolate fill the window. Finally, the Israel Museum, Bible Lands Museum, Anna Ticho House, and David's Tower Museum are also excellent places for gift buying.

Value-Added Tax

When shopping, note that a price quote may or may not include the value-added tax (VAT). Inquire before agreeing to buy, because the tax ups the price by 17 percent.

Tourists who use foreign currency to make purchases of more than $50 and at Tourism Ministry–approved stores can receive a refund on the VAT when they leave the country. To get that refund, the invoice must be attached to your purchase and placed in a sealed bag. Carry the item with you to Ben-Gurion Airport or Haifa Port, where you can get the VAT back in dollars, minus commission. At other departure points, a customs official will stamp the invoice, and you will eventually get the refund at the address abroad that you wrote on the invoice.

8
IS THERE LIFE AFTER DARK IN JERUSALEM?

Y ou bet there is. Plenty goes on in Jerusalem at night, and I don't mean only lectures on religion (though admittedly there are lots of those) or all-night shopping at Super-Sol.

Reputations have a way of sticking like Velcro, even when they long have been outlived. Tel Avivians from "the Big Orange—the city that never sleeps" still say they wouldn't dream of being trapped in Jerusalem at night. They are convinced, as one critic put in, that Jerusalem is "half the size of the New York City cemetery and twice as dead."

But that was years ago. Jerusalem has learned to stay up at night and go out on the town. To relax after a hard day's touring, you can choose from a variety of events. You'll find information in the *Jerusalem Post*'s Friday edition and in hotels.

Classical Music

The **Israel Philharmonic Orchestra**, with world-famous conductors, performs about ten times a season from October to May in Jerusalem's Binyenei Ha'uma near the Central Bus Station. Although tickets are hard to come by, you can almost always find people outside the theater just before a performance trying to sell tickets they can't use. It's worth taking a chance on landing one or two.

While the **Jerusalem Symphony Orchestra** doesn't have the glamor of a Zubin Mehta, some magnificent music comes from this younger, more adventurous orchestra. Its soloists are stars whose full brilliance is yet to shine internationally. The JSO performs at the Henry Crown Symphony Hall at the Jerusalem Theater, Rehov Marcus 20, in the city's Talbia neighborhood.

Other classical music events include the **Etnahta** series, (02) 530-2208, free concerts at 5 p.m. Monday at the Jerusalem Theater. The **Anna Ticho House,** (02) 624-5068, holds concerts at 11 a.m. Friday. **Bible Lands Museum,** (02) 561-1066, across from the Israel Museum, has 8 p.m. Saturday performances with different types of music each week—classical, jazz, ethnic, and blues. The admission fee includes wine and cheese. Check the newspaper or call to verify performance information.

Jazz

The center of the Jerusalem jazz world is **Pargod,** at Rehov Bezalel 94. In addition to scheduled performances, every Friday a jam session starts at 1 p.m. Admission is free. While listeners nurse Kinley orange pop, tea, coffee, or Maccabee beer rather than hard liquor, the smoke gets as thick as a Chicago jazz joint. For a more sedate environment, the **Hyatt Regency** in French Hill has jazz at 8:30 Sunday, Tuesday, Thursday, and Saturday.

Pop Music

At an Israeli pop concert, you'll sink in amid sabras and be surrounded by Israeli life. Israelis are out to have a good time, and they do. When a song touches them, a surge of emotion sweeps through the crowd. You'll be carried along on its wave, too. Listeners freely clap their hands with the music and sing along. They seem to know every word of every song. If you catch a mizrachi singer, so much the better for atmosphere. The crowd will be dancing in the aisles.

Melave Malka is the festive weekly leave-taking of Shabbat. The **Diaspora Yeshiva** on Mount Zion near King David's Sepulchre often has a rock band playing from 9 p.m. Saturday. Shows often overflow with enthusiasm and dancing in the aisles.

Theater

While dance and music need no translation, plays performed in an unknown language can be forbidding. Occasionally, you can see English-language theater in Jerusalem. Not only could a British troupe be here but local English-speaking groups might also be performing. **Jerusalem English-Speaking Theater** is one of the latter, presenting plays and musicals. Its standards are surprisingly high. I was dragged there to see yet another performance of *The Music Man*, and I left amazed by the talent and exuberance found in the small pool of native English-speakers.

The **Palestinian National Theater** is located at Abu Obeida Street 2, off Salah ad-Din Street behind the Tomb of the Kings in eastern Jerusalem. Its children's puppet shows don't use spoken language. Other productions are in Arabic, but often an English synopsis is available. For information on performances, call (02) 628-0957.

Folk Dancing

You can dance your stay away every night but Friday at Israeli folk-dance sessions. There's always a dance somewhere—almost every community center offers folk dancing.

Israeli folk dance uses certain basic steps, and all you have to remember is their order within any particular song. There's something especially liberating about Israeli folk dance. And you don't need a partner to participate—most dances are done in a welcoming circle. If partners are required for a certain dance, one will be found for you. Most dances open with a beginners' session.

Sunday nights in summer, the courtyard at **Hebrew Union College**, 13 Rehov King David, is a glorious site for dancing. The **International Culture Center for Youth** (ICCY), Rehov Emek Refaim 12a, (02) 566-4144, holds dances on Tuesday throughout the year. From 7 to 8 p.m. you can learn the steps, and dancing continues until 11:30. At the ICCY you have only to be young at heart. Nobody checks your birth certificate.

Dance Performance

At 9 almost every night, the **Tsbarim Troupe** puts on a dance program in which you can see the *debka*, the Yemenite step, and the *hora* the way they should be done. Performances are held at the YMCA Auditorium, Rehov King David 26. Call 050-233-210 for information. Concerts by major Israeli and visiting dance companies usually are held at the Jerusalem Theater.

Nightclubs and Pubs

Nightlife to some people is synonymous with nightclubs or, as they're called in Jerusalem, pubs. Local familiarity with alcohol has become far more sophisticated since the time when, out of nostalgia, I ordered a Margarita from a drinks menu. I was served a wide-rimmed champagne glass of pure tequila.

But Jerusalem's nightspots come and go, and their names change from week to week. Listing them would be useless. It's best just to head to areas where pubs are found. These include the Russian Compound neighborhood (especially Rehov Helena HaMalka), Nahalot Shiva, and the Talpiot industrial area. The legal drinking age in Israel is 18.

Festivals

Two festivals require setting everything else aside and rushing to the concert halls: the **Israel Festival** and **Liturgica**.

The Israel Festival every May and June is the biggest, with music, dance, and theater groups from around the world gathering for an explosion of artistry. At the festival, I have seen the British *Coriolanus*, a wordless antiviolence production by a Polish theater, and Moroccan trance painters who flung paint all over the place. The most unusual performances were the first production of *Turandot* at which I didn't want to nod off, performed by the Swedish National Folksoper, with Italian music sung in Swedish and supertitles in Hebrew and Arabic (I often wondered, where am I?); and Shakespeare's *The Merchant of Venice*, performed in German by German actors, directed by an Israeli, and set in a Nazi death camp. The Israel Festival also offers free daily performances in the Jerusalem Theater plaza, special sculptures, banners, and balloons. The cotton-candy maker does a runaway business.

Liturgica is basically a festival of religious choral music, most of it Christian. Again, performers are international. One year, I heard the Mormon Tabernacle Choir perform Berlioz's *Requiem*.

A particular goal of both festivals is to feature Jewish music. I have witnessed a thrilling performance of Jewish liturgical songs as jazz, a concert by Jewish and Moslem musicians in which an Israeli pop singer joined in to sing liturgical melodies, and an evening showcasing music of various Jewish ethnic groups, such as those from India, Ethiopia, and Uzbekistan.

Tickets and Schedules

To know what performances are taking place in town—I know this sounds like a broken record—read the Friday *Jerusalem Post.* For events at the Jerusalem Theater, you can buy tickets at its box office close to Rehov Marcus. Commercial ticket agencies are **Ben Na'im**, Rehov Yafo 38, (02) 623-1273; **Bimot,** Rehov Shamai 8, (02) 624-0896; and **Kla'im,** Rehov Shamai 12, (02) 625-6869.

Brain Food

Yes, there are lectures. English-language talks on any number of subjects take place throughout the week but are held regularly at 8 p.m. Monday at the **Conservative Center** at the corner of Rehov Agron and Keren HaYesod.

Many lectures deal with religion. The Hebrew Bible is constantly examined, with each speaker offering his or her own insight. Speakers who especially spur the intellect and touch the heart are Rabbi Mordechai Gafni, a young man who refers to God as "she" as well as "he"; Rabbi Adin Steinsaltz, who, besides being a preeminent scholar and translator of the Talmud into English, exudes warm humanity in his twice-a-year English talks; and Anita Zornberg, a trailblazer in religious scholarship. Their speaking schedules can be found in the *Jerusalem Post.*

And then there's **Yakar**, a Jewish learning center that has events such as "Song, Silence and Soul," "Poetry Slam," and discussions on social concerns. The center is located at Rehov HaLamed Hey 10; phone (02) 561-2310. The Web address is www.cyberscribe.com/yakar.

9
TOURING
JERUSALEM

J erusalem is an endless, million-calorie serving of sights and sites. It is easy to be intimidated by so many choices all at once. If you feel daunted, just remember, even an elephant can be eaten one bite at a time.

Visit the **Municipal Tourist Information Office,** (02) 625-8844, currently in Building 3, Safra Square (off Rehov Yafo), directly across from the entrance to City Hall, for free maps, listings of events, and advice.

The **Christian Information Center,** (02) 627-2692, near the Jaffa Gate post office has lists of church services and hospices. The center is open 8:30 a.m. to 1 p.m. Monday through Saturday.

Guides and Tours

For the feast that is Jerusalem, there's nothing like a good guide to help you digest it. You might look on what a guide has to offer as spoon-feeding, but I see it as a proper education. Jerusalem might be the most complex city in the world to understand.

Beware of individuals who approach you on the street and offer to show you around for a price. They abound at Jaffa Gate. It's illegal for non-licensed guides to accept money. Licensed guides have had 18 months of intensive training and testing by the Ministry of Tourism. They wear a distinctive pin and don't do business by cornering wide-eyed tourists. To hire your own licensed tour guide, contact the Association of Guides, (03) 751-1132.

Excellent tour groups operate as well. You can find schedules for the following and other group tours in *This Week in Jerusalem* or *Your Jerusalem*, free in hotels and at the tourist information offices mentioned above.

- **Archaeological Seminars**, Rehov Habad 34 in the Jewish Quarter of the Old City (above the Cardo), has seminars and tours usually lasting three hours. The price is reasonable, and tours are prefaced by a talk about the area to be visited. The group also publishes an excellent review of Jerusalem's archaeological history: *Getting Jerusalem Together* by Fran Alpert. You can contact the company by telephone: (02) 627-3515, e- mail: office@archesem.com, or Web site: www. archesem.com.

- **Zion Walking Tours, Ltd.**, (02) 628-7866 or (050) 305-552, located past the Tower of David entrance next to Bank Leumi, specializes in various aspects of the Old City, including walks on the wall ramparts and in nearby neighborhoods such as Mea She'arim and the Bucharan Quarter. Tours average three to three-and-a-half hours.

- The municipality has free walking tours in English to a different site each week. Tours leave from Rehov Yafo near the Russian Compound at 10 a.m. Saturday. Friday's *In Jerusalem* has listings.

- **Solan Tourist Information,** (02) 628-0382, a private company, is located just inside Jaffa Gate, next to the H. Stern store. Besides information and maps, for about $10 a day you can rent an "audio guide," a green contraption that resembles a telephone handpiece, to guide you throughout the Old City. The office is open 8 a.m. to 4 p.m. Sunday through Thursday, until 1 p.m. Friday and holiday eves.

What's Open on Saturday in Jerusalem

Christian and Moslem sites are open on Saturday. In addition, you can visit these attractions:

- Bible Lands Museum
- Bloomfield Science Museum
- Church of the Holy Sepulchre
- Tower of David Museum
- Ein Kerem Christian sites
- Garden Tomb
- Hebrew Union College Skirball Archaeological Museum
- Holyland Hotel—Model of Second Temple Jerusalem
- Israel Museum
- Mardigian Armenian Museum
- Mayer Museum of Islamic Arts
- Ramparts Walk
- Rockefeller Museum
- Sherover and Haas Promendes
- Stalagmite and Stalactite Cave
- Temple Mount Islamic Museum
- Tisch Family Biblical Zoo
- University Botanical Gardens
- Wohl Rose Garden
- Zedekiah's Caves

As a general rule, museums and sites that are open on Shabbat are also open on Jewish holidays, including Rosh HaShana. On Yom Kippur, all museums and sites are closed, except Christian and Moslem.

- The **Society for the Protection of Nature** has a few Jerusalem tours in English, especially during summer. They usually take place in Jerusalem's historical neighborhoods outside of the Old City. Check *In Jerusalem* or contact SPNI, Rehov Helena HaMalka 13, (02) 625-7682.

  You can also become oriented to the Golden City through Egged's Bus 99. Designed for tourists, it zigzags through the city to reach 36 major attractions. You can buy tickets on the bus for on-and-off privileges for one or two days of sightseeing. The trip starts at the bus stop below Jaffa Gate at 10 a.m., noon, 2 p.m., and 4 p.m. Sunday through Thursday, and 10 a.m. and noon Friday and holidays (more frequently in summer), but you can board at any Bus 99 stop. Contact Egged for additional tour information.

Helpful Hints

Dress modestly on tours or while sightseeing on your own, since you are likely to visit religious sites or pass through conservative neighborhoods. Men will need a head covering at synagogues. Indeed, a head covering for any sightseer is a good idea, for the sun can be fierce. Respect it.

To see in action what inspires Jerusalem, feel free to enter churches on Sunday morning and synagogues on Shabbat—Friday evening after sunset and Saturday morning. (Many Orthodox synagogues request no visitors on Yom Kippur, however.) Non-Moslems are not welcome at mosques during prayers.

Don't be discouraged by the enormous number of places to visit in the Golden City. Even lifetime residents complain that they haven't been able to get to them all. What's more, it seems as if any time anyone digs up so much as a teaspoon of Jerusalem's rocky earth, another archaeological site is uncovered. But that's one of the reasons to return again and again.

Itineraries

The next three chapters contain suggested itineraries for one-week, two-week, and extended visits to Jerusalem. There's nothing sacrosanct about the itineraries, however. I know my favorite ways of showing Jerusalem to newcomers, but you know your own interests. The heart of Jerusalem is small enough that you can walk from place to place and explore neighborhoods. Some of your most memorable moments will come from spontaneous excursions. Or you may want simply to pass the time watching little children swinging in a park or splashing in the Lions Fountain at the lower end of Rehov King David. After all, it's your visit.

So put on your most comfortable shoes, plop a wide-brimmed hat on your head, grab a bottle of water, and let's go.

10
IN THE BEGINNING: WEEK ONE

S o you won't miss the choice delicacies of Jerusalem, the "absolutely must-see" sites, I have put together itineraries for one- and two-week visits and a third for those who have visited the city before or are staying put for weeks or months. (And I weep for those sights that space limitation requires me to leave out.) The first two itineraries will help you become grounded in Jerusalem. As I see them, they form a basis for everything else. Beyond these, if it suits you better, each day's suggestion can be swapped for another, and parts may be interchanged. And if a day seems too strenuous as outlined, you might want to substitute part of it for a visit to a sight described in Chapter 12, "Linger Awhile."

The First Day

You might be feeling an irresistible urge to embrace as much of Jerusalem as you can as soon as you can. You may even look at the itinerary I recommend for your first day and think that it will hold you back from the thick of Jerusalem, the Old City particularly, and its sites, shops, aromas, crowds, and excitement.

You're right. That's exactly what I want to do. "A" comes before "B," and today's tour is "A." This first tour is the prerequisite for everything else you will see in Jerusalem. Besides, there is plenty of excitement on this tour—but without the crowds and strong aromas. On this first day, you will be introduced to the country's vast cultural and ancient heritage as presented in the Israel Museum. Most importantly, you will touch Israel's soul at Yad Vashem. Physically, this isn't a lot for one day of sightseeing. Emotionally—well, that's another story.

Yad Vashem

For a fundamental understanding of Israel, you must visit Yad Vashem. It is set in a forest on Har HaZikaron (Mount of Remembrance) near Mount Herzl on Shderot Herzl. Its name means "a monument and a name," from Isaiah 56:5: "I will give them in my house and within my walls a monument and a name better than sons and daughters; I will give them an everlasting name which shall not perish."

Almost everything and everyone in Israel has some sort of relationship, some link, to the Holocaust in which 6 million Jews were killed by the Nazis and their sympathizers. In ways, the very existence of modern Israel is an outcome of the Holocaust, although in no way a quid pro quo. Guilt felt by the world community, for its failure to help save the Jews, was no small factor in the United Nations' 1947 vote to establish an independent Jewish state. But most significant, especially in the face of the bloody war the new country had to fight, was the Jewish people's determination never again to be at the mercy of others.

Sometimes I detect impatience in the non-Jewish world over Jews' everlasting memory of the Holocaust. It is one of life's challenges for one person to understand another's pain. And in this case, those affected, the Jews, are people with a memory. The lessons of the past are a constant in their lives. Reminding the world of the Holocaust is seen by Jews and many others as a way of preventing anything like it from happening again to any people. The tragedy of the Holocaust, however, has been compounded, for it seems as if the world doesn't want to learn the lesson.

And what can one say about those who deny the Holocaust ever happened? Are they stupid, evil, or both? The book *The Anatomy of Auschwitz*, published by both Yad Vashem and the American Holocaust Memorial in Washington, has a section asking if it is true that 6 million Jews were killed. The researcher, a non-Jewish Pole, examined all the evidence—much of it available only with the fall of the Eastern bloc—and concluded that that unfathomable number remains unchanged. Would that it were not so. The "monument and name," Yad Vashem, stands as a witness.

The memorial, extensively redesigned under Yad Vashem Masterplan 2001, is composed of several parts, each with its own purpose and theme. The Visitors Center removes you from the familiar world. Beyond it, you will walk the tree-lined Avenue of the Righteous Among the Nations. Before each tree is a plaque honoring a non-Jew who risked his or her life to save Jews.

The new **Historical Museum** shows communal life before its destruction, traces the rise of Hitler in 1933, and documents as annihilation, resistance, and the death camp closings in 1945. Most of the photographs were taken by the German military. The route continues into the **Hall of Names** with its millions of pages of testimony.

The complex has a learning and information center where visitors can access information at computer stations. The screening center not only shows documentary and commercial films about the Holocaust but also contains master copies of tens of thousands of video interviews of Holocaust survivors from Steven Spielberg's Survivors of the Shoah (the Hebrew word for the Holocaust) Visual History Foundation.

The **Hall of Remembrance** is near by, a somber structure of concrete and black basalt, and invites reflection. Inside, heavy silence fills the dimly lit, cryptlike room. There, an eternal flame burns from a stone slab on the floor in memory of the murdered. It is a symbol of the unquenchable human spirit and will to live. Chiseled in the dark uneven paving stones surrounding the flame are names of the 21 largest Nazi death camps.

A park on the grounds is named for Janusz Korszak, who headed a Warsaw Jewish orphanage. By choice, he went with the 200 children he

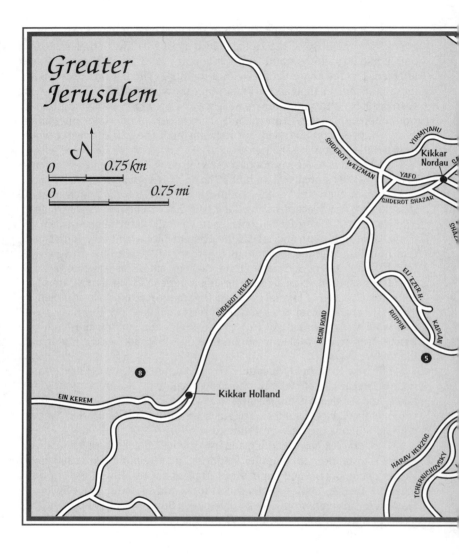

Greater Jerusalem

N

0   0.75 km

0   0.75 mi

YIRMIYAHU

SHDEROT WEIZMAN

Kikkar
Nordau S

YAFO

SHDEROT SHAZAR

SHA

ELI 'EZER H.

SHDEROT HERZL

RUPPIN

KAPLAN

BEGIN ROAD

⑤

⑧

EIN KEREM

Kikkar Holland

HARAV HERZOG

TCHERNICHOVSKY

cared for into the Treblinka gas chambers, rather than abandon them in
their time of greatest need.

The **Hall of Mirrors** memorializes the 1.5 million Jewish children
killed in the Holocaust and was built by the parents of one such child.
Designed by famed architect Moshe Safdie, with great inventiveness, it is
unlike any other memorial anywhere.

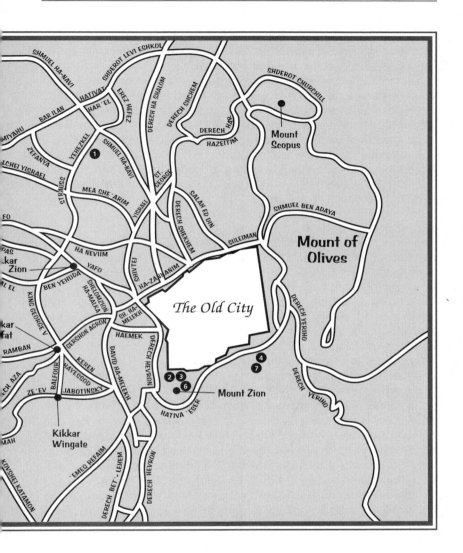

Greater Jerusalem Sights

1 Baba-Tama Synagogue	5 Israel Museum
2 Church of the Dormition	6 King David's Tomb
3 Coenaculum	7 Pool of Siloam
4 Hezekiah's Tunnel/Warren's Shaft	8 Yad Vashem

Down the road is the **Valley of the Destroyed Communities.** Its colossal wall is shaped like Europe. Inside, carved into large stones, are names of 5,000 Jewish communities that were obliterated.

A visit to Yad Vashem is harrowing, saddening beyond words. But you must experience Yad Vashem to understand much that you will encounter in Israel. After I leave the grounds of Yad Vashem and feel the burst of Jerusalem's vitality around me, it is as if I have stepped from one world to another, from death to life. Surrounded by Jerusalem's exuberance, I am in the midst of an affirmation of life. To see Yad Vashem is to touch Israel's heart, beating strongly against all odds. *Details: (02) 675-1611. Sun–Thu 9–4:45, Fri 9–12:45. Tours in English Sun at 10 and 2; Wed, Thu, and Fri at 10. Admission is free.*

The Israel Museum

The Israel Museum is spread across a hill off Rehov Ruppin. It actually is a collection of museums: the Samuel Bronfman Museum of Biblical Archeology, Billy Rose Sculpture Garden, Shrine of the Book, Nathan Cummings Pavilion for 20th Century Art, and others.

The main building, which houses three museums, is up a long flight of stairs from the entrance gate. A shuttle bus will take you there, if you wish. (But new construction might change that.) Inside is a sumptuous collection of archaeological and ethnographic artifacts; ceremonial art; a reconstructed Indian synagogue; paintings by Cezanne, Chagall, Van Gogh, and Picasso—and perhaps a janitor or two spontaneously dancing. One of the prize exhibits is of traditional Jewish dress from several countries.

In the **Billy Rose Sculpture Garden**, designed by Isamu Noguchi, you will see sculptures by Rodin, Picasso, Lipchitz, Maillol, Henry Moore, and others. The unusually shaped **Shrine of the Book,** which houses the Dead Sea Scrolls, is a much-photographed Jerusalem image. The exterior of this unique building is shaped like the lids of the jars that contained the scrolls. (But locals often describe the building as looking like a breast.)

Entering the shrine is like stepping into the cave at Qumran, where the scrolls were discovered. Inside are originals and copies of the Dead Sea Scrolls, religious writings from 100 B.C.E. to 68 C.E. The first scrolls were found in 1947 by Bedouin youths in a Judean Desert cave near the Dead Sea. Also on exhibit are other Qumran finds, portions of Genesis, and the Book of Psalms. The only reproduction on exhibit is that of the oldest known version of the Book of Isaiah, which appears on a turning drum so all of it can be read. I have seen young Israelis going through it word by word. An original portion of the book is also on exhibit, along with letters written by Bar Kochba, whose disastrous revolt against the Romans was put down in 135 C.E.

For lunch, you might go on to the Israel Museum's moderately priced cafeteria. Alternatively, sandwiches, beverages, and cakes are available at a snack counter outside the gift shops, downstairs in the main building. Bus 24, not the most frequent of buses, goes to the museum from Shderot Herzl. Note that the museum doesn't open until 4 p.m. Tuesday. *Details: (02) 670-8811. Open Sun, Mon, Wed, Thu 10–5, Tue 4–10, Fri 10–2, Sat 10–4. Free guided tours daily.*

After an intensely emotional day such as this, you might be ready for a stiff dose of the positive. Perhaps an Israeli pop singer is performing tonight. It would be good to be in the midst of an enthusiastic, warm, boisterous crowd whose existence collectively communicates the words to a famous song, "Am Yisrael Chai" ("The People of Israel Live").

The Second Day: The First Half of the Old City

Now comes tour "B," which yesterday led up to. Today's tour will give you an understanding of the depth of Jewish history in Jerusalem. This day's journey through the ages is within the physical distance of about one kilometer. It starts beside the Western Wall that supported the Temple Mount, then leads through the Jewish Quarter, most of it re-created from ashes after 1967. Later, the journey introduces another of Jerusalem's fabled human mosaics—the Armenian community—and continues to Mount Zion.

There are two Christian cemeteries of note on Mount Zion. The grave of Oskar Schindler, the unlikely hero of the movie *Schindler's List,* is easy to find in one. The other cemetery has an array of historically notable persons buried there, but can be entered only by first calling St. George's Cathedral, (02) 627-1670, which will direct your admission.

Start early. You can prepare yourself for the Old City's confusing lanes by bringing along one of Aharon Bier's clearly marked Old City maps, available from the Christian Information Center. Allow three hours for the Western Wall and the Jewish Quarter; two-and-a-half for the Armenian Quarter and Mount Zion, if a tour of the Mardigian Museum is included.

As you walk through Jerusalem, examine architectural expression through designs of windows and doors and the different types of stonework. Religious expression is found in decorations on doors, gates, and windows and in *tzedaka* boxes on the sides of buildings for people to slip in donations for the less fortunate. Sheer practicality is expressed by railroad ties used as house beams outside the Old City and the now covered-over cisterns in courtyards. Look above first and second floors to see if different stonework and windows indicate that floors have been added. And always, Jerusalem's symbol, the lion, will be looking at you from innumerable places.

83

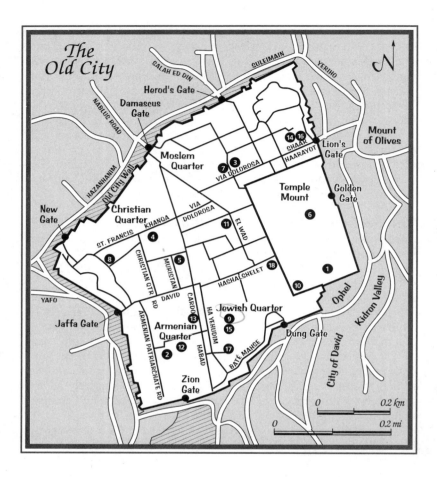

The Old City

Old City Sights

1 al-Aqsa Mosque	10 Islamic Museum
2 Cathedral of St. James	11 Madrassa Resaiya
3 Church of the Condemnation	12 Museum of the Old Yishuv
4 Church of the Holy Sepulchre	13 One Last Day Museum
5 Church of the Redeemer	14 Pool of Bethesda
6 Dome of the Rock	15 Ramban Synagogue
7 Ecco Homo Arch/Convent	16 St. Anne's Church
8 Greek Patriarchate Museum	17 Sephardi Synagogues
9 Hurva Synagogue	18 Western Wall

Eight Gates to the City

It is in the Old City that the elements that give Jerusalem one of its names, "the navel of the world," come together. Here, side by side and often built on top of each other over the centuries, are some of the holiest sites of Judaism, Christianity, and Islam.

These, along with living quarters, schools, museums, bazaars, bakeries, restaurants, synagogues, churches, mosques, post offices, and parking lots are squeezed into an area of only one square kilometer and wrapped in Suleiman the Magnificent's wall, built in 1543. Like virtually every other structure in Jerusalem, Suleiman's wall had its predecessors, for it rests on walls built by Crusaders and Romans.

Suleiman's powerful wall, reflecting golden sunshine by day, golden lights by night, has at least eight gates. The ones commonly referred to are Jaffa Gate on the western wall facing western Jerusalem, New Gate on the northern wall, and, continuing east, Damascus Gate, Herod's Gate, Lion's (St. Stephen's) Gate, Golden Gate, Dung Gate, and Zion Gate. Jerusalem's City Council might open another gate—the Newer Gate?—to relieve traffic jams into the Old City.

Jaffa (Yafo) Gate is named for the road that began here and ended at the city of Jaffa on the Mediterranean Sea. It sits at the western end of the Romans' east-west main road, and it is the busiest entrance into the Old City, for most tourists and traffic enter here. A moat between it and the Citadel (David's Tower, now a museum) was filled in to make an appropriately grand reception for German Kaiser Wilhelm II's celebrated entrance on horseback in 1898. In contrast, when the British took control of Palestine in 1917, General Edmund Allenby dismounted his horse and walked through Jaffa Gate as an expression of his humility on entering the Holy City.

New Gate was built in 1889 to make an easier connection between the Christian Quarter and Christian properties across the road, outside of the Old City.

Damascus Gate, in eastern Jerusalem, is the largest and most impressive of the eight. It faces Damascus and was the northern end of the Romans' Cardo, their north-south road following the Tyropoeon Valley through the city—which they renamed Aelia Capitolina. In Hebrew, Damascus Gate is called Sha'ar Shchem, because it opens onto the road to what was the city of Shchem. When the Romans, under Vespasian, built the city of Neopolis (Arab pronunciation changed the name into Nablus) near ancient Shchem, they constructed two arched gates of classic design in their walls. These have been excavated and can be seen on either side of Damascus Gate.

Herod's Gate is beyond Damascus Gate to the east. Its name comes from Christian pilgrims in the Middle Ages who thought Herod's palace was nearby. In both Arabic and Hebrew, it is known as the Gate of Flowers.

It was through the steep entrance to **Lion's (St. Stephen's) Gate** that the Israeli army fought its way into the Old City in the Six-Day War. One name of the gate comes from lions carved on both sides, and the other from the belief that St. Stephen was martyred nearby. The Via Dolorosa, Jesus' path to crucifixion and burial (also known as the Way of the Cross), begins inside this gate.

The present double **Golden Gate** (Gate of Mercy in Hebrew and Gate of Repentance and Gate of Mercy in Arabic), near the middle of the wall's eastern side, was built by the Byzantines in the fifth century. It is said that Jesus rode on an ass into Jerusalem from the Mount of Olives through a predecessor of the gate standing today. With its two arches, it is the most beautiful of the gates and the one through which the Messiah will enter Jerusalem, according to Jewish tradition. It was blocked up under Moslem rule in 1530, to prevent the Messiah's entrance, Jews maintain. Israelis, even after winning control of the Old City in 1967, have let the gate remain blocked.

Dung Gate is the gate closest to the Western Wall. It acquired its lowly name after the area around it became the city's dumping ground for refuse—often to humiliate Jews— in the second century C.E.

Zion Gate (Prophet David Gate in Arabic) connects the Armenian Quarter with Mount Zion. An engineering mistake regarding this gate is described below in the Second Day tour.

The Western Wall

Rabbi Abraham Isaac Kook, appointed Chief Rabbi of Palestine in 1921 and remembered for his erudition and compassion, wrote of the Western Wall, "There are men with hearts of stone and stones with hearts of flesh."

While nothing remains of the Second Temple, parts of the retaining wall that raised the Temple Mount (Haram ash-Sharif

Inside Damascus Gate, Old City

in Arabic) exist, namely on the west and south. Only part of the western section can be seen above ground.

The Western Wall is considered the holiest site in Judaism because of its proximity to the location of the temple. Among devotedly believed traditions is the notion that the Divine Presence rests eternally over the wall. The area before the wall isn't used only as an outdoor synagogue. It also serves as a national gathering place. What you see from the plaza is the largest section of the Western Wall left standing after the Roman destruction of Jerusalem in 70 C.E.

In Hebrew, its name is HaKotel HaMa'aravi, or simply HaKotel. It is not—I repeat, *not*—the Wailing Wall, no matter what the *New York Times* writes. That title, a misnomer, was given to this stretch of wall by the British, because Jews who prayed there lamented the destruction of the temple as well as the pain of their country not being restored to them.

There are several ways to reach the Western Wall. One is through Dung Gate. This is the most convenient entrance because Buses 1 and 2 stop outside, but I'd rather leave than arrive from that direction. Another entrance is by the Arab *souk* from Jaffa Gate, down David Street to Bab el-Silsileh Street (Street of the Chain), and right on Western Wall Road. To me, that route makes too tumultuous a preface into the wall area.

My preferred route, for sheerly aesthetic reasons, is through Jaffa Gate (Buses 19, 20, and 30), right on Armenian Orthodox Patriarchate Road, and left on St. James Road, which leads into Rehov Or HaHayim. That lane leads down hill and, after a flight of stairs, to the Jewish Quarter Plaza.

The lane at the opposite side, Tiferet Yisrael, leads to dozens of stairs—down, down, down. An alternative is to take the Old City Bus 38 to the end of the line next to the Jewish Quarter parking lot. Head away from the parking lot entrance, which will bring you into the Jewish Quarter Plaza, and you can continue down from there.

The most dramatic first view of the wall is from the stairs, and there's nothing like a smashing first impression. From a major landing on the stairs, the wall is below to the left across a plaza. You can see the gleaming Dome of the Rock on the Temple Mount above the wall.

Ahead, the arches of a Jordanian-built hotel top the Mount of Olives, a deliberate insult during wartime to the cemetery that seems to cascade down the mountain. This is the oldest Jewish cemetery in the world and is still used today. The clunker of a building a bit to the right is the Panorama Hotel, about which one could say the same as was said about the former Hilton Hotel, now the Crowne Plaza: "The best view in Jerusalem is from the Hilton Hotel, for then you don't have to see the Hilton Hotel."

Jerusalem Syndrome

Every so often, a tourist on pilgrimage comes down with "Jerusalem Syndrome," an ailment peculiar to the Holy City. The fictional Bradley Wilson is typical. He manages a supermarket in Missouri. While he enjoys a good joke, no one would ever call him eccentric.

After many years of dreaming and saving, he and his wife made a pilgrimage to the Holy Land with their church group. Bradley couldn't sleep for days beforehand. When he stepped from the plane at Ben-Gurion Airport, he resisted an urge to get down on his knees and kiss the tarmac.

His elation remained unabated while the group toured Nazareth and other places important in Jesus' life. Then, with his spirits soaring, Bradley and the group journeyed to Jerusalem. Coming on top of everything else, Jerusalem overwhelmed him.

His second day here, he disappeared from the group. He'd had a message that he was John the Baptist. With a beatific expression on his face and his eyes glazed, he stood at a busy Jerusalem intersection and began preaching. Jerusalemites paid him scant, sometimes bemused, attention.

He was John the Baptist, he shouted. He had walked the streets of Jerusalem in an earlier time and now he was home again, ready to baptize one and all. Plainly ecstatic, he preached on and on. Then he started taking off his clothes.

At that point, a policeman appeared and gently ushered this latter-day John the Baptist to the police station. It was plain to the authorities that Bradley was another victim of Jerusalem Syndrome. With Bradley's drivers' license as identification, the police called his home in Missouri. It was 5 a.m. there, and Bradley's teenage son sounded sleepy when he spoke to his father: "Hi, Dad, how's the trip? Did you find me a Coke bottle in Hebrew?" It didn't take long for this victim of Jerusalem Syndrome to realize that instead of John the Baptist, he was Bradley Wilson, in search of a Coca-Cola bottle.

Victims of Jerusalem Syndrome might be embarrassed but they aren't sorry. Bradley said that the time he had Jerusalem Syndrome "was just about the happiest I've ever known." As Leon Uris wrote in his book *Jerusalem*, "This tinge of glorious madness is an integral part of the city."

But let's think of more positive things: Beyond are the Judean Desert and, if the day is clear, the shimmer of the Dead Sea.

If it is Monday, Thursday, or Shabbat morning, 13-year-old boys will be having their bar mitzvahs, ceremonies that usher them into adult religious responsibilities, in front of the wall. Singing, ululating (the joyful high-pitched crying of Sephardi women), drumming, clapping, and chanting will waft across the plaza and up the stairs. On Friday night and Saturday morning, the hum of people praying and the buzz of spectators rise. Yeshiva (Jewish religious school) students put their hands on each other's shoulders and come singing down the stairs in a line on Friday night. At the wall, they form a circle and perform a simple, swaying, shuffling dance as they sing. Late at night, followers of certain Hasidic groups sometimes stand alone in the dark before the wall and shout their prayers to the heavens. When soldiers take their oath of service at the wall, the young men's firm voices resonate off the stone. But during the heat of a summer afternoon, barely a murmur can be heard.

The vast plaza from the bottom of the stairs to the wall wasn't there before the Six-Day War. For centuries, only a narrow lane ran between the wall and a mass of shacks for Moslem North African immigrants. To the scene, the Jordanians and local Palestinian Arabs added the rubble left from their house-to-house battle to oust the Jews in 1948. During the 19 years of Jordanian occupation, contrary to armistice agreements, Jews weren't allowed access to the wall. During the preceding British Mandate, Jews could go to the wall on most occasions, but they were never allowed to blow the shofar (a ram's horn and an important part of High Holiday observance), bring a Sefer Torah (the Hebrew Bible), or even bring chairs so they could sit.

Now, the part of the plaza closest to the wall, set off by a fence, is reserved for religious observance. Men and women have separate (but unequal) areas for worship. On Shabbat, even visitors outside the prayer area are forbidden to take photographs or smoke.

What can be seen of the wall reveals seven rows (the bottom two uncovered after 1967) of Herodian Stone from the Second Temple. They are massive but elegant, with their distinctive narrow frame and smooth center.

The stone layers above are vastly different, far less refined in style, as the stonecutters took fewer aesthetic pains with them. Four rows are from the Arab period. The remaining rows were constructed by the Ottoman Turks.

There are another 17 rows of stone below the Herodian stone we see. As archaeological excavations proceed, more and more history is being revealed. In 1996, a new section of the Western Wall—separated from the main place of prayer by the slope up to the Temple Mount—was dedicated. Near the Dung Gate is an entrance to both the Ophel Archaeological Garden along the southern wall of the Temple Mount and a newly excavated area along the Western Wall.

An entrance in the **Western Wall Tunnel**, is near the men's side of the Western Wall. The tunnel leads to Wilson's Arch, which once provided a path for priests to reach the Temple Mount. A thoroughfare during Hasmonean times, the tunnel exits near the beginning of the Via Dolorosa. Entrance is by advance reservation only, (02) 627-1333 or (02) 627-1334, and usually in the afternoon Sunday through Thursday. There is an admission fee. You will be sure to get in with Archaeological Tours, which offers tunnel visits three mornings a week, or Zion Walking Tours, which has visits three afternoons and one morning a week.

The Jewish Quarter

The southeast quadrant of the Old City became known as the Jewish Quarter in 1267. The present Jewish Quarter only slightly resembles the Jewish Quarter that existed before the Jordanian occupation (1948–1967). During that time, most of the quarter was destroyed, and all Jews were banished. After 1967, some of the buildings were restored, but many more are new (none even hinting at the hovels that used to be here).

The new buildings were designed to blend with the old, architecturally. This is happening as they weather. The quarter is losing its just-built appearance and is settling in as an authentic community, despite the hordes of tourists who fill its narrow lanes and peek into its enticing courtyards. In the process of digging foundations, many archaeological sites were uncovered. Construction had to adapt to the finds. The discoveries exist side-by-side with, even as part of, modern buildings.

Begin the ascent from the Western Wall Plaza to the Jewish Quarter by returning to the Stairs of Rabbi Judah HaLevi. The buildings on the left are Yeshivat Porat Yosef, another site designed by the famed Israeli architect Moshe Safdie of Montreal's Habitat fame. To the right of the stairs are ruins of a Crusader period church destroyed by Saladin in 1187.

At the top of the last stairs, tucked away on the right and opposite several refreshment stands, is the **Burnt House**. This home, owned by a well-to-do priestly family, was among those destroyed when Romans burned Jerusalem and killed its inhabitants in 70 C.E. One of the poignant finds inside was the burnt-in image on the stairs of a young women's arm reaching for escape. An excellent audiovisual show that re-creates the events can be seen in English every two hours between 9:30 a.m. and 3:30 p.m. *Details: (02) 628-7211 Sun–Thu 9–5, Fri and holiday eves 9–1. Admission fee.*

The snack stands opposite the Burnt House make a good rest stop. Public lavatories are located in an alcove around the corner from the snack stands. Or you can climb up for some food at the Quarter Cafe.

If you exit from the café upstairs, you will find a bridge in front of you. As you cross, you will be traversing the emptiness that was left by Arab occupation of **Tiferet Yisrael Synagogue**. Built by Hasidic Jews in 1867, it was one of the largest and most famous synagogues in Jerusalem. Its dome could be seen from every part of the Old City. Its beauty is hinted at by the elegantly carved windows, which you see from Rehov HaKara'im.

Opposite Tiferet Yisrael is the **Karaite Synagogue**. Whether or not someone will be there to show you the synagogue and its museum is unpredictable. It is described in detail in Chapter 12: "Linger Awhile."

Karaites are a non-mainstream Jewish group that abides strictly by the Torah, so strictly that while mainstream Orthodox Jews leave lights on over Shabbat and even have lights connected to timers, Karaites will have no lights whatsoever over Shabbat.

As you face the Karaite synagogue, go left and turn left sharply when you can, then go straight ahead and under an arch. Turn left and you will find yourself in Batei Mahse Square, with buildings financed by German and Dutch Jews. Remember this square, for it figures prominently at the One Last Day Museum. **Beit Rothschild**, the large building with its two floors of arches, was built by the Austrian branch of the famous family as residences for the poor.

Backtrack and go under the arch again. You will come out at the quarter plaza. On your right is the **Wohl Archaeological Museum** and its lavishly styled Herodian Palace. This was once the wealthy part of ancient Jerusalem. (If time is running out, you can catch this sight later.) *Details: Sun–Thu 9–5, Fri 9–1, holiday eves. Admission fee.*

Back into the plaza, walk along its left side as you face away from the Western Wall. Turn left at the first street, and remember, this is a street. Look out for cars. After the arch, you will find a long staircase going down on your left. Descend these stairs, and you will enter the first of the four **Sephardi Synagogues**. (During Moslem rule, synagogues and churches were often built below street level because of a decree that they had to be lower than mosques.)

Perhaps the most famous of Old City synagogues, these were founded beginning in the sixteenth century by Spanish Jews or Jews of Spanish descent. These synagogues, interconnected in one building, were the community center for Old City Jews. During the 19 years of Jordanian occupation, the synagogues' contents were stolen or destroyed, and the buildings were turned into warehouses.

Despite being below ground level, the four synagogues are bright with

91

sunshine and exude an air of simplicity and peacefulness. The first and largest of the synagogues, **Ben-Zakkai,** is named for Rabbi Yohanan Ben-Zakkai, who taught his pupils on this site in the first century C.E. Its front door and twin ark doors were designed by Boris Schatz, founder in the early 1900s of Jerusalem's Bezalel School of Art.

A door at the rear of Ben-Zakkai Synagogue leads to the **Elilyahu HaNavi Synagogue**. This is the oldest of the four, dating from 1586, with a chair near the door reserved for the Prophet Elijah. A traditional story is that Elijah was the 10th man at this synagogue—thus there were enough men for a *minyan* (the required number for prayers) one Yom Kippur eve.

In Ben-Zakkai Synagogue again and toward its front is the door to the **Emtza'i (Middle) Synagogue**. This is the smallest and newest of the synagogues. It was a courtyard, but ruler Mohammed Ali gave permission in 1835 for it to be covered. The plaster artwork on the ceiling is original.

From the Emtza'i, you can enter the **Istanbuli Synagogue**, founded by Turkish Jews in 1764. Its gilded ark and its *bima*, on which persons leading the prayers stand, were brought from Italy after 1967 to replace those destroyed.

Also in the complex is a one-room museum. It has a wealth of fasci-

View of an old synagogue from a window in the Jewish Quarter

92

nating photographs of people, these synagogues, and others going back to the early twentieth century. Daily prayers take place at Ben-Zakkai. An Ashkenazi minyan uses the Eliyahu HaNavi Synagogue on Saturday, while the Istanbuli is used Saturday before the new moon and holidays and is devoted to preserving its traditional liturgy. *Details: Sun–Thu 9–4, Fri and holiday eves 9–1. Admission fee.*

Out on the street again and to the right, near a minaret, is the **Ramban Synagogue**, the oldest known Jewish house of prayer in Jerusalem, dating from the fourteenth century. The synagogue is named for the important Rabbi Moshe Ben-Nahman, though he may not actually have had a connection with it. Great rabbis are known by several names, one usually being an acronym. Ramban is an acronym of the rabbi's title and name. He is also known as Nachmanides. A Spaniard, the Ramban was forced to leave Spain after he bested a Catholic priest in a religious debate before the king. He then came to Jerusalem to help rebuild the Jewish community. The synagogue exhibits a plaque showing a copy of an ethical will he wrote in 1267, the year he arrived here. What you see of the synagogue is a post-1967 reconstruction.

To the right of the synagogue, or left and then right on Rehov HaYehudim, are entrances to the single, sweeping arch and four broken walls—all that remain—of the **Hurva Synagogue**. Built on previous synagogues, it was once the largest Ashkenazi synagogue in Jerusalem. Twice it was destroyed by Moslems; it was rebuilt the first time. What exists now is a memorial to the destruction after 1948.

Both on nearby Rehov Plugat HaKotel and at a place in the Cardo you can see remains of the **Broad Wall** from the First Temple period. King Hezekiah (of tunnel fame) had the Broad Wall constructed around what then was the northern boundary of Jerusalem in approximately 701 B.C.E. (Incidentally, the post office on Rehov Plugat HaKotel may be the only post office that also is an art gallery.)

The Cardo is a Byzantine extension of Hadrian's main north-south street of his built-over Jerusalem. Because of the historical importance of the Cardo, it was a particularly exciting archaeological find when it was uncovered during excavation for new construction after the Six-Day War. Reconstructed with some original pavement, columns, and arches, it now contains mostly shops.

Anyone who loves the immediacy of trenchant photography should not miss the little-known **One Last Day Museum**. To find it, in the Cardo look for the Culinaria, a first century–style Roman restaurant that caters to tour groups. Diners and waiters wear Roman dress and the food simulates that of upper-class Romans.

Climb the stairs to the restaurant, and you will find the entrance to the one-room museum. On May 28, 1948, *Life* magazine photographer John Philips accompanied the Jordanian Arab Legion into the besieged Jewish Quarter. There he photographed inhabitants as they surrendered to the Jordanians. Fires burn and people are distraught yet incredibly brave in this "you are there" series of photographs. In one of the most touching, the Jordanians have demanded from the assembled population that all the fighters step forward. A bearded, ultra-Orthodox octogenarian does so. *Details: (02) 628-8141 or (02) 628-8142. Sun–Thu 9–5, Fri and holiday eves 9–1. Admission fee.*

Backtrack on Rehov Habad past the Habad Synagogue. Because it was used by Arabs as a private home and workshop, it is almost the only synagogue in the Jewish Quarter that survived the 1948 war.

If you haven't taken a rest or eaten lunch, now is a time to do so. The Bird of Paradise, Habad 56, not only serves lunch but also has live entertainment Thursday night. Or, on Jewish Quarter Road toward the parking lot, are HaHoma Restaurant, a tiny Arab bakery where you can buy pita with spice for $1, and a falafel stand. Another choice is the Armenian Tavern, to the right and downstairs when you reach Armenian Patriarchate Road.

From Rehov Habad, go up steep Rehov Or HaHayim. At number 6 is the **Museum of the Old Yishuv** (Old Settlement), a restoration of one of the oldest houses in the quarter. It provides a rare picture of Jewish life during the last years of Turkish rule. *Details: Rehov Or HaHayim 6, (02) 628-4636. Sun–Thu 9–4. Admission fee.*

Rehov Or HaHayim becomes St. James Street in the Armenian Quarter, which brings you out at Armenian Orthodox Patriarchate Road, another heavily traveled, narrow road. To the right, the road leads to Jaffa Gate and out of the Old City; to the left, to the Cathedral of St. James and the entrance to Mount Zion.

Detour toward the Moslem Quarter from St. James Street at Ararat Street, named for the Armenians' holy mountain and the place where Noah's Ark is believed to have come to rest. On the right, where Ararat makes a jog, is the **Syrian Orthodox Monastery** with its St. Mark's Church. Here, Syriac, a language close to ancient Aramaic, is still spoken. Syrians believe that this location, not the Coenaculum on Mount Zion, is the site of St. Mark's house and the Last Supper (see Chapter 13: "Heavenly Jerusalem"). *Details: (02) 628-3304. Mon–Sat 8–5.*

The Armenian Quarter and Mount Zion

The Armenian Quarter, reached most easily through Jaffa Gate and down Armenian Orthodox Patriarchate Road past St. James Road, is a walled enclave in the southwestern corner of the Old City. Continuing on Armenian Orthodox Patriarchate Road, the Armenian Seminary is on the right; the entrance to the Armenian Quarter is on the left. Some two thousand people live in this walled "town" with its own language, school, churches, social life, and soccer field. It is a tight enclave, made all the tighter because its gates are locked from 10 p.m. until 6 the next morning. Sightseers aren't encouraged to wander beyond the quarter's major attractions, but they aren't actively discouraged. During the average day, few residents are out and about. The quarter can appear to be deserted.

In 303, Armenians were the first people to convert as a nation to Christianity. The quarter focuses on the **Cathedral of St. James**, said to be built on the place where Herod Agrippa I decapitated the apostle James the Greater in 44 c.e. A head, thought to be that of James, is entombed in the chapel inside the cathedral. The cathedral is also named for St. James the Lesser, Jesus' brother and the first bishop of Jerusalem, according to Armenians.

Crusaders helped Armenians erect the present cathedral in the twelfth century on the ruins of two previous churches. A wooden clapper, instead of bells, is still used to announce services. (Bells were forbidden by the Moslems until after 1840.) *Khachkars*, stone crosses, are inlaid in the walls around the cathedral courtyard. They are memorials for people and events, and each of the 22 is unique. Inside are altars to St. James the Lesser, the Virgin Mary, and St. John the Baptist. The church is startlingly beautiful in a fairy-tale way, with blue tiles, carvings, and dozens of hanging metal lanterns. It is open only during prayer services. *Details: (02) 628-2331. Mon–Fri 6–7 a.m., 3–3:30 p.m., Sat and Sun 6–9 a.m., 2:30–3:15 p.m.*

Outside, a stone-covered walkway leads to the main compound and courtyard. In it are the Armenian Press (established in 1833, it was Jerusalem's first printing press), Gulbenkian Library, and, facing a landscaped courtyard, **Mardigian Museum of Armenian Art and History**, located in the old seminary. The small museum gives a powerful view into the world of this little-known people. I highly recommend visiting the museum at this time, if your endurance allows. It is described in detail in Chapter 12: "Linger Awhile." *Details: Mon–Sat 10–5. Admission fee.*

Outside again, down a few stairs to the right, under an archway and to the right again, is the **House of Annas** (Convent of the Olive Tree). Annas was the father-in-law of Caiaphas, the high priest. It is said that Annas had Jesus bound overnight to the nearby olive tree before he delivered Jesus to Caiaphas.

Back on Armenian Orthodox Patriarchate Road and left (watch out for cars from behind you) is Zion Gate, on the right side of the road. Through the gate is **Mount Zion**, outside the Old City walls.

95

Mount Zion has been enclosed by the Old City walls at various times. One Arab tradition says that after Suleiman the Magnificent had the walls reconstructed and discovered that his two engineers neglected to include Mount Zion and its reputed Tomb of King David within, he ordered the two men executed. They are said to be buried in the two graves inside Jaffa Gate, next to the H. Stern store. If the story is true the deaths were in vain, for modern archaeologists deny that King David is buried on Mount Zion.

Zion Gate, as improbable as it appears, is a thoroughfare for cars, so be careful walking through it. Inside, the road to the right leads to the black-topped Romanesque **Church of the Dormition**. It was built by German Catholics in 1910 and badly damaged during the fierce fighting in the War of Independence. It was constructed over a series of ruined predecessors marking the spot where, according to tradition, Jesus' mother, Mary, died. The interior is impressive for its many mosaic designs. The one on the floor is of three interlocking circles and the words in Latin, "Holy, holy, holy." *Details: Daily 7 a.m.–12:30, 2–7 p.m.*

To the left is a building complex whose various parts reflect Jewish, Christian, and Moslem religions. However, neither Jews nor Christians were allowed inside for centuries until the Israelis won control of Mount Zion in 1948. Christians (except the Syrian Orthodox) believe the smaller

Armenian Easter services outside the Cathedral of St. James

room above to be the site of Jesus' Last Supper and the Holy Ghost's appearance to the Apostles. **The Coenaculum** is built in classic Crusader style. *Details: Daily 8–5, Fri 8–1.*

Downstairs, or entered directly from the road before you turn toward the church, in a dark, narrow room, is what some believe to be **King David's Tomb**. The stone coffin, covered by a synagogue altar cover, dates from Crusader times, but the room might have been a post–Second Temple synagogue. Men will need a head covering, handed out free inside. *Details: Sun–Thu 8–6 (to 5 in winter), 8–2 Fri and holiday eves (to 1 in winter).*

This complex also houses the Diaspora Yeshiva, site of energetic and enthusiastically received religio-rock performances on Saturday night.

To see Oskar Schindler's grave in the German Catholic cemetery, keep walking down the hill, through the parking lot, and across the busy road that circles the Old City. The cemetery will be in front of you. You enter on the right and walk down, down, down for Schindler. Everyone knows where he is buried. Everyone expects you to look for his grave.

The Protestant cemetery is more difficult to find. Note that you must receive prior permission from St. George's Cathedral to visit. Look for the Jerusalem College of the Holy Land. From the Church of the Dormition, go down the path toward Jaffa Gate, then take a sharp left and keep walking. Ring the office bell at the college gate. Among the graves are a communal grave for residents of the American Colony and those of builders of late nineteenth- and early twentieth-century Jerusalem.

Along the east rim of Mount Zion, near Jerusalem College, you might be able to see a cable and its dangling container crossing the Hinnom Valley above the Cinematheque building. During the War of Independence, the cable car ferried guns, ammunition, and even wounded soldiers back and forth. During the day, the cable lay on the valley floor. At night, it was raised and put to work.

From Zion Gate, you can follow the road left back to Jaffa Gate for a bus or take the road to the right to the Jewish Quarter parking lot to catch Bus 38 to western Jerusalem. Or, if you actually found the Protestant cemetery, keep the Old City walls on your right and you will come to the Jaffa Gate bus stop.

After this day, with its visits to ancient sites that go back 2,500 years, the juxtaposition of buildings from different centuries, and the exposure to the complex Jewish and Armenian cultures, you might feel as if you have been bludgeoned with history. History does come at you from all sides in Jerusalem. And there is another half of the Old City yet to be explored. I feel strongly about the order of the first two tours. The arrangement of the remaining tours is a suggestion, based on a logical sequence.

The Third Day: The Other Half

The two other parts of the Old City, the Christian and Moslem Quarters, are the setting for a walk that is traditionally seen as following Jesus' footsteps as he labored to carry the cross to his crucifixion. The backdrop is the sights, sounds, and smells of the ancient city's crowded, narrow lanes. The last part of the walk will take you to important examples of Islamic architecture, their beauty almost obscured by the darkness of the streets, the ravages of time, and human indifference.

Allow three hours for the Christian Quarter and about two for the Moslem Quarter, depending on how many shops entice you on the way.

The Christian Quarter and the Via Dolorosa

The Christian Quarter of the Old City was established when the Church of the Holy Sepulchre was built in the fifth century. The market streets, David Street and Khan es-Zeit, divide Christian from Moslem Quarters. But since little is arranged neatly in Jerusalem, a visit to the major Christian sites in the Old City takes you through the Moslem quadrant as well.

Few Arab Christians live in the Christian Quarter these days. The most Christian things about the Christian Quarter are the religious sites and the people who staff them. Some sites on this tour are closed on Sunday. If, on Friday, you want to see the 3 p.m. procession, the following morning and afternoon tours could be reversed.

Buses 23 and 23a go to Herod's Gate. Through it and to the left, the street becomes Aqabat Darwish. It ends at al-Mujahideen Road. A left turn here leads directly to Lion's (St. Stephen's) Gate, rebuilt by Suleiman in the sixteenth century and through which Israeli forces broke into the Old City during the Six-Day War.

Turn left and through a gate to the Crusader-built **St. Anne's Church**, believed to be located where the house of Anne (Hannah), mother of Mary, once stood. The building was destroyed and rebuilt many times. The present church dates from 1192 and is an example of the transition between Roman and Gothic architecture. It was preserved because Suleiman the Magnificent used it as a Moslem school. The church is famous for its excellent acoustics. Stand quietly at the back and pilgrims might give you a demonstration by singing a hymn.

Beyond the church door is the **Pool of Bethesda**—in a cool, tranquil spot surrounded by greenery—where Jesus is said to have healed the sick. Excavations have uncovered the original structure with its steps leading down into the water. *Details: Mon–Sat 8–noon and 2–5 (to 6 in summer). Admission fee.*

A right turn back on Al-Mujahideen Road will take you to the **Via Dolorosa** (Path of Sorrows). It is both the name of the route that Jesus is said to have taken to his crucifixion and a street in the Christian Quarter. Actually, they aren't one and the same. The street was first constructed during Crusader times and has deviated since then.

Archaeological findings have changed Jesus' route and even increased the number of Stations of the Cross from 7 to 14. But for pilgrims who follow the 14 stations, the spiritual and emotional factors of the journey far outweigh the historical. What might come as a shock is that until the stations fall within the Church of the Holy Sepulchre, they are found in the midst of vivid, ongoing life, often in the heart of a marketplace. What you see and feel might seem like a paradox, but Jesus had to pass through a similar scene almost two thousand years ago.

At 3 p.m. every Friday, Franciscan priests lead a procession along the route. It begins at Station I and is open to everyone. Perhaps, once in a while, pilgrims along the route will send grateful thoughts toward Israel. Before Israel gained the Old City in the Six-Day War, Via Dolorosa storm drains ran with sewage, and the walkway itself was often littered with garbage. The Israelis dug up the route, laid sewage pipes and utility conduits underground, and repaved the street with new cobblestones. Whenever they uncovered the original massive Roman paving stones, they inserted them into the walk. The effort enabled pilgrims to think about their mission, instead of what they were smelling and where they were stepping.

The courtyard of the el-Omariyah School on al-Mujahideen Road is **Station I** of the cross. Entrance isn't always possible, but if you can, walk up the stairs to the school for a wonderful view of the Temple Mount.

Only few remains exist of the colossal Antonia Fortress, which once stood here. It was built by Herod the Great on an existing Hasmonean (the family of the Jewish Chanukah heroes) fortress and named for his friend Mark Antony. After Herod's death, Roman governors used the fortress to keep an eye on anti-Roman locals during festival days such as Passover. Pontius Pilate was based here (some scholars maintain he was located in the Herodian Palace near today's Jaffa Gate) when Jesus was brought before him for a private trial in the courtyard.

Station II, a little farther on and opposite the exit to the Hasmonean Tunnel, is in the **Church of the Condemnation** (also called Flagellation), built in 1929 over the place where Jesus took up the cross. Despite the centuries of artwork on the subject and pilgrims today who struggle with a heavy cross as they follow the Via Dolorosa, researchers say that victims of this cruel Roman punishment didn't carry a cross, only the cross bar, which was later nailed to a tree stripped of branches. Inside the Franciscan monastery, on the left, is the Chapel of Judgment, with flagstones from the Antonia Fortress. On the right is the Chapel of the

Flagellation, where Jesus was scourged. *Details: Daily 6–noon and 2–5 (to 6 in summer).*

Ahead on the Via Dolorosa, the **Ecce Homo Arch** spans the street. The way becomes more crowded with tourists, residents, and merchants at this point. Rather than thinking of the increasing commotion and cars in the street as a distraction, you can think of them as simulating the events Jesus endured. Tradition has it that at the Ecce Homo Arch, Pontius Pilate looked down on Jesus while he was being presented to the waiting crowds and declared, "Ecce homo!" ("Behold the man!"). However, the arch is actually part of a gate constructed by Roman emperor Hadrian in the second century C.E. to commemorate his victory over the Jewish revolt led by Bar Kochba.

Inside the adjacent **Ecce Homo Convent** in the Lithostrotos, you can see the arch's continuation and pavement stones that were thought to be from the Antonia Fortress—until a Dominican scholar proved in 1972 that this area lay outside the fortress. The stones were grooved to allow water to run to a cistern, which still exists below the paving, and were scratched into squares and triangles by bored Roman legionnaires who passed the time playing games. *Details: Mon–Sat 8:30–12:30 and 2–4:30 (to 5 in summer). Admission fee.*

The street leads into el-Wad Road. Narrow as it is, it's a main Old City commercial artery. Turn left and almost immediately on the left side is **Station III**. This is where Jesus fell from exhaustion the first time. Above the door of the small Polish chapel here is a relief showing Jesus fallen under the weight of the cross.

A short distance ahead, past a vegetable market and a café, a relief on the arch over the entrance to the Armenian Church of Our Lady of the Spasm marks **Station IV**, where Jesus met his mother. Two sandal prints inside represent the place Mary stood as she watched her son go by.

After you pass Barquq Road on the left, Hebrew signs appear over a door, also on the left. This is the **Yeshivat Torah Hayim**. The Arab family that looked after it during Jordanian occupation protected it from looters. Religious services resumed here after the city was reunited.

Around the corner to the right into the Via Dolorosa is **Station V**, where Simon of Cyrene, a passerby, was recruited by Roman soldiers to help Jesus carry the cross, probably so Jesus could survive this difficult journey long enough to be crucified.

Just before an arch is **Station VI**. Here, Veronica wiped Jesus' face with her handkerchief. Whether or not Veronica knew Jesus before this moment is debated by historians.

At the junction with bustling Khan es-Zeit Street, the marker for **Station VII** is above the entrance to a Franciscan chapel facing you.

This station marks where Jesus fell a second time. It is believed that a gate leading out of Jerusalem for those condemned to death stood here during Jesus' time. It is possible he saw his own execution notice on the gate.

Across the street and up the slope of Aqabat el-Khanqa, on the left, is a cross on the wall of the Greek Monastery of St. Chara-lambos. The cross marks **Station VIII**, where Jesus consoled the women of Jerusalem and warned them of catastrophes ahead.

Back to the corner and right into the Khan ez-Zeit Street there is a stairway on the right. Up the stairs and to the right is the Coptic Orthodox Queen Helena Church. Ahead is the Coptic Orthodox Patriarchate, **Station IX**, where Jesus fell a third time.

The Coptic community has been on this site since 1219. Beyond the steps to the left is the Ethiopian Compound, on the roof of the Chapel of St. Helena, within the Church of the Holy Sepulchre below. Ethiopian monks live in huts here. They say that the olive trees here, enclosed by a wall, were once the bush where Abraham found the ram caught in a thicket, which became his sacrifice.

Back down the stairs, turn right and right again at the corner, which leads you to the **Church of the Holy Sepulchre** and the final stations of the cross. The Holy Sepulchre, the holiest shrine to much of the Christian world, is a dark confusing warren with a jumble of chapels. It stands over what the Byzantine Queen Helena determined was the hill of Golgotha. The name is derived from the Hebrew word for skull. Perhaps the hill was given the name because that was what the barren height resembled centuries ago, or because of the legend that Adam's skull was buried here.

Apparently, the site actually was a burial ground at the time of the crucifixion. Later, Hadrian erected a temple to Venus here. The Byzantine emperor Constantine had the

Station IV on el-Wad in the Moslem Quarter

temple destroyed so his mother, Helena, could have the first church built on this spot in 335 C.E.

The church, in turn, was destroyed by the Persians in 614, restored, and alternately destroyed and rebuilt several more times. Fire severely damaged the structure in the nineteenth century, and a 1927 earthquake left its mark. Today the church seems to be constantly under repair, although the dome over the sepulchre has been finished at last and sits up there gleaming and rather sedate, a far cry from the rest of the church. What is seen now closely resembles the Crusader building of 1149. Only the rotunda above what is held to be Jesus' tomb resembles Queen Helena's fourth-century church.

Six Christian communities, none of them Protestant, share responsibility for the church. Each is wildly jealous of the others, and each fiercely guards its own turf and rights. They even battle over the prize of which community gets to clean the church. The powerful Greek Orthodox Church has won almost two-thirds control, so the Greeks tend to sit serenely by while the five other churches fight over what is left. The crumbs have gone to the Ethiopians, whose rooftop monastery you saw earlier in this walk. Because they have the least, they fight most often with the Copts, who have the next-least and have a monastery nearby. For the sake of peace, keepers of the church keys are Moslem.

Inside the church entrance, on the floor, is a slab of red stone. This is the Stone of the Unction, which dates from 1810 and covers the spot where it is said Jesus' body was anointed after being taken down from the cross.

The Greek Orthodox Chapel of Adam is to the right, before the stone. The cleft in the rock here is held to have split apart during an earthquake at the time Jesus died.

The steep stairs on the right of the red stone lead up to Calvary. The Chapel of the Sorrows has two naves. The one on the right is **Station X,** where Jesus was stripped of his garments. Close by is **Station XI**, where he was nailed to the cross.

In the adjoining Greek Orthodox chapel is **Station XII**. This is believed to be the place of the Crucifixion and is richly decorated with precious metals, icons, statues, and suspended lamps. Tradition says the cross stood in the silver-inlaid hole in the rock.

Jesus' body was taken off the cross at **Station XIII**, marked by the small Roman Catholic Stabat Mater Dolorosa Altar between Stations XI and XII. The wooden statue was sent from Lisbon in the late seventeenth century.

On ground level, to the right, a curved passageway leads to the left. Just past a flight of stairs and directly opposite the entrance to the edicule under the rotunda, on your right, is the Armenian Chapel of the Division of the Raiment, where soldiers distributed Jesus' clothing.

On your right and curving left are seven arches, each with a different column. These are remains of a Byzantine church called Archway of the Virgin. A left turn leads to **Station XIV,** the Holy Sepulchre, in the center of the rotunda.

The rococo nineteenth-century edicule, with its onion-shaped cupola, is the focal point of the church. Inside are two tiny, claustrophobia-inspiring rooms. The Chapel of the Angel is first. This is where an angel is said to have sat on a stone and proclaimed the Resurrection. The sepulchre, the tomb, is next and is reached through a low, arched doorway. The marble chest in the small chamber is considered by many to be Jesus' grave. A priest in these tight confines will offer to burn a candle for you.

Around to the rear of the tomb is the Chapel of the Copts. The Coptic Christians are based in Egypt and claim descent from Christian Egyptians who held fast to Christianity despite the Moslem invasion and pressures that continue to this day. A Coptic monk sitting in darkness at the entrance will invite you to put your hand through a small hole and feel the rock that was Jesus' tomb.

At the opposite side of the church, down 13 steps, past crosses scratched on the walls by Christian pilgrims, is the Chapel of the Discovery of the Cross, where Queen Helena found the reputed original cross during her stay in Jerusalem. *Details: Winter 4 a.m.–8 p.m. (to 9 in summer). Modest dress is required.*

Outside the church, leave the courtyard via the gate to your left. Take the first right turn into Muristan Road. The Lutheran **Church of the Redeemer** is at the corner. Prussia built the church in the last half of the nineteenth century, in twelfth-century architectural style, on the site of the original church. That one was destroyed by Moslems in 1009 along with the rest of the area, known as the Muristan District. The church was consecrated by Kaiser Wilhelm II on his 1898 visit. For a great bird's-eye view of the Old City and beyond, climb the church tower. *Details: (02) 627-6111. Mon–Sat 9–1, 1:30–5. Admission fee.*

Continue down the Muristan (a corruption of the Persian word for hospital), where the Crusader Order of the Hospitaliers, the Knights of St. John, had its hospital and headquarters. The area now is a Greek bazaar, Souq Aftimos. The ornamental fountain in the middle of the Muristan was built by the Greek Orthodox Church in the nineteenth century.

Throughout this walk, various sites and the Church of the Holy Sepulchre especially indicate the importance of the Greek Orthodox Church in Jerusalem. It is the strongest Christian presence here. If you would like

103

a more complete picture of the church, visit the **Greek Patriarchate Museum**, appropriately on Greek Orthodox Patriarchate Road. (The priest-curator I encountered during one visit was from Prospect Park in Brooklyn.) Pilgrims' gifts, various patriarchate acquisitions, and writings are on view in this Crusader building. *Details: (02) 628-2048. Mon–Sat 10–1, 2–4.*

If you wish to remain within the Old City walls for lunch, in the Moslem Quarter, Abu Shukri on el-Wad is one of many restaurants known for having "the best hummus in town." Closer is Samir Said's Friendly Falafel at Christian Quarter Road 11.

The Moslem Quarter

From the more familiar Christian sites, this walk goes to the more remote Moslem world. The Moslem Quarter of the Old City used to be considered the "mixed" quarter, because Jews as well as Moslems lived there. But Jews were killed in Arab riots, particularly in 1929 and 1936, and many fled or were removed by the British authorities. Finally, after the Jordanian occupation, no Jews remained anywhere in the Old City. In 1948, women and children were sent to western Jerusalem; the men were taken to Jordan.

Since the city's reunification in 1967, Jews have returned to what now is known as the Moslem Quarter. Although not in great numbers, they are back to pray in their synagogues, to study in *yeshivot*, and even to live. More than 60 Jewish families now have their homes here. On any walk through the Moslem Quarter, it is intriguing to look for signs of the Jewish presence, past and present. It's like uncovering a secret.

The largest quarter, the Moslem Quarter is in the northeast part of the Old City. Almost lost in its hectic jumble are glorious examples of Mameluke Moslem architecture from the thirteenth and fourteenth centuries. Also hidden are remnants of former Jewish occupants. But happily blazing away are buildings covered by many-colored polka dots, plus doves and images of Mecca. These structures are homes of people who made the pilgrimage to Mecca.

If this is where you are starting today, enter the quarter through Damascus Gate. You have to make two turns to get inside (the better to stymie invaders with their long lances). Inside is a jumble of stores, street vendors, sights, smells, and a few stairs to negotiate. Angling off to the right is Khan es-Zeit Street (with its tempting pastry shops). This is the beginning of the Roman Cardo, following the natural descent of the Tyropoeon (Cheesemaker's) Valley. The street straight ahead is el-Wad. Follow el-Wad in the midst of this heavily Moslem atmosphere, and you find the Stations of the Cross III, IV, and V, which you saw before.

Jewish institutions are another non-Moslem presence here. Before Station IV, note a Star of David built into the metal door on the left. After Barquq Road, you see again on the left and just past the Via Dolorosa Yeshivat Torah Chaim, where the Moslem caretaker hid its holy books during the Jordanian occupation. Farther down el-Wad, the Institute for Talmudic Studies and Hazon Yeheskel Synagogue are on the right.

Turn right at Aqabat at-Takiya Street. On the left is a theological seminary, **Madrassah Resaiya,** distinguished by its striped facade of black basalt, pink marble, and white limestone and blending both Mameluke and Ottoman features. (The Mamelukes, slaves who became kings, are remembered for their architecture, which features rows of alternating colored stone, arches like clamshells or the roofs of stalactite caves over entrances, and projections on either side of these entrances for guards.) Up the stairs to the left is a Moslem orphanage built in 1398 as a palace.

In the reverse direction, the street on the other side of el-Wad is Ala Uddin (Aladdin). This street is the African Quarter. It is quiet here compared to el-Wad, and the quarter seems isolated and poor. The inhabitants are descendants of either sixteenth-century pilgrims, slaves, or those who came here in the 1930s from Chad, Senegal, Nigeria, and the Sudan. They number 200 families. The buildings in which they live date to the thirteenth century. On the left is the oldest Mameluke doorway in Jerusalem.

These decorations indicate that the home's owners have made the pilgrimage to Mecca.

At the end of the street, leading to the Temple Mount, is Bab el-Nadir (Prison Gate)—named for a prison that was housed in one of the nearby buildings. Back to el-Wad and left at Bab el-Hadid Street, you will pass the fifteenth-century Madrassah Muziriya on the right. You will know you're on the right street because Hebrew writing is over a door facing you on the left. Keep going, past the colorfully painted houses. Just before the green Bab el-Hadid (Iron Gate) leading to the Temple Mount, you turn left. Go under the arch and you will see a short stretch of the Western Wall. This stretch, called **HaKotel HaKatan** (the Small Wall), is closer than the famous portion of the wall to the location of the Holy Temple. Shabbat services take place here.

Backtrack and turn left through a dark tunnel. Pay attention to the stairs. You will come out at the **Souq el-Qattanin** (Cotton Market). A flourishing market when it was built in 1329, it looks rather forlorn now, but merchants sell odds and ends and trinkets. The Bab el-Qattanin (Cotton Gate) to the Temple Mount, at the end of the Cotton Market, is one of the most beautiful gates, typically Mameluke with its shell-like arch, stone "stalactites," and many colors.

At the opposite end of the Cotton Market is el-Wad again. Cross it into Aqabat el-Khalidieh. Besides signs of residents' pilgrimages to Mecca, watch for places to the right of doorposts that look as if the stone has been gouged. It has been. The damage is the result of non-Jews' efforts to remove *mezuzahs* (rectangular containers of Biblical verse) that previous Jewish occupants affixed to their doorposts in accordance with religious law.

This area, around Aqabat el-Khalidieh especially, has housed synagogues, yeshivot, and other Jewish institutions. One of the most intriguing, **Yeshivat Torah HaKohanim**, is found in a three-story building on the right that once belonged to a charities trust for North African Jews. The men studying here learn the religious responsibilities of the Jewish priestly class—the Kohanim—so they will be ready when, as they believe, the Messiah comes and the temple will be restored.

The route returns to el-Wad. Go right. Instead of entering the security gate to the Western Wall, go up the stairs to the left, and you will find yourself on Bab el-Silsileh Street (Street of the Chain). Left, opposite the beginning of Rehov HaKotel leading to the Western Wall Plaza, is the Jaliqya Building. Opposite it is el-Khaldiya, a library now closed. Before the Gate of the Chain on the right is the Madrassah et-Tankiziya, a lovely Mameluke building constructed in 1329 that is now a Moslem college.

Turn around and walk away from the *bab* (gate). On the right, just before Rehov Misgav Ladach, is the Tashtamuriya Building, one of this street's several examples of outstanding architecture, with a fountain by its entrance. This building dates to the thirteenth century.

To get to Jaffa Gate and its many bus lines below, continue straight ahead through the souk. At the T, turn right and left immediately and continue up the stairs.

A tour of the Christian and Moslem Quarters can be a turbulent experience, raising emotions about Jesus and the impact of his life. Although Jesus, too, was surrounded by a crush of humanity as he made his way up the Street of Sorrows, you might find yourself squelching introspection as you dodge donkeys and slide through crowded, narrow lanes. And despite the time you spend in the Moslem Quarter, with its graceful, imaginative architecture, this culture remains, frustratingly, behind closed doors.

Perhaps this is the time to find a quiet place to sit and reflect. Some options are Independence or Liberty Bell Parks.

Fourth Day: From the Mountain to the Valley

For a change of pace from sunless, narrow lanes and crowds of people, this walk goes to a part of Jerusalem that is like the countryside. The tour starts at the top of the Mount of Olives (Har Tzeitim), where Jews believe Elijah will announce the Messiah's arrival by blowing a shofar. The descent includes visits to some of the loveliest churches in Jerusalem and one of the oldest cemeteries on earth. The tour continues into the Kidron Valley, with its ancient tombs and examples of burial customs from thousands of years ago.

The longer you are in Jerusalem, in all likelihood, the more tombs you will visit. This might seem macabre, but in Jerusalem, tombs have historical as well as religious significance. The ways in which they were used, their architecture, and their artwork speak about the people who are buried there.

Be doubly sure to protect yourself from the sun and dehydration on this walk. Refreshment stands are scarce, so along with water, you might want to bring a snack. Also bring a flashlight for viewing tombs. It's best to avoid this walk on a Sunday, when church services limit sightseeing. On Saturday, the Jewish burial site on the Mount of Olives (the world's oldest Jewish cemetery) is closed, but the tombs in the Kidron Valley will be open. Keep in mind that Christian sites close from about noon until 2 or 3 p.m. To reach the Mount of Olives by public transportation, take Arab Bus 75 at the Suleiman Street Bus Station across the street and a little past Damascus Gate.

In the afternoon, you should have time to visit Bethlehem, a short (five-mile) ride south of Jerusalem. Bethlehem is not as simple to traverse as it was when it was under Israeli control, but the tour is still doable, although more expensive. You will need your passport for this segment.

Allow two-and-a-half hours for the descent from the Mount of Olives and at least that much for Bethlehem.

The Mount of Olives

From the summit of the Mount of Olives, you can see, if not forever, at least Jerusalem's yesterday and today. The view carries the eye into the Kidron Valley and its tombs, across the ruins below Dung Gate of the Jerusalem that was King David's, to Mount Zion, to the walled Old City, to the towers of new Jerusalem beyond, even to Nebi Samuel, where the Prophet Samuel is said to be buried. Try to see this view at night, when Jerusalem is golden not from its stones but from its lights.

The Mount of Olives, 2,600 feet high, was once thickly covered by the trees that gave it its name. Now it is covered with graves, shrines, churches, monasteries, and an Arab village—and topped by a hotel. To most Jews, the large hotel, built close to the Mount of Olives' highest point during the Jordanian occupation, is a jarring presence. The original road to the hotel was laid over Jewish graves. Israelis installed a new road and reconstructed the graves.

The Mount of Olives is Judaism's most select place of burial. Jews believe that when Elijah blows his shofar from the top of the Mount of Olives, the dead will be resurrected. Those buried here will be the first to get the wake-up call. It was from this mountain that rabbis waited for the sight of the new moon to signal the start of a new month. With its appearance, they built a huge bonfire. When watchers on other hills spotted the fire, they built their signaling bonfires, and so the word was spread.

For Christians, churches on the mount commemorate events in Jesus' final entry into Jerusalem. But to make things confusing, there are at least two Gethsemanes (from the Hebrew words for oil press), from where Jesus descended toward Jerusalem and was seized by the Romans, and two places credited as the location for Jesus' ascension to heaven. At the Russian Orthodox Monastery, behind the hotel, a six-story bell tower was constructed on the spot from which Russians believe Jesus rose to heaven. The monastery is closed to the public.

From the hotel, the main road leads to a string of churches, Christian religious sites, and the Jewish cemetery on the mount. Keep in mind that in Jerusalem's typically "layered" architecture, churches were often built on mosques, which in turn were built on churches.

Backtracking to the village of A-Tur, the first church you'll reach is **Pater Noster**, where Jesus is believed to have taught the Lord's Prayer. It was built in 1874, financed by a French princess. Inside, the Lord's Prayer is written on plaques in some 63 languages. At the end of the church courtyard is a reconstruction of the Byzantine Church of Eleona, originally built by Queen Helena, destroyed by Persians, then rebuilt by Crusaders. *Details: Mon–Sat 8:30–noon, 3–5.*

The octagonal **Church of the Ascension**, opposite the Pater Noster, really is a mosque. It is on the highest point of the Mount of Olives and is one of the claimed locations of Jesus' ascension to heaven. Located on an earlier church, it is the focal point of the celebration of the Feast of the Ascension. A rock inside shows what is said to be the imprint of Jesus' foot. To enter, ring the bell.

108

From the road that leads to the hotel, a stairway heads down a steep incline. On the left are the **Tombs of Prophets** Haggai, Malachi, and Zechariah, plus some 50 others. Farida, a woman who lives in the house above the tombs, will unlock the gate. She also will sell drinks—lemonade costs about $3.50—and offer the use of toilets standing in the yard. *Details: Daily 9–3. Admission fee.*

Farther down the slope, you will find an illegible orange sign over a grave on the other side of the fence. To get to the grave, you will have to figure out the route from the opening to the cemetery still farther down the road. This is the **Common Grave of the Fallen of the Old City**, the resting place of 48 fighters who fell in the battle for the Jewish Quarter in the War of Independence.

A plaque you might have noticed in the Jewish Quarter of the Old City marks the site of the Israelis' common grave, used between 1948 and 1967. The grave was found after the Six-Day War reunited the city, and the bodies were reburied here. Check the ages on the stones to see how young some of the fighters were.

If you haven't entered the Jewish cemetery from below the hotel, you can enter it past the common grave. You'll find graves of great Torah scholars, rabbis, writers, and leaders, including former Prime Minister Menahem Begin. Feel free to stroll through this sun-bleached cemetery. It is covered, mostly, by flat headstones. The height of the memorial stones might give the impression that the bodies aren't in the ground, but be assured they are. Jewish law requires it. Pebbles on top of the slabs are left by mourners, fulfilling Jewish custom.

Off the road continuing down, the **Basilica of Dominus Flevit**, with a tear-shaped cupola, was built in 1955 to mark the spot where Jesus wept. In the apse, architect Antonio Barluzzi preserved a Byzantine mosaic floor left from the original Crusader church on this site. Just before entering the church, take a look at the nearby collection of ossuaries, used by Jews for burial. *Details: Daily 8–noon, 2:30–5.*

Continue on the road. To the left is a cut-off called **Kohanim Observation Point**. Descendants of the priestly class, the Kohanim, are forbidden from entering cemeteries. This cut-off was made so they could watch funerals while not actually being in the cemetery.

The Russian **Church of Mary Magdalene**, farther down to the right, has seven golden onion domes, making it the most distinctive sight, along with seven arches at the Arches Hotel, on the Mount of Olives. The church was built in sixteenth-century Russian style by Czar Alexander III to honor his mother. Consecration was in 1888. The church claims Gethsemane is on its grounds. *Details: (02) 628-4371. Tue and Thu 9–noon or 10–11:30 a.m. Admission fee.*

109

Continue to the end of the road, turn left, and enter the **Grotto of Gethsemane** (the second Gethsemane), next to the Church of All Nations, built in 1924. With its ancient olive trees with enormous and multiple gnarled trunks, the grotto is a peaceful rest stop. The Franciscans have owned this site since the fourteenth century.

Contributions from 12 nations paid for the **Church of All Nations** (Basilica of the Agony). It, too, was designed by Antonio Barluzzi, the Dominus Flevit architect. Byzantine in style, its colorful mosaic facade shines brilliantly as it reflects the sunset. *Details: (02) 628-3264. 8:30–noon, 3–6 (to 5 in winter).*

Carefully crossing the main road that runs in front of the Church of All Nations, go left to find an entrance to the Kidron Valley. At the far end, you'll reach the Kidron Valley Tombs.

Kidron Valley Tombs

The Kidron Valley, at the foot of the Mount of Olives, was once far deeper than it is now. It was probably more like a canyon. Accumulations of ruins, garbage, and silt have changed the configuration over the centuries. In the valley are examples of Second Temple–period memorials and tombs, standing like sentinels. No fence protects them and no ticket takers sit before them. They are open to all who want to explore. But visitors need tools for exploration: a flashlight and a body that can fold like a pretzel, for climbing in and out of the small tomb openings.

During the Second Temple period (536 B.C.E. to 70 C.E.) and after, well-to-do families buried their dead in natural or quarried caves. Inside, the dead were laid on cut ledges. Then the cave entrances were closed until nothing was left of the bodies but bones. The bones were gathered and interred in ossuaries, stone containers, which were placed farther back in the caves. A cave could hold generations of bones. Thus a dead person's bones almost literally were gathered unto his father's.

Ossuaries and caves were carved with floral and geometric decorations. Images of humans and animals weren't included because of

Kidron Valley/Mount of Olives Sights	
1 Absalom's Memorial Pillar	7 Tomb of Jehoshaphat
2 Basilica of Dominus Flevit	8 Tomb of the Sons of Hezir
3 Church of All Nations/Gethsemane	9 Tomb of Zechariah
4 Church of the Ascension	10 Tombs of the Prophets
5 Church of Mary Magdelene	
6 Church of Pater Noster	

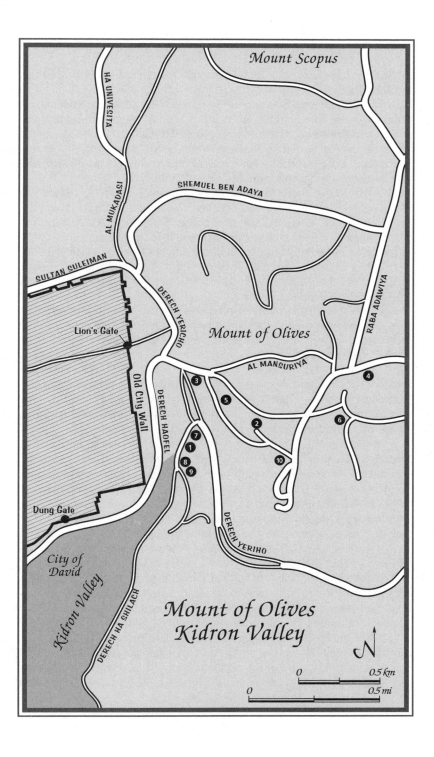

Mount Scopus

HA UNIVESITA

AL MUKADASI

SHEMUEL BEN ADAYA

SULTAN SULEIMAN

Lion's Gate

Old City Wall

DERECH YERICHO

DERECH HAOFEL

Mount of Olives

AL MANSURIYA

RABA ADAWIYA

3

5

4

2

6

7

1

8

9

10

Dung Gate

City of
David

Kidron Valley

DERECH HA SHILACH

DERECH YERIHO

Mount of Olives
Kidron Valley

N

0   0.5 km

0   0.5 mi

rabbinic interpretation that the Second Commandment forbids their reproduction.

The first tomb reached and the last one built is **Absalom's Memorial Pillar**. It dates from some nine centuries after Absalom's life. Absalom, said to be King David's favorite son, turned on his father and led a revolt against him. The structure acquired its name, for some inexplicable reason, during Crusader times. Freestanding, the memorial shows an amalgam of Egyptian and early and later Greek influences.

Nearby is the **Tomb of Jehoshaphat**, uncovered only in 1924. Jews of Jerusalem used the tomb to bury their worn-out holy books. Since the books carried the name of God, they couldn't be destroyed. As it turned out, this practice has led to major historical finds in our day.

A few steps south is the **Tomb of the Sons of Hezir**, an artificial cave with pillars in front. The priestly Hezir family is mentioned in the Book of Nehemiah. The tomb has several rooms and is a classical example of a Second Temple–period burial site.

Next is the **Tomb of Zechariah**, carved out of rock and topped by a pyramid. This tomb had several names over the centuries, but finally its present name stuck. Like the Hezir Tomb, it was probably built during Hasmonean times, between 129 and 63 B.C.E.

Why tombs for Zechariah both on the Mount of Olives and in the Kidron Valley? Some rabbis point out that because he told the king and the people what they didn't want to hear, he was stoned to death. That was an unforgivable act against a prophet, so the construction of two tombs was a (belated) way of making amends.

The Kidron Valley tombs aren't the last tombs to see during a visit to Jerusalem. The tombs of the Kings, the Sanhedrim, Jason, and Simon the Just are others. And it isn't only their artwork that makes them intriguing. The bones have been removed, but the spirits of the dead rattle around inside. It's almost as if you can feel these spirits and touch their laughter, ambitions, and tears. This feeling is characteristic of all Jerusalem. The way the city entwines past and present is among its magical aspects.

Be sure to look up from here at the view of the sun-bleached tombstones climbing the Mount of Olives and the Arab (formerly also home to Yemenite Jews) village of Silwan clinging to its hillside. This sight inspired Saul Bellow to write in *To Jerusalem and Back* that the city reminded him of sun-bleached bones. Standing closer to you might be some silvery olive trees and shiny, ample-leafed fig trees.

If you get to Derech HaOphel, the road below the Old City, walk toward the Dung Gate on the promenade. At a marked overlook is a "tomb finder." One tomb is just at the edge of the houses in Silwan. You can see the opening in a stone wall, which is a First Temple burial site. It is called

Pharaoh's Daughter's Tomb—exactly why, no one knows. It resembles an Egyptian structure and has some traces of a pyramid on its roof. Some believe the woman in question was one of Solomon's wives.

If your next stop is Bethlehem, it is most convenient to return to eastern Jerusalem and the Suleiman Street bus station via taxi. From there, take Arab Bus 22, which runs about every 15 minutes. Bring your passport for identification.

If you wish to have lunch in Bethlehem, try the Granada Grill Bar or El Andalus Restaurant (both of which serve Arab food despite their historically evocative names) in Manger Square or the St. George Restaurant in the Municipality Building.

Bethlehem

Rachel's Tomb stands about one-and-a-half miles before the city. This is the division between Israeli and Palestinian lines. According to the Book of Genesis, Rachel, Jacob's most beloved wife, was buried on the road to Efrat (Bethlehem). The hardworking, Italian-born Englishman Sir Moses Montefiore won Jewish ownership for the tomb. In one of its two rooms is a large tomb, usually encircled by red twine and surrounded by fervently praying women. (The other room is for men.) *Details: Sun–Thu 8–6, Fri and holiday eves 8–1. Free.*

In Hebrew, *Bethlehem* means House of Bread; in Arabic, House of Meat. Besides being near the place of Rachel's death some 3,600 years ago, Bethlehem is significant to Jews as the city in which Ruth, loyal convert to Judaism ("Whither thou goest I shall go ... and thy people shall be my people"), met and married Boaz. Their great-grandson, David, born in Bethlehem, was a shepherd and became Israel's second and greatest king.

Bethlehem is most famous as the site of Jesus' birth. But despite the tradition, songs, and artwork, some scholars believe Jesus was born in his hometown of Nazareth. At any rate, the **Church of the Nativity**, commanding Manger Square, marks the place where it is believed Jesus was born. The Samaritans destroyed the first church built here in 326 C.E. Byzantine emperor Justinian erected the present church in the sixth century. Persians invading in 614 spared it. Its physical changes have been minimal.

Like the Church of the Holy Sepulchre, ownership of the Church of the Nativity is shared. But here, fewer denominations are involved. Still, Greek Orthodox, Armenians, and Latins (Roman Catholics) must adhere strictly to the protocols worked out under the Turks.

To enter the church through the Door of Humility, it's necessary to bend (or bow, according to one's interpretation). Stairs on either side of the altar in the nave lead to the Grotto of the Nativity, dimly lit, its air

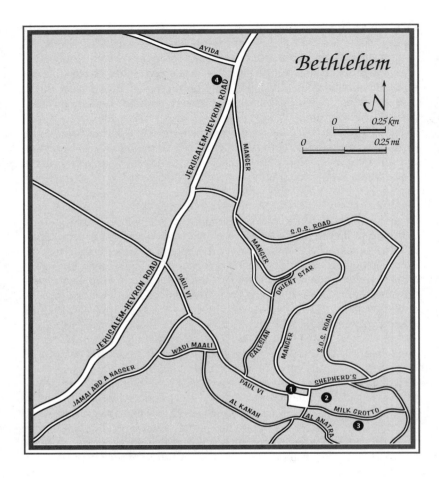

Bethlehem Sights

1 Bethlehem Museum
2 Church of the Nativity/Latin Church of St. Catherine
3 Milk Grotto
4 Rachel's Tomb

heavy with incense. *Details: (02) 274-2425. Daily 5:30–5 (to 6 in winter). Modest dress required.*

Part of the complex of chapels and grottos attached to the Church of the Nativity is the **Latin Church of St. Catherine**, dating from 1881 and reached through a door in the apse of the older building. It is from this bright church that the Christmas midnight mass is televised to the world. Not all those packed into the church that night are Christians. The Palestinian hierarchy, almost all of whom are Moslem, also watch the pageantry. *Details: (02) 274-2425. Daily 5–noon, 2–5 (to 6 in summer).*

The **Milk Grotto** is on the street named for it, to the right of the Church of the Nativity as you face it. The Franciscans built a church over the place where Mary was believed to have spilled milk while nursing Jesus. *Details: Daily 8–11:45, 2–5 (to 6 in summer).*

Aside from its religious significance, Bethlehem is a charming town with winding streets, white buildings, and views out to the Judean Desert. It also has a souk, beginning off Manger Square, which some avid shoppers prefer to the one in Jerusalem's Old City.

Across Manger Square, with the Church of the Nativity away from

---

Getting Around When It's a Challenge

It's no secret that accommodations for the disabled in Israel are behind those in the West. Slowly, Israel is catching up. A few accessible museums are David's Tower Museum, Bloomfield Science Museum, and Bible Lands Museum. Neot Kedumim, the Biblical Landscape Reserve northwest of Jerusalem, is also wheelchair accessible. Hebrew Union College's hostel, Beit Shmuel, has rooms designed for wheelchair access. The Jewish Quarter of the Old City has a wheelchair-accessible route, as does the Western Wall Tunnel, and Ministry of Tourism projects and hotels that receive government aid must provide access.

Anyone who needs a wheelchair, walker, electronic medical rehabilitation equipment, or special transport may contact Yad Sarah, Rehov HaNevi'im 43 and Rehov Yermiyahu 70, (02) 644-4444, which has a free lending service. The Advisory Center for the Disabled (Milbat) at the Sheba Medical Center in Tel Aviv, (03) 530-3739, can provide additional information.

you, take Paul VI Street and turn right into a narrow street to reach the **Bethlehem Museum**. It shows traditional Bethlehem crafts, costumes, and lifestyles. *Details: Mon–Sat 10–noon, 2:30–5. Admission fee.*

Except for Rachel's Tomb outside the city, Bethlehem's place in Jewish history isn't obvious. You have to carry its importance to Judaism in your memory of Bible stories. In its Christian aspect, Bethlehem is the reversal of the Church of the Holy Sepulchre where Jesus died. Bethlehem celebrates life.

The Fifth Day: Further into the Past

This walk includes the further reaches of Jerusalem's history, a bit of adventure, and some delicate beauty. It begins in the morning at the City of David—the Jerusalem that King David built on the slopes of the Kidron Valley. Near to it, you can travel through a tunnel that King Hezekiah's men worked desperately to build before invaders arrived. These places have dramatic stories to tell. In contrast, the afternoon offers the tranquil beauty of the Temple Mount.

Allow two-and-a-half hours for the City of David, Warren's Shaft, and the tunnel walk. Allow two hours for visiting the Temple Mount. Since Moslem authorities close the Temple Mount, or Haram ash-Sharif as it is known in Arabic, at 3 p.m., you might consider reversing these two sites. Keep in mind that the Temple Mount is also closed Friday.

Gear up for walking through the tunnel with shorts, shoes that can get wet, and a flashlight. Wear clothes that provide modest coverage for the Temple Mount.

The City of David can be reached by descending the slope opposite Dung Gate (Bus 1 will drop you there). Across from the parking lot you'll see what looks like a park. In it is a tourist office especially for the City of David. Since it isn't easy to find your way around these sites on your own, the office can provide tour guides for the area, including Hezekiah's tunnel, as well as an audio-guide you can carry with you. Or you can join an organized tour. Wading through the narrow, unlit tunnel is more comforting in the company of others.

The City of David and Hezekiah's Tunnel

The oldest part of Jerusalem is outside the walls of the Old City. The original Jerusalem, called the City of David, wasn't built on the heights by the Temple Mount but on the slopes of Ophel south of it. Solomon built the First Temple on the mount, and eventually the city extended farther up the slope in the area we know today.

You will begin the story of the City of David from the park above it. A wooden platform at the edge of the park overlooks the valley. It is believed that King David's palace was here. From this height, you can imagine how easy it was for him to look down and find Bathsheba bathing on her rooftop.

Excavations below began in 1859, but they have been conducted systematically only since 1978. Archaeologists have uncovered 25 strata going back to the Chalcolithic Period in the fourth millennium B.C.E., as well as those of King David's and King Solomon's reigns, and even after Jews returned from Babylon in 538 B.C.E. Jerusalem's oldest houses—5,000-year-old, one-room, early Canaanite structures—have been uncovered on bedrock in Area E. Among items found were two stone toilet seats from the eighth century B.C.E., which Israelis love to note are in sharp contrast to the Turkish holes in the floor that were standard in Jerusalem even in modern times. Another find was arrowheads from Babylonian King Nebuchadnezzar's siege of Jerusalem in 586 B.C.E.

Cities preceded David's here by two thousand years, because this place was both high enough to defend and close to a stream in the valley. The Jebusites built a shaft to obtain water from the Gihon Spring without leaving the city walls. One story tells of David discovering and scaling the shaft. David's army then took control of the water supply, so the Jebusites were forced to surrender.

Named for the man who found it in 1867, **Warren's Shaft** is entered below the City of David excavations. A spiral staircase gets you partway down, then you're on your own. Have your flashlight handy. *Details: (02) 628-8141. Sun–Thu 9–5, Fri and holiday eves 9–1. Admission fee for Warren's Shaft only.*

The entrance to **Hezekiah's Tunnel** is below Warren's Shaft. The proverbial profound Jewish memory saved the day, when, in 700 B.C.E., King Hezekiah remembered how David conquered the Jebusites. Chronicles II:32 says the Assyrian Sennacherib and his army descended on Jerusalem "like wolves on the fold." Hezekiah prepared for their arrival by building a new wall to the north and taking action to keep control of the city's water supply. First, he stopped the waters of Gihon. Then he had a tunnel dug that brought water from outside the city walls into the city. The tunnel, dug simultaneously from either end, is an engineering marvel. With the tunnel accomplished, Hezekiah, having learned from the Jebusites' mistake, blocked the entrance from outside the city walls.

You can walk ("slosh" is more accurate) the 570 yards through Hezekiah's Tunnel in your "may-get-wet" clothes. Water height varies, but averages thigh level. This is an experience not to be missed. On one hand, you can feel as adventurous as a kid. On the other, you can feel the anxiety of the men who hastily labored to achieve this startling engineering feat to protect Jerusalem from Sennacherib. The water level, which used to rise and fall unexpectedly, is mechanically controlled, so there is no danger of suddenly finding yourself swimming.

Tool marks on the walls tell the direction from which the excavators were coming. The tunnel was barely finished when King Sennacherib's army arrived. But the invaders mysteriously succumbed to disease, beat a quiet retreat, and left the Jews victorious—and with a remarkable and handy water tunnel.

You exit at the **Pool of Siloam** (Shiloah). Jews come to the pool during Rosh HaShana to symbolically cast their sins into the water. Christians believe this is where Jesus told a blind man to wash and he would see. The man did, and he saw. Because of this story, some people consider the pool to have healing powers.

Now that I have waxed so enthusiastic about a slosh through the tunnel, I must in good conscience warn that to do so in winter might be unbearably cold. The walk takes about half an hour. *Details: (02) 625-4403. Sun–Thu 9–4, Fri and holiday eves 9–2.*

To get back to the Old City, the still energetic can hike up the slope to Dung Gate, a moderately strenuous walk of about half an hour. The less energetic should look for a taxi. Back in the Old City, the most convenient place for lunch is the Jewish Quarter, perhaps at the Quarter Cafe, up the stairs from the Western Wall Plaza, close to the Burnt House and with a splendid view.

The Temple Mount

For non-Moslems, entry to the Temple Mount is free through two gates: one at the eastern end of the Street of the Chain, the other via the ramp from the Western Wall Plaza. But tickets to enter the Dome of the Rock, al-Aqsa Mosque, and the Islamic Museum may be purchased only at the top of the ramp.

The Temple Mount, Mount Moriah (mor-ee-YAH)—called Haram ash-Sharif by Moslems—is considered in the Zohar, Jewish mystical writings, to be the center of the world. This is where Abraham is said to have followed God's orders and offered his beloved son, Isaac, as sacrifice—an offer God refused, thus ending human sacrifice.

King David put an altar here, and his son, Solomon, built the First Temple on this rise in the tenth century B.C.E. The Babylonian Nebuchadnezzar destroyed the First Temple in 587 B.C.E. Some 70 years later, after Jews returned from exile in Babylon, the temple was rebuilt.

The Second Temple, which Herod had raised to become an elevated plateau, was destroyed by the Romans. The site became a shrine to Jupiter which, in turn, was transformed into a Christian church.

With the Moslem conquest, evidence of Christianity was wiped from the mount, and the Dome of the Rock was erected in 691 over what was believed to be the rock on which Abraham offered his son. But Moslems claim that the son was Ishmael, not Isaac. The Crusaders turned the building into a church, but it was restored to its original purpose when Moslems regained Jerusalem.

Although Israel was the most recent conqueror of the Temple Mount, it has made no move to alter the status quo. Shortly after Israel captured the Old City in 1967, the keys to the Temple Mount were returned to the Moslem authorities with no provision made for Jewish worshippers. Therefore, take note: The Moslems in control of the Temple Mount allow neither Christian nor Jewish prayer to take place there. Visitors who appear to be praying will unceremoniously be ejected from the mount.

The **Dome of the Rock** isn't a mosque. Besides being the site of expected sacrifice, it enshrines the rock from which Moslems believe Mohammed made his Night Journey astride his horse to visit Allah in Heaven. But there was also a strong political purpose for the Dome of the Rock. The Moslem world at the time was torn by conflict over which faction could claim to be Mohammed's heir. Khalif Abd el-Malik, an Umayyad whose seat of power was Damascus, wanted to discourage his followers from making the pilgrimage to Mecca and possibly falling under the influence of his rivals. He constructed the Dome of the Rock in hopes of establishing Jerusalem as the major Moslem pilgrimage destination. He didn't achieve his objective, but he left a magnificent building. Guides will point to an indentation in the rock as from Mohammed. But there is no evidence that Mohammed was ever actually in Jerusalem.

Dome of the Rock (background)

The eight-sided building, blue and golden, is one of the loveliest and most graceful anywhere. Many of its 45,000 exterior tiles were installed under Suleiman the Magnificent in the

1500s. Its golden dome, which provides a signature view of Jerusalem, was re-covered with gold leaf in the mid-1990s, thanks to Jordan's King Hussein.

Inside, mosaics cover the walls. The mystical, mythical rock under the dome is surrounded by a wooden fence. A structure on a nearby pedestal is said to contain hairs from Mohammed's beard, sent to Jerusalem by a Turkish sultan in 1609.

Opposite the entrance to the Dome of the Rock is **al-Aqsa Mosque**, built on the site of previous churches and mosques destroyed by war, earthquakes, and fire. *Al-Aqsa* means "the farthermost point" and refers to the farthest point the Prophet reached from Medina in his flight on his miraculous horse. While Jerusalem is never mentioned in the Koran, that distant point was interpreted as meaning Jerusalem.

Little remains of the original mosque built in 670. The spacious rectangular building, with its 12 white pillars of Carrara marble, can hold five thousand worshippers. Much to be seen inside is the result of extensive restoration in the 1930s and 1940s. Outside, the lead-plated dome contrasts with the golden dome opposite like night and day. It was at the al-Aqsa entrance that King Abdullah of Jordan, King Hussein's grandfather, was murdered in 1951 by a Palestinian Arab.

The trapezoid that forms the mount is a pleasant, parklike space with fountains and small buildings. To the right of the ramp from the Western Wall Plaza is the **Islamic Museum**, which houses a rich display of items from the Temple Mount. The Islamic Museum shouldn't be confused with the Museum of Islamic Art in western Jerusalem. *Details: (02) 628-3313. Dome of the Rock, al-Aqsa Mosque, and Islamic Museum, Sat–Thu 8–12:30, 1:30–4. Hours differ during Ramadan and some other Islamic holidays. Admission fee.*

One of the most overpowering aspects of this walk and those through the Old City is the layering of cultures and religions right before your eyes. Whoever is the most powerful at the moment gets to knock down what existed before. Even in the mid-twentieth century, Arabs destroyed Jewish houses of worship, as well as almost everything else in the Jewish Quarter of the Old City, and with no outcry from the rest of the world.

The notable exception to past practice is that the current "ruler" of all Jerusalem, the Israelis, have let Islamic and Christian religious sites be. They have improved some (such as the Via Dolorosa), opened them to all, and turned their administration over to their respective parent religious authorities. Does this mean the world has improved since 1967, that Israelis are more sensitive and less cruel than their predecessors, or that Israelis are just more aware of the international repercussions that would fall on them?

The Sixth Day: A Great Leap Forward

This day's walk takes you centuries forward from the previous ones. Most of your surroundings will be little more than 100 years old—scarcely a hiccup in time compared to the other walks. Ethnically, you will go from Central Asia and Iran to Eastern Europe.

This walk goes through some of the most picturesque and religiously orthodox neighborhoods in western Jerusalem. Be sure to dress modestly. If you go on a Friday, Mea She'arim should be full of hustle and bustle while its residents prepare for Shabbat. The walk also takes you to old neighborhoods that have been reconstructed: Mishkenot Sh'ananim, Yemin Moshe, and an artisan's quarter, Khutsot HaYotzer. Plan on three hours for each walk.

Bucharan Quarter, Mea She'arim, and Nahalat Shiva

The Bucharan Quarter was built beginning in 1894 by wealthy Jews who came from the Asiatic-Russian province of Buchara. Today, Buchara is part of the Uzbekistan Republic. Persian and Afghani Jews also have been integral to the neighborhood from its early years.

The neighborhood is untypical of early Jerusalem for its spaciousness. Streets are straight and wide. Some of the homes are palatial and almost all are of Italian influence, often symmetrical in form, and with elaborate stonework on doors and windows. But now, sadly, they are in need of repair. Poverty, new construction, and the ultra-Orthodox are greatly changing the atmosphere.

Buses 3, 4, 9, 39, and several others pass the quarter. Start off at the Rehov Ezra intersection with the main street, Yehezkel. At Ezra 14, west of Yehezkel, is the **Koj'hinaieff**, a one-story building of one of the neighborhood's founders, a rabbi of Samarkand. On the left side of the street is the most ornate of the houses on Rehov Ezra, the **Yehudaieff House—** called The Palace—with a long Italian Renaissance facade. On the roof is a moveable glass pyramid over an inner balcony that can serve as a succah during the holiday of Succot (See Chapter 15: "The Cycle of Celebrations"). During World War I, the house served as Turkish headquarters. Under British occupation, Jewish British soldiers celebrated a Passover Seder here and a reception was held for General Allenby, who stood at the top of the double curved exterior staircase with Chain Weizmann, future president of Israel. Twenty years later, the house was the center for Etzel, Menahem Begin's anti-British organization. The Palace is now home to two ultra-Orthodox girls' schools. Upstairs are murals high on the walls.

At the corner of Rehovs Ezra and Fischel is the **Bucharan Old Age Home**. Right one block to the far right corner with Rehov Yissa Bracha is

121

the L-shaped **Simhaieff House**. Continue on Yissa Bracha and turn left at the lane that leads to stairs to Rehov HaBucharim.

Across the street is the **Davidaieff House**, distinctive for its double roof. The mansion is getting a new lease on life as host to technical and jewelry-making schools, a dental clinic, day-care center, and, most famously, Kuzari, where North African and Middle Eastern folk embroidery is made and sold (see Chapter 7: "Shop Worn"). Feel free to visit the building to see how the architect combined the old and new. *Details: (02) 582-6632. Sun–Thu 8:30–5, Fri and holiday eves 9–noon.*

Turn right on leaving the Davidaieff House. At number 18 is the **Mash'hayaieff Courtyard**, the largest in the quarter. The Turks used the house as a prison. Inside is a fine vaulted arcade on the northern and eastern sides, but these cannot be seen for the building has been gutted. What it will become, we will have to discover.

Head down Rehov David Hazzan and turn right at Rehov Adoniyahu HaCohen. At number 28 is the **Haji Yehezkel House**, built by Haji Muhammed Ismail, the first immigrant from Meshhed, Iran, where Jews had been forced to become Moslems. In Jerusalem, the Haji reverted to Judaism and became Yehezkel Levi. He wrote an inscription below 18 windowsills in which he leaves the building to his father and children and asks that it never be sold and should be named for him. The building stretches the entire block.

Continuing on Adoniyahu HaCohen, you will find on your left the courtyard of the **Meshed Adoniyahu Synagogue**, recognizable by the Armenian plaques on either side of the entrance. This was once the center for Meshed's forced Moslems. The gate and doors are profusely adorned with six-pointed stars, perhaps expressing Jews' joy at their release from forced conversion to Islam. You can enter the lush courtyard and climb the stairs to look into the synagogue.

Turn left at Rehov Yehezkel. Close by, at number 33, is the **Aharonaieff Courtyard**, once a lovely private courtyard but now unkempt. Beyond number 33, a giant eucalyptus and a cypress protrude into the street. Bucharans planted rows of trees, most of which the Turks chopped down. Across Yehezkel is the Bucharan market, a rather forlorn place.

Cut through the market. Turn left at Rehov Moussaieff and you'll find another historic house at number 13. On the other side of the street at Rehov Adoniyahu HaCohen 6 is a house attacked in 1913 by Arabs, who killed the owner's son. Go back to Moussaieff and turn up the hill. On the left, a rectangular building at number 8 is noted not for architectural interest but because it was the first house built in the quarter, in 1894. You can recognize it by the market inside, through a wide door. Enter to get an idea of the building's once-grand interior.

On the right side, before the corner of Rehov HaBucharim, is a large building wealthy Bucharans built for their less-fortunate compatriots—that is, while the wealthy still had money. You can enter from Moussaieff and leave at the Rehov HaBucharim exit—if you can find the building. The patched-together homes and their outhouses facing the courtyard give a hint of the statistic that Jerusalem is the poorest large city in Israel.

Turn right on HaBucharim. At the corner with Yehezkel is the **Baba-Tama Synagogue**. Hopes for a grand synagogue in the quarter never materialized, and this one became the central synagogue, even though most of the grand houses included their own synagogues. If the synagogue is open, inspect its humble interior.

Next stop: **Mea She'arim**. Turn left on Yehezkel, left again on Rehov Ezra, and right on Rehov Yoel. The simplest way to Mea She'arim is to continue on Yoel and then turn left at Rehov Mea She'arim, although your map will show you shortcuts. Mea She'arim means "one hundred fold," from a line in Genesis. It is important to remember that this was an ultra-Orthodox neighborhood from the beginning—established by ultra-Orthodox Jews for ultra-Orthodox Jews.

Mea She'arim, also a poor neighborhood, is a series of row houses in a near-fortresslike setting, almost rectangular. When initial construction was completed in 1875, the community was situated in a dangerous wilderness. The need to protect the population from marauders was paramount. The houses in the center of the rectangle were added later.

If you are there on Friday, the bearded men of the neighborhood might already be in their various styles of holiday dress. The flavor of Mea She'arim, with men in black frock coats, women with scarves covering their hair, and the frequent sounds of Yiddish instead of Hebrew, is Old World Ashkenazi, almost as if the clock has been set back a few hundred years. (Ask for permission before taking anyone's picture.)

Don't be surprised by the posters and graffiti that heap epithets on the State of Israel. Many people here refuse to recognize the nation's existence. Their position is that only God can create the Jewish nation.

Enter at any gate. Mea She'arim's market is on Rehov Ein Ya'acov, off Rehov Mea She'arim and next to the Bratzlav Yeshiva. It's said that you can't get lost within Mea She'arim, but I never know quite where I am. But wander at will and observe how people with little means and many mouths to feed manage to cope in their physical space. An exit at the far side of Mea She'arim will put you on Rehov Avraham Mislonim. Turn right and at Rehov Shlomo Baharan (named for a Mea She'arim founder), then turn left.

You might not find these streets at all. If you see you are approaching busy Rehov Strauss, you're going in the wrong direction. Ask for help finding Ethiopia Street. Look for the dome of the Ethiopian Orthodox Church, which should be on your left. Now you are in another world.

Most of the houses here were built by a wealthy Arab Nashishibi family, notable in the late 1990s when one of its prominent members growled about U.S. Secretary of State Madeleine Albright, "Her husband didn't want her, why should we?" Every other house is set back on its lot, so each house has four exposures. With houses not set in a straight line as they usually are, the street was given greater interest than it otherwise would have had (what a pity that idea has been lost).

On the left is the **Ethiopian Orthodox Church**, described in Chapter 13: "Discover Heavenly Jerusalem." Across the street, marked by a plaque (unless it's been removed by anti-Zionist Jews), was the home of Eliezer Ben-Yehuda, the dedicated man who revived Hebrew as a living language at the end of the nineteenth century.

You will see some of the city's loveliest houses here. One of them, at number 3—a Nashishibi-built house—was once the British Council Library and is now a private residence. It underwent extensive renovation in 1998. A hideous wooden structure that had been added to the top floor was removed and new top floors were added.

Cross Rehov HaNevi'im and continue on Rehov HaRav Kook (named for the same Abraham Isaac Kook quoted earlier about the Western Wall). On the right, at number 7, is a lane. Inside, the house on the right was built in 1926 for Rav (Rabbi) Kook, known not only for his erudition and modesty but also for his strong Zionism. *Details: (02) 623-2560. Sun–Thu 9–3, Fri and holiday eves 9–noon.*

At the end of this same lane is a garden and an 1860s house. Now a museum and dairy restaurant, it was last the home of artist Anna Ticho and her ophthalmologist husband. Inside the thick-walled Arab-style house are the Tichos' extensive chanukiah collection and Anna's splendid paintings of the Judean Desert. *Details: (02) 624-5068. Sun, Mon, Wed, Thu 10–5, Tue 10–10, Fri and holiday eves 10–2. Restaurant open 10 a.m.–midnight. Admission fee to the museum.*

This might be your chance for a lunch break. If the weather is good, you have the peaceful garden to enjoy. Otherwise, there are plenty of restaurants in Nahalat Shiva.

On the left on the same street at number 12 is an elegant, endangered two-story building set back from the street. It used to be the Italian consulate and later functioned as Maskit, a high-quality store founded by Moshe Dayan's first wife, Ruth, to sell immigrant crafts. Next to it is an intrusive new building.

Cross Rehov Yafo. Turn left and pass Kikar Zion. **Nahalat Shiva** (Estates of the Seven) has been tucked out of sight by new buildings on

Rehov Yafo, but most of the original construction has been preserved. This was the third neighborhood founded outside the Old City walls, the second that was permanent, and the first by and for people who already lived in Jerusalem. The seven men who established it in 1869 were led by the dedicated (and, some said at the time, crazy) Yosef Rivlin.

Enter the neighborhood by descending the stairs on Ma'alot Nahalat Shiva to the right of the Beit Yoel building at 33 Rehov Yafo. Along the lane to the right is a Sephardi synagogue, the **Tent of Yitzhak**. Closest to the synagogue, you will find open courtyards of buildings that face Rehov Yoel Salomon. Returning to the lane and continuing, you will find another synagogue, this one Ashkenazi.

The neighborhood might appear to be falling down, but it costs a pretty penny to buy into it, and it has been regentrified with trendy restaurants and shops (some are described in Chapter 7: "Shop Worn"). Feel free to stroll through. At one time, all the cooking was done in courtyards, where rainfall was collected in cisterns and provided the only water supply.

After you have investigated the nooks and crannies, find your way to Rehov Yoel Salomon, lined on both sides with more enticing shops and restaurants. If you haven't done so, now you must stop for lunch and to rest your feet. You will have many choices. Afterward, several bus lines on Rehov King George will drop you at the end of Rehov Keren HaYesod close to your next walk.

Mishkenot Sha'ananim, Yemin Moshe, and Khutsot HaYotzer

The adjacent neighborhoods known as Mishkenot Sha'ananim and Yemin Moshe are on a mountain slope with a breathtaking view of the Old City, Mount Zion, and the Judean Desert. The top of the slope is at the intersection of Rehov King David and Rehov Keren HaYesod (the continuation of Rehov King George) and through the Bloomfield Garden to the east. The blades of the **Montefiore Windmill** (described in Chapter 12: "Linger Awhile") make a good landmark.

Montefiore had the windmill built to provide jobs for Mishkenot Sha'ananim's residents as millers. (This area was once studded with windmills.) Inside are exhibits devoted to Montefiore's colorful life. He retired at age 40 and henceforth devoted himself to Jewish causes. He died at age 100.

If you stand on the terrace in front of the windmill at sunset, just as the horizon is turning violet over the Judean Desert and with a full moon rising in the east, I guarantee you will carry the image forever. *Details: Sun–Thu 9–4, Fri 9–1. Free.*

Going down the slope, Rehov Yemin Moshe is the dividing walkway between Mishkenot Sha'ananim on the right and Yemin Moshe on the left. **Mishkenot Sha'ananim** (Dwellings of Tranquility) was Moses Montefiore's attempt in 1860, with the financial contribution of New Orleans Rabbi Judah Touro, to lure Jerusalemites out of the hovels in the Old City to live in fresh air. Even though he built a wall around the buildings and paid residents to move to what was then a dangerous wilderness, Montefiore's effort failed. Every night, residents would scurry to the higher-walled safety of their former homes.

Mishkenot Sha'ananim consists of two long, low buildings. Above them is the Jerusalem Music Center, established with the help of American violinist Isaac Stern. The lower, longer building, the first of the two, now provides quarters for visiting artists of all kinds. From their apartments, they have box seats to view the Old City's changing shades of gold.

A restaurant, the Montefiore, is located in the Guest House, (02) 624-3811. The more famous and expensive Mishkenot Sha'ananim Restaurant is in the upper building.

Jerusalem Scene

On the road south of Bethlehem, Morty, who is driving his battered car to Tekoa, the Jewish community near Prophet Amos' ancient home, sees a truck facing the opposite direction stopped at the edge of the road. A man sits at the wheel and several others stand around it. They are Arabs.

Morty, a cheerful, outgoing, middle-aged man, says to a passenger, "They might be having car trouble." He stops his car and asks in a cheery voice in Hebrew if they need some help. The man at the wheel, in his 20s, sullenly says in English, "Speak English." In the identical cheery voice in which he asked the question in Hebrew, Morty asks in English, "Do you need some help?"

Now he gets an answer. The man snaps, "No." Still with the same tone of equanimity he had used before, Morty says in English, "I just wanted to know if I could be of help." The man in the car is silent, and Morty drives on.

Because of its location, side by side with Mishkenot Sha'ananim, **Yemin Moshe** often is assumed to have been the next settlement outside the walls. Not so. Yemin Moshe, named for Montefiore, arose 30 years and several other settlements later.

In the 1950s, Jerusalem's poor lived here and had to put up with pot-shots from the Arab Legionnaires across the valley. With post-1967 development, the entire neighborhood received a dramatic facelift. Property values soared, and the poor and the artists who lived here took the money and moved elsewhere.

Two beautiful synagogues are on this slope. The one next to the stairs leading from the park is Sephardi. The other, in a more austere building near the center of the neighborhood, is Ashkenazi.

You can simply wander the streets here and study the differences in gates, windows, and gardens. In one direction, you can climb the stairs at the north end of Yemin Moshe back up the hill and stop for refreshments in the King David Hotel. In the other, down a staircase to the left at the bottom of Yemin Moshe, you will reach **Khutzot HaYotzer**, another redevelopment area, with shops selling high-quality arts and crafts. The area is described further in Chapter 7: "Shop Worn."

From the shops, go left up the hill. Below Jaffa Gate is the bus stop for various alternatives into the city center. Across the street from Jaffa Gate is the recent **David's Village** development of million-dollar flats, unfortunately owned mostly by part-time residents. Attractive as it is—it is again work by Moshe Safdie—it always looks deserted. But then, it is.

It often comes as a surprise to visitors that Jerusalem's older neighborhoods are newer than most American cities. Outside the Old City, pent-up energy once confined to ancient narrow lanes was able to explode and express itself in new ways. Perhaps that is one explanation for the electricity in the air in western Jerusalem. After all, it is still a young city.

If you haven't done so, tonight might be ideal for lingering over dinner and the nighttime, stage-set view of the Old City from Mishkenot Sha'ananim, the Zionist Confederate House restaurant, or Montefiore Restaurant.

The Seventh Day: To the Desert

The Lord may rest on the seventh day, but the tourist? Rarely. No visitor should miss a day at Herod's desert- fortress palace, Masada; a refresher at Ein Gedi; or a float in the salt-thick Dead Sea. Bring your bathing suit and a towel. The Egged Bus Company has service Sunday through Friday morning from Jerusalem to all three, so you can go on your own, but

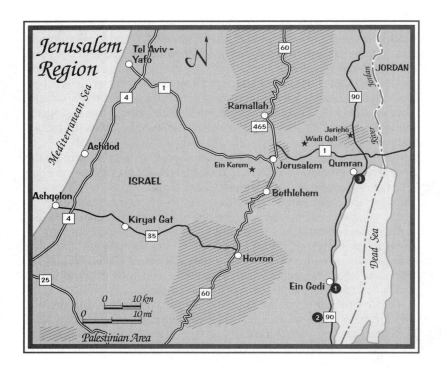

Jerusalem Region

Tel Aviv – Yafo

JORDAN

Ramallah

Jericho
Wadi Qelt

Ein Kerem

Jerusalem

Qumran

Bethlehem

Ein Gedi

Mediterranean Sea

Ashdod

ISRAEL

Ashqelon

Kiryat Gat

Hevron

Dead Sea

Jordan River

Palestinian Area

0 10 km
0 10 mi

Regional Sights	
1	Ein Gedi
2	Masada
3	Qumran

Egged-Tlalim, United Tours, and other tour companies will get you there more easily and usually on a daily schedule. Some hotels will make arrangements.

The Dead Sea

Oh, to be lazy and simply float in the Dead Sea (Yam HaMelech—Salt Sea). And that's about all you can or dare do in that extremely saline and chemical-filled body of water. Its salt content is almost nine times that of the Mediterranean Sea. Getting the salt, magnesium, bromide, and iodine into your eyes or on an open wound hurts a lot.

The **Dead Sea**, at 1,069 feet below sea level, is the lowest spot on the face of the earth. It is also in an incredibly bleak landscape. Still, there are plenty of luxury seaside hotels on the 49-mile-long lake for the many people who come from far and wide, attracted by the Dead Sea's famed therapeutic properties.

Visitors should make sure they take their Dead Sea dip in an area where they can shower with fresh water afterward. The **Ein Gedi Beach** has lots of facilities. It isn't a good idea to leave all those chemicals on your body for a long time. Smearing black Dead Sea mud over your body and face is supposed to do wonders for you, however, besides giving your friends a hoot over your appearance.

The Biblical Sodom and Gomorrah story took place on these shores. Geologists maintain that the shallow southern tip of the Dead Sea was formed by an earthquake at a time that is close to that of the Biblical account. The earthquake could explain Sodom and Gomorrah's swift destruction. Today's Sodom (Sdom in Hebrew) is an industrial city near its Biblical location.

Other visible Biblical connections are on the opposite (Jordanian) side of the sea. Moses is said to be buried farther north in the pink Moab Mountains. Moslems will show the grave site, but Jews don't acknowledge it, for they deliberately and conscientiously avoided

Tourists under Dead Sea mud

establishing any sort of shrine to the man considered the greatest Jewish prophet.

If you are traveling with a tour group, a lunch stop will be part of your day. If you are on your own, you can eat at Masada or the Ein Gedi Beach.

Ein Gedi Nature Reserve

Ein Gedi is a bit of lush greenery—including waterfalls and pools and a wildlife haven—in the midst of the parched desert at the lowest spot on earth. **Qumran**, where the Dead Sea Scrolls and other antiquities were discovered, is north of the reserve. The Egged bus stops at the base of Ein Gedi, and you must hike up. Some tours include a stop at Qumran. Ein Gedi is closed on Shabbat and holidays.

Masada

About one-and-a-half miles west of the Dead Sea, a boat-shaped mountain rises 1,300 feet from the flat plain. It is Masada (Matza-DAH in Hebrew), where one of the most dramatic events in Israeli history took place almost two thousand years ago. Its impact resonates through the subconscious of Israelis even today.

Herod the Great built a marvel of a palace atop the mountain and surrounded it with a 13-foot-thick wall with 35 towers more than 80 feet high. About one hundred years later, in 66 C.E., the Jewish rebellion against Rome burst forth. A group of Zealots struck out for the desert and captured Masada from the Romans. With giant cisterns on the grounds with capacity for eight years' worth of water, conceivably, the Zealots could remain indefinitely.

After the fall of Jerusalem in 70 C.E., the Zealots were joined by other refugees from the Romans. The number of people in the mountaintop fortress grew to 960 men, women, and children.

The Jewish historian Josephus told of how the Romans returned to Masada in 72 C.E. with the Tenth Legion and thousands of Jewish slaves to lay siege to the fortress. The siege lasted three years. With construction of a huge ramp to the top of the mountain and a battering ram rolled up to that height, eventually, the Romans broke through the walls and entered the fortress.

Inside, the soldiers were met by silence. They found an ample amount of provisions, which proved starvation hadn't been a threat, but the men, women, and children were dead. The Jews had decided they would never become slaves or be abused by the Romans, so they committed suicide.

Two women and five children survived by hiding in caves. They told the details of the suicide and reported how the Zealot leader, Eleazar Ben

Ya'ir, exhorted men not to be taken alive or allow their families to be taken alive by the Romans. His speech has come down through history.

To reach Masada, you can hike up the winding **Snake Path**, which takes about an hour; take the **Roman Ramp** on the west side, which takes half an hour; or ride the cable car in a few breathtaking minutes. In any event, don't hike when the sun is high.

The view of the Dead Sea, like a turquoise gash in the sand, the pink Moab Mountains beyond it, and the desert all around are spectacular from this height. From various places on Masada, it is possible to look down and see, even these many centuries later, the outlines of the eight Roman ramps at the base of the mountain.

Yigal Yadin, probably Israel's most famous archaeologist, led a team uncovering Masada in 1963. Digs and reconstruction are still underway. A black line distinguishes the original site and the reconstruction.

Herod's private palace for his leisure is at the northern end of the mountain. In it are original frescoes and columns, as well as a bathhouse where Yadin uncovered skeletons (probably those of a Zealot family), arrows, potsherds, and parts of a Jewish prayer shawl.

On the summit is the **Zealots' Synagogue**, overlooking the Roman camps. It is one of the oldest synagogues in Israel. Parchment scrolls discovered here contained portions of the books of Deuteronomy and Ezekiel.

Like the synagogue, the mosaics in the **Western Palace** are among the oldest in Israel. The only colored Herodian mosaics are on the entrance hall to the throne room. But the finest Masada mosaics, of oranges, grapes, figs, and pomegranates, are on the floor of the **Byzantine Chapel**. They were left by Christian monks who were ensconced in this secluded spot for a short while during the fifth century C.E.

The desert ride back to Jerusalem after the impact of Masada can be a welcome time to reflect on how the past informs the present in this part of the world. Some Israeli observers say the country has a "Masada complex." Standing on Masada where the tragedy happened, hearing its history and the moving story of the Zealots, it's possible to understand this expression. Between the Jews' twentieth-century history and their ancestral memory, Israelis know how it feels to be cornered. The expression means that Israelis have made a promise to themselves and to Israelis of generations to come that Masada shall never fall again.

131

11
A SECOND WEEK
IN JERUSALEM

With a second week in Jerusalem, the pressure's off—a bit. The city's pell-mell impact may have communicated to you by now its own Levantine sense of order—or disorder. A second week in the Golden City offers a chance to absorb what you have already learned and experienced, to expand that into finer detail, and to continue learning and experiencing, but at a less hectic pace.

With the itineraries in this section, you can do additional archaeological exploring in the Old City area, become more familiar with western Jerusalem, and discover eastern Jerusalem. You can delve into some of the small, specialized museums scattered throughout the city or even take a break from history, but not the Bible, at the Tish Family Zoological Gardens (Biblical Zoo). Or you might want to return to the museums on the one-week itinerary, which you could only skim, or perhaps even had to skip, earlier.

The following chapter has itineraries for six days of your second week in Jerusalem. Keep in mind that closing hours make some of the itineraries impossible on certain days. But since the trips are arranged for starting on a Sunday, if you follow them in sequence, closing hours shouldn't present a problem.

On the seventh day, if you haven't had a chance to do so before, spend the morning at a Jewish or Christian house of worship. I guarantee the experience will be different from that at any of its counterparts back home.

However you choose to juggle your sightseeing this week, keep walking. At every opportunity, explore neighborhoods. Jerusalem is one of the world's great cities for walking. A mere turn around a corner can lead you into a totally different way of life from the one behind you. Adventure awaits.

First Day: Back to the Old City

Today you will be above if not all of Jerusalem then a lot of it. From Suleiman's Wall and the Tower of David Museum (the Citadel), Jerusalem's backyards and frontyards will be spread out below you. A visit to an intriguing archaeological park at the Southern Wall abutting the Temple Mount will end the tour. If you start with the Ramparts Walk at Damascus Gate, your direction will always be downhill.

The Ramparts Walk

From the ramparts of Suleiman's magnificent wall, you will see the slope of the Tyropoeon Valley and into residents' backyards. You can check out families' laundry and their chickens, as well as count the number of TV antennas versus minarets.

Your view from on high will allow you to study a classic example of

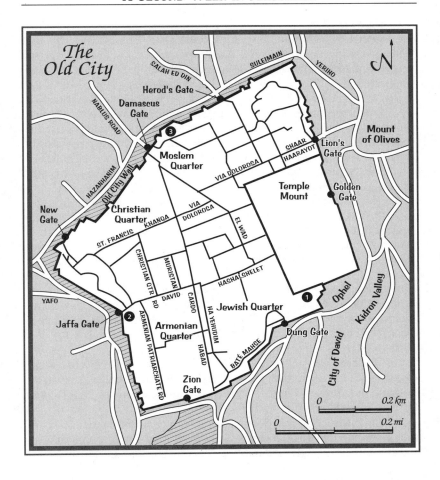

Old City Sights

1 Ophel Archaeological Garden	3 Zedekiah's Cave
2 Tower of David Museum	

local architecture: the dome-roofed house. To create it, builders piled up sand within the structure's four walls until they achieved the desired shape of the dome. Then they laid stone in mortar on the sand. When the stone and mortar were firm enough, the house had its roof. The sand was scooped out, and the residents moved in.

135

Entrances to the ramparts are at Jaffa Gate, between the Old City wall and the back of the Citadel, and at Damascus Gate. You can descend at several places. At Damascus Gate, you enter through the adjacent, elaborate, second-century Roman Gate. The walk can be prefaced by a visit at that spot to **Roman Square**, a small museum of the Roman garrison.

From here you walk toward Jaffa Gate, while below you the Moslem Quarter dissolves into the Christian Quarter. Jordanian soldiers used to patrol these ramparts, often aiming their guns indiscriminately into the homes of Jewish refugees in the neighborhood across from the Old City.

If you begin at Jaffa Gate, you can walk toward either Damascus Gate or Dung Gate, depending on where you enter. Suleiman's Wall ran continuously around the Old City until Germany's Kaiser Wilhelm II visited in 1898. The wall was opened at Jaffa Gate to allow the Kaiser and his horseback-riding entourage to enter. The original Ottoman Gate, with its 90-degree-turn, is next to the opening. Hang onto your ticket: It's good for two days. *Details: (02) 625-4403. Daily 9–4, Fri and holiday eves 9–2.*

Tower of David Museum (The Citadel)

At the Ottoman Gate, you can take a break and visit David's Tower (the Citadel)—the Museum of the History of Jerusalem. The tower is a good place for a bird's-eye look at the Old City and new Jerusalem as well. Climb to the top for a great view.

The Citadel was built by Herod in 24 B.C.E. and had nothing to do with King David—but fact is relative in Jerusalem, as you've noticed. When the Romans demolished Jerusalem, they left one of Herod's three towers because it could serve as a good watchtower.

Herod's structure now is a melange of overlays of construction and handiwork by Romans, Moslems, Crusaders, Mamelukes (who built the tower's minaret), and Suleiman the Magnificent. Sultan Suleiman was responsible for most of the Citadel's current appearance.

Inside is the city's historical museum, with dioramas, holograms, and videos. The charming **Museum of Modern Religious Dress** displays clothing worn by thick-ankled dolls that look as if they shared ancestry with— remember them?—Cabbage Patch Dolls.

A model of nineteenth-century Jerusalem, now on exhibit, has had quite an odyssey. It was built in Jerusalem in mid-century, displayed for the first time in Vienna in 1873, then landed in storage in Geneva. It was discovered in 1984 and brought to Jerusalem a year later. You will recognize places you have visited and see how some sites that are in ruins today, such as the Hurva Synagogue, appeared when all was well.

A multimedia Sound and Light Show in English is presented in the courtyard at 9:30 p.m. Monday and Wednesday and 9 p.m. Saturday from

April through November. Dress warmly, even in summer. *Details:* (02,
5333. *Sun–Thu 10–4, 10–2 Fri, Sat, and holidays. Admission fee.*

It's probably lunchtime. You can have a snack in the museum or leave
the building and find a restaurant in the Jaffa Gate area. Afterward, you
can resume your Ramparts Walk. The entrance is behind David's Tower.
From the museum exit, walk straight ahead and left at the bend.

The Kishle police station is near the Tower's main entrance below. It's
believed that south of the Kishle, King Herod's Palace is buried. Some
also believe that Jesus was sentenced to death here. On the other side of
the rampart, you can see the red roofs of Yemin Moshe and Mishkenot
Sha'ananim beyond.

At the wall's southwest corner you can see the square tower of St.
Anthony's Scottish Church, which lies on the watershed that Jerusalem
straddles. Beyond the church, rainwater flows to the Mediterranean. From
the Hinnom Valley, which looks eastward, water flows to the Dead Sea.

After passing the Armenian Quarter and Mount Zion, you get the
sweep of the view toward the Mount of Olives and the desert beyond.
The last promontory is the confluence of Jerusalem's three major valleys
and the place where the City of David began three thousand years ago. A
new staircase takes you down to Dung Gate.

Ophel Archaeological Garden

Inside Dung Gate is the entrance to the Ophel Archaeological Garden, along
the corner of the western and southern walls of the Temple Mount.
Excavations here keep uncovering surprises. Digs along the end of the
Western Wall, the newest, reveal the building stones of the Second Temple
in a smashed heap, just as the Romans left things when they destroyed
the temple. Centuries upon centuries of debris covered the stones until the
1990s.

The southern side of the site includes the remains of an Arab palace
complex (previously unknown to even Arab scholars), a Byzantine house
with a well-preserved mosaic floor, some 60 ritual baths used by priests
and pilgrims before entering the Second Temple, and two stairways leading to double and triple gates into the temple area.

Pilgrims at the time of the Second Temple approached the Temple
Mount up the restored grand stairway. And it is grand. They were continuing the First Temple tradition of entering the Temple Mount from the south.

When I last was here, the first time on my own, I noticed an absence
of explanatory signs. Consider joining up with Zion Walking Tours or
Archaeological Seminars so this mass of stonework acquires an identity.
Remember, the sun here is especially fierce—this being the southern wall.
Details: Sun–Fri 7–6 (to 5 in winter). Admission fee.

137

From outside Dung Gate, you can take Bus 1 or 2 back to central Jerusalem or hike uphill through the Jewish or Moslem Quarters. By now, you have probably learned your way through the Old City streets. Its host of first impressions is becoming familiar. What is surely emerging this second week are the details, even in the manner of dress you see around you: the variety of ways Orthodox women tie scarves to cover their hair from everyone but their husbands, how their scarf-tying differs from that of Moslem women, and the many different kippot worn by men—Jewish and sometimes Moslem—that communicate religious as well as political positions. Do you get the feeling that if you close your eyes for a moment in Jerusalem, stop to relax, and turn the rest of the world off, you'll miss something?

Second Day: Go East

Jerusalem's other side, its predominantly Arab side, is to the east. Governments might draw boundary lines between people, but people's lives reveal how artificial these lines are. Eastern Jerusalem might be looked on as Arab, but Jews, Armenians, and Protestants also have claim to parts of this area.

Eastern Jerusalem close to the Old City is a lively commercial area, where, during the day, Arab music emanates from stores and restaurants, and sidewalks are crowded with food vendors and residents leisurely chatting. But a few blocks away, eastern Jerusalem is more like a peaceful mixture of a small town and the countryside.

For a walk through eastern Jerusalem, allow all day with a stop for lunch. Because you will be so close to western Jerusalem, there is no strategic problem in your calling it quits any time your feet tell you to. Also bring a flashlight for more tomb exploring and a sweater for the cool of Zedekiah's Cave.

Eastern Jerusalem

An example of the area's cultural mix is opposite Damascus Gate, which, at least for the time being, is closed—but know that it is there. It is the *Mosaic of the Birds*, an Armenian work from the fifth century. The 26-by-14-foot mosaic might be the first memorial to an unknown soldier. It was probably part of a chapel honoring Armenian soldiers who died fighting the Persians in 451 C.E. The lovely mosaic shows a variety of birds perched on grapevines.

On a stretch close to Damascus Gate, as you've noticed before, is an outdoor market under green canopies. You can stroll through later, but for now, turn left. Between Damascus and Herod Gates is **Zedekiah's Cave** (also known as Solomon's Quarries, Suleiman's Cave, and a few other names), thought to have been the source of the white "Melekeh" lime-stone for the First Temple.

It is believed that Judean King Zedekiah tried to flee from the conquering Nebuchadnezzar in 587 B.C.E. through these quarries via a passageway connected to his palace. The caves are important to Freemasons, who claim that their group descends from Solomon's masons.

This five-acre underground expanse has paths that lead to separate rooms, nooks, and crannies. It is lighted the entire way, so the claustrophobic need not be intimidated. But visitors should bring a sweater—it is cool and damp in the cave. Details: (02) 625-4403. Daily 9–4, Fri and holiday eves 9–2. Admission fee.

Farther east, almost opposite the corner of the walled Old City, is the **Rockefeller Museum**, one of the most important in Israel. It was planned and built during the late 1920s under the British Mandate. John D. Rockefeller's gift of $2 million insured that the museum would carry his name.

The oldest item in its collection is the remains of a 10,000-year-old man found on Mount Carmel, near present-day Haifa. Notable are flint utensils from Stone Age cave dwellers, Roman sarcophagi, and sculptures and stone tablets from the Egyptian Pharaohs Seti I (1313 B.C.E.) and Ramses III (1198–1167 B.C.E.), which were found at Beit She'an south of Tiveria. From the entrance, the best route to the exhibits is to the left. *Details: (02) 628-2251. Sun–Thu 10–5, Fri, Sat, and holidays 10–1. Admission is free to Israel Museum members.*

Around the northeast corner of the Old City is a Moslem cemetery. In it is a monument to Arabs who died in the Six- Day War.

The Garden Tomb

From Nablus Road (Derech Shchem), turn right at Rehov Schick. You will find a quiet sanctuary of Aleppo pine and almond trees amid the hurly-burly of this part of eastern Jerusalem. Signs on the street give directions.

General Charles Gordon of Khartoum fame popularized this site, not the Holy Sepulchre, as Jesus' true grave. It is a two-chambered tomb carved out of rock on a hill that looked to him like Golgotha, the skull-like rise where Jesus was crucified. Anglicans and other Protestants hold to that belief, but archaeologists date the tombs from the fifth century C.E. At any rate, it's a peaceful place to sit and catch your breath. *Details: (02) 627-2745. Mon–Sat 8:30–12:30, 2–5. Free.*

If you are ready for lunch, you can catch a light snack at a restaurant in the neighborhood or a superb mezze at the Philadelphia Restaurant, downstairs at 9 az-Zahra Street off Salah ed-Din Street. An alternative is to wait until you reach the gorgeous, but pricy, American Colony Hotel.

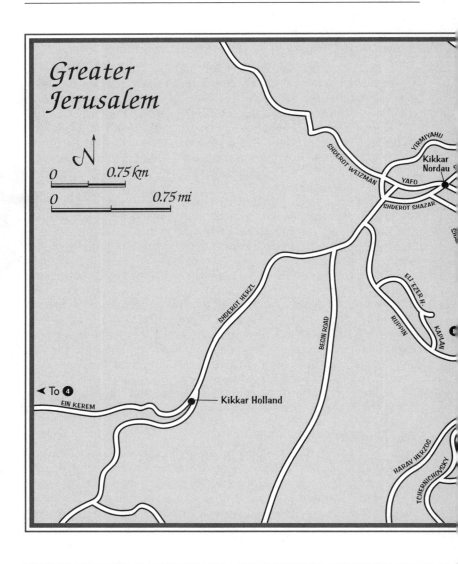

Greater
Jerusalem

N

0   0.75 km

0   0.75 mi

◄ To ❹
EIN KEREM

Kikkar Holland

SHDEROT WEIZMAN

YIRMIYAHU

Kikkar
Nordau

YAFO

SHDEROT SHAZAR

ELI 'EZER H

RUPPIN

KAPLAN

SHDEROT HERZL

BEGIN ROAD

HARAV HERZOG

TCHERNICHOVSKY

Greater Jerusalem Sights

1 American Colony Hotel
2 British War Cemetery
3 Garden Tomb

4 Hadassah Medical Center
5 Hadassah-University Hospital
6 Hebrew University
7 Jason's Tomb
8 Knesset

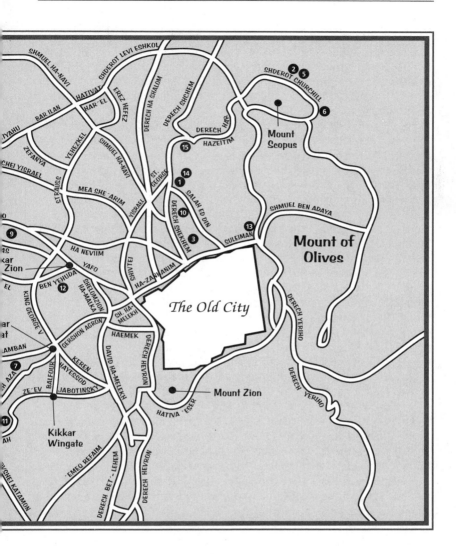

9 Mahane Yehuda
10 Monastery of St. Stephen
11 Museum of Islamic Art
12 Nahon Museum of Italian Jewish Art
13 Rockefeller Museum

14 Tomb of the Kings
15 Tomb of Simon the Just

Farther up Nablus Road is the Dominican **Monastery of St. Stephen** (St. Etienne). Within this complex of buildings are a church, a monastery, tombs hewn from rock, and the **French Institute for Biblical Archaeology**. The present church was built in the late 1800s on the ruins of a fifth-century basilica, said to house the bones of St. Stephen, the first Christian martyr.

Still farther up Nablus Road, surrounded by an iron fence near the American Consulate, is a remnant of "the third wall" around the city from the Second Temple era. Opposite the American Consulate, located in a former private home, is Palestine Pottery, which has nothing to do with anything Palestinian, but everything to do with Armenian creativity. Lovely Armenian pottery is made and sold here. The shop is closed Sunday.

Continuing up Nablus Road, **St. George's Cathedral** can be found to the right. It is distinguished by its tower, named for King Edward VII of England. The cathedral has a lovely garden with lush citron trees. Citrons look like grapefruit-sized lemons. Reportedly, they make great marmalade.

At the intersection of Nablus Road and Salah ed-Din Street, above St. George's, is a sign that points to the **Tombs of the Kings**. It was long thought that this impressive necropolis 18 feet below street level was the burial site of Jewish kings, hence the name. But its story is more interesting even than that. The tombs were cut in 45 C.E. by Queen Helena—not the later Christian Queen Helena but Helena (as she was called by the Greeks) of Adiabene, Mesopotamia—for herself and her sons. They settled in Jerusalem and all converted to Judaism. Queen Helena was known for her generosity to Jerusalem's poor.

These are truly grand tombs. The edifice, cut out of rock, even includes *mikvot* (Jewish ritual baths). The richly decorated sarcophagus of the queen is in the Louvre, for these tombs are the property of the French government. Other sarcophagi have disappeared. By stepping through the small tomb opening, you can see a sequence of rooms and elegant stone carvings. Here you will need your flashlight. My latest information is that these tombs, like those in the Kidron Valley, are open to all, all the time.

The **American Colony Hotel**, even farther up Nablus Road, was once the home of a wealthy sheikh. Its attractive courtyard makes for an ideal pause. The hotel is named for Americans who bought these buildings from a sheikh in 1881. They came for spiritual reasons, but a group of nineteenth-century hippie equivalents gathered around them. Eventually the people in the American Colony were considered scandalous, but all that was long ago. Today, the hotel is a favorite of United Nations personnel and journalists.

Ahead on Nablus Road, the next road to the right takes a left fork

142

that leads through a field and to a burial cave said to contain the **Tomb of Simon the Just**. It is surrounded by other burial caves. This is where the Jewish festival of Lag B'Omer is celebrated in spring, with crowds of Orthodox Jews gathering to give three-year-old boys their first haircuts (see Chapter 15: "The Cycle of Celebrations.")

The Sheikh Jarrah neighborhood extends before you as Nablus Road climbs the slope. This neighborhood has many luxurious homes, and its residents include some of the most illustrious Arab families. The streets invite exploration. To get back to where you started, all you have to do is go downhill.

Eastern Jerusalem's open spaces are one of its greatest charms. Even in the city, don't be surprised to see a young boy leading a herd of sheep past you.

Third Day: Get Out of Town

Jerusalem might be on a mountain but it isn't on an island. Bethlehem and Masada are the big out-of-town attractions, not to be missed, but at least five other places are worth a visit and will get you out of town: Ein Kerem, the Soreq Stalagmite and Stalactite Cave, Bethany, and Wadi Qelt.

Because Israel is so small, these places only seem far away. Ein Kerem and Bethany can be half-day trips. The caves can be a half-day tour if visited by private car, although the Society for the Protection of Nature in Israel (SPNI) includes the caves in a day-long Wednesday tour that also visits other sites. Wadi Qelt can take up to an entire day.

Ein Kerem

True, Ein Kerem is within Jerusalem's city limits. But it is a big enough change from the center of Jerusalem (as long as environmentalists succeed in fighting city hall, which wants to erect a massive apartment development there) that you'll feel as if you have made a huge trip. Actually, it won't be huge, but, as Bus 17 takes you over hills and into valleys, it will be slow—perhaps 45 minutes from the city center.

Bucolic Ein Kerem has many fine old Arab houses and, as the traditional birthplace of John the Baptist, contains several Christian sites of note. The Franciscan **Church of St. John the Baptist,** to the right of the main road, was built over what is believed to be St. John's birthplace. Downstairs, mosaics from the original Byzantine chapel here decorate the grotto. *Details: (02) 641-3639. Sun–Fri 8:30–11:45, 2:30–6.*

On the other side of the main road, next to an abandoned mosque, is the **Spring of the Virgin**, from which Ein Kerem gets its name. Beyond it is the **Church of the Visitation**, built on the traditional summer home of John's parents. It is believed that during a pregnant Mary's visit to

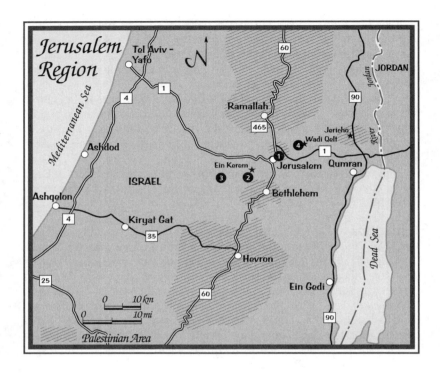

Regional Sights

1 Bethany	3 Soreq Stalagmite and Stalactite Cave
2 Ein Kerem	4 Wadi Qelt

Elizabeth, John's mother, Mary was visited by the Archangel Gabriel. *Details: (02) 641-7291. Sun–Fri 8:30–11:45, 2:30–6.*

At the top of the hill is a Russian convent, **Mar Zakariya**, visited by appointment only. *Details: (02) 565-4128.*

Soreq Stalagmite and Stalactite Cave

The Soreq Stalagmite and Stalactite Cave in the Avshalom Shoham Nature Reserve is about 12 miles (19 kilometers) southwest of Jerusalem, near the village of Nes Harim. The cave, an awesome 5,000 square meters, was discovered only in 1968 and was opened to the public in 1977. Lighting highlights the myriad colors in the stalagmites and sta-

144

lactites that grow continuously but minutely. *Details: (02) 991-1117.
Sun–Thu 8:30–3:45, Sat, Fri, holidays 8:30–12:45. Admission fee includes
audiovisual show and guided tour. Photographing is allowed Friday
morning only.*

No public bus goes to the caves, but there is one excellent tour, SPNI's
tour, which includes **Beit Guvrin**, caves and a tunnel system created by
Bar Kochba's warriors, and **Neot Kedumim**, the only Biblical landscape
preserve, which also has a trail for the blind.

Bethany

Bethany, on the Jericho Road and about two-and-a-half miles (four kilometers) from Jerusalem, is the village in which Christians believe Jesus
raised its most famous resident, Lazarus, from the dead. Now an Arab
village, Bethany is known as el-Azariye, from Lazarus.

Jesus is said to have visited Bethany on the eve of his fateful Passover.
According to the Gospel of John, Jesus raised Lazarus after Lazarus had
been dead for four days. Another well-known Bethany resident was Simon
the Leper, whom Jesus is said to have cured.

The Franciscan **Church of St. Lazarus**, built in 1954, has mosaics
that depict Lazarus's resurrection. Antonio Barluzzi, the man responsible for both Dominus Flevit and the Church of All Nations on the
Mount of Olives, designed this church as well. **Lazarus's Tomb**, down
a flight of stairs, is looked after by Moslems who might deliver a dramatic account of his resurrection. *Details: Daily 8–noon, 2–6.
Admission fee.*

Bethany can be reached by taking Bus 36 from the eastern Jerusalem
Central Bus Station on Sultan Suleiman Street. Two buses are numbered
36, so you must ask for the 36 to el-Azariye.

Wadi Qelt

The gorge of Wadi Qelt, a spring east of Jerusalem, makes for an adventurous and dramatic day-long hike. But you *must* partake of this adventure with a group—no "ifs" or "buts" about it. The SPNI takes groups
through every Monday. Bring your own lunch, lots of water, a bathing suit,
and a towel. Wear clothes that cover your legs and shoulders for the
monastery visit.

Besides walking along the top of a Roman aqueduct (not for the faint-
hearted or anyone who fears heights), the hike stops at the Greek Orthodox
Monastery of St. George, which has clung to its cliffside since the sixth
century. According to legend, after he fled Samaria, the prophet Elijah
hid in a cave over which the monastery was built. Currently, only eight
monks live in this huge edifice.

145

Fourth Day: From Italian Beauty to Judah's Camp

Arabs have their souk and Jews have their *shouk,* which usually refers to the semi-covered and open-air market of Mahane Yehuda. This day includes a visit to the Nahon Museum of Italian Jewish Art and a stroll through Mahane Yehuda and its aging neighborhoods, Mazkeret Moshe and Ohel Moshe.

Nahon Museum of Italian Jewish Art

The Nahon Museum of Italian Jewish Art at Rehov Hillel 27 is reached through a courtyard and up to the second floor at the end of the building on the left. On the landing, a short corridor has entrances to both the museum and the **Italian Synagogue**. The synagogue, open for viewing during museum hours, is described in Chapter 13: "Heavenly Jerusalem." At this point, we will discuss only the four-room museum.

At the entrance to the Italian Synagogue are Hebrew words that read: "Do not leave this place in haste." Indeed. The words apply spiritually to the synagogue, but because of its art collection, the museum too is a place to tarry.

While the Jewish community in Italy goes back some 2,500 years, probably the oldest object in the museum is a plaque that advises, "Know before whom you stand." It dates from the end of the fifteenth century

Monastery of St. George in Wadi Qelt

146

and is decorated with neoclassical, Renaissance designs. The plaque was originally above the Holy Ark in the Great Synagogue of Padua. Although the Great Synagogue was badly damaged by bombs during World War II, the ark and plaque escaped harm.

In the museum's third room are the Holy Ark of Mantua and a pair of chairs beside it. The chairs are a beehive of carved wood. An inscription on the ark dates it to 1543, which makes it the oldest dated holy ark in Israel.

A *maftir* book from Urbino stems from a lovely, unusual tradition. In that city, each boy who reached bar mitzvah age received a book with the portion of the Torah that was his to read during his first time participating as an adult in a worship service. This particular book was written and illustrated by hand in 1704 by the bar mitzvah boy's grandfather.

Lacy embroidered clothes for a baby boy during his circumcision ceremony are astoundingly luxurious. Time has taken little toll, and these shining threads aren't Lurex.

In the last room is a machine for making *matzo*, the flat, brittle unleavened bread eaten during Passover. You might find examples of the machine's end product on the table. Perhaps some scholar will research the variety of matzot produced by Jews in different parts of the world. Italian matzo is white, round, and shot with pencil-size holes. It looks like a clumsily crocheted doily. (A Jewish-Italian woman in Jerusalem confided to me that she punched the holes in her matzot with her fingers.)

The examples in the Museum of Italian Jewish Art reflect a rich and exuberant lifestyle. The museum has identified and explained the displays well and also provides a free four-page guide in English that takes a viewer through the museum virtually step by step. *Details: (02) 624-1610. Sun–Tue 9–2, Wed 9–5, Thur 9–1. Admission fee.*

Mahane Yehuda

Heading up Hillel, you come to "Little America," with Blockbuster Video and Tower Records on either side of the street and Ben & Jerry's up the hill. McDonald's and Burger King aren't far away. At Tower Records, you can buy the Sunday *New York Times* in its skinny West Coast edition two weeks late (don't snort—that's wonderful service compared to three months late and worse by mail) and Peanuts greeting cards in Hebrew. At King George, you might pop into **HaMashbir Lazarchan**, Jerusalem's largest and finest department store (such as it is).

On leaving HaMashbir, turn left. At Rehov Agrippas, turn left again and keep going. Eventually you will see utter congestion on the right side of Agrippas. Join it, and when you see a covered lane with food stalls on either side, enter and gaze, listen and stroll—but not too slowly or your backside will ache from being nudged decisively by frenzied shoppers.

The atmosphere at Mahane Yehuda (Camp of Judah) is combative, especially in that major part of the market that sells fresh produce. Located between Rehov Agrippas and one of the more dingy portions of Rehov Yafo, the market includes not only the street named Mahane Yehuda but also the covered street parallel to it and a warren of lanes that run from either side.

The market's narrow aisles are crowded with shoppers determinedly making their way between stalls and pushing away anyone in front of them. Plugging the aisles are boys, sometimes men, pushing carts with fresh produce and shouting "Allo, allo" as a warning to hapless souls in their path.

Stall owners try to out-shout each other with the price of produce. But instead of offering shoppers efficient, kindly service, the stall owner usually acts as if he has better things to do than wait on them, like continuing to shout. This offhand treatment is part of the Mahane Yehuda tradition. The challenge for the shopper is to appear to be unintimidated. Never mind how you really feel: You must show a tough exterior.

The market is noisy, but rich with color. Ripe watermelon halves cover a table. Freshly killed chickens, pink, plucked, and shiny, lie limp on top of each other on a counter, their yellow feet scratching passersby. Dark green, light green, red, and yellow peppers are stacked in gravity-defying towers. Fish helplessly flip and flap their last. Containers offer varieties of green and black olives to please every taste. These and many more sights of the fruits of the earth and sea and slaughtered barnyard creatures are repeated stall after stall. Punctuating all these are stalls full of kitchenware, linens, clothing, shoes, Middle Eastern salads, baked goods, candy, and pop music tapes and CDs, usually blaring into the noisy atmosphere.

Much of Mahane Yehuda has become less and less of an open-air market over recent years. Most aisles have been covered, so shoppers and sellers can laugh at the weather. What's more, the shouk is about to be moved to a new, modern (so they say) facility. Sentimentalists decry any effort to make Mahane Yehuda look like just another place to shop. But it is doubtful that whatever happens to it physically will alter the traditional disposition of its stall owners. Philadelphia's Reading Station Market it never will be.

Near the end of the main covered lane is a bakery on the right side that has warm spiced pita and heavenly warm *sambusak*, chunky chickpea-filled pastry, an Iraqi-Kurdi specialty.

Out at Rehov Yafo, you're not done yet. Turn left, until you can turn left again onto a street named Mahane Yehuda. This genuinely is an open-air market. Keep your eyes out for narrow lanes where more fresh produce and shouting abound.

Back at Agrippas, you might want to buy a falafel or a fish patty or omelette in a pita and cross the street. Look for an archway with a plaque over it and enter. You will find a park of sorts where you can sit and eat.

You have reached the twin neighborhoods **Mazkeret Moshe** and **Ohel Moshe**. Prestigious when built in 1883 by the Moses Montefiore Foundation, they are yet another example of the dedicated Englishman's influence. The twin neighborhoods were planned to be fraternal, not identical. Mazkeret Moshe ("Remembrance of Moses") was constructed for Ashkenazim and Ohel Moshe ("Tent of Moses") for Sephardim. The buildings were arranged in a rectangle around an open courtyard. Each neighborhood was to be self-contained. Over the years, parts of the central courtyard have been filled for community needs, and private courtyards were built up to meet family needs.

The twins are divided by a narrow street, Rehov Ohel Moshe. If you enter the neighborhood on the far right, under the arch with the plaque, you are in Ohel Moshe. You can recognize it by the covered cistern on your left and the diagonal path into the garden.

It is easy to stroll about in these neighborhoods. In both, small homes—some now a jumble of additions over the years, some being regentrified—surround the courtyard and a small park. Both neighborhoods, largely, are poor. A building close to the Rehov Agrippas entrance of Mazkeret Moshe is a community center. Women from the area gather here to sing. At the opposite end of the central area is a nursery school. If you pass by in the morning, prepare to be charmed. Opposite the nursery school, at the corner of Rehov Arye, is a jewelry and crafts shop worth checking out.

To get back to Rehov King George, narrow lanes at the far end of the neighborhoods and to the left lead to Rehov Mesilat Yesharim. This street will bring you close to the rear of HaMashbir, and from there to King George.

Tonight, you can maintain the Italian mood by having dinner at Pera-e-Mela at Rehov Ma'alot 7, Mamma Mia's around the corner facing King George, or Angelo at Rehov Horkanos 9.

Fifth Day: From Hadassah to Hadassah with Several Places in Between

How about a break today and a chance to rest your feet during long bus rides? This trip will take you literally from one end of Jerusalem to the other. The Knesset (Parliament), one of the sights included today, is open only on Sunday and Thursday from 8:30 a.m. to 2:30 p.m. There are free guided tours. Bring your passport.

The link between these visits to Mount Scopus, Hadassah-University Hospital, Hebrew University, the Knesset, and Hadassah Medical Center at Ein Kerem is art and architecture—of masters, ancient and modern. Bus 99 can chauffeur you, if its times and yours coincide, but it doesn't go to Ein Kerem.

Mount Scopus

During the 19 years of Jordanian occupation, Mount Scopus (Har Ha-Tzofim) was an Israeli island surrounded by warring Arabs. Every two weeks, the United Nations supervised a convoy of people and supplies to the embattled outpost. UN supervision came about partly because of the murder by ambush of 78 doctors, nurses, and university personnel traveling to Mount Scopus during the War of Independence.

Out of necessity, Hadassah Medical Center in Ein Kerem and the Hebrew University campus at Givat Ram, near the Knesset, were built during the years Jerusalem was a divided city. From the top of Mount Scopus down the slope, the sites are the Hebrew University, Hadassah-University Hospital, and the British War Cemetery.

Buses 4A, 9, 23, 28, and 99 can take you to Mount Scopus. The last stop is **Hebrew University**, founded in 1925. You get off the bus in a tunnel, take an escalator upstairs, and step into one of the most confusing campuses anywhere. Besides that of Arabs and Jews rushing around on the same college campus, the best sight is into the desert from the amphitheater. At 11 a.m. Sunday through Thursday, you can take a 60- to 90-minute tour in English, leaving from the Forum in the Administration Building, if you can find it.

Walk down to **Hadassah-University Hospital**, which has a more relaxed, pleasant environment than Hadassah at Ein Kerem. Both hospitals are world-renowned. Many an Arab sheikh from countries that have only ugly things to say about Israel has discreetly entered the hospital as a patient. Both Hadassahs are additional places to see Arabs and Jews going about their lives side by side and often helping each other.

The next stop below the hospital is the **British War Cemetery**, for those who died in World War I. As in all such cemeteries, it is the youth of the fallen that appalls.

Bus 9 or 99 can take you to the **Knesset**, which means "assembly." Israel's Knesset building is off Rehov Eliezer Kaplan in the same neighborhood as the Israel Museum. This 1966 building is the Knesset's third home in Jerusalem since 1948. Earlier, it was located in the Jewish Agency

150

Building and then in a building that now houses the Government Tourist Office, both on Rehov King George.

Across from the entrance stands a large bronze *menorah*, the seven-branched candelabra that symbolizes Israel. It is the work of Benno Elkan and a gift of the British Parliament. The iron gate at the entrance to the Knesset Plaza was made by Jerusalemite David Palombo.

Inside, major attractions are Marc Chagall's tapestries, wall paintings, and floor mosaics in the upper foyer. The huge tapestries show moments in Jewish history.

To see the Knesset in action, visit between 4 and 9 p.m. Monday or Tuesday. The proceedings can be quite a show, but they are in Hebrew and occasionally Arabic—no subtitles provided. Note the informal clothing and manner of the legislators. The Knesset has a cafeteria for visitors.

In the Knesset area, known as Museum Mile, you will also find the Bible Lands Museum, the Bloomfield Science Center, the Hebrew University–Givat Ram campus, and the Supreme Court, in addition to the Israel Museum and other government buildings. If your schedule permits, walk up to the Supreme Court, considered by many to be one of the most beautiful government buildings in Israel. *Details: (02) 675-9612. Sun–Tue 8:30–2:30. Free tours in English Sun and Wed at 11.*

Hadassah Medical Center–Ein Kerem

Bus 99 won't get you there, but Buses 19 on Rehov Aza and 27 on Shderot Herzl will—the end of the line. The bus ride west to Hadassah Medical Center in Ein Kerem is a leisurely, picturesque trip. Hadassah has as its non-medical attraction 12 stained-glass windows by Marc Chagall. Chagall, who lived in France for many years before his death, made a gift of the windows, depicting the 12 tribes of Israel, in 1962. They are in Hadassah's synagogue. The famed painter of a fiddler on a roof later replaced four windows that were shattered during the Six-Day War.

Because these stained-glass windows were made for a synagogue—and a Jerusalem synagogue at that—Chagall followed the Biblical injunction that has been interpreted as a prohibition against representation of the human figure. He looked on this rule as a challenge and took such imaginative flights as transferring human characteristics to animals.

One can't help wondering about the wrench someone like Chagall felt when he left behind a small, conservative Jewish village in Russia to go to the cosmopolitan capitals of Europe to fulfill a dream. His work makes it plain that he never left that village behind in his artistic imagination. Perhaps he reflected on the Second Commandment, which says in Exodus 20:4, "You shall not bow down to them (graven images) or serve them," and decided he wasn't making idols to be worshipped, he only was putting

151

his dreams on canvas. *Details: (02) 677-6271. The windows may be viewed Sun–Thu 8–1:15 and 2–3:45, Fri and holiday eves 8–12:45.*

Sixth Day: "God's Expanse" and Its Neighbors

This outing takes you through a neighborhood that was and still is one of the most famous in Jerusalem. It was where the makers and shakers of modern Israel and its founding fathers and mothers lived—some still do. Also on the agenda are views of the prime minister's and president's official residences and a visit to the exquisite Museum of Islamic Art. This is a relatively easy day. The walk and visit to the museum should take about three hours. You could preface it with a tour of the Wolfson Museum in Hechal Shlomo, around the corner from the walk's starting point. Or you could return there afterward. (See Chapter 12: "Linger Awhile.")

Rehavia, Homes of the Famous, If Not the Rich

Modern Jerusalem began in Rehavia, the pie-shaped area wedged east of the juncture of Rehov King George and Rehov Keren HaYesod, south of Rehov Keren Kayemet, and north (more or less) of Derech Aza, and west to the ridge of the Vale of Rehavia (Valley of the Cross).

When it was founded in 1921 by middle-class Ashkenazim, Rehavia ("God's Expanse") was to be one of several new "garden" communities.

Bible Lands Museum on "Museum Mile"

Bible Lands Museum Jerusalem

That it certainly became. From barren rock, it now is packed with bougainvillea, eucalyptus, cypresses, palms, cacti, roses, and giant trees. People from new neighborhoods complain that Rehavia is "too dark— you don't see the sun." But real estate agents will tell the unwary that almost anything within a day's walk is in Rehavia, so strong is the neighborhood's lingering chichi aura.

The British introduced twentieth-century architecture to Jerusalem when they took over Palestine from the Turks in 1917. They also made it a law that buildings had to be faced with Jerusalem stone. In Rehavia, you can see how the old stone and the then-new architecture first came together. The buildings often have flat roofs, square windows, and, frequently, curved art deco lines on the balconies.

During the later Mandate years, the neighborhood bristled with Jews' illegal planning for independence. Building after building was a site of secret activity.

With Israeli independence, Jerusalemites also asserted their independence from the past by rescinding British law requiring use of the city's characteristic stone. Fortunately, that ruling didn't last too long. Thoughtful observation of the results led to that law's reinstatement. You can see a few buildings in Rehavia and some other locations from that brief hiatus.

After visiting the old, poor neighborhoods of Mazkeret Moshe and Ohel Moshe, Rehavia's well-being and cosmopolitanism are strikingly apparent. For years, Rehavia smacked of snobbery. However, the community declined because of the intrusion of offices into apartment buildings, and its population has become more ethnically mixed. It remains a pleasant, convenient, and expensive place to live.

Start at the corner of Rehov Keren Kayemet and King George, in front of the Jewish Agency Building. From its balcony at the front facing Rehov King George, such people as David Ben-Gurion and Golda Meir gave speeches about independence to tumultuous crowds. This also was the site of a car-bomb explosion during the turbulent years before independence.

Continue down King George to Prima Kings Hotel at the corner of Rehov Ramban. The hotel's next-door neighbor on Rehov Ramban is a shopping center built around Jerusalem's second famous windmill (the first was built by Moses Montefiore). This newer one was built by the Greek Orthodox Church in 1875. At the entrance to **The Mill**, as this shopping center is called, is a permanent exhibit of the history of the mill and Rehavia.

Continuing on Rehov Ramban away from Prima Kings Hotel and right at Rehov Alharizi, a narrow street leads to the back of the Jewish Agency. Right on Rehov Ibn Gabirol, left on Rehov Keren Kayemet, then straight ahead is the **Hebrew Gymnasium**, founded in 1909 as the first high school in Palestine in which all subjects were taught in Hebrew. It is part of the public school system. The Haganah, while still an illegal army, gathered in its basement during the Mandate.

Across the street, between numbers 19 and 21, a walkway descends some stairs to another segment of Rehov Alharizi, a quiet enclave of tucked-away houses. Turn left to see, at number 22, an unusual Spanish colonial–style house built by a Jerusalem lawyer from Canada, Dov Joseph. He was responsible for trying to feed starving Jerusalemites during the Arab siege of 1948.

Backtrack. Next to a green metal wall is a narrow path. The wall encloses **Yad Ben-Zvi Institute**, once the residence of Israel's second president, Yitzhak Ben-Zvi. He and his wife, Rahel, studied the various Jewish ethnic communities, work continued by the institute.

Continue on the narrow walk, and you will cross Rehov Abravanel (another attractive, secluded street). Continue through a tunnel of trees back to Rehov Ramban. Take Ramban to the right, past a variety of interesting houses, many of them reflecting the 1930s International Style, until you reach Rehov Sa'adya Gaon, which curves left at a signal light.

Follow Sa'adya Gaon down the hill. It overlooks the Vale of Rehavia (Valley of the Cross). The street offers one of Jerusalem's grandest views, including the brooding Monastery of the Cross in the valley, the Israel Museum, and the Knesset on the heights.

Sa'adya Gaon connects to the left with Rehov Alfassi, which climbs a hill. Rehov Alfassi 25 was one of Menahem Begin's many secret residences during the Mandate period. The British tried to arrest him at this address, but as he was coming down from the top of the hill on his way home, a colleague gave him a prearranged signal. Begin turned around and never came back to that address again.

Little can bring home the amount of history hidden under Jerusalem more than a stroll along the crooked bends of Rehov Alfassi. There is no question but that you are surrounded by modern life, albeit with the look of the first half of the twentieth century. Then you reach Rehov Alfassi 10 and 12 and a gap on the street between those numbers. What you find here whisks you back in time more than two thousand years.

Jason's Tomb

Where you would expect another building on Rehov Alfassi, there is a wall and what looks like a park behind it. It is a park in a way, but the greenery is a carpet leading to small, graceful Jason's Tomb. It was constructed toward the end of the second century B.C.E. in the Hasmonean Period, apparently by a well-to-do family. It is much less grand than the tombs in

154

the Kidron Valley, and its pyramidal roof and arched gateway, and especially its stillness, are in striking isolation from the modern life around it.

The tomb is named for the unknown Jason, referred to in one of several inscriptions written in Hebrew, Aramaic, and Greek in the burial chamber. Beside the words about him on the wall are charcoal drawings of boats, a crouching deer, and some of the earliest representations of the seven-branch menorah.

The tomb was built far from the Jerusalem of that day, for burial within the city was forbidden under ancient Jewish law. An earthquake in approximately 30 B.C.E. damaged the structure, but it was used at least once again after that. Then the burial chambers were sealed, entrances were blocked, and the courtyard filled with stones. As the centuries went by, debris piled up, grass grew, and eventually the tomb itself was buried.

In 1965, during excavation for a new building, workers discovered masonry blocks. With more digging, Jason's Tomb emerged. The discovery ended the future of any new construction on this spot. The tomb was cleaned, restored, and turned into yet another Jerusalem archaeological site. This one, however, is enveloped by one of the choicest residential neighborhoods in the city.

So who was Jason? Could he have been a seaman? Is that the significance of the ships? Or, since according to the Bible, Simon Maccabee of the Hasmonean dynasty used drawings of boats to decorate his father's tomb, were ships simply a motif of the period? Another curiosity is that Jason is a Greek, not a Hebrew, name. Was it fashionable among upper-crust Jews of the time to adopt Greek names? As fashionable as it is today for Jewish boys to be named Scott or Brandon? The references to Jason in his tomb say only that his friends promised to grieve and mourn for him. So far, and maybe for always, Jason's identity remains a mystery.

The people who live on Rehov Alfassi know one thing

Jason's Tomb

about Jason for sure: He makes for a quiet neighbor. Details: Mon and Thu 10 a.m.–1 p.m. (But don't count on it.)

Continue up the hill, right on Rehov Radaq, left at Derech Aza (that's "Gaza" in Hebrew), and right at Rehov Balfour. The house on the left at the corner of Balfour and Rehov Smolenskin is the prime minister's official residence—not that you could miss it with the guard towers, limits on nearby parking, and wary security men standing around glowering. And not that you can see much of it.

The house was formerly the residence of an Egyptian-Jewish family. If you could see it, you would know that it isn't much grander than many others in the area. You used to be able to see the upper floor, but after Prime Minister Rabin, who actually preferred his Tel Aviv–area home, was murdered in 1995, the surrounding wall was raised and cement blocks were installed in the sidewalk in front of the house. Demonstrators used to sit on the low wall across the street and block the sidewalk, but now they are kept far, far away.

If you want to rest or eat lunch at this point, Savion is behind you and nearby at the junction of Derech Aza and Rehov Ben Maimon. Savion, which has a fish and dairy menu, is like an island in a sea of traffic. In its heyday, Savion hosted journalists, who sat and drank coffee here for hours while they waited for news from the prime minister's home.

Rehov Balfour continues to Kikar Wingate, named for a British army officer who audaciously broke ranks with his peers and helped develop what would become the Israeli army. The Brits then transferred him to Southeast Asia, where he was killed during World War II.

On your right, at the corner, is Villa Salameh, built in the 1930s as the private residence of an Arab contractor and now the Belgian consulate. Across the street and right on Rehov Jabotinsky (the "J" in this name is pronounced by Hebrew speakers), which then becomes Rehov HaNassi (the President's Street), is the much more sumptuous residence of Israel's presidents. After all, prime ministers come and go, but a president holds office for at least five years.

Neither residence has visiting hours. The best most of us can do is just look. But during the holidays of Succot in the fall and usually Passover in the spring, the president has a garden reception for anyone who wants to show up, stand in line, and bring identification.

Museum of Islamic Art

Past the president's house, Rehov HaNassi turns left and then right and becomes Rehov HaPalmah. At this corner, you will find a large attractive building of pink stone. Not to be confused with the Islamic Museum on the Temple Mount, the Museum of Islamic Art is formally known as the L.A. Mayer Memorial Institute of Islamic Art.

And how does it come to be that this museum of the art of the Moslem world is located in the heart of a middle-class Jewish neighborhood? This is the story: Vera Frances Bryce Salomons, daughter of Sir David Salomons, the first Jewish mayor of London, was a longtime Jerusalem resident. Unhappy over the squalor around the Western Wall where Jews prayed, she tried, unsuccessfully, to buy the Western Wall from the Turkish rulers. When the British took over from the Turks, she tried again, but with no greater luck. After Jerusalem was divided in 1948 and the Western Wall fell under Jordanian control, her goal seemed hopeless.

Meanwhile, Salomons developed an interest in Islam out of her long and close friendship with Leon Arie Mayer, a Hebrew University professor of Islamic studies. Finally, with the same amount of money she would have spent to buy the wall, she established the Museum of Islamic Art and set up a residence next door to it for retired academics. Mayer was to be museum director, but he died in 1959, before the museum opened.

Exhibits are clearly laid out and displayed. They draw from the entire range of the Islamic world—from the Atlantic coast of Africa to East Asia. The more than two floors of exhibitions are awesome for their breadth, depth, and beauty. In most cases, information on the exhibits is extensive and detailed.

Each display—like one on pottery—not only points out variations in artistry from community to community but also gives historical background and tells how outside influences affected the art. The glass-blowing exhibit explains the process step by step and how different effects, such as the luminous colors, were achieved. A huge amount of information is packed into each room.

But, alas, the Islamic Art Museum isn't what it used to be. One of its greatest attractions—which had nothing to do with Islam—has been reduced to a smidgen of its former self. A multimillion-dollar collection of antique timepieces that had belonged to Salomons' father, the London Lord Mayor, once occupied the museum's ground level. Some of the pieces dated back to the early seventeeth century. Marie Antoinette owned one of the watches.

In 1983, in the largest such loss in Israel's history, burglars hauled away an estimated $7.5 million worth of the horology collection while leaving their lunch wrappings behind. To date, the burglary hasn't been solved. *Details: (02) 566-1291. Sun, Mon, Wed, Thu 10–5, Tue 4–10, Fri, Sat, holidays 10–2.*

Like other museums, the Islamic Art Museum offers more than insight into art. It also offers insight into Israel itself. One day, museum visitors

157

included a class of Jewish schoolchildren escorted by their teacher, a group of Arab teenagers on their own, and a large group of Israel Defense Forces soldiers on a lecture tour. The diversity of viewers that day was typical. What was startling was not only that soldiers were being taken to an art museum but also that they were learning about the art of the Islamic people—most of whom refused for many years to recognize Israel. This paradox of military tension combined with cultural admiration is part of Jerusalem's mystique.

Wander back in the direction from which you started and turn left on Rehov Arlozoroff, before the Belgian Consulate. Between Rehov Bartenura and Aza on the left side of Arlozoroff is a 1930s version of Mea She'arim and Ohel Moshe, communities with their backs to the street and facing a courtyard. You must enter a gate to see the buildings, designed as a "workers' paradise" with separate entrances to each living unit. Notice that the complex was built of stucco instead of stone. There might be one or two original "workers" living here, but if so, they now possess a fortune in real estate.

12
LINGER AWHILE

The number of sites that Jerusalem has to offer is enormous—and ever-increasing as archaeologists do more work. If you are staying on in the city or returning for a repeat visit, how lucky you are. You can get to know the city beyond its major tourist attractions. You can visit the not-so-famous museums and sites that tourists often miss.

More Museums

The following museums offer broader insights and a more intimate picture of Jerusalem. At some, you might find yourself the only non-Israeli. At others, you could be one of only a few adults.

Bible Lands Museum

Bible Lands, located across Rehov Granot from the Israel Museum and on Museum Mile with the Bloomfield Science Museum, Knesset, and Supreme Court, opened in 1992 with two purposes. One was to create and produce exhibits on the history of the Bible period and the lands of the Bible. The other was to develop educational programs to encourage people to discover the wonders of the ancient world and their own heritage.

Bible Lands is unusual for several reasons. First, it is the fruition of a dream held by a single person, Elie Borowski, and based on his own collection of Near Eastern antiquities from the dawn of civilization to the early Christian era. Also, it is reputed to be the only museum dedicated to the Biblical period.

Its permanent exhibit is set up like a journey through history, with galleries first showing artifacts of the area's hunting civilization and then moving to urban civilizations in Sumer, Egypt, Persia, Assyria, and Mesopotamia. Interwoven with these galleries is the story of the Hebrew people and their march through early history until the Talmudic period in Babylon.

Along the way is an interactive computer program to help visitors explore the meaning and use of ancient cylinder and stamp seals, among the earliest means of communication. One of these seals was Borowski's first collected item.

The museum's temporary shows have traveled to other countries. One about the great cities of the ancient Middle East was extremely successful. Another was the *Seven Species of the Land of Israel*—barley, wheat, pomegranates, olives, grapes, dates, and figs. Besides showing how each food was represented in artwork and artifacts, the exhibit explained the meaning of each one in various cultures, including Buddhism.

Wednesday evening, when the museum is open until 9:30, you might encounter a talk on ancient Sumerian poetry. Saturday night, the museum has a wine-and-cheese concert with music that could be Mozart or Marsalis.

The museum is open Saturdays and holidays (except Yom Kippur and Rosh HaShana) and does something classy. To maintain separation of the mundane from the spiritual on Shabbat, Jews aren't supposed to handle money. So visitors arriving on Shabbat are given a stamped, self-addressed envelope. Those who don't want to handle money take the envelope home and mail in the fee later. It's an honor system, and it works.

Bible Lands Museum is surely one of the most beautiful museums anywhere. It is ironic that Ze'ev Schoenberg, the architect who gets the credit for the building (it's said that someone on his staff actually did the design), is guilty of the ugly, intrusive, and totally inappropriate-for-Jerusalem blue and stone tower off Rehov Hillel and the dismal hotel-office building at Kikar Zion. At least Schoenberg had the sense to let his assistant (rumored to be a woman) have a good day with Bible Lands. Buses 9, 17, 24, and 99 can take you to the museum. *Details: (02) 561-1068; biblelnd@netmedia.net.il. Sun–Thu 9:30–5:30, Wed to 9:30, Fri and holiday eves to 2, Shabbat and holidays, 11–3. English tours daily.*

Ammunition Hill

With its solid new buildings and colorful playgrounds, the neighborhood of Ramat Eshkol is settled, comfy, middle-class, and monotonous. It's hard to imagine what this part of formerly divided Jerusalem was like before the Six-Day War in 1967. Then, there was no Ramat Eshkol and the area was in Jordanian hands.

Harder still is to contemplate the bloody battle that took place here while Israelis, inch by inch, forced the Jordanians out. The museum, Ammunition Hill (Givat HaTahmoshet), across the divided highway Shderot Eshkol, helps give a picture of that brief, tumultuous upheaval.

The museum is in an idyllic setting at the top of a hill covered by a pine grove. Children play and birds sing, while the elderly rest on benches. Only the sight of deep trenches sliced into the hill hint at the history of this lovely place.

For 19 years this was Jordan's most fortified and heavily guarded position in eastern Jerusalem. The museum is in part the reconstruction of the Jordanian bunker and mess hall that stood here. The rest is new construction with arches, rough stone walls, and soaring ceilings.

Inside, maps and aerial photos show the area before the war and during battle. Huge photos capture the perspective of Israeli soldiers as they fought their way up the hill. It was the capture of Ammunition Hill from the Jordanians that allowed Israeli forces to enter the Old City, reach the Western Wall, and bring about reunification.

A rotating exhibit near the front of the museum gives a glimpse into the lives of the 183 Israeli soldiers who died in this battle. Hebrew

161

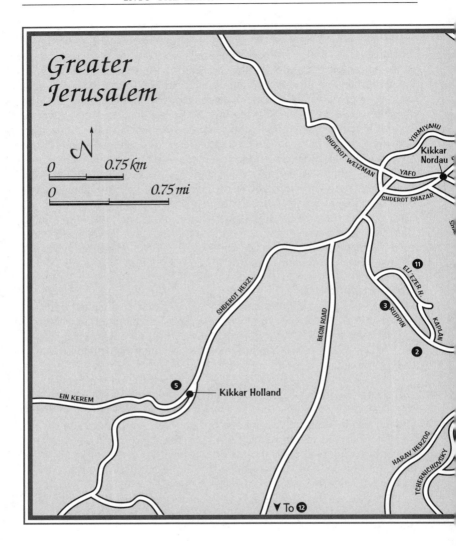

Greater Jerusalem

Greater Jerusalem Sights

1. Ammunition Hill
2. Bible Lands Museum
3. Bloomfield Science Museum
4. Hall of Heroism-Museum of Underground Prisoners
5. Herzl Museum
6. Karaite Museum and Synagogue
7. Mardigian Museum

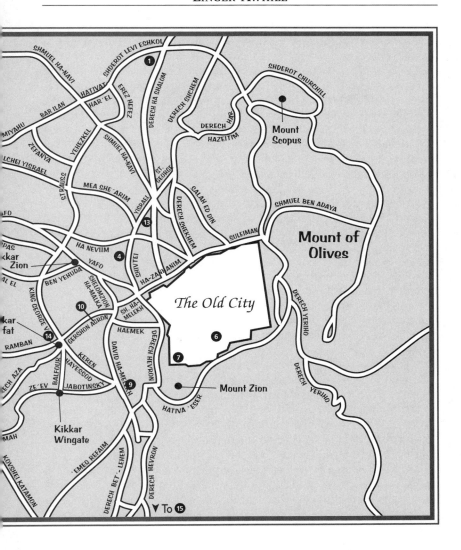

8 Monastery of the Holy Cross
9 Montefiore Windmill
10 Museum of Taxes
11 Supreme Court

12 Tisch Family Jerusalem
   Zoological Gardens
13 Tourjeman Post
14 Wolfson Museum
15 Sherover and Haas Promenades

documents are translated into English. They include soldiers' letters, poems, and essays. In an excerpt from Ofer Feniger's *The World Lives Within Me*, Feniger writes to a friend about the emotional impact he felt after reading, for the first time, a book about the Holocaust. Feniger was killed in hand-to-hand fighting on Ammunition Hill. He was 24 years old.

The soldiers' writings are astoundingly eloquent, as is their artwork and photography. These young men had the emotional freedom to look inward and the artistic talent to express outwardly what they found within. Buses 4, 9, 25, 26, and 99 will take you to the museum. *Details: (02) 582-8442. Sun–Thu 8–6, Fri and holiday eves to 2. Admission fee.*

Monastery of the Holy Cross

The hulking Greek Orthodox Monastery of the Holy Cross squats like a silent behemoth at the southeastern end of the Valley of the Cross—known also with a less religious title, the Vale of Rehavia. For years the ancient edifice seemed dark, gloomy, and inhospitable. It had, in fact, only two monks and the elderly mother of one of them rattling around in its 300 rooms.

In 1986 a portion of its vast interior was opened to visitors. Behind the forbidding monastery walls are quiet courtyards, one of the loveliest churches in all Jerusalem, and an unpretentious museum. Only two monks remained.

After the monastery opened to visitors, I spent many a lovely Saturday afternoon in deep, friendly discussion with one of the monks, talking about religion and politics in Jerusalem (you often wonder if there's anything else to talk about here). The idyll ended when the Greek Orthodox powers that be decided to use more of those 300 rooms and brought seminarians to study. My monk friend decided the place was too noisy and went elsewhere. The rest of us can still find plenty of peace within these walls.

The first church on this site, believed to have held the cross on which Jesus was crucified, was built in the early fourth century. Persians destroyed the church in 614. Moslems destroyed its Georgian-built replacement in 1009. Around 1038, construction began again. Much of what you see today dates from 1038, while an ersatz Spanish-style rococo tower is only 130 years old. The Greek Orthodox Church assumed responsibility for the monastery from the Georgian Orthodox Church in 1840.

What is so ingratiating about the church, compared with other Jerusalem churches built before the mid-1800s, is that it is both bright inside and devoid of religious overstatement. The floor is an eleventh-century mosaic (stand on the step to the right of the iconostasis and you can see the remains of a sixth-century mosaic floor).

Seventeenth-century frescoes adorn pillars and walls. Many consider these frescoes the finest in Israel. They have clean lines, expressive portraits, and intense colors. In one fresco, two church fathers gaze off into the distance. At their feet is a small white-bearded, red-robed figure. This is Shota Rustavelli, the Georgian Shakespeare and Cervantes, who came to the monastery in the twelfth century and remained until his death.

On the upper floors you can see the old kitchen with its huge vats and wall ovens, and the refectory with three long tables topped with white and pink marble. Another display contains photographs of solemn seminary graduates with their black gowns, tall black hats, and black beards. A painting, a large triangular piece, shows Jesus on the cross, myriad events taking place around him, and the monastery itself.

The monastery is tucked away near the intersection of Rehov Aza, Herzog, Tchernichovsky, and Valley of the Cross Road. Follow the path into the valley. Buses 31, 32, and 19 will get you there. *Details: (02) 679-0961. Daily 10–1:30. Admission fee.*

Hall of Heroism-Museum of Underground Prisoners
Jerusalem is a haunted city and one that doesn't forget its ghosts. Among the city's hovering spirits, those at the Hall of Heroism, dedicated primarily to the fight for a Jewish homeland and against the British Mandate's severe limitation of Jewish immigration, are among the most poignant. The men memorialized here appeared to be reckless for challenging the British Empire. Few contests could have been so lopsided. Yet these men fought with complete dedication to a seemingly impossible dream—a home in their ancestral land for homeless Jews.

The museum is tucked behind a parking lot in the Russian Compound, behind City Hall. Inside, against stone walls in a small room, is a photo exhibit of Jewish men, some scarcely old enough to be called men, who were put to death by the Turks in 1917, by the Syrians in 1965, and by the British and Egyptians during the intervening years.

Past the portrait gallery, you enter what was Jerusalem's Central Prison during the Mandate period (1917–1948). Inside the prison is a long, shabby corridor hung with impressive and intriguing maps, documents, and large photos related to the prisoners and their resistance to the Mandate. But, alas, as at many Israeli museums that aren't top tourist attractions, English translations are frustratingly rare.

Once, when I was the only visitor, my footsteps were frighteningly loud. Creaking sounds added to the eeriness and seemed ghostlike in this forsaken place, as if all of its terrible memories were stirring. As it turned out, the sounds came from an open window swaying in the breeze, but such is the atmosphere of this prison. The ordinary assumes unreal proportions.

165

Display cases exhibit the inmates' craftwork, done while they waited for their fate. A tiny, neatly woven container for cigarettes looks like a gift for Dad made at summer camp. Also on display are *tzitzit*—the fringed undergarments worn by religiously observant Jewish men—woven by a prisoner, perhaps for himself.

Thirty to forty men at a time were jammed into the small cells here. Some were locked up for overt acts against the Mandate forces. Others had committed "crimes" such as blowing the shofar during High Holiday prayers at the Western Wall—an integral part of Rosh HaShana and Yom Kippur, but banned by the British.

In one of the death cells, a mat and a pair of shoes seem as if they had been left there only moments earlier. Around a corner, almost hidden, is the gallows, the hangman's noose and pulley at the ready.

Actually, for fear of sparking an uprising, the British didn't execute Jews in Jerusalem. Instead, on execution day they spirited the prisoners far away to Akko, then a largely Arab city north of Haifa, and hung them there.

A plaque in the corridor relates that two prisoners condemned to death refused to let the British have their way. Two hours before their scheduled execution, the prisoners pressed grenades—smuggled to them inside oranges—against their hearts and blew themselves up. One was 17 years old.

Sunshine in the courtyard, where prisoners were allowed to spend a half hour a day, seems to mock the dark history of the Hall of Heroism. All city center buses travel here. *Details: (02) 623-3166. Sun–Thu 8–4. Admission fee.*

Herzl Museum

When Captain Alfred Dreyfus of the French army was convicted of treason in 1885, journalist Theodor Herzl covered the Jewish officer's trial for a Viennese newspaper. (Years later, it was proved the case had been based on false documents.) Dreyfus's blatantly anti-Semitic treatment made such an impact on the 35-year-old Herzl that it changed the course of his life, not to mention history.

Remembering the prejudice he had endured as a child in Budapest, Herzl concluded that Jews never would be freely accepted in any country, no matter how long their families had lived there or what patriotic contributions they made. The only solution for them, he decided, was to create their own homeland. And so it was that Herzl, virtually alone, started the modern Zionist movement with the First Zionist Congress in 1897 in Basel, Switzerland.

Herzl predicted that within 50 years there would be a Jewish state.

In 1948, his bold campaign came to fruition with the reestablishment of the State of Israel.

The small museum, on Mount Herzl off Shderot Herzl, is dedicated to Herzl's life story. It is tucked at the bottom of a slope between the entrance to Yad Vashem and the Military Cemetery on Mount Herzl.

Included are Herzl's handwritten letters and a re-creation of his study. The Hebrew and English comments beside each display provide a continuous, if sometimes abbreviated, glimpse into this visionary's life. It may

Jerusalem by Night

If you linger in Jerusalem, you will have the good fortune of beholding the city at night. The golden glow of streetlights against the city's stones can make you feel as if you have accidentally wandered onto a stage setting.

Recently, the city has instituted nighttime illumination of certain sights. First came specially designed lighting of the Old City walls. That was so successful that more sites were illuminated. To date, Mishkenot Sha'ananim, the Montefiore Windmill, the Jerusalem Theater, and the Sergei Hospice in the Russian Compound are lit at night. The Mount of Olives churches glow at night, including the Church of All Nations. Tombs in the Kidron Valley take on an especially dramatic, even otherworldly, aspect under their night-lights.

In the Old City, lights shine at the destroyed Hurva Synagogue in the Jewish Quarter, the Coenaculum on Mount Zion, and the Muristan in the Arab souk. In addition, East Jerusalem Development Ltd. has provided Old City shopkeepers with lights outside their establishments. The purpose is to encourage businesses to keep longer hours for the benefit of tourists.

More night-lights are found at the Ramparts Walk, Haas Promenade, St. Andrew's Church, and the Hebrew University on Mount Scopus. Plans are for additional sites to be illuminated.

These lights, making Jerusalem even more magical, more spellbinding, more entrancing at night than ever, are the work of French illumination designer Ronald Geoll, who has also performed his art in Lyons, Paris, and St. Petersburg.

come as a surprise to learn that this intense man with an all-consuming mission had a less serious side to his personality and professional life. He was the author of 20 plays, most of them comedies.

The exhibit includes a collection of oval photos of the delegates who came to Basel for that fateful First Congress. The men and women appear to be comfortable, middle-class Ashkenazim—not world shakers. The exhibit also points out the bizarre historical fact that in the early 1900s, the British first tried to establish a Jewish home in the northern Sinai. Failing that, they offered Eastern European Jews a portion of Kenya that later became Uganda.

Herzl's personal life was starkly tragic, and he died on July 3, 1904, with his dream dismissed as a fantasy by most people. But, he said, "If you will it, it is no dream." A copy of Herzl's will, on exhibit, states his request for "a poor man's funeral." He also asked that his body be re-interred in Palestine. In 1949, his body was indeed re-interred in the land he sought for the Jewish homeland. It rests at the top of the mountain named for him. His grave is marked by a simple black slab of stone on which one word is engraved: "Herzl." Buses 13, 17, 20, 23, 27, 39, and 99 will take you here. *Details (02) 651-1108. Sun–Thu 9–6, Friday and holiday eves to 1. Free.*

Karaite Museum and Synagogue

Among the mosaic of Jerusalem's people are the Karaites—members of a Jewish sect founded by Anan Ben-David in Persia in the eighth century. It is said that he emigrated to Jerusalem and built the Karaite Synagogue—located at Rehov HaKaraim 3, Jewish Quarter, Old City.

Karaites accept only Tanach—an acronym for Torah (the Five Books of Moses), Nevi'im (Prophets), and Ketuvim (writings such as the Psalms and the Books of Daniel and Ruth). They believe Tanach is binding and to be interpreted literally. Out of this, they have developed traditions that vary from those of mainstream Jews.

During Shabbat, for instance, Karaites don't eat cooked food or leave lights burning, as mainstream Jews do. Karaites do not use lights at all. Nor do they leave their homes on Shabbat, except to go to the synagogue and pray.

The Karaite compound—synagogue and museum—faces the ruined Tiferet Israel Synagogue in the Jewish Quarter between Rehov HaKaraim and Tiferet Israel. When the original museum was open, the caretaker's wife told me that some 50 Karaite families live in Jerusalem and about 20,000 individuals in all Israel. Karaite communities also exist or have existed in Turkey, the Crimea, Poland, Lithuania, Egypt, and, in the United States, in Chicago, San Francisco, and Los Angeles.

For centuries, the center for Karaites was Egypt. The establishment of an independent Israel inspired some Egyptian Karaites to move here. But most arrived after they were forced out in 1956, when Israel briefly won control of the Sinai.

A new, bigger Karaite Museum features exhibits from the original one-room museum. One exhibit is a delicate, 100-year-old white bridal gown from Egypt with a pair of pearl-covered slippers beside it. There are also photos of dignified Karaite rabbis from another era. Many of the religious leaders wear white-topped black turbans.

At the far end of the museum, visitors can look into the synagogue below. The synagogue was originally completely underground, built that way both as a shelter against violence and because the ruling Moslems required synagogues and churches to be inconspicuous. Improvements after the Six-Day War raised the synagogue floor, adding natural light.

Still, this house of worship remains quite dark inside. Displays emerge only slowly from the shadows. Its Torah scroll sits in a cabinet in the corner. There is a small *bima* (platform from which services are conducted) by the holy ark. A screen at the rear reserves a tiny portion of the room for women. Richly colored carpets cover the stone floor. The room has no furniture because worshippers, who must leave their shoes outside, often prostrate themselves during prayer. Call the museum caretaker, (02) 628-6688, or the Municipal Tourist Office, (02) 625-8844, for information.

Mardigian Museum

"Who remembers the Armenians?" Hitler was said to have asked that rhetorical question before he embarked on the slaughter of 6 million Jews. The Nazis learned well the lesson of history and concluded that it would be as safe for them, as it was for the Turks in 1915, to annihilate a people.

Wars and politics unfortunately put the largest chunk of the ancient Christian land of Armenia within the border of Moslem Turkey. Under the cover of World War I (as the Germans later used World War II), the Turks massacred Armenians. Armenians say the toll was 1.5 million people. The rest of the world paid scant attention and, afterward, quickly forgot.

But survivors and their descendants aren't about to let the Turks forget. They want the Turks to acknowledge what happened to Armenians in the early years of the twentieth century. And they have hopes that even at this belated date, the rest of the world will learn from it.

That is one purpose of the Helen and Edward Mardigian Museum, past the Armenian Cathedral of St. James in the Armenian Quarter of the Old City. The museum's other purpose is to exhibit centuries' worth of

Armenian art, especially that which praises God and expresses devotion to the church. Edward Mardigian, a Detroit industrialist, endowed the museum with $250,000 in the 1970s.

Three thousand years of Armenian history are surveyed in a series of ground-floor rooms in a two-story, nineteenth-century building that once housed seminarians. Through maps, audiovisual presentations, and pictures, the vivid story is told. The Armenians' expertise with metal turned them into chariot drivers in 2000 B.C.E. Between 70 and 50 B.C.E., they briefly became conquerors, spreading their territory from between the Black and Caspian Seas to an area that included Syria and northern Israel.

In a stunning photo, Mount Ararat, the spiritual symbol of the Armenian people, rises out of a rocky wasteland. The mountain is echoed in the black pointed headdresses of Armenian Orthodox priests and in the pointed, conical towers of their churches.

Photos of these churches line the walls in a first-floor room. The churches are significant as the link between Byzantine and Islamic architecture. The ones on view are those that, at least until the time of the photos, survived the region's bitter winters and what Armenians allege is deliberate Turkish destruction.

On the second floor, photographs recount Turkish genocide. In one, a group of Turkish men proudly stand beside a pile of severed heads of Armenians. In another, orphans who managed to escape the Turkish storm gaze forlornly at the camera.

Another room shows examples of Armenian art, such as a 1685 world map drawn by an expatriate residing in Amsterdam. His map includes a vast area called America. Next to America is a large island called California. On seeing this, some Americans today might say that the mapmaker was prophetic, for perhaps some day California will float out to sea.

Newer museum additions hold examples of the rich collection of religious art belonging to Jerusalem's Armenian Orthodox patriarchate. In 301 C.E., Armenia was the first nation to adopt Christianity as its state religion. Pilgrims from Armenia have been coming to Jerusalem ever since, always bringing the best they could as a gift to the patriarchate. Gifts range from copper pots to illuminated manuscripts, intricately patterned carpets, and altar curtains emblazoned with gold thread.

The exhibit of religious art changes about every six months. Bit by bit, the Armenian patriarchate's immense collection will see the light. Perhaps someday, the exhibit will satisfy rumors that the patriarchate owns what is purported to be the world's largest pearl (an inch wide) and the longest piece of amber (four feet, eight inches).

Meanwhile, art exhibited at any given time is awesomely rich: vestments of such fine gold and silver thread that the designs are as smooth

170

as paintings, chalices of gold filigree inlaid with pearls and gemstones. The never-repeated designs of the crosses, alone, are bedazzling.

The cross of the Armenian Church is distinctive for usually being equilateral and having four open, split branches. It is said that each cross is different. But rarely is there a crucifix. Former museum curator Kevork (George) Hintlian explained this absence by saying, "The cross should represent victory—not pain."

Entrance to the museum is from Jaffa Gate, along the Armenian Orthodox Patriarchate Road to the right, then, after the second archway, through a modest doorway on the left and through a courtyard. Buses 13, 19, and 20 can take you to the museum. *Details: (02) 628-2331. Mon–Sat 10–4:30. Admission fee.*

Montefiore Windmill

Funny that a windmill should be one of the most famous landmarks of Jerusalem. More than a hundred years ago, this windmill of northern European design, built by Sir Moses Montefiore, was one of many in the uninhabited rocky countryside outside the Old City. Almost all have disappeared.

The Montefiore Windmill stands near the top of a hill, adjacent to the Yemin Moshe neighborhood. It is now a museum commemorating Montefiore's long life and astounding impact on the development of Jerusalem. The windmill, even to its huge blades, is beautifully restored. Next to it is a small building that houses the carriage Montefiore used in Europe and on some of his journeys to the Holy Land. The family crest on the carriage door has a lion and buck holding up banners of Jerusalem. Between them is the family slogan: "Think and Thank." In 1986, arsonists destroyed the original carriage; what you see here is a replica.

From the terrace in front of the windmill, you can see some of the more spectacular vistas of the Old City, the Hinmom Valley, and the Judean Desert. This is a view to be treasured when a full moon rises.

The display within the windmill is excellent for its clarity and breadth. Eight well-lit panels have photos and reproductions of documents, paintings, and drawings pertaining to Montefiore's life. Beside each panel is an explanation in Hebrew and English, and above each is a blown-up photo of old Jerusalem. The photos date to the 1840s.

Montefiore was born in Livorno, Italy, in 1784, into a family that already had settled in England. Wealthy, he retired at an early age and devoted himself to the Jewish people. He and his wife, Judith, visited what then was southern Syria seven times.

Montefiore saw that the Jerusalem of his day, totally within the walls, was impoverished and pestilence-ridden. He believed that for their health and welfare, Jews had to move outside the walls. If they were afraid—for outside the walls was a dangerous wilderness—he would offer them inducements such as employment and a stipend.

The three-story windmill went up in 1855, to provide flour at a reduced price as well as work for poor Jews. In 1860, Montefiore built Mishkenot Sha'ananim, tiny apartments for millworkers and their families from the Old City, just below the windmill. But being paid to live in Mishkenot Sha'ananim wasn't enough for these Jerusalemites. Fear of marauders persistently drove them back to the safety of their old, wall-protected homes every evening.

Both the windmill and Mishkenot Sha'ananim were failures. The mill wasn't designed to grind rough Middle Eastern wheat, and Jerusalemites weren't yet ready to be pioneers. But Montefiore wasn't discouraged. The exhibit in the windmill chronicles the many Jerusalem neighborhoods that Montefiore and the foundation that continued after his death successfully created. Montefiore was an expert fund-raiser. The money for Mishkenot Sha'ananim, for example, came from the will of Judah Touro, the first American Jew to make a large contribution to Israel.

One of the neighborhoods built by the Montefiore Foundation was Yemin Moshe (the Righteous Moses), named for the English philanthropist. Located next to Mishkenot Sha'ananim and the windmill, it is often called the first permanent neighborhood outside the walls. Not true. The first successful neighborhood outside the walls was Mahane Yisrael, off Rehov King David, built in 1868 for North African immigrants.

Yemin Moshe was begun in 1891, after Montefiore's death. The upper streets were for Sephardim, the lower for Ashkenazim. Between 1948 and 1967, the area became a refuge for the poor—a jumble of hovels. After the Six-Day War, it became an artists' colony, then a high-priced neighborhood largely inhabited by Anglo-Saxon Jews.

The windmill almost didn't survive the British Mandate. Before the British—notoriously and disgracefully pro-Arab—left Palestine in 1948, they blew off the windmill's top, reportedly to make it more difficult for the Jews to defend the soon-beleaguered city from Arab attack. Jews dubbed the British act Operation Don Quixote. Ironically, when Montefiore built the windmill almost a hundred years earlier, it could have been called the same thing.

Montefiore died in England at the age of 101 and was buried there. Because of his steadfast devotion to Jerusalem, a stone from the city was placed beneath his head before he was buried. Buses 4, 4a, 7, 8, 15, 18, 21, 30, 38, 48, and 99 all reach the windmill. *Details: (02) 625-4403 or (02) 625-4404. Sun–Thur 9–4, Fri to 1. Free.*

Museum of Taxes

The Tax Museum at Rehov Agron 32 is said to be one of only two such museums in the world. It is just inside the entrance to the Customs and Value-Added Tax Building, distinctive for its ornate grillwork at the windows, neat sidewalk in front, and modernistic iron fence on the traffic island in Agron. Israelis ruefully insist that these elaborate touches are sure signs that the government collects more tax money that it knows what to do with.

A museum devoted to taxes may seem merely to offer a good way to duck out of the rain or sun. The reality comes as a surprise: This place is amusingly quirky and has items any sightseer will enjoy. Inside is a single large room. The walls and floor exhibit a variety of items, some of which look like discards from the Israeli equivalent of attics. In the midst of the clutter, uniformed officials stand at attention, and you might also find a young woman at a computer and a man at a desk. After a moment, you realize that the woman and man, who seem to have no connection with the museum, are moving and are real, while the uniformed officials are not. The sight of the uniforms and the documents hanging along the walls might produce angst in a beholder, as if yesterday was the deadline for filing tax returns and nothing had been done about it.

In a tiny section about taxation in ancient times you'll see a clay slab with a painted line of awkward young women dancing. The slab dates from fourth century B.C.E. Persia. An explanation in English states that by dancing in a Persian temple, the women could square their "labor tribute"—whatever that was.

In an ominous vein, the *Taxation in the Diaspora* section has an official notice from eighteenth-century London. It warns Jews that if they don't want to be stoned on the street they had better promptly pay the special tax levied on them.

Nearby, a neat parchment printed in Hebrew from seventeenth-century Mantua, Italy, reminds Jews that their taxes to the Jewish community are due and advises that they should be paid in "moral and strict righteousness."

One part of the museum shows the many clever ways people tried to smuggle items into Israel and thereby avoid import taxes. Of course, these ways weren't all that clever. Otherwise, the shabby coat with 97 silk scarves sewn into its lining or the cute baby doll that now is without the load of jewelry that had been stuffed into its body wouldn't have been confiscated and put on display.

Another example of inventiveness is a gorgeous inlaid table. Why is this here? Mira Dror, the museum's dedicated director, pointed to what was below the table's top—a roulette wheel. "Gambling is illegal in Israel," she said, "but should it become legal, we'll have the first casino!" Buses 6, 15, 18, 21, 22, and 30 can get you to the museum. But because it's a one-woman operation, Dror urges prospective visitors to call in advance. *Details: (02) 625-8978 or (02) 670-3201. Sun–Thu 9–3. Free.*

Tourjeman Post for Dialogue, Understanding, and Coexistence •

The museum, at Rehov Hel HaHandassa 4, was simply the Tourjeman Post Museum until 1999. But even that name needs explaining. The structure was built in the mid-1930s by the Arab Baramki family, who bought land from Ahmed Bey Tourjeman. They built a graceful, pink-and-white stone, four-family house, with Crusader arches and Corinthian columns. Strangely, the house retained the name of the landowner, not the builder.

After the Arab residents fled during the War of Independence in 1948, Israeli forces turned the house into a fortified blockhouse at the edge of "no-man's land." That's when it acquired the name Tourjeman Post.

For 19 years, Tourjeman Post overlooked the Mandelbaum Gate—the makeshift border between Israel and what only the Jordanians, British, and Pakistanis then called Jordan. The gate split the heart of Jerusalem from 1948 to 1967.

With the city's reunification, the house became a museum dedicated to the story of a divided Jerusalem. The building's shell-blasted balcony was left as it was when the fighting ended. The poignant sight made the events described within seem as if they had happened yesterday.

Among the exhibits in the original museum were the photo-story of a nun on the Israeli side of the border who dropped her false teeth from a window into no-man's land. United Nations personnel, white flags flying, embarked on a search. At the end of the series of photos, the nun was seen grinning with her newly retrieved teeth.

In another exhibit, a short film showed people's reaction to unification on both sides of the border. After 19 years apart, Arabs rushed to visit their old Jewish friends, and Jews rushed to visit their old Arab friends. An Arab eyewitness called the result "the biggest traffic jam ever" as both sides converged in the middle.

The redesigned museum opened in 1999 with new goals. It will now concentrate on the causes of conflict and resolution—not just among Arabs and Israelis but among all people. Museum director Danny Shalem noted, "Our goals aren't political. We want to stimulate people's imagination in ways of solving conflict. We will be a center for learning. The building will stand as it is. Damaged by war, it's a symbol for the goal of resolving conflicts without weapons." Buses 1, 2, 11, 27, and 99 will take you to the museum or close by. Call for more information: (02) 628-1278.

174

Bloomfield Science Museum

Step into the Bloomfield Science Museum and the first thing that might hit you will be the sound of children shouting, laughing, clattering around, and having a marvelous time. This isn't a museum in which kids have to whisper, tread softly, and keep their hands to themselves. Here everything is to touch, feel, and investigate.

But you don't have to be 10 years old to have a terrific time here. Perhaps, if you're a physicist or engineer all these exhibits will be old hat to you. But the rest of us will learn what the Leonardo Bridge is and how to cross a river even without material long enough to reach to the other side. In another exhibit, you'll learn how to make your own miniature St. Louis Gateway Arch.

A Rube Goldberg–like black metal contraption fills a room, part of a special wing designed for children from ages three to eight. On this contrivance, children send balls down twisting, turning tracks, while, incidentally, learning about simple machines and the impact of levers. The lavatory nearby is designed for young children, with sinks at their level and faucets that turn off automatically.

Upstairs, among other hands-on items, are computers on which you can play endlessly with color and design and an electric piano from which you can see how pitches register on an electronic scale.

Youngsters especially like the Bloomfield Science Museum.

Shimi Nachtailer

175

The museum, located on Museum Boulevard between the Hebrew University at Givat Ram and Bible Lands Museum (take Bus 9, 17, 24, 28, or 99), opened in 1992. It came about through the Hebrew University, the Jerusalem Foundation, and a gift from the Bernard M. Bloomfield family of Canada. Together they created a place that simply is a lot of fun. Information is written in Hebrew, English, and Arabic. If you have children old enough to read, you can leave them alone to explore. There is a cafeteria, but it is open only during summer and the Succot and Passover holidays. Children (or anyone else, for that matter) can bring snacks, but they must eat them outside. *Details: (02) 561-8128, www.mada.org.il. Mon, Wed, Thu 10–6, Tue 10–8, Friday and holiday eves 10–1, Shabbat 10–3. Admission fee.*

Wolfson Museum

Directly across the street from the Sheraton Jerusalem Plaza Hotel rises Hechal Shlomo at Rehov King George 58 (Buses 4, 7, 8, 9, 14, 19, 31, 32, 48, and 99 will take you there). It isn't named for King Solomon but for the father of Sir Isaac Wolfson, an English millionaire who built it out of filial respect.

The tall, domed building, the former headquarters of the Ashkenazi and Sephardi Chief Rabinates, houses various offices, a charming small synagogue and, on the third floor, the Wolfson Museum of Jewish Religious Art and a collection of miniature, three-dimensional scenes from Jewish history. One drawback is that the museum is skimpy on identifications.

Judaica involves only a certain number of objects, which must meet certain requirements—a limitation for artists, you would think. But look around you. The human imagination is astounding. Take chanukiahs, for instance. They must have eight candles or oil lamps in a row, plus the Shamas, the candle or lamp from which the other eight are lit. Yet the spectrum of styles and materials seems endless.

I was here one day when a young Italian engineer from Milan, a silversmith of Judaica, arrived to show a few of his creations to the curator. In this one limited showing of one person's work were three styles of silver chanukiahs.

The museum is small and just right for a visit of an hour or so. Drawing from countries as disparate as Yemen and Holland, it displays a rich variety of religious objects—old and new—used at home and in the synagogue. The permanent collection contains jewelry, amulets, Passover Seder plates, and even such humble objects as charity boxes and circumcision clamps that, through embellishment, have become works of art. Changing exhibits focus on different themes.

Among the treasures inside are a pair of rare Persian rugs more than a hundred years old that together portray Moses, Aaron, and the aborted sacrifice of Isaac. They contrast with a seventeenth-century Florentine tapestry showing Moses receiving the Ten Commandments from a shadowy representation of a white-bearded God. While the Persian weavers' Biblical characters have the clothing and stylized faces seen in classic Persian miniatures, the Italian Moses wears red leggings and a jaunty cape, as would any seventeenth-century Florentine blade. Framing the Italian scene are four chubby cherubs holding up towering piles of fruit.

The museum exhibits two art forms that became particularly Jewish: paper-cutting and micrography. From the fifteenth century, especially in eastern Europe, Jews (even yeshiva students) did paper cutting. It lost its prominence before World War I, but recently several Jewish artists have revived the intricate skill. The museum has a large nineteenth-century Moroccan paper cutting with an exotic cast to it, with shiny colored papers as a background.

Micrography is a richly symbolic art form developed by Jews in the ninth century. The practice involves using minute Hebrew letters to form representational, geometric, and abstract designs. Like paper cutting, it is an intricate and demanding art form that has been revived.

A startling object here is a round, blue Hungarian matzo cover for Passover. Look closely. Amid the embroidery are luminous fish scales.

One small room is devoted to photos of Sir and Lady Wolfson at the many places in Israel and England they have endowed, as well as standing side by side with the doers and movers of the world, including the classic figureheads, the British royal family. The Wolfsons weren't collectors themselves. They gave the money so the items could be collected.

Across the hall from the museum is a display of three-dimensional scenes from Jewish history. These are in miniature, with the figures about one inch high. The display begins with Abraham and his family leaving Ur and ends with Chaim Weizmann, Israel's first president, on the White House lawn presenting President Harry Truman with a Sefer Torah on May 25, 1948, shortly after the establishment of modern Israel.

Scenes include casts of thousands. There is Pharaoh's army about to be swept away by a huge wave of the Red Sea. There is Jerusalem under siege by the Roman army, which swarms around the city's walls.

The artist shows not only the main characters but also parallel lives: While Queen Esther begs her Persian husband to save her people's lives, three bare-breasted women do a wild dance out in the courtyard. While Philo pleads with Emperor Caligula to annul his anti-Jewish decree, far from that emotional scene a slave serenely hauls water from a pool. *Details: (02) 624-7112. Sun–Thu 9–1. Admission fee.*

Downstairs in Hechal Shlomo is Rananim, the more endearing (to me) of two synagogues in the complex. Its neighbor is the **Great Synagogue**, whose services are attractive to tourists as well as Israeli prime ministers, who have only to cross a couple of streets to get there. To see the likes of the Great Synagogue, you don't have to leave Beverly Hills—but take a peek anyway. The stained-glass windows are gorgeous and the Friday night music is a concert in itself.

The **Rananim Synagogue** is infinitely more intimate than its grand neighbor. Within its gray-blue, unadorned walls is a Baroque brown-and-cream eighteenth-century bima and holy ark brought from Padua, Italy.

More Sights and Attractions

Tisch Family Jerusalem Zoological Gardens (Biblical Zoo)
Nothing could be more earthly than a zoo. But in the heavenly city of Jerusalem, religion finds a place even here. The city's zoo not only has the same features as its counterpart in, say, Detroit, but also has its own specialty. It contains a gathering of birds, snakes, insects, and plants mentioned in the Bible. Biblical verses referring to animal life appear in Hebrew, Arabic, and English next to the appropriate animal ("The lion hath roared, who will not fear?" Amos 3:8, or "And the cow and the bear shall feed, their young ones shall lie down together," Isaiah 11:7.)

Surely, few zoos have had such a rough history. The Jerusalem Biblical Zoo, founded in 1939, was originally located on Mount Scopus, which fell to the Jordanians in the War of Independence. In 1950, the 18 animals that remained from the pre-war 122 were moved by armored convoy to a site in Romema's Schneller Woods. In 1967, a Jordanian shell hit the zoo, killing 110 animals.

Few people expected the financially strapped zoo to survive this second blow. It was already so impoverished that a few years before the bomb hit, its main keeper was arrested for stealing vegetables from the municipal dump. He did so to feed the animals.

But miracles tend to happen in Israel, and the zoo survived, flourished, and outgrew its postage stamp–size turf. Now in architecturally notable facilities, some 140 species live on more than 80 acres. The exhibits note species that once were common in Israel and now are extinct, the Syrian bear as relatively recent as 1917. One of the major activities here is breeding endangered species. The zoo has a train to get you up the hills, bamboo umbrellas and screens to protect you from the sun, and a children's zoo with playground equipment.

The drive to the zoo alone is worth the trip, although with the mad pace that Jerusalem is developing, the view might be quite different when you get here. The zoo is south of the Jerusalem Canyon neighborhood. On the way there, you'll see hills and valleys that are reminders of the time-lessness and antiquity of this land. You can take Bus 26, 33, or 99, or a train from the Jerusalem station. The zoo itself is set in a valley. New construction hovers on some of the nearby hilltops. Elsewhere, what you see is what has been for millennia. *Details: (02) 643-0111.Winter 9–5, spring and fall 9–6, summer 9–7:30.*

The Supreme Court
The year 1992 was a flourishing one in Jerusalem, with the opening of two new museums, plus the new dramatic Supreme Court building. From Israel's beginning, the law said that the Supreme Court had to be based in Jerusalem. The law was fitting, for Jerusalem has been the city of Solomonic judgments; of prophets exhorting people that God wanted not sacrifices but justice; and of Rabbi Hillel, who set a standard of moral behavior when he said, "Don't do to others what is hateful to yourself."

For decades the Israeli Supreme Court was squeezed into a hostel for Russian Orthodox pilgrims in the center of Jerusalem. Then a contribution arrived from the fabled Rothschild family, who earlier had funded the nearby Knesset building. The contribution covered the entire cost of the impressive Supreme Court building.

Ram Carmi and Ada Carmi-Melamed, a brother-and-sister team of

Supreme Court Building

architects, spent seven years on the design. For inspiration, they drew from the meaning of justice, the Bible, and Jerusalem itself. Outside, rough-cut stones sit at the base of the building, smoother-cut stones above. Stone is everywhere inside, often contrasting with a plain white wall opposite. A staircase landing has an enormous curved window that looks out on the red-tiled roofs of Jerusalem's Nahlaot and Mahane Yehuda neighborhoods.

The entrances to the five courtrooms resemble enormous gates, for in Biblical times, justice was determined at the gates. Each courtroom feels like an outdoor space set between stone walls. The play of light in the interiors and the effect of the unadorned arches are some of the delights of this building. Take Bus 9, 24, or 99. *Details: (02) 675-9612. Free English-language tours Sun–Thu at noon.*

A Train Trip

The Jerusalem–Tel Aviv train trip, except in winter when the highway is closed by snow, is primarily for the scenery. As these words are being written, the train resembles a Toonerville Trolley. But there is talk of buying newfangled tilting trains, which will reduce the trip from an hour and a half to an hour or less.

The train line has a glorious history. When built in 1892, the line linked Jerusalem and Jaffa. (There was no Tel Aviv then.) Its purpose,

The Soreq Valley, seen from the train to Tel Aviv

180

investors deemed, was to provide a safer, faster way for pilgrims to reach the Holy City. But every item needed to build the line had to be rowed ashore like the pilgrims themselves. And then the challenge was to lay the tracks on a convoluted path from sea level to 2,297 feet.

When the railway finally reached Jerusalem, it may have been the first (and possibly last) bloodless major event here in thousands of years. Suddenly, isolated, impoverished, and disease-ridden Jerusalem was connected with the outside world.

Bands played to a carnival atmosphere at the maiden outing, and celebrating Jerusalemites rode the train down the mountain. But Arabs derailed the train, and the celebrants had to hike back up the mountain in the dark.

Arabs continued damaging the tracks and, during the Jordanian occupation, hurling rocks at the cars. Because the new Jordanian border was so close, travelers were warned, "Don't lean out of the country." These problems disappeared after the Six-Day War.

The most striking part of the trip is in the Soreq Valley. Tortuously, the train makes its way through this rock-ribbed land. You'll pass the Arab village of Battir, formerly the Jewish Bitar. This is where Shimon Bar Kochba, thought to be the messiah who would rescue the Jewish people from the Romans, was killed by the Romans in 135 C.E.

Then comes Samson country. Samson hid in a cave here from the Philistines, Aegean people who caused the Hebrew people enormous grief, then disappeared from history. This is where Samson disastrously fell in love with Delilah and was buried. Let your imagination choose the cave in which he might have hidden.

Branches now thrash the train windows, but as recently as 1960 these slopes were barren. The forests that now surround the route were lovingly planted with the help of contributions to the Jewish National Fund—Karen Kayemet. The view widens close to Beit Shemesh. Here, you can take the train back to Jerusalem or continue to Tel Aviv. The train station is at Kikar Remez on Derech Hevron, reached by Buses 7, 8, 30, 38, 48, and 99. For schedule information call (02) 673-3764 at around 8 a.m. or 4 p.m.

Hevron (Hebron)

During a tour to Hevron, you have an opportunity to see what the headlines are written about. Artzeinu Tours offers trips once a week. You might have trepidations, but you should have greater trepidations about crossing the street in Jerusalem.

With Artzeinu, you leave Jerusalem at 9:15 a.m. and return at 6 p.m. The bus makes its first stop at **Rachel's Tomb**, just before Bethlehem,

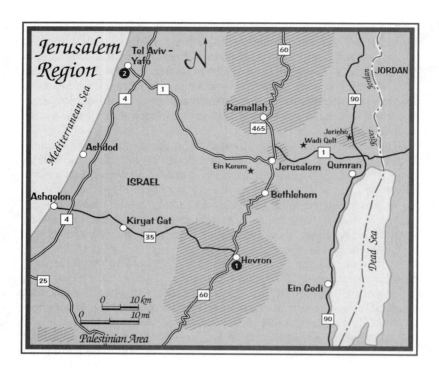

Regional Sights
1 Hevron
2 Tel Aviv

where Jacob's favorite wife is said to be buried. Surrounded by red string, the tomb attracts the fervently religious, many of whom will be making this trip with you. (Pieces of the red string, by the way, are also tied around the wrists of newborns and their mothers as good-luck amulets.)

The next stop will be at communities in **Gush Etzion**, an area that suffered harrowing attacks before Israel's independence. The stories of the residents' bravery and the atrocities committed against them are legion. Eventually, these few residents, defending their homes against Arab armies, especially the Egyptian army, could hold out no longer and the area fell to the Arabs.

182

Then comes Hevron, a city that evokes passions. In 1997, Israel turned over most of Hevron to the Palestine Authority but kept a small part, where intrepid, sometimes called crazy, Jews live. But there is reason to their "madness." Hevron is one of four holy Jewish cities, bound up with the Patriarch Abraham and the site of a burial place he bought for his wife, Sarah, in the first known real-estate transaction by a Hebrew purchaser in the Holy Land. The site, covered at least since Herod's time by a grand building (he didn't know how to build anything less), is known as the **Machpelah**. It is said to be the burial place not only of Sarah but also of Abraham, Isaac, Jacob, Rebekah, and Leah. David was crowned king in Hevron and ruled from there, until he established Jerusalem as the nation's capital.

Hevron, inextricably wound into Jewish history, has a past almost as bloody as Jerusalem's. One of the most chilling events was the 1929 slaughter of 67 Jewish men, women, and children, orchestrated by Haj Amin Husseini, whom the British appointed head of Jerusalem Moslems. The British evacuated the survivors, thus breaking more than 3,500 years of Jewish connection with Hevron.

With the Six-Day War, Gush Etzion and Hevron came under Israeli control. Survivors of the 1929 massacre and the 1947–1948 wars and their children returned to those areas despite initial Israeli government objections. With Israeli control, a dramatic change occurred at the Machpelah. During centuries of Moslem rule, Jews weren't allowed to get any closer to the Machpelah than the seventh step up to the entrance. Inside it to pray? Never. Now there is a synagogue inside, and the facilities are shared by Moslems and Jews.

The tour includes visits to the Machpelah, the old Jewish quarter, a rebuilt synagogue, and the new Jewish quarter. You will probably have a chance to meet with some residents and ask questions. *Details: Artzeinu Tours, phone: (02) 587-1718, fax: (02) 587-1719, e-mail: artzeinu@ netvision.net.il.*

Western Wall (Hasmonean) Tunnel

When you look at the Western Wall, you are seeing only part of it. Layers of buried stone sit below the exposed portion of the wall. Because of the centuries-old buildings against it, you can't see the Temple Mount as it once stood. Not long after Jerusalem was reunited, Israelis, every one of them an archaeologist at heart, began a project to get to the bottom of things (so to speak) at the Western Wall.

Millennia of debris slowly was stripped away, some by hand, until the entire length of the Western Wall came into view. But the project uncovered more than the wall and its bedrock. It revealed structures from Second

Temple Hasmonean times to the fourteenth century, lost under the accu-
mulation of years.

Among the finds were public rooms, a section of a Second Temple
road, a pool, a water tunnel, a Second Temple Hasmonean cistern, a four-
teenth-century cistern, the largest building stone ever uncovered in
Jerusalem, and the quarry from which Western Wall stones came. Also
discovered was a gate to the Temple Mount, the site of a synagogue during early Moslem times, and far more.

Today the excavation is an archaeological treasure trove open to visitors. When you enter the Western Wall Tunnel, most of it a thoroughfare
during Hasmonean times, a sound-and-light show introduces you to the
excavation. At several places, as you walk along a catwalk, it looks as if
there's an opening below your feet and you might fall through. Actually,
you're walking on windows, through which you can see down to bedrock
or water.

The tunnel first opened to visitors in 1990, both its entrance and exit
at the Western Wall Plaza. A new exit, so visitors wouldn't have to backtrack, opened into the Moslem Quarter in 1996. The new exit brought a
riot and bloodbath—the word in the Arab community was that Israelis
were digging under the Dome of the Rock. Fifteen people were killed, most
of them Israeli soldiers, in the rioting. The inflammatory results of rumor
echoed events in Hevron in 1929.

The fact was, the digging wasn't anywhere near the Dome of the Rock.
None of the excavations were under the Temple Mount; all were along
the outer western walls of the Temple Mount.

After the riots, the tunnel became one of the most popular sites in
Jerusalem, and tours now operate in total peace. The exit on the Via
Dolorosa brings additional, and welcome, tourists to the businesses there
and along el-Wad Street. *Details: (02) 627-1333 or (02) 627-1334 for individual reservations, usually Sun–Thu afternoons. Archaeological Tours has
tunnel visits three mornings a week. Zion Walking Tours has visits three
afternoons and one morning a week. Admission fee.*

Sherover and Haas Promenades

You know how you feel when someone who loves you enormously, and
whom you love back, opens his or her arms all the way and sweeps you
into them? That's the feeling you will have when you stand on the Sherover
and Haas Promenades. There is Jerusalem before you, as wide as you
can open your arms, welcoming you, receiving you, and there you are,
overwhelmed and a bit breathless.

The focus of this sweeping view is the golden shimmer of the Dome
of the Rock. From there, you can begin to pick out sites: the Old City walls,

the Mount of Olives, Silwan, the YMCA tower, dense western Jerusalem descending the slope to the left, the sparsely settled Arab neighborhoods with Jebel Mukaber below to the right, and the Augusta Victoria spire topping the space between Mount Scopus and the Mount of Olives.

You wish you were a vacuum cleaner that could suck this expansive view into your consciousness all at once. For help, if you are at the far end of the upper promenade (*tayelet* in Hebrew), go down the stairs, past the lavatories, and past the restaurant. Ahead you will find three stones that look like sawed-off pillars. Below them is a path to a "view finder," which identifies the major sites before you. You can descend the path into the gardens below, then climb back up. The view is hypnotic any time of day or night. The promenades are east of Derech Hevron in Armon HaNatziv, East Talpiot. Buses 8, 44, and 99 will take you there.

13
HEAVENLY JERUSALEM: CHURCHES AND SYNAGOGUES

The myriad alluring paths in Jerusalem can turn you into an explorer. The paths can take you outward and into the Jerusalem around you, or they can turn you inward and, eventually, back into yourself. This chapter is devoted to guiding you toward a discovery of yourself.

I have written much in this book about earthly Jerusalem—its movie theaters and its all-over-the-place pedestrians. Jerusalem is a real, down-to-earth city. But the greatest opportunity for discovery is in the spiritual realm.

There is an undeniable spiritual factor in Jerusalem that lifts the city into a heightened sphere. A clerk might be cranky, an ultra-Orthodox Jew and a secular Jew might carry on a shouting match, trash might sit on the streets because of a sanitation workers' strike. All this goes on. But no matter what else occurs, this is Jerusalem after all—and somehow heavenly. In Jerusalem, you feel closer to God—or at least to the divine spark within yourself.

Through its Jewish, Christian, and Moslem houses of worship, the spiritual avenues you can travel in eternal Jerusalem are many. But Jerusalem's spirituality isn't confined to its varied houses of worship. It flourishes at homes, hotel ballrooms, and ancient tombs. It flourishes whenever and wherever families and friends share life's milestones. It floods the streets when the city celebrates religious festivals and when it cries over the lost 6 million or its fallen defenders.

The paths have no end; the search is limitless. To pray in Jerusalem is the dream of people around the world. To Jews Jerusalem is God's home, to Christians it is where Jesus walked, to Moslems it is where Mohammed made his mythical visit.

King David made the city on the hill holy when, as one story goes, he bought a threshing floor from a Jebusite some three thousand years ago. He turned that space into an altar and the home for the Ark of the Covenant, and thus laid the foundation for the Holy City.

From that time, through destruction, dispersal, reconstruction, and gathering, Jerusalem has been the center of Jewish spiritual life. Jerusalem is named almost 700 times in the Torah, is included in daily prayers, and is in the fervent wish, "Next year in Jerusalem," said in the Diaspora at the end of Passover and the High Holidays. The name, pronounced in Hebrew "Ye-ru-shah-lay-im," is like the main theme of a symphony.

A thousand years after King David, Jesus, like all Jews, made his required Passover pilgrimage to the Holy City. His last days and his death took place in and around Jerusalem. Christians established magnificent churches here in Jesus' honor, and every place in the city that had a connection to him.

More than 600 years after Jesus, Moslems swept in from the Arabian peninsula and conquered Jerusalem. While Jerusalem isn't named in the Koran, nor did Mohammed ever actually come here, Jerusalem became the third holy city in Islam, after Mecca and Medina. Moslems believe that Mohammed's winged horse carried him to heaven from the rock atop Mount Moriah. Jews believe that was the location of their First and Second Temples. Jesus might have prayed at the Second Temple. Thus three great religions intertwine in one small spot on the globe.

A babble of prayer resounds through Jerusalem, with Moslems calling Friday their sacred day of the week, Jews keeping Friday sunset to Saturday night as their holy time, and Christians marking Sunday as their special day of the seven. During the rest of the week, each group designates several times of day for prayers.

Guests are usually welcome in every synagogue and almost every church, not only to view architecture and history but also to observe worship services. On a visit, keep in mind the proprieties. Some synagogues have strict dress codes for women (see Chapter 1: "Getting There"). Churches also expect a certain amount of decorum from women, such as no shorts or bare shoulders; some require women to cover their heads. Men are expected to cover their heads in a synagogue.

Entrance to the Church of the Holy Sepulchre, Old City

Visits to mosques are another matter. The religious leader of Moslem Jerusalem insists that non-Moslems, women as well as men, are welcome to observe services. But my own experience as well as that of others contradicts this claim. I've been shooed from Islamic services like a chicken strayed from its coop. However, a non-Moslem man might have better luck.

Following are brief descriptions of three churches and four synagogues. Each has a flavor not duplicated anywhere else. To call these churches and synagogues representative would be like saying that enchiladas represent all Mexican food.

In Christianity alone, there are vast differences in style and content between Protestant,

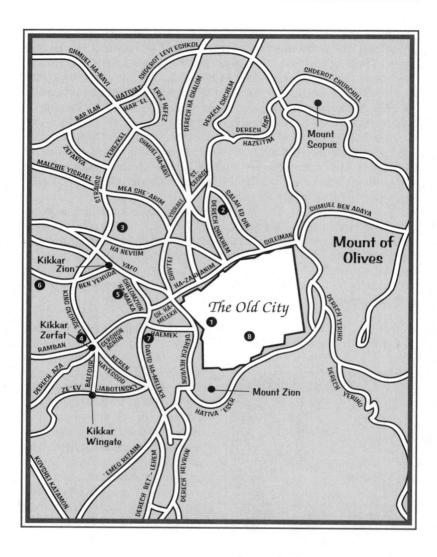

Greater Jerusalem Sights

1 St. Mark's Church
2 Cathedral of St. George the Martyr
3 Ethiopian Orthodox Church
4 Great Synagogue

5 Italian Synagogue
6 Urfali Synagogue
7 Hebrew Union College Synagogue
8 Istanbuli Synagogue

190

Roman Catholic (Latin), Eastern Orthodox, and monophysites or Oriental Orthodox churches. Similarly, each synagogue and mosque has its own *ta'am* (taste), as the Jews say.

So go taste. Try a church here, a synagogue there. And do try to visit a mosque. Discoveries will occur, some of them wonderful, no matter what your state of religious observance.

Churches

St. Mark's Church

St. Mark's Church is the Jerusalem home of the Syrian Orthodox congregation, reputed to be the oldest Christian denomination. The church originated in the first century.

You can find St. Mark's near Jaffa Gate at a bend in Ararat Road, in the opposite direction from the Armenian Quarter. A red sign on the wall identifies the church. The twelfth-century building is true to Jerusalem's churchly tradition: It is dark inside and far removed in spirit from the outside world.

Also typical for Jerusalem is the layering of new houses of worship on this location. A church that existed here in the seventh century was demolished by the Moslems. One of its pillars remains. A mosque and hospice then occupied the site, until Crusaders built the present church. The church and its monastery were restored in 1940.

St. Mark's is rich in tradition. A sixth-century inscription on a wall explains that this was the site of the house of another famous Mary, the mother of John the Evangelist, known as Mark. The Syrian Orthodox maintain the Last Supper and Washing of the Feet took place here and not the Coenaculum on Mount Zion. This, they also believe, is where the disciples gathered for holy communion. And it was to this house that Peter came after he was released from prison.

A painting of Mary and the baby Jesus hangs above a baptismal font opposite the colorful entrance. It is said that the portrait of Mary was painted from life by St. Luke (historians maintain it originated later, in the Byzantine Period) and that she was baptized here by the apostles. The small church is brightened by the shine of gold, decorating everything except the wooden pews. Enormous chandeliers hang overhead.

The Syrian Orthodox monks who serve a congregation of some 150 families, far less than the thousand that were here before the Six-Day War, maintain that many of their rites resemble Jewish practices. Religious rites are in Syriac, a language that is close to Aramaic, the language of the Talmud.

Perhaps the Church of St. Mark's major contribution to the city is its

191

youth marching band, which beats its drums and blows its horns through the lanes of the Old City at many Christian festivals. The youngsters invariably appear at Christmas and during Easter week. This, the oldest Christian denomination, was innovative in accepting girls into its marching band. *Details: (02) 628-3304. Mon–Sat 8–4. 8:30 Mass. Sunday services take place in its chapel in the Church of the Holy Sepulchre.*

Cathedral of St. George the Martyr

Sunday service at St. George's Episcopal-Anglican Cathedral on Nablus (Shchem) Road can seem like a meeting of the United Nations. A string of tourist buses arrive for the 11 a.m. English-language service, and worshippers from a number of countries descend. One Sunday they included a delegation from Sarawak, Borneo.

Step into the gate and you find yourself in a courtyard, with the cathedral entrance straight ahead. The cathedral looks the way a cathedral should, lofty and inspiring. Despite its soaring heights, this cathedral is actually quite small. Only about six people can sit on either side of the center aisle.

This is a bright, cheery cathedral, its white walls set off by black marble pillars. High above, the ceiling is composed of stained wooden slats. Each chair has hand-embroidered cushions for kneeling, each with its own artwork and message.

While the organ plays and the congregation sings a four-square hymn, the priest and his white-robed assistants (two of them young women) come to the front of the cathedral in a solemn procession, carrying a decorated golden cross with a lamb in its center, a Bible, and candles.

The service gives you a little bit of England, with traditional prayers and hymns, except that one priest is an Arab and another speaks with an American accent. They make much of the fact that visitors are in Jerusalem and that the service here can bring about "a minor incarnation."

A closed-off playroom for children is near the entrance, which explains the absence of wrigglers during the service—though one morning, at least six children accompanied one young woman to the altar for communion.

Outside, an archway from the courtyard leads to a garden. Inside, close to the center of the garden, is the church's old citron tree. As early as mid-May, enormous citrons ripen on the branches. *Details: (02) 628-3261. English-language Eucharist 8 and 11 a.m. Sun and 7 a.m. daily, evening prayer at 6 daily. Arabic Eucharist Sun at 9:30 a.m.*

Ethiopian Orthodox Church

A church that seems disarmingly plain after the darkness and rich decor of so many others is the circular Ethiopian Church at Ethiopian Street 10.

192

But this plainness is only relative, for the church actually contains a multitude of decorations and artwork, illuminated by sunlight streaming from the many high windows.

Entry is under a stone lintel topped by two Lions of Judah, the symbol of Ethiopia. Ethiopian kings claim descent from the Queen of Sheba and King Solomon.

The altar is in the center of the building, said to follow the design of the Second Temple. Around it are salmon-colored pillars with bright blue trim. Walls are hues of blue and on the ceiling is a splash of gold stars. Painted flowers decorate the tops of the encircling pillars. Many large icons hang from pillars and walls. It comes as a surprise that these paintings don't reflect Ethiopia: the faces are pale.

The Ethiopian Church has a New Testament written by hand on parchment. A priest pointed out to me with pride that that is how Jews make their Torah scrolls.

The church is divided into men's and women's sections, but not by partitions. Men and women simply congregate in separate areas during services. Wooden partitions do designate a separate monks' area. In it, directly opposite an opening to the altar, is a thronelike chair for the bishop.

For a 4 p.m. vesper service, worshippers enter the church, fall on their knees, and almost touch the floor with their foreheads in a motion that is more Moslem than Christian. The service begins in silent prayer. The bishop enters wearing a sumptuously embroidered red-and-gold gown with a green-and-gold cape. Then soft singing begins. The sound is repetitive and finally a drone is established. Eventually, the singing is like the wind or even an organ and becomes hypnotically enveloping. The vesper service becomes a sort of reverie. At the church's Easter services, drums add to the sounds of the distinctive singing.

The church maintains a gift shop in the courtyard near the entrance. Inside are Ethiopian-made baskets, embroidered

Interior, Ethiopian Orthodox Church

items, and horsetail fans. *Details: (02) 628-6871. Vespers 4 p.m. week-days, 3 p.m. Sun. Liturgical services 4 a.m. weekdays, 6 a.m. Sun.*

The Beit Knesset (Synagogue)

The English word *synagogue* comes from the Greek word for assembly. The Hebrew name for a synagogue is *beit knesset,* which has a simpler, more down-to-earth connotation. It means meetinghouse.

Each beit knesset is strikingly different from the next. It isn't simply a matter of Orthodox or non-Orthodox—at least 99 percent of Israel's Jewish houses of worship are Orthodox. Each beit knesset reflects, first, the distinctions between Ashkenazim and Sephardim. After that division, each takes on the special character of the major ethnic background of its worshippers.

The **Great Synagogue** in Hechal Shlomo is the grandest, but to me the most off-putting Jerusalem synagogue, particularly on Friday nights and major holidays. It is stuffy and distant—at least from the woman's designated bird's-eye view near the roof. The greatest interest in this synagogue lies in the fact that the prime minister might be seen in prayer here. Menahem Begin was a regular; Yitzhak Rabin, never. He preferred tennis on Saturday morning. Binyamin Netanyahu? Sometimes.

Some beit knessets built by Hasidic sects are even larger than the Great Synagogue. They might be enormous, but surely not stuffy. But I don't know if women get even a bird's-eye view there. I am happy to ignore the so-called grand and glorious in favor of grassroots, neighborhood houses of worship. These are the most enjoyable and informal.

But while visitors are welcome at certain times, women face a challenge. From puberty, the sexes are strictly separated in synagogues, so as not to distract the weaker sex from concentrating on his prayers. So a woman visitor first must figure out where the women's section is located and how to get there. At some synagogues, men and women enter through the same main door and then separate. At others, women must go around a side of the building and climb stairs to the women's section. It might be confusing. If a woman blunders into the men's section, she causes a minor ruckus as the men turn (some smiling benignly) and wave her off in the proper direction.

The separation of men and women in synagogues can be disconcerting to a lot of Western Jews accustomed to more liberal ways. In the Orthodox synagogues, women (if they can see at all through curtains or latticework) are merely observers of men when anything physical takes place during services—like removing the Torah scrolls from the ark and carrying them to the bima. In some tiny synagogues women can't even see that much, for they are in a separate room.

Still, if a woman is able to see, it can be immensely pleasurable and somewhat awesome to watch the warmth and camaraderie among the men. But watching isn't the same as doing. At festive times, women are free to dance with each other, but attention focuses on the men's dancing. It seems implicit that women are the act's "second bananas."

Ultra-Orthodox synagogues are sticklers when it comes to women's dress (see Chapter 1: "Getting There"). Other synagogues are more laissez-faire, as long as good taste is used. Men need only be sure that they wear a head covering and, in ultra-Orthodox synagogues, long pants. A clean white shirt is formal enough for men in most synagogues.

The greatest difference between worship service in synagogues and churches is that in churches the feeling is of reverence and restraint; in synagogues it is of reverence and exuberance. Synagogues often house a constant buzz, either from children running between their father's legs, their mothers in the women's section, or the men greeting and chatting with old friends. Occasionally, there can be a feeling of chaos.

While this activity might strike people not used to Orthodox services as undignified, I'm inclined to look on it the way composer John Cage looked on extraneous sounds during a concert. "It's all music," he said once as a fire engine went by during his performance.

Jews pray three times a day: morning, afternoon, and evening. But

Ultra-Orthodox Jewish men leave the Western Wall after prayers.

195

the custom is for afternoon prayers to take place late enough to merge with evening prayers. Prayer times are determined by the setting and rising of the sun. The *Jerusalem Post* Friday edition tells when Shabbat begins and ends.

A festive dinner at home follows Friday night services. A *kiddush*—a blessing over wine—usually takes place after Saturday morning services at the synagogue. The kiddush might include cookies and cakes and might be even more elaborate if there is a celebration. You are invited, simply because you are there.

Assuming the kiddush takes place outside, as you leave the synagogue someone will be standing by the door with small paper cups of wine or grape juice. Take one and hold it. Do not so much as sip until after the rabbi or male in charge chants the blessing over wine. Then it's bottoms up. Usually, there is a blessing over bread before you can dive into the cakes, but follow the lead of the crowd.

Italian Synagogue

At the entrance to the Italian Synagogue at Rehov Hillel 27, these words are written: "Do not leave this place in haste." A person wouldn't want to, especially if he is the male of the species and may enjoy a clear, unobstructed view during services of the synagogue's glories.

The Italian Synagogue occupies the far corner of a large building that has one side on Rehov Hillel. The synagogue is at the other end of the courtyard, on the left side and up one flight of stairs for men, up another flight for women. The entrance for men is across the hall from the Museum of Italian-Jewish Art.

The design of this beit knesset is authentically and lavishly Baroque. The interior belonged to a 1719 synagogue in Conegliano Veneto, some 60 kilometers from Venice. It was removed in its entirety after the Holocaust, when Jews no longer lived in that city, and was installed in Jerusalem in 1952. Since the Jerusalem location has slightly different proportions than the original building, the layout isn't identical to what it once was. Nevertheless, the Italian Synagogue is a brilliant sight with its shining chandeliers, gilt curlicues around the ark, and strings of stucco grapevines along its walls.

In front of the lavish ark is a curtain with row upon row of bright colors. From the ark comes a Torah scroll with a high silver crown topping its velveteen cover, its silver finials tinkling as it is carried around the bima.

Upstairs, a narrow balcony lines three sides of the synagogue. It swiftly becomes crowded. Women must peer through carved lattices that are pushed away from the balcony at an angle. But in a certain place a woman can sit in the balcony and peer down at the open Torah over the shoulders of the reader. Ancient *ketubahs* (marriage contracts) cover the balcony walls.

The service is neither Sephardi nor Ashkenazi. It is based on ancient Roman traditions. Primarily, it's a solo for the reader and person leading the service. Sometimes, especially on the High Holidays, you really know this place is Italian, for it can seem as if the cantor is delivering his solos with many operatic flights. Only at the end of the service does the congregation join in with two rousing songs.

One Saturday morning, a young man was called to the bima to read from the Torah as an honor before his forthcoming marriage. When he finished, his future in-laws, of Tunisian background, flung candies from the women's section in their traditional North African way of wishing him a sweet marriage.

As the candies whacked the wooden floor, the Italians were shocked. Nothing so indecorous happens in their synagogue, they grumbled. Clucking their tongues, they insisted, "That's not Italian."

Urfali Synagogue
The beit knesset of the Urfalim—Kurds from the town of Urfa, politically in eastern Turkey but culturally and emotionally within the ancient borders of Kurdistan—is at Rehov Bezalel 19. Men go upstairs from the sidewalk and enter directly into the sanctuary. Women enter a door at the right of that entrance and must climb a flight of steep stairs that demands the agility of a cat. Then they find themselves in a small balcony.

There, a lacy white curtain hides the women from men's wandering eyes below. The curtain is parted briefly during the reading from the Torah and while the Torah scroll is joyously carried around the room. At that time, some of the women blow kisses toward the Torah.

And if there is a special *simha*—a happy occasion such as an impending marriage—the curtain is thrown back again so the entire congregation may see and participate, even if from afar.

The Urfali Synagogue is in one of Jerusalem's poorer neighborhoods, and the women's dress reflects that poverty. Many wear scarves tied under their chins, babushka style. Others are bareheaded.

The building is freestanding; windows on all four sides let in a flood of light. The walls are whitewashed, and the room has a particularly cheerful atmosphere. Six chandeliers hang from the ceiling; two are light violet in color. The bima is made of stone and has large, round glass decorations at each corner. Benches around the bima are covered by red Turkish rugs.

The most startling sight to a newcomer to Sephardi synagogues is that

197

in many, fluorescent lights snake around the ark. Here, green lights in the shape of a crown top two stone tablets that contain the Ten Commandments. The commandments themselves are encircled by blue lights and seem to rest on a jagged green outline of the Old City walls. Red lights make a colorful emphasis below. All this tops the white stone ark, whose curtain is embroidered with palm trees, an ancient symbol of Israel. The Urfali worshippers are energetic participants during services. The reader says the prayers loudly and enthusiastically.

One Saturday morning, the simha was special blessings for the arrival of a new baby boy, who would have his *brit milah* (ritual circumcision) during the coming week. The father was called to the bima and given the honor of reading a portion of the Torah. Upstairs, the baby's grandmother went from woman to woman in the balcony and poured cologne into their hands. Later, she gave each woman a little sack of hard candy. When the father finished his reading, the women showered the candies on him while uttering ululating cries.

On that particular morning, after services ended, women shook hands and took a heady whiff from a jar full of aromatic greenery, a reminder of sweet Shabbat, before they descended the steep stairs. Meanwhile, downstairs, the men also shook hands, and in the Eastern custom of honoring someone else, after each handshake lightly kissed the knuckles on his own hand that had been held by the other man.

Hebrew Union College Synagogue

Hebrew Union College (HUC) on King David Street is the Reform movement's Jerusalem home. When the Reform movement bought this property in the preunified Jerusalem years, people said it was crazy: the college was right under Jordanian guns from the Old City. The King David Hotel stubbornly sat up the street and kept the college company.

These days, what plot of real estate in Jerusalem could be considered more prime? Now the college has the grandiose new Hilton Hotel on one side and the la-di-da expensive King David's Village on its backside.

Reform rabbinic and cantorial students from overseas and Israel spend their first year here. The Shabbat morning service strongly reflects their presence. What you see are men and women sitting side by side with many women wearing kippahs and tallits. You also see a lot of young people—all those students and their friends. What you hear is lots of music, sung by students and the congregation with piano and perhaps flute accompaniment. HUC encourages new musical settings for the prayers. The music is largely unique to HUC and can range from "generically spiritual" to hints of the Eastern European shtetl to 1960s American rock.

The room in which the service takes place is large and basically uninteresting. The congregation is almost completely American, including many tourists, with a few Israelis. With so many students, it's a lively congregation, given to clapping with any music that has a strong rhythm.

The service itself is abbreviated. Only three people come to the bima to read from the Torah. And instead of the added prayers one hears at the end of Orthodox services, this congregation hears a sermon, which is in English and often veers into left-wing politics.

Afterward, there might be a tour of the college complex, famed for its "Hanging Gardens of Babylon" courtyard, again the work of the ubiquitous architect Moshe Safdie.

Istanbuli Synagogue

One of the four Sephardi synagogues in the Old City, the Istanbuli might be the hardest to find. The entrance is on Rehov Beit-El. As if you were heading to the Western Wall, walk on the right size of the Jewish Quarter plaza and up some stairs. The door to the Istanbuli Synagogue will be on the right. Enter and go downstairs.

The Istanbuli doesn't have services every day or even every week—only on Saturday morning before the new Jewish month or on special occasions. The small and almost all-English-speaking congregation exists because of determination to preserve the ancient Sephardi traditions of this synagogue.

Sephardi Jews became an important presence in the Ottoman Empire after their expulsion from Spain in 1492. The Turkish sultan invited them to his empire, saying that Spain's loss was his gain. Jews flourished in the Turkish empire for centuries.

Few of the people who come to the Istanbuli Synagogue have direct Spanish roots. One man is from Surinam, where his first language was Dutch. Another is from Cuba. Several English-born congregants do claim Spanish descent. Because of the goal of preservation, the melodies heard here are quite different from those heard in an Ashkenazi synagogue. Indeed, one Ashkenazi visitor asked, "Why do you sing those awful melodies?" At first the melodies do seem remote, but you get used to them. Adding a certain otherworldliness here is that almost the entire synagogue is under a high dome, and sounds resonate as if in a cathedral. Women don't sit in a balcony but next to the men, separated by a thin gauze curtain.

This small synagogue is like a pearl. It is unadorned, simple in its way, but luminous from this very simplicity. The Torah rests in a midnight-blue case and is set on its end for reading from the bima, Sephardi style. At the top of the high dome is the only color in the room, arches filled with blue, green, and a bit of orange cut glass.

The holy ark and the bima are made of carved wood, brought here from a synagogue no longer in use in post-Holocaust Italy. A picture on the wall near the entrance hints at the fate of the original ark and bima. It shows the extensive damage wrought by Arabs while Jordan occupied the Old City.

As in most synagogues, children wander around during the service. One Shabbat morning, the prayer leader's seven-year-old daughter, in a long pink dress, wrapped herself in the end of the gauze dividing curtain and twirled herself around. But when her father walked toward the ark to receive the Torah, she was right by his side.

14
FAMILY TIES

To partake of Israel means to partake of family life. From the *brit milah* (ritual circumcision) of the infant son to his first haircut at age three to his bar mitzvah at 13 to marriage and finally death, the family and the extended family gather. In Judaism, when you share in these events, you are performing a *mitzvah* (loosely translated as "a good deed"), and you are sanctified.

It might come as a surprise that here, the extended family encompasses people who other societies regard as strangers. Israelis tell you that when you are in Israel, you are with family. Their behavior bears this out. When they celebrate major events in their own lives or their cousins' or nephews'—it's all the same to them—they will invite you. *Invite* might be too formal a word. They expect you to come to family events. And their invitations aren't for Jews only. Non-Jews too feel as if they suddenly discovered relatives they never knew they had.

You might be invited to a wedding or a bar mitzvah or a brit milah. You might never have laid eyes on the bride or groom or any of the other actors in these major life events. The person who invited you might be only an aunt or cousin of the hosts. What's more, the invitation doesn't mean you only are to observe the ceremony. It also means you are to stay and eat. Indeed, often the ceremony and the food are in the same room.

Rabbi Shlomo Riskin, holding the oldest of twin boys, reads prayers at a brit milah. The happy father looks on.

Because of that, you might hesitate to accept the invitation. You might feel it would be an imposition for you to show up. After all, you don't even know the host family. You'd probably never dream of accepting such an invitation back home. But, my dear, this is Jerusalem. Go. In Israel, joy is to be shared. That's all there is to that. You will be welcomed. You will be fulfilling a mitzvah. In Judaism, it is the host's mitzvah to welcome the stranger. It is the stranger's mitzvah to share the host's happiness.

Brit Milah

Let's go to the beginning. Ceremony and tradition follow a Jewish child all his or her life. If the child is a girl, even though she isn't the focus of certain rituals in Orthodox circles, she participates in all of them.

Boy babies are ushered into their lives as Jews with a brit milah, the ritual circumcision, when they are eight days old—when they are over the shock of being born and when they will bleed the least.

Yes, it might seem strange to celebrate while the baby loses a little part of himself. And yes, it does seem a bit scary because there is that tense moment just before the *mohel,* the circumciser, does his job. But it is we who are tense. Thanks to that great invention, baby aspirin, the baby might be halfway in dreamland at this moment. Also, mohels are far more expert than pediatricians.

The baby is held during the circumcision by someone honored with this responsibility. The grand chair that sits empty nearby is Elijah's. A story goes that because Elijah had no faith in the Jewish people's survival, God told Elijah he would be proved wrong by having to attend every brit milah to witness the group's continuation. With the baby having symbolically entered a covenant with God, after the circumcision his name is announced to the guests. They nod with approval.

No one wants to hear a baby cry, and it usually lasts just for a moment as he's scooped into his parents' loving arms and is lulled with a little wine. Now you can relax. And now you can reflect on this tradition going back some 3,500 years.

The ceremony usually takes place first thing in the morning, before people go to work. But there's a big spread of food, for Judaism says not only the heart and mind should enjoy but the body, too. Afterward, going back to bed might seem more tempting than going to work.

The celebration isn't common, but when a baby girl was born to my Iraqi friends, the parents held a "brita," as they called it. They hired a hall, a caterer, a band, and video and still photographers and had a blast. The eight-day-old baby girl wore a white dress, white socks, and a big white ribbon around her bald head. It seemed as if everyone at the party danced around the room with her. How the mother survived all this, I don't know.

Her baby often dozed through it. And maybe the family paid off the brita in time for their daughter's wedding.

Bar Mitzvah: Rite of Passage

Monday and Thursday mornings are the prime times boys become bar mitzvah at the Western Wall. Twelve or twenty bar mitzvah ceremonies could be going on simultaneously. They also occur on Saturday mornings, but weekdays are more popular, because then people who live beyond walking distance may drive.

The bar mitzvah marks a Jewish boy's coming of age religiously. From this point on, he assumes all the religious responsibilities of an adult male. Having reached the age of 13, the bar mitzvah boy will read from the Torah while wearing for the first time a tallit (if the event isn't on Saturday) and tfillin (phylacteries). The latter are two small leather boxes, each containing parchment inscribed with relevant quotations from Hebrew scripture. As a reminder of the commandments, first the left arm is bound with a leather cord, then one box is strapped to the forehead.

One Thursday morning in March, it was Elon's day. Despite the auspicious occasion, he, like most 13-year-old boys, still looked like a gawky kid. The night before, his parents had held an open house, and family, family friends, and friends' friends showed up. They brought gifts and were served cakes, cookies, bourekas, and other foods cooked in Elon's grandparents' native Iraqi style. Spurred on by wine and brandy, the men especially sang loud and strong into the night. Afterward, when he finally climbed into bed, Elon was too excited to sleep.

At 8:30 in the morning, under a gray sky, Elon's bar mitzvah began at the Western Wall. He and male relatives and male family friends gathered around a high metal table in the men's prayer section. They were only a few feet from a fence separating them from the spectators' area. That way, women attending Elon's bar mitzvah, standing behind the fence, could be as close as possible.

While a video-cameraman recorded the occasion, Elon, a slender boy with olive skin and large, earnest brown eyes, began reading the prayers. For the occasion, he wore a white long-sleeved shirt, white trousers, and a white kippah. A yellow T-shirt under his shirt showed at his neck.

At a certain point in the prayers, Elon's grandmother's brother, Mordechai, draped the boy in a white linen tallit with black stripes at either end, ceremoniously covering his head for a moment. Elon lifted an edge of the prayer shawl to his lips and kissed it. This was now his very own tallit, an outward sign of his new responsibility.

Mordechai then rolled up Elon's left shirtsleeve, wrapped tfillin around

204

the boy's thin arm, and centered a small shiny black box anchored by a leather strap on Elon's forehead.

Prayers continued. Elon was escorted by the men to a corner of the Western Wall where they walked under an archway into a synagogue inside a tunnel. A few minutes later, they emerged. Elon proudly carried a Torah scroll in a metal case with fluttering, colorful scarves tied to it. He set it on the metal table for the next stage in his ceremony.

When the men and Elon returned to their prayer stand near the fence, the women, as they did at every high point in the ceremony, burst forth in high-pitched ululations and pelted the bar mitzvah boy with hard, wrapped candies. Little children, both boys and girls, playing around the prayer stand during the service, scrambled to pick them up. Grown men, too, reached for some, whisked the hard candies out of their wrappers, and popped them into their mouths.

With the resumption of the ceremony the sun emerged, bright and warm. It would be a lovely day, after all. The metal Torah case was opened, and Elon read from the scroll with assurance. He looked pleased with himself (but what an advantage he had over the bar mitzvah boys and bat mitzvah girls around the world: After all, Hebrew is his native language).

Afterward, he and the men returned the Torah to its place in the

Bar mitzvah celebration

tunnel synagogue. When they emerged into the sunlight, instead of Elon carrying the Torah, this time the men carried Elon. He was on their shoulders, and they were singing lustily.

The cameraman walked backward in front of them to preserve the precious scene. A rent-an-accordionist serenaded the happy group. Seeing the joyous procession, the women grew more fervent in their ululating and candy throwing.

When Elon was set on his feet, a piece of candy remained lodged in the folds of his tallit. He was smiling broadly now—for the first time all morning, but still more like a kid than a man.

This high point in a young man's life was being played out, with minor variations, all over the worship area beside the wall. Songs by one group collided with songs from another group in the musical style of Charles Ives, while ululations rose and fell and candies glinted in the sun as they sailed through the air.

Time was, the celebration after the bar mitzvah could take place right there in the huge plaza in front of the wall. But no more. What with all the elegant rebuilding in the area, that kind of Israeli down-homeness has been banished.

Instead, Elon's parents led their guests away from the wall, out of the plaza, across the street, down some stairs, and into a parking lot. There, they hauled food out of their car. Cookies, cakes, bourekas, fruit, and brandy were consumed on the spot. That night, at a rented hall, the real celebration would take place with a sit-down dinner, a band, endless dancing, and the video-cameraman.

Should you be invited to a bar mitzvah, if you are a female and confined merely to watching, make the most of the situation. Arm yourself with a sack of wrapped candies for pelting. And if the woman beside you ululates, open your mouth, strike a high pitch, and let it rip.

Weddings: Oh, How We Danced!

In Israeli terms, the young couple's wedding was an intermarriage. The bride was an American from a Long Island family of Ashkenazi background. Her parents weren't Orthodox. The Sephardi groom was the son of strictly observant Iraqi immigrants. Joanne and Avner had known each other for five years before they were married in Jerusalem, in exuberant festivities replete with Jewish disarray. (More and more such cultural mergers are taking place in Israel. I know of two Norwegian sisters whose husbands' families are Iranian.)

Guests were invited at 7 p.m. to a hall that is among Jerusalem's popular wedding sites. One large room would hold the prenuptial reception, the wedding ceremony, the dinner, and the festivities. Tables were set for a sit-down dinner for 150. Fewer than that number had been formally invited, but friends of relatives and friends of friends were expected to show up.

Joanne and Avner's families stood in a reception line, greeting guests as they arrived. The next stop after the reception line was a long table of appetizers—hot peppers, pickles, hummus, marinated beets, a creamed vegetable salad, and lots more to be scooped up by huge, twisted buns. Against one of the long walls, a band of young musicians was getting itself organized.

When Joanne and Avner walked into the room together, women emitted high-pitched ululation, and the band burst into a song that inspired people to stop eating and start dancing. Men and women danced separately, of course, for this was an Orthodox wedding. Men put their arms over each other's shoulders as they danced and shouted out the words to the song. Later, they formed two lines facing each other and moved toward each other and away, back and forth. Meanwhile, women had their own enthusiastic circle dance going.

Evening prayer time arrived. The music stopped, and the men went into a corner, bowed their heads slightly, and let their bodies sway to the rhythm of their chanted prayers. While this was going on, Joanne, in a white dress and with the veil behind her head, sat in the center of the room in an elaborate white peacock chair, like a throne, and was greeted by guests.

After prayers ended, she remained there while the men gathered at a table, and two witnesses and Avner signed the *ketubah*—the marriage contract guaranteeing the groom's economic support of the bride. Presiding over things at this point was the nation's chief Sephardi rabbi, whose presence bestowed great honor on the marriage and the groom's family. The rabbi looked regal in a blue turban and a black caftan with yellow embroidery outlining the front opening.

With the ketubah signed, the wedding could begin. Avner approached his bride-to-be in her elaborate chair and, tenderly smiling at her, gently lifted the veil from behind her head and allowed it to fall over her face—a tradition said to date from the time the patriarch Joseph found he had married Leah instead of Rachel because he didn't see his bride's face before the wedding.

Four men appeared, each holding a pole attached to a green satin *chuppah*—the canopy under which the couple would stand during the ceremony. The men arranged themselves so the chuppah was upright in a clearing in front of the band. With Joanne, Avner, and the rabbi now in their places under the canopy, guests and family crowded around them. The crush of people close to the young couple obstructed the view for most of the other guests. A voice over a microphone pleaded for everybody to take seats at the tables, so all could see. Some actually did, probably because they had no hope of seeing the ceremony in the first place and figured they might as well save their feet. But most remained pressed in close. Only a few caught sight of the bride slowly walking around her husband-to-be seven times.

After the rabbi's readings, with a man now on either side of the couple pulling a tallit taut above their heads, Joanne and Avner took a sip of wine from a silver goblet. Avner placed a plain gold ring on Joanne's finger and said in Hebrew, "With this ring, you are consecrated unto me according to the laws of Moses and Israel." The rabbi read the terms of the ketubah and together with other men chosen for the honor took turns chanting seven time-honored blessings. The couple took another sip of wine, Avner stomped on a glass wrapped in a napkin placed at his feet, the glass shattered with an explosive pop, and the two were married. The ceremony lasted 15 minutes.

With a shout of joy from family and friends and ululations from the women, the band struck up celebratory music and dancing resumed. No shmaltzy public kiss between the couple sealed the deal, but they left the crowd for their first married moments in privacy. When they returned to the festivities, Avner's male friends and relatives lifted him high in a chair and carried him about the room. He was ecstatic. His outstretched arms kept time to the surging music. Joanne's women friends and relatives lifted her, too, on a chair. Above the crowd, the couple's arms reached out to each other. Later, the men scooped up Avner's father and carried him on their shoulders. Now off their perches, Avner danced with the men and Joanne danced with the women. When Joanne stopped to rest, she took a seat in front of the male dancers, who seemed to perform especially for her. Meanwhile, her American parents watched, as if in as daze, the dancers' abandonment and the guests' noisy celebration.

Between the athletic, energetic dances, the guests (if not the bride and groom) ate dinner. The first course was a pastry cup filled with meat. Heaping bowls of rice, corn, and potatoes and a variety of salads were on each table, so guests could help themselves. Then waiters went from person to person to serve chicken, beef, and schnitzel. Dessert was cakes and the fresh fruit that was each table's centerpiece. Steaming Turkish coffee was the finishing touch. While each table had been laden with mitz, brandy, and arak, and the alcoholic beverages were imbibed freely, no one seemed to be drunk. Boisterously happy, yes; inebriated, no.

The dancing became more and more adventurous and flamboyant. Four men formed a circle with their arms on each other's shoulders. Faster and faster their circle turned, when suddenly two of the men's feet came off the floor and their bodies stretched away from the circle as if they were carried by the wind. In another demonstration of bravado, a young man put a bottle filled with water and flowers on his kippah-covered head and proceeded to dance. He held everyone's rapt attention and drew applause when he performed push-ups, still with that bottle perfectly balanced.

And the band played on. Israeli pop music is a mixture of secular and sacred words. One song includes words of the Rebbe Nachman of Bratislav. "Gesher Tzar Me'od" says, "The world is a narrow bridge; the important thing is not to be afraid." One wouldn't assume that such advice would make for a hit song, but that is what the song became and now is

Jerusalem Scene

Yelena and Victor were two young immigrants from Russia. They met and fell in love in Israel. When they decided to marry, neighbors in the Jerusalem building in which Yelena and her family lived realized that the family didn't have the wherewithal for a wedding party.

So the neighbors in that building and elsewhere in the area got together and put on the wedding for the couple. A family living in a single home made their kitchen available and opened their spacious garden so the wedding could fulfill tradition and take place under the stars. Neighbors cooked and cooked for the event. Someone in the neighborhood wrangled donations of liquor. Someone else secured a band. Another person persuaded a particularly lovely hotel at the edge of the city to host the couple on their wedding night. And the rabbi, an Anglo-Saxon from Denver who invited me to the wedding, not only performed the wedding ceremony but also spent the day barbecuing chicken for the event.

Well into the celebration, Yelena's mother took the microphone and eloquently described how they arrived in Israel knowing no one, bringing with them practically nothing, and questioning their future. But now, like a miracle, they had neighbors, friends and, best of all, a community. "This is Israel," she said. The tears in her eyes were matched by those in the listeners'.

something of a standard. At this wedding, as the song, slow at first but increasing in speed, reached its exultant climax, it gave family and friends yet another chance to express wild jubilation.

Another colorful wedding event is the Yemenite Jewish henna ceremony. Few Jews remained in Yemen at the southern tip of the Arabian peninsula after "Operation Magic Carpet" flew the bulk of the population to Israel in 1948. Since then, Yemenite Jews have made major cultural contributions to Israel.

By now, weddings of Yemenite Jews more and more resemble typical Israeli weddings, except for the henna ceremony that takes place a few nights earlier. It proceeds as follows:

On this night, the bride and groom wear traditional Yemenite festive dress as if they were royalty. The groom is bedecked for the occasion in a silk caftan, necklaces, and silk scarves. The bride wears a silk caftan embroidered with gold thread and decorated with layers and layers of ornaments, from coins and trinkets to gold and silver filigree bracelets. Under the caftan, the bride wears "harem" pants that hang loose but are held tight to the ankles with embroidered leggings. Ornaments attached to her pants jingle with every step she takes.

On her head is a magnificent, bejeweled, conical headdress, almost like a helmet, part of it coming down to her chin on the sides. Fresh flowers frame the tall headdress. Only the bride's face can be seen, and, whoever she is, she always looks stunningly beautiful.

An esteemed, older female relative applies the red henna, a pasty substance, to the bride's palms and soles. In Yemen, henna designs were drawn on the bride's face, but that part of the ceremony has been dropped here. Henna is also applied to the hands of the groom and relatives.

Guests, too, are included. At a henna ceremony I attended, a hunk of henna was pressed into the palm of my hand, and I clutched it for hours. I think I was supposed to sleep like that. At any rate, my palm was orange for days afterward.

The red dye is said to give protection from the "evil eye." The idea is that bad spirits are fooled into thinking that this ceremony is the wedding, so then they won't be around at the real thing. Chanting, singing, dancing to drums and cymbals, and eating are also part of the celebration.

The henna ceremony is so colorful and is considered so special in Israel that often in "mixed" marriages, if the bride is not Yemenite but is marrying a man who is, she will go through the ritual.

Funerals

The Hebrew word for funeral means "to accompany." Jews' responsibility is to accompany the dead body to its final resting place.

When you see a large white sign with black letters and a black border affixed to a wall, you know that someone close by has died. In ultra-Orthodox neighborhoods, a car drives through the streets with someone using a loudspeaker to announce the name of the deceased and when and where the funeral will take place. The word needs to be spread as quickly as possible. Often Jewish funerals take place the day of the death.

People gather at a memorial hall for eulogies (if the time of the year and the deceased's wishes allow them). Before that, mourners tear their clothing. After the eulogies, the mourners follow the body to the hearse.

If time allowed planning, buses could be waiting for the trip to the cemetery. In theory, widows and children aren't supposed to be at the cemetery. But a Jerusalem tradition gets around that by having the widow and children walk in front of the hearse.

Jewish dead are buried in four places in the Jerusalem area. The Mount of Olives cemetery is the oldest. The most usual location is Har HaMenuhot, the official Jerusalem cemetery at the city's western edge, where Jerusalem residents receive a free grave. You can see the cemetery if you look up on the left side of road that leads to Tel Aviv. Another is the cemetery at Beit Shemesh, west of Jerusalem, where the Association of Americans and Canadians in Israel owns plots, as do several other organizations and religious groups. The fourth Jewish burial area in Jerusalem is the Military Cemetery atop Mount Herzl.

The first funeral you attend in Jerusalem could be a shock, because of the Jerusalem tradition of not using coffins. Only soldiers are buried in coffins, and these are of the simplest wood. In the Jerusalem tradition, the deceased, even former prime ministers like Menahem Begin, are simply encased in a shroud and lowered into the ground. At Beit Shemesh, since it is outside Jerusalem, coffins are optional.

The graveside service includes Kaddish (if 10 men are present), the traditional prayer often mistakenly called "the prayer for the dead." The prayer contains no words relating to death; it is simply a prayer, with a powerful rhythm, to glorify God. A prayer to God the Merciful and Psalms follow.

The sons of the deceased begin to cover the body with earth, followed by other men, then the grave diggers finish. Those attending form two parallel lines, and mourners walk away from the grave site and pass through these lines to hear their first condolences. Said a rabbi, "It's like the whole world is comforting you."

A source of water is just outside the cemetery gate, where those at the funeral can fulfill the tradition of washing their hands before leaving.

The family goes to the home of one of its members where shiva, the seven days of mourning, will be observed (*shiva* is Hebrew for seven).

211

Usually the first things eaten after a funeral are hard-boiled eggs, which symbolize the continuity of life. Neighbors and friends bring the family food during this week.

It's at this home that people pay condolence calls, but often not until the third day, when mourners are beginning to come out of their initial shock. Visits take place day and evening, but visitors try to avoid meal and nap times.

Visitors aren't supposed to bring anything, but it isn't forbidden. Sometimes a charity box is at the home for people to make contributions in the name of the deceased.

Traditionally, visitors will find mourners sitting on low chairs or pillows on the floor and wearing slippers or socks. The tradition is also for visitors to wait until mourners acknowledge their presence and for mourners to speak first of the dead. But these days, there is flexibility. Don't worry about what to say. Your presence is more eloquent than words, but if you have an anecdote or memory of the deceased, tell it.

If the deceased left a son, he begins a year of reciting Kaddish at prayers. If 10 men are present in the house when prayer times arrive, they recite Kaddish together. Usually, men make a point of being at the shiva location early in the morning and late in the afternoon for Kaddish.

After the seven days are over, mourners leave the home for the first time since the funeral. They might merely walk around the block, but they discover that children are playing, birds are singing, and life continues. It's almost like waking up. The walk is also a public statement that mourners are returning to their normal routines.

In Israel, the gravestone is set after 30 days, not a year as usually is the case in North America. Notices might appear in the newspapers. You're on your own to get to the grave this time. Prayers are from the Psalms, and one by one, the verses' first letters spell the name of the deceased.

A Jewish tradition when visiting a grave site is to leave a stone. But in Israel, perhaps because flowers are an important part of the economy, it is a new custom to leave flowers at grave sites. That is especially so in the military cemeteries, where the young men buried there often are compared to flowers cut down too soon.

15
THE CYCLE OF
CELEBRATIONS

At any given moment, somebody is celebrating or commemorating something in Jerusalem, and a cacophony of ringing bells, muezzin calls, and dancing in the streets fills the Holy City's sweet air.

As Moslem, Jewish, and Christian Sabbaths follow one after the other, week after week, so Moslem, Jewish, and Christian holidays follow each other, one after the other, year after year.

Here, in "the navel of the world," time is measured in cycles of anticipation and experience. Members of each faith count their year by the events in their religion. For all, preparation feeds the excitement of the approach of a particular event. Then the event itself blossoms forth and is savored. And so, yet another landmark in the year becomes shared communal history.

But five major cycles of anticipation and experience revolve simultaneously in Jerusalem. Each within its own time frame, Jewish, Moslem, Roman Catholic and Protestant, Eastern Orthodox, and Armenian Orthodox events often overlap. With all this, Jerusalem is like a person who wears multiple wristwatches so he or she can contemplate several time zones at once.

Of course the dominant time zone, the one with the most festivities that meet the eye and affect the course of the year, is Jewish. Jews who didn't grow up in Israel may be astounded when they experience religious holidays here. For a change, the world revolves around them. Here Christmas and Easter are just ordinary days to most people, and it is the minority Christians who are being deeply worshipful while everybody else goes shopping, to the tennis courts, or to work. For Diaspora Jews who have grown up feeling that their religious life is a sort of underground subculture, being a member of the majority for a change can be an invigorating surprise.

The impact of the robust Jewish celebrations raises a question: How can a people with such a tragic history have such a joyous religion? Except during Yom Kippur, Tisha B'Av, and a few less strongly observed occasions, Jews always seem to be feasting, tossing down celebratory drinks, and kicking up their heels at religious holidays.

In contrast, when Christians observe their important religious events, pomp, ceremony, and solemnity are the keynotes. Another thing Christians do that Jews don't, except at Purim, is offer more than one chance to experience a major occasion. Because of Christianity's schisms, there are three Christmases and two Easters in Jerusalem. If you miss one of these the first time around or want to go through it again and again—and even again—you may have at it.

The Christian calendar is packed with less-known holidays. The Greek Orthodox, for instance, mark the beheading of John the Baptist with a special service on September 11 at St. John's in the Old City; Roman Catholics have a procession in Jerusalem on Ascension Day.

Jerusalem Moslems aren't out on the streets with their observances (other than protests) the way Christians and Jews are. Nor are their holidays generally publicized in advance. Keeping track of important Moslem events requires closer scrutiny than the average citizen can give, especially since precise dates aren't announced by religious leaders until a day or so in advance. And since the Islamic calendar, even more so than the Jewish calendar, seemingly wanders in relation to the West's Gregorian calendar, it is harder to anticipate the dates. The most precise information you can get in advance is a ballpark figure for the current year alone.

It isn't that Jewish and Moslem events occur according to some inscrutable Oriental mystery. They have definitely assigned times within their own years. The Jewish calendar of 12 months of 29 and 30 days is lunar-solar and is adjusted by the addition of a 13th month at regular intervals, so a particular holiday occurs within a range of the same few weeks each year. Many Jewish holidays are timed to coincide with the full moon. The Moslem calendar is purely lunar and makes no adjustment. So over the years, Islamic holidays ease their way backward from one season to another.

Not all celebrations and commemorations in Israel are religious. Independence Day and Remembrance Day, for those who fell defending the country, are secular. But their dates of observance, too, are tied to the Jewish calendar.

Of course, any city whose residents insist with no trace of modesty that their hometown is the center of the world would have its own holiday. So every spring Jerusalem observes Jerusalem Day, celebrating its reunification.

Some celebrations have no official standing and might be legacies left from the British or simply carried into the local scene in immigrants' luggage. One is Sylvester's Day, which the Western world knows as the New Year's Day that occurs a week after Christmas—the first of Jerusalem's three Christmases, that is. Another is April Fool's Day, which hardly seems Israeli at all but is observed by the media, which finds lots of fools in the political world.

Then there are festive events imported out of sentiment for the Old Country, wherever that is. Americans have their Fourth of July, and the Scottish have their Robert Burns Memorial Dinner.

With this many holidays in Jerusalem, a person well might wonder, are businesses ever open? Does anyone ever get any work done? For several weeks during the year, the answer is no. So let's follow the year chronologically in Jerusalem to find out who is celebrating what, when, where, and how.

Shabbat: The Seventh Day

Shabbat is Jews' holiday every seventh day. It is more than simply the Sabbath, however, and to say only that it is a day of rest barely brushes its meaning. Shabbat's importance can be recognized by the fact that it is the only religious observance included in the Ten Commandments and the only one personified in religious poetry: Shabbat as the bride, Shabbat as an honored guest, Shabbat commemorating the creation of the world, Shabbat remembering the exodus from Egypt.

From sunset Friday until three stars are visible in the sky on Saturday night, Jews are to obey the Fourth Commandment: "Six days you shall do your work. And the seventh day shall be a holy day, a Sabbath rest." As the Book of Genesis says, "And God blessed the seventh day and made it holy." Rabbi Abraham Joshua Heschel wrote of the revolutionary concept introduced by the ancient Hebrews, "Six days a week we seek to dominate the world, on the seventh day we try to dominate the self."

Jerusalem pursues its fast pace Sunday through Thursday. Friday morning, that pace picks up even more as people rush to finish what they have to do before Shabbat begins. Flower sellers are out in force, as custom is to buy flowers for one's own home or for friends.

Businesses begin to close at noon. By mid-afternoon, Jewish parts of the city are shut down. Traffic thins, buses stop running, some traffic lights only blink instead of changing colors, sidewalks become empty, and a hush descends on the city. When the weekly siren sounds, Shabbat officially begins. Shabbat "the bride" arrives and is welcomed and treated as such.

I find an almost selfish pleasure in knowing that for 25 hours, I can't possibly run errands and that there are few people I can even telephone, for many don't answer the ring on Shabbat. I must stop my daily race with myself and simply let time be.

Observant Jews, in addition, won't ride in a car, light a fire, or turn on an electric light or appliance. Certain lights are left on all night. Food is cooked in advance and kept warm.

Before the siren sounds, the table has been set with the best dishes for Friday dinner, the most festive meal of the week, and family members have donned their nicest clothes. As the sky fades, the women of the household light candles and say a prayer over them honoring Shabbat.

Then, whole families can be seen heading for their synagogues. At the Western Wall, a colorful sight every Friday night is the procession of singing yeshiva (religious school) students descending the stairs from the

Old City. They come down in a line, each man with his hand on the shoulder of the man ahead. When they reach the area in front of the wall, they form a circle and to their joyous singing they dance a sort of two-step shuffle (the Yeshiva Two-Step?).

After services, families return home to their welcoming dinner table. They say traditional prayers over a brimming cup of wine and challah, the special braided Shabbat bread. The food varies according to the ethnic background of each family, but an important part of the meal is the singing of songs, some of which go back centuries.

In synagogues on Saturday morning, the Torah is removed from the Ark and a portion of it is read. After services, synagogues often have a kiddush, a serving of wine and cakes. *Kiddush* means "to make holy." In Judaism, where every aspect of life is sanctified, partaking of wine and bread after services is a holy act.

The afternoon meal almost always includes *cholent* (the "ch" is pronounced as in *choke*), a dish of endless variety that has been cooking overnight and usually includes beans, vegetables, potatoes, and beef or chicken. A must afterward is a nap. After eating a heavy meal of cholent, there really isn't much else you can do.

Following evening services, with three stars in the sky, Shabbat the bride is ceremoniously bidden farewell with Havdalah, which separates Shabbat from the week, the sacred from the ordinary. A glass of wine is filled, a candle is lit, and a box of sweet-smelling spices is passed from person to person to inhale and remember the sweetness of Shabbat. Then wine is poured over the candle to extinguish the flame.

Jerusalemites—those in the Old City, particularly—open their homes to strangers who wish to share Shabbat with them. You might receive an invitation by chance. I was invited to Shabbat when I happened to ask a question of a couple at the wall one Friday night. It turned out, after their invitation to me, a total stranger, that they knew my family.

Often, men who are active in certain synagogues or yeshivot spend time at the Western Wall Plaza, usually behind the men's side, looking for people to invite to spend Shabbat in the Old City. They are especially interested in inviting Jews who never have participated in an Old City Shabbat observance. Scruffy young men in blue jeans catch their eyes the fastest. If these emissaries don't find you, you should feel free to ask around for them.

You can also arrange to observe Shabbat through the Israel Center, the Center for Conservative Judaism, Hebrew Union College, or postings on bulletin boards around the Jewish Quarter of the Old City. Often, everything will be arranged for you—a place to sleep and places to eat. Sleeping arrangements are a must if you will be in an Orthodox situation, especially in the Old City. No public transportation will be available to take you any-where else. Aside from that, spending the night ensures that you will par-take of the experience to its fullest.

You might sleep and eat in the same home, but usually you will eat at several different places. Be sure to arrive with all your gear (and flow-ers for the family) at the place you will be sleeping well before Shabbat begins.

Sleeping arrangements aren't likely to resemble the Ritz. It's possible that you will have to share a bed or sleep on a cot, so princes and princesses need not apply. At meals, you might be one of a few or, liter-ally, dozens of other guests.

Out of this might come an exhilarating experience, with high points being the heady singing and intellectual Torah discussions around the din-ing table. The Havdalah ceremony after sunset is a sweetly poignant way of saying goodbye to Shabbat.

With that, Jerusalem springs back to life. It seems as if the whole town converges on the Ben-Yehuda Mall, and every teenager in the city is around the metal fence below the old clock in front of HaMashbir.

If you are reluctant to leave your retreat and face the now bustling world again, don't be surprised. You have experienced the peace of Shabbat. But next Friday you will have the chance to do it all over again.

Moslem Holidays

One of the many Jerusalem "time zones" is Islamic. It is the new moon that determines the Islamic calendar, in a year of 354 days. Instead of cal-culating days on the basis of sunset as Jews do, Moslems (like Christians) figure the day from midnight to midnight ("like normal people," a Moslem religious figure told me).

Most Moslems in Jerusalem, like the majority of Moslems, are Sunni Moslems. The main Moslem holidays are Awwal Muharram (the first day of the New Year), the Prophet's Birthday, Ramadan, Id el-Fiter, and Id el-Adha. The word that Ramadan is being observed gets around non-Islamic Jerusalem via Moslem workers, who show up half the day or sporadically, but observances of the other holidays can escape non-Moslems' attention.

Moslem institutions close for the happy time of Awwal Muharram. A pastry called *mushabek* is the treat of the day. It looks like a hardened, shiny yellow and pink glop of fat spaghetti and is incredibly sweet for a sweet new year.

The Prophet's birthday is celebrated with services at mosques. Stores are open on this day.

The Moslem holiday best known to the rest of the world is Ramadan, the name of the ninth Moslem month. Like Jews during Yom Kippur,

218

Moslems now contemplate atonement. The entire month is devoted to fasting during daylight hours—so that everyone can experience what it is like to be poor. Besides food, abstinence is required—at least during daylight hours—from beverages, smoking, and sex.

Work continues during the month of Ramadan, but only halfheartedly at best, especially in the afternoons as energy levels drops. Ramadan is primarily difficult when it occurs during summer, when the days, especially to Moslems, seem endless.

Arab restaurants are closed during Ramadan. Moslems, even those who don't observe the holiday, don't eat in the streets. Jews who have reason to visit Moslems during business hours during Ramadan pass up their hosts' customary offer of coffee or tea, so as not to make their hosts' fast more uncomfortable.

Before the fast ends for the day, customers line up at pastry shops. It is the custom to break the daily fast with something sweet. The favorite delicacy at this time is a special Ramadan pancake, *katayif*. Moslems take the pancakes home and fill them with almonds or fruit and honey and fry them. You can find them in the Old City souk already filled and fried.

With the end of the day's fasting, friends and family gather for a sumptuous meal or just to eat the cakes after sunset. This isn't a time for celebration, however. Before dawn, drummers and muezzin calls wake everyone to eat again.

After Ramadan, three days are given over to Id el-Fiter ("feeter"). This is a happy social time, and stores and businesses close down completely. Especially important during this holiday, men visit their sisters and bring them the unbeatable combination of money and chocolate.

Id el-Adha marks God's command to Ibrahim (Abraham) to sacrifice his son, who is, according to Moslem belief, Ishmael, not Isaac. The holiday lasts four days.

Mosques, especially al-Aksa, are full. This is one of the pilgrimage festivals when many Moslems go to Mecca, as they are expected to do at least once in their lives. While they are there, on this holiday, they go to nearby Mount Arafat to "stone the devil." After that, they travel to Islam's second holiest city, Medina.

To get ready for Id el-Adha, people go on buying sprees for presents, clothes, and food. The observance includes the sacrifice of a lamb. Wealthy Moslems give lambs to the poor at this time. During Id el-Adha, businesses are open.

Another event, depending on the religious-nationalist mood, is a pilgrimage to what Moslems consider to be Moses' tomb near Jericho. In Arabic he is called Nebi Musa (Prophet Moses). The Jewish religion has no connection whatsoever to the site, for Judaism has always maintained that Moses' grave is unknown.

The High Holidays (Rosh HaShana and Yom Kippur)

The new year most Israelis celebrate, Rosh HaShana (Head of the Year), occurs in fall on the first day of the Jewish month of Tishrei. The holiday generally occurs in September, occasionally in October.

Lasting two days, Rosh HaShana is a happy time, even though it marks the beginning of 10 days of repentance. During that period, Jews examine their thoughts and deeds for repentance, renewal, and return. It is said that God evaluates their actions. It is believed that on Rosh HaShana, all the destinies of humankind are recorded in heaven for the New Year. The righteous are recorded in the Book of Life; the wicked get the opposite. But Judaism isn't a fire-and-brimstone religion: People have 10 days in which to shape up and mend their ways.

Actually, the month before Rosh HaShana ushers in a period of introspection, which culminates with Yom Kippur. During this time, special prayers (called *slichot*) ask for forgiveness. You might hear footsteps outside during the middle of the night, for Sephardim have a tradition of praying that entire month, and slichot prayers take place usually at 4 a.m. or very late at night—when the world is quietest and it is easiest for a person to reflect. Ashkenazim, who are usually the more strict, don't begin slichot prayers until a minimum of four days before Rosh HaShana.

Rosh HaShana heralds three weeks of holidays. To assess the impact of these three weeks on Israeli life, multiply what happens in the Western world during the week between Christmas and New Year times three.

From Rosh HaShana to Yom Kippur (collectively called the High Holidays), Jerusalem's streets are crowded with tourists. For many Jews, spending these days in Jerusalem is a spiritual pinnacle.

For the month before the High Holidays, you might hear the sound of the shofar wafting from synagogue windows. Huffing and puffing inside are young men hoping to master that ancient instrument. Not only is it tough to elicit a sound from the ram's horn in the first place but it is also murderously difficult to blow the precise pattern required for the High Holidays.

Like Shabbat, Rosh HaShana begins at sunset. Stores close by 1 in the afternoon and buses stop running at about 4. A siren sounds as the holiday starts, just as it does for Shabbat. In homes, burning candles usher in the new year in light.

Then it seems as if Jerusalem en masse is off to the synagogues. The Municipal Tourist Office might be able to direct you to a synagogue. Even

220

though most synagogues sell tickets for High Holiday services, doors are open to all. Tickets only guarantee a seat. An empty seat is for the taking. For many people, participation in evening prayers at the Western Wall, where nearby yeshiva students arrive together singing, seems like the most inspiring way to start the new year.

Afterward, it is time for a holiday family feast. Tradition calls for apple slices dipped in honey to symbolize the wish for a sweet year ahead. Pomegranates are on every table. One belief is that pomegranates have 613 seeds—the number of *mitzvot,* or commandments. Another is that the many seeds represent the Jewish people. And the challah, instead of rectangular or oblong, is now round and sweet.

The shofar's fearsome bellow can be heard at morning services the next day. Also on that first day of Rosh HaShana, families fulfill the ceremony of Tashlich, in which they symbolically cast out their sins. They throw bread crumbs on a fresh body of water—an interesting requirement of a former desert people. The ultra-Orthodox, especially, descend to the Pool of Shiloah below the Old City for this tradition.

After two days, Rosh HaShana ends. Buses begin to run again, and worldly life resumes. Until Yom Kippur, the following days ostensibly operate as normal, but the city is really in a holding pattern.

Yom Kippur is the most solemn day in the Jewish religion. It is called "the Shabbat of Shabbats." For more than 25 hours, Jews partake of neither food nor drink and are to reflect on their lives and determine how to return to the "right path." They confess their transgressions communally. But before they can stand before God, they must make amends with people they have wronged. To make sure nothing has been overlooked, sometimes one person will approach another and say, "If I have inadvertently hurt you, I want you to know I'm sorry."

Dinner begins early before Yom Kippur, so it will be finished approximately an hour before sundown. The last bit of food must be swallowed before the siren signals the start of this most holy day.

Of course, stores have closed and buses have stopped running, this time at 2 p.m. An awesome stillness grips the city. After hearing Kol Nidre chanted in the synagogue, a person steps into darkened Jerusalem and finds the city transformed. Cars exist only as deserted hulks, occasionally resting over curbs as if they had been abandoned in a hurry. The city belongs to the people who walk smack down the middle of what yesterday was busy Rehov King George or Rehov Yafo. The only sound in the streets is the echoing clack of heels on the pavement, the hum of subdued conversation, and, I'm sorry to say, the eerie whoosh of bicycle tires against pavement.

The next day, such simple things as birds twittering, leaves rustling,

221

and children laughing can be heard with startling clarity. Now, it's the children's turn to take to the streets in earnest. Last night was only a rehearsal. Even near pious Mea She'arim, a group of boys, their *payot* (side locks) flying, chase each other in the middle of the street. At the intersection of Rehov King George and Rehov Yafo, girls jump rope where at other times cars snarl at each other.

People wear white on Yom Kippur. Even in the Reform synagogues, many people are in white. You will see an array of footwear. An incongruous sight in the ultra-Orthodox neighborhoods is bearded men in long white coats, but with cloth sneakers or even rubber flip-flops. These aren't signs of repressed athleticism or a rush from the shower, but of strict adherence to rules—not wearing leather shoes is part of the observance of Yom Kippur.

Inevitably, seeing the city at a complete standstill, a person can't help but realize how vulnerable Israel is on such a day and remember with a chill that it was on Yom Kippur 1973 that Arab armies invaded Israel.

As color begins to drain from the sky, intensity in the air increases. Yom Kippur, this deeply introspective period, goes out in a blaze of glory with triumphant blasts from the shofar.

Strange as it might seem after so many hours without food or drink, a wish might sneak in to slow the clock. The separation of this day from every other has been absolute. The peace the day brings is fragile, precious, and all too brief.

On leaving a synagogue in the darkness, the sounds of car ignitions, engines accelerating, and a sudden quickening of the city's tempo brashly intrude on the night. Breaking the fast usually involves a light meal with family or friends. (Another round of repentance can begin the next day for anyone who makes the mistake of stuffing him- or herself with food.) A growing tradition in Jerusalem after the fast is broken is for people to gather at the Western Wall.

The Feast of the Cross

For pageantry, pomp, and mystery, few religious events can match the Armenian Orthodox Church's observance four times a year of the Feast of the Cross. It occurs twice in the fall and twice in the spring on dates that can change.

The feast marks various events. The first, in September or October, marks the time when, "by a miracle, the cross was seen in the sky all over Jerusalem in the fourth century," said Armenian priest Father Razmig. The second celebrates Queen Helena's find of the cross on which Jesus was crucified. Another marks the Persian invasion and kidnapping of the cross in 612, and the fourth celebrates the cross's return in 629.

And where is that cross now? "Churches all over the world have a piece of it," said Father Razmig.

The first two Celebrations of the Cross follow or sometimes coincide with the chaotic exuberance of the Jewish holidays that stretch from Rosh HaShana through Simchat Torah. Nothing could highlight better the difference in styles—indeed, in worlds—between Jews and Christians than these observances. Jews may have created Broadway and Hollywood, but for a show of sheer grandeur, one that is awesomely beautiful and dramatic, Christians take the prize—with popes and patriarchs and an elaborate hierarchy.

The first of the four feasts occurs in St. James Cathedral, with this most colorful church made even more so by greenery. In the special afternoon service, aromatic greens, especially fragrant rosemary, fill the air. Perfumed water is sprinkled on the remains of what is believed to be the original cross. All this is accompanied by wondrous Armenian religious music.

When the celebration of the feasts takes place in the Church of the Holy Sepulchre in the Old City a few weeks later, the Armenian congregation is given the rotunda, and mass is sung before the shrine that houses the tomb where it is said Jesus' body was laid.

After the sunlit courtyard, it takes a moment for your eyes to become accustomed to the dim light inside the church. But then the gowns and capes of the Armenian priests, and especially the patriarch, dazzle the beholder with the glint of gold thread on shimmering fabric of brilliant colors. Assisting the mass are altar attendants, young men and boys in red and tan gowns with delicately flowered yokes, who stand in lines on either side of the sepulchre. Occasionally during the ceremony, the scene becomes cloudy with pungent smoke from swinging incense burners.

About midway through the celebration, schoolchildren troop in to witness the event and take their places behind the altar attendants. Girls in green uniforms sit sedately on chairs behind one line, while the boys, with much shushing from their teachers, plunk down on the stone floor behind the other line.

Twice during the mass, the patriarch, priests, and altar attendants march in solemn procession around the sepulchre. As they make their way they sing, and their voices fade and return, always resonating against the church's stone walls and hollows. The procession is led by two elders, not part of the clergy. The two men wear dark business suits and black shearling hats, reminiscent of dress in their Armenian homeland. Each carries a tall, heavy wooden staff. With every other measured step, the men pound the stone floor with the staffs—not simultaneously, but with a slowly tolling kerplunk-pause-kerplunk-pause. The sound is ominous.

With the backdrop of otherworldly music and pageantry, the impression is spine-tingling. An aura of doom hovers in the air. Armenian church music is melismatic, quasi-Oriental, and awesome. It is an integral part of the magnificence of the mass. The ceremony ends with the deafening but triumphant peal of bells from the tower above, followed by the clergy and congregation joining in joyous song.

Succot

After Yom Kippur, you will have four days to take a breather before the next holiday begins. Israelis will be moving ahead full blast, but ignore them. They like to travel without a speed limit.

Yom Kippur ends. People break their fasts. And without a pause, they're off making preparations for Succot. Succot (beginning on the 15th of Tishrei—full-moon time—and lasting seven days) is a combination harvest festival and commemoration of the years the Hebrews lived in the Sinai wilderness. As it says in Leviticus, "Ye shall dwell in booths [succot] seven days." Up and down the streets of Jerusalem, the thwack of hammers can be heard as succot are built on balconies and in gardens.

The *succah* (the singular of succot) is a temporary dwelling with sides of wood or canvas. The roof is a covering of palm branches, through which one can see the stars at night. Just before the holiday begins, the city gives out free palm branches, but most people already have completed their booths by then. Decorations inside are dictated by one's own imagination.

In preparation for Succot, stands on street corners sell what are known as "the four species." A Jewish man is supposed to have a palm branch, three myrtle twigs, two willows, and an unblemished etrog (a sort of overgrown lemon). Men hold these in both hands and shake them toward the four compass points, while saying a special blessing over them each day of the holiday (except Shabbat).

A *midrash* (Jewish allegory of scripture) says that each item's taste and aroma, or lack thereof, can be compared to the degree to which individual Jews keep the commandments, perform good deeds, and study Torah. Therefore, bringing the four species together represents different kinds of Jews joining together.

The plaza in front of HaMashbir and the upper reaches of Rehov Strauss are full of "four species" stands. Shoppers closely scrutinize each selection to make sure it is blemish-free. There also is a brisk sale of succah decorations: multicolored streamers, paper pineapples, colored pinwheels, shiny paper cutouts, and such. Someone from the West can't help but be reminded of Christmas. Indeed, inside HaMashbir it seems even more Christmaslike, for the toy department does a booming business.

When the holiday actually begins, the city's usual commercial hubbub is dimmed, for many offices and stores open only half days. Some are closed completely, for this is a major vacation time.

As you walk down residential streets during Succah, the sounds you hear can seem like another Middle Eastern version of a Charles Ives symphony. From time to time, while families feast in their succot, they break into cheerful song. The song at one end of the block collides with the song in the middle of the block, and they and any number of others on the street entwine abrasively. But the spontaneous joy of the music brings a sort of harmony, musical and otherwise, from dissonance.

Some people sleep in their succot, just as Leviticus says to do. Most Jerusalemites, however, only take their meals there. Eating in a succah isn't just an option for an observant male but a requirement. So restaurants and hotels, too, have their succot.

Among Succot events is the chance to get a good look at two of the most important people in the country—the president of Israel and the mayor of Jerusalem. The president is in the garden at his official residence in Talbia for one day to welcome anyone willing to leave his or her weapons at home (as requested on the invitation published in the newspapers) and stand under a blazing sun in a line that moves forward by millimeters. The reward might be a personal word with the president.

On this occasion, children are everywhere, scrunched down in

Buying palm branches for Succot

strollers, carried on their fathers' shoulders, swinging on railings. Meanwhile, the waiting crowd (observed by sharpshooter soldiers on nearby rooftops) might be entertained by an orchestra of teenage musicians playing tunes by Israel's (unofficial) composer laureate, Naomi Shemer, and from Broadway's *Fiddler on the Roof.*

The mayor has his annual Succot reception at the Tower of David (Citadel) just inside Jaffa Gate. The succah here has pomegranates dangling from its beams and children's drawings pinned to its fabric walls.

Outside the succah, guests sip mitz, chat with the mayor who casually wanders about, check out the dress of the various Christian priests, count the number of Arab dignitaries who showed up, and listen in awe to the Tennessee twang of an International Christian Embassy official. Meanwhile, the mayor's reception might be serenaded by the same teenage orchestra that played at the president's reception and with the same music.

On the third day of Succot, starting early in the morning, there is a special ceremony at the Western Wall for Kohanim, Jewish men who claim descent from the ancient priests. The area before the men's side of the wall becomes a sea of white-shrouded heads as the men envelope themselves in their tallitot.

On the fifth day of Succot, the annual Walk Around Jerusalem begins at 6 a.m. north of the city. Walkers have their choice of 12-, 15-, or 22-kilometer routes. Afterward, they gather for a parade early in the afternoon down Rehov Yafo to the heart of Jerusalem. Plan very carefully if you intend to ride anywhere in a car this day—the traffic jams are monumental. Better to walk.

Israel's Jewish Kurdish community takes to a park to celebrate Saharana during Succot. Sometimes they choose Sacher Park in Jerusalem. Otherwise, they meet elsewhere in the country. The festivities echo Kurdistan—an area that includes portions of Iran, Iraq, and Turkey—where Jews used to leave their homes during Succot and live in the wilderness, just as their ancestors did in Sinai.

Saharana doesn't get a lot of publicity, except on Israel's Mizrachi radio stations. Kurds aren't interested in the general public's participation, for this is a family affair. Kurdi Jews are known as the "wild ones" of Israel, and they prefer to be wild in private. But should you show up for the celebration, you'll be welcomed.

Simchat Torah

All this celebrating doesn't wind down at the end of Succot. Instead, it explodes with Simchat Torah immediately afterward. On Simchat Torah ("Rejoicing in the Teachings"), the year-long cycle of synagogue Torah readings ends and immediately begins again. The men designated to read the last and the first of the Torah are called "bridegrooms of the teachings." They have been greatly honored.

Torah scrolls are carried around the interior of the synagogue seven times, each time accompanied by lusty singing and dancing. Men dance with children on their shoulders or in their arms. In one synagogue, a sturdy young bearded man stands amid the crowd and holds the Bible in book form high in one hand. With his free hand, he conducts the men singing. He belts a solo and the others answer as a group. Sometimes, he slows the tempo way down and then, with a flourish, leads an accelerando to a vivace while he dances about, putting everything he has into his song of reverence for the teachings.

In another synagogue, a wizened old man hobbles on a cane into the middle of a circle of dancing men. He pulls his head into his shoulders like a turtle pulling into its shell, waves his cane in the air, grins from ear to ear, and breaks into a wild dance that could have had its origin on the steppes of Russia.

But for women, who sit and dance separately from the men (or simply stand and watch the men), and for men as well, the culminating expression of celebration is their descent from new Jerusalem to the Old City and the Western Wall. The descent takes place from synagogues all over the city.

Simchat Torah procession— celebrants hold a tallit above the Torah scrolls.

The procession from the Great Synagogue has its genesis when the men who had been dancing in the wide lobby move outside into the blocked-off street. Two circles of dancers— one of men, the other of young women—become even more animated than before. Finally, dancers and onlookers form a procession around the men carrying Torah scrolls. The scroll carriers are treated in a way that again symbolizes a wedding. Little boys on men's shoulders hold the ends of a tallit so it forms a canopy—like the wedding chuppah—over the heads of the scroll carriers.

Dancing young women lead the singing throng down Rehov Agron to the Old City. Men, too, dance, even as they and the accompanying crowd fight against gravity pulling them down the sloping street. More skip along the sidewalk to keep up with the exuberant parade.

Onlookers in upstairs flats along the route toss candy onto the celebrating mass below. As the multitude approaches a government building, a pot-bellied guard leaves his post, cuts into the line, kisses a Torah scroll, and protectively wraps his arms around it. With his treasured bundle, he dances down the street until he reaches the next intersection. He kisses the scroll again, carefully hands it back, and returns to his guard post.

The jubilation continues as the procession moves on down the hill and through Jaffa Gate into the Old City. As the celebrants turn the corner in front of the Tower of David, a bent old women with a scarf over her wispy gray hair looks up at the advancing throng and ululates with gloriously gutsy abandon. She slides like a piece of paper between the men and approaches a Torah scroll. The dancing men accommodate her by marking time in place and turning the front of the scroll toward her, so she can kiss it.

The parade follows Armenian Patriarchate Road. As celebrants, like a stream composed of countless rivulets, flow through the tunnels of the Armenian Quarter, the singing resonates with grandeur, as if from a mighty army of pilgrims instead of a disorganized spontaneous gang of disparate people bound by their commonality as Jews.

The road sweeps east and suddenly there is an enormous view of the Kidron Valley, the sun-bleached village of Silwan beyond blending into the mountain to which it clings, the pink and purple Judean Desert in the far distance, and straight ahead at the end of the road, the shimmering golden Dome of the Rock above the Western Wall.

The throng continues singing and dancing as the parade descends the steep road. As it nears the wall, people sing with even more exultation. Sweating after the strenuous trip, but too exhilarated to feel tired, they have brought the teachings to the most meaningful symbol of Judaism that stands—and it is here in Jerusalem.

Simchat Torah ends that night, but without a sudden letting go. Partying continues with a free program in Liberty Bell Park. Hasidim, Yemenites, and various Jewish ethnic groups present dance performances on stage. Often it is the wild Kurds who steal the show. Then, for days afterward, huge palm branches—no longer needed as succot roofs—lie forlornly in the gutter, waiting to be collected by the trash men.

Sigd

For innumerable years, the Jews of Ethiopia made a pilgrimage every November to the mountaintops near their isolated villages. During a day of fasting, they celebrated the giving of the Torah in Sinai, the return of exiled Jews to Zion from Babylonia in 536 B.C.E., and the renewal of the Jewish covenant and spirit by prophets Nehemia and Ezra. They saw the ancient return to the Holy Land as a paradigm for their own fervently prayed for return to Israel.

The holiday is called Sigd (one syllable; translated as "prostration"— an act that wasn't carried to Israel). For almost all Ethiopian Jews, their prayers have now been answered. Many small actions to rescue them began in 1979, followed by two dramatic rescue operations, Operation Moses in 1984 and Operation Solomon in 1991. These probably were the only times in history that a nation of lighter-skinned people brought black Africans to their country to live as equals.

Said by some to be descendents of the Tribe of Dan, Ethiopian Jews might have numbered a million during their zenith, when they controlled the northern part of their African country. During some of those years they had their own rulers, including a queen. Since their defeat by the Portuguese in the sixteenth century, they were forced to convert to Christianity, imprisoned, sold into slavery, and terrorized in many other ways.

During the height of the killer drought that gripped northern Ethiopia in the mid-1980s, also a time of dangerous political upheaval, hundreds of thousands of Ethiopians fled to the Sudan, where they were placed in refugee camps. For the Jews, who call themselves Beta Israel, joining the flight was a chance to escape a country that neither wanted them nor allowed them to leave for Israel. The drought was their cover.

Their journey was perilous, often beset by murderers and starvation. The disease-ridden camps offered little respite. Death still stalked them. Some four thousand Ethiopian Jews died in their attempt to reach Israel.

Then, in what came to be known as Operation Moses, the Israeli government surreptitiously and daringly airlifted thousands of Jews out of camps in Sudan, an enemy Arab land, and brought them to Israel. They joined a few hundred of their countrymen who had preceded them by a decade and longer.

In 1991 Ethiopia was torn apart by revolution. The remaining Ethiopian Jews were trapped between the warring factions. Most of them left their mountain villages and headed for Addis Ababa. There, in another daring mission, while war guns boomed in the city, Israel flew 14,500 Ethiopian Jews to Israel in the space of 30 hours.

Since 1982, Sigd has been replicated in Jerusalem every November,

229

50 days after Yom Kippur, by these former Ethiopians who were disparagingly called *falashas* (strangers) in their native land. In Jerusalem, Sigd includes the reading of Nehemiah 9, thanks for the return to Zion, and prayers for any family or friends still in Ethiopia.

Sigd takes place in a grove of pine trees at the end of the Sherover-Haas Promenades in Armon HaNatziv (East Talpiot), with a stunning view of the city. Not only do Ethiopian-born Jews and their sabra children from all over Israel attend, but so do their paler-skinned co-religionists, who choose this time to demonstrate their solidarity with their fellow Jews.

With the Israeli president and other government officials usually offering a greeting, the ceremony is led by white-bearded *kessim* (priests) garbed in white from their turbans to their leggings. As they did in Ethiopia, they read the Ten Commandments, passages from the book of Nehemiah, and prayers especially composed for this day. Readings are in Ge'ez, an ancient language, and the chanting is a hypnotic drone. In the high priests' hands are horsetail switches, classical African artifacts.

Ethiopian women wear white, too, but with accents of bright colors on embroidered bands on their dresses. Their scarves are wrapped like turbans around their heads. To the chanting, they add their high-pitched ululation.

One of the loveliest aspects of Sigd is that it brings together Ethiopian friends and relatives who have been dispersed in Israel. There is much kissing, as many as six times from cheek to cheek, between men as well as women. Happiness over these reunions spreads to non-Ethiopians.

Sigd culminates, after prayers and readings, with some Beta Israel going to the Western Wall (some were there before Sigd began) and the rest enjoying a festive meal.

Chanukah

Some time in December, occasionally as early as the end of November, Chanukah arrives on the 25th of the month of Kislev for eight increasingly colorful days.

Chanukah might be the first recorded celebration of religious freedom. It commemorates the victory of the Maccabee family and its followers over the Greek-Syrian king who attempted to destroy Judaism. The story goes that when the victorious Maccabees returned to the temple in Jerusalem to cleanse it after desecration by the Syrians (acting on behalf of Greek rulers), there was only enough ritually pure oil to last a day. But through a miracle, the oil burned for another seven days—enough time to prepare a new supply.

So Jews all over the world light a "servant" candle (*shammash*) from which they light one candle the first night of Chanukah and an additional candle each following night, until all are burning on the eighth night.

In Israel, the candelabra is called a *chanukiah*, not a menorah, as in the Diaspora. And more and more in Israel, instead of lighting candles people light oil, as in ancient times.

Jerusalem during Chanukah truly is aglow. Chanukiahs are everywhere—in apartment windows, atop buildings, in public areas, in hotel lobbies, and at the Western Wall. Late every afternoon, people gather at the wall to watch enormous vats of oil set ablaze—surely the biggest chanukiah in town.

An enormous metal chanukiah is also set up in the plaza in front of the department store HaMashbir. There you find black-coated rabbis rising to great heights aloft a "cherry picker" to illuminate the chanukiah each night. When they are finally in position—accomplished with the cherry-picker pilot making a little adjustment here, a little adjustment there—the rabbis say prayers, to which passersby join in and add their Omayne. Afterward, yeshiva students offer any takers a shot of schnapps and some cookies.

Of course, there is something special to eat during Chanukah. To Ashkenazi Jews in the Diaspora, the special Chanukah food is potato latkes (pancakes) under a dollop of sour cream or applesauce, and most Ashkenazim continue to eat them in Jerusalem. But the truly special Israeli Chanukah treats are *sufganiot*—sugar-dusted jelly doughnuts.

Just as Christmas decorations appear as early as November in the West, sufganiot might appear as soon as Simchat Torah is over. But during the actual eight days of Chanukah, sufganiot are everywhere, not only in pastry shops but also at hotel chanukiah lightings and *ulpan* (Hebrew class) parties. Might as well dig in, although your eyes might bulge like your waist at the sight of them by the end of the eight days. They are especially tasty warmed up, and it's possible to find some with butterscotch instead of the ubiquitous cherry jam filling. Check out the bakeries.

Make sure to stroll through neighborhoods like Sha'are Hessed and Mea She'arim during Chanukah, especially on the last night, when every chanukiah is fully lit. The lights are placed where passersby can see them. In these neighborhoods especially, instead of a candelabra residents use a rectangular glass case, resembling a small aquarium, which they set outdoors. Inside these cases burn containers of oil—the glow of the flames reflected in the glass. I have seen houses with as many as five such cases filling the night air with their radiance. A particularly brilliant, large chanukiah is on Rehov Ibn Shaprut, near Keren Kayemet, adding yet another bewitching dimension to the Golden City.

Christmas

To be a Christian in Israel during Christmas is to acquire an inkling of what it's like being Jewish anywhere in the world other than Israel—or perhaps parts of Brooklyn. Stores are open, kids are in school, Christmas decorations are absent from streets and stores. Radio airwaves carry no repeated strains of "Hark, The Herald Angels Sing" or "Rudolph the Red-Nosed Reindeer." All that might come as a surprise in Jerusalem, where Bethlehem used to be considered something of a suburb and where Christians mark three Christmases—not just the one.

Christians with allegiance to the pope in Rome and Protestants mark their holiday on December 25. Eastern and Oriental Orthodox—including Romanian Orthodox, Russian Orthodox, Ethiopian Orthodox, Copts, and, the biggest group, Greek Orthodox—follow the Julian calender and celebrate Christmas on January 6. Bringing up the rear on January 19 is the last Christmas, that of the Armenians.

Celebrations of the three Christmases follow similar patterns. Only faces, languages, and religious dress differ. To keep it all straight, the Christian Information Center and the Municipal Tourist Office have schedules of which church is having services when, where, and in which language. You want Danish? You can get Danish. You want French? You can get French.

Just as Jerusalem gives out palm fronds so Jews can build their booths at Succot, the city ecumenically gives away Christmas trees to Christian residents. Actually, there's an ulterior motive: the gifts keep people from chopping down trees in the Jerusalem Forest.

Now that Bethlehem is no longer under Israeli jurisdiction, special buses no longer whisk people from Jerusalem to Bethlehem. If you're on your own and not with a tour group, an alternative is Egged Bus 30, which goes south to the Jerusalem neighborhood of Gilo, close to Bethlehem.

Christmas Eve, you can take Bus 30 as far south as it goes on Derech Hevron, then walk the rest of the way. Or you can take Arab Bus 22 from the bus station opposite Damascus Gate (depending on its schedule) or a taxi.

Festivities on December 24 begin shortly after noon when the Latin patriarch begins his traditional procession from the Old City to Bethlehem's Manger Square. Modern times have made their inroads, for he now rides in a limousine in a convoy. In Bethlehem at the southern edge of Jerusalem, the procession picks up an escort of mounted police and Christian Arab Boy and Girl Scouts beating drums, blowing trumpets, and playing bagpipes. Mayors of Bethlehem and nearby Christian towns, as well as Palestinian officials, greet the patriarch in Manger Square.

As night falls in Shepherds' Field in Beit Sahur near Bethlehem,

232

Protestants enjoy a carol service and Bible reading in English, Arabic, and Swedish on a rocky outcropping overlooking the Judean Desert.

From 7 p.m. until midnight mass begins in the Roman Catholic St. Catherine's Church, local and foreign choirs, some from as far away as Fiji, sing in Manger Square. Among them might be a Baptist choir leader from Atlanta who invites the milling crowd to sing along with "Happy Birthday, Dear Jesus."

But it's when the Atlanta choir sings "O, Little Town of Bethlehem," with its line "How still we see thee lie," that it's time for a look at modern Bethlehem. Quiet it isn't. At least not at Christmas.

Stores lining the square remain open at least until midnight mass begins. A clerk might ask a browser, "Wouldn't you like to buy yourself a diamond for Christmas?" Everyone has hopes.

Outside the stores, the atmosphere is even less like Christmas Eve in the West. The square is full of people, most of them young, from various parts of the world. And they behave just like young people in most small towns: Whether they are Arab, German, Scottish, or American, they hang out in the square looking for action.

Most of the action consists of buying food from vendors, then dropping greasy paper wrappers on the pavement and kicking empty pop cans across the square. For many visitors and locals alike, drinking excessive

Christmas procession in Bethlehem

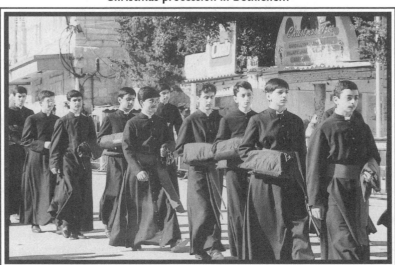

233

amounts of alcohol is a prime activity. The most interesting actions to behold are the interchanges between young Arab men and young blond foreign women. Their peers gather around to eavesdrop and check on the progress.

Finally, mass begins at the Church of St. Catherine. It is for this that churchgoers have gone through the tumult of Manger Square. Admission is by ticket, available beginning in November from the Franciscan Pilgrims Office, P.O. Box 186, Jerusalem 91-001, Israel, (02) 627-2697, in the same building as the Christian Information Center inside Jaffa Gate.

However, tickets aren't available to just anyone—only Roman Catholics. A Franciscan official explained: "There are no seats in the church. You will have to stand from 11 p.m. until 1:40 a.m. We don't want people taking up space who will leave when their feet start hurting."

"But," I replied, "I used to see on TV, Israeli officials and now Yasser Arafat sitting in the first row."

"That's protocol," the official said with a sigh. "We are strangers here. We can't do as we would like."

The Franciscans limit groups to 35 people and a priest. An individual can get in, but only with proof of being Roman Catholic—a signed document from his or her parish priest. "And," the official noted, "the signature has to be legible."

With the mass beginning, the commercialism, nationalism, hustle, and high jinks in the square outside are forgotten. Inside the white-columned church is pageantry and joy. Carrying a doll in his arms, a replica of the Baby Jesus, the Latin patriarch leads a procession up the aisle. Guards carrying swords and silver staffs surround the patriarch, who is accompanied by prelates and officials. When he reaches the altar, the patriarch lays the doll on a cradle of straw. For those who can't get inside the church, the mass is televised live on an enormous screen in the square, as well as internationally.

Meanwhile, in Jerusalem, Christmas Eve services take place in churches all over the city. Protestants usually have services early in the evening, 6:30 or 8. Other churches often begin mass at 10 and end around midnight. While Jewish and Moslem Jerusalemites go about their routine lives, they are serenaded by a bell concert from the YMCA tower, which spreads the sound of Christmas over its corner of the city.

Fewer tourists come to partake in the other two Christmases. But the Orthodox Christmas offers even more color than does the Latin. At the Orthodox Christmas, not one, not two, but three separate processions make their way from Jerusalem to Bethlehem on the morning of January 5. First the Syrian bishop makes his journey, then the Coptic bishop an hour later, followed an hour-and-a-half later (the extra half-hour is in deference to his greater influence) by the Greek Orthodox patriarch. The separate services held in Bethlehem that night are staggered by the same intervals.

On the morning of January 6, the streets of Bethlehem are packed with people who come to see the parades of Arab Boy and Girl Scouts. Each troop has its own uniform. Even headdresses vary, from tams with pompons to red and white keffiyahs worn in the style of the Jordanian Legion. One of the most intriguing sights in the parade is of adolescent girls who insist on marching in high heels for vanity's sake, struggling to keep up and not be undone by the bumpy streets.

After the parade, the Greek Orthodox patriarch and other high churchmen majestically march from one end of Manger Square to the other in their colorful vestments. Then they proceed to the Church of the Nativity, built over the Holy Grotto where, tradition has it, Jesus was born. The main religious ceremony is the midnight mass. It begins with a stately procession around the church and culminates in the small, incense-filled Holy Grotto itself.

On January 18, Armenian Christmas Eve begins with yet another procession from Jerusalem to Bethlehem. As in the previous ones, the mayors of Bethlehem and smaller Arab villages, along with Palestinian officials, greet the dignitaries. Usually, the main service begins in the church at 10:30 p.m. and continues in the grotto at midnight. A second mass follows from 2 a.m. to 5 a.m.

Not to be outdone by Latin Christmas, the Greek service is also televised. The Armenians' is broadcast only on radio. Despite the larger world attention on the December 25 Christmas, it is the Orthodox celebration that resembles a hometown party. By the time the third Christmas is over, one wonders if the Atlanta Baptist choir leader had any idea that "Happy Birthday, Dear Jesus" would be sung in one fashion or another again and again.

New Year

Depending on who your friends are in Jerusalem, you might barely notice when the Gregorian calendar flips to its new year. The Gregorian New Year (as in "Ha-a-a-ppy New Year" and popped champagne corks), if referred to at all here, is usually called Sylvester's Day.

Some Anglo-Saxim and Western European Jews have parties on the evening of December 31. The ultra-Orthodox are steamed about that. But unless December 31 falls on a Friday, the day Pope Gregory called New Year is just another workday, except for international money transactions. If you go to a party on Sylvester's Day, chances are it will end close to midnight because tomorrow will be merely a workday.

Why is it called Sylvester's Day? No one has a definitive answer. Sylvester was the name of two popes. Which of the two is tied to the day is a mystery. But one ironic fact is known—both were notably anti-Semitic.

Serious celebrators of New Year's would do well to trundle down to Tel Aviv, where people party hard and often, and nightclub revelries continue not until dawn but until noon the next day. In hearth-loving Jerusalem, a few establishments have parties. One Jerusalem restaurant's Sylvester's Eve celebration included caviar, champagne, lobster thermidor, chocolate log, and, lest revelers forget where in the world they were, belly dancing.

Tu B'Shvat

Come to think of it, new years outnumber Christmases in Israel better than two to one. In the Jewish calendar alone, there are six occasions on which a new year is celebrated. But most of them don't get a lot of attention.

So far, we've had Rosh HaShana in the fall and Sylvester's Day on January 1. The end of January or the beginning of February brings another new year: Tu B'Shvat, the New Year of the Trees, on the 15th of the Jewish month of Shvat.

Tu B'Shvat is the Jewish way of celebrating the coming of spring. The brave assumption is that most of the winter rains are over, the almond trees, the first ones to do so, have bloomed, the soil is ready for saplings, and clear days are ahead. Maybe in Beersheva, but in Jerusalem, it's only an assumption.

Rain or not, Tu B'Shvat is a festive time. The number-one activity is planting seedlings. Planting trees in Israel has long been a big deal. Since the birth of the Zionist movement more than a century ago, Diaspora Jewish homes haven't been complete without blue-and-white containers into which coins are dropped and eventually sent to the Jewish National Fund, primarily for reforestation.

In Israel, children go off with their classes to plant trees. Drivers can stop on certain highways, plant trees, and drive on. Tourists can go on outings to forests and, as publicity tells them, "plant a tree with your own hands." I've done it. Hype aside, it's an emotionally satisfying experience.

Are there special foods for Tu B'Shvat? Of course. To mark the abundance that spring portends, people taste from 7 to 12 kinds of dried and fresh foods, including nuts.

Vietnamese New Year

Are you ready for one of the biggest surprises about Israel? It's the sight of a dragonlike creature accompanied by a pot-bellied man wearing red, undulating through the streets to the staccato of exploding firecrackers. But that's a scene from eastern Asia, not the Middle East, you say?

That's right. It's the Vietnamese New Year, which occurs sometime in February, according to the old Chinese lunar calendar adopted by the Vietnamese.

Whoa! Has yet another previously unknown Jewish ethnic group surfaced, like the Bnei Menashe near India's border with Burma? No. These New Year's celebrants number about 330 former "boat people"—refugees whom the Israeli navy rescued in 1977. They celebrate together in a community center in Azor near Tel Aviv. Israelis come from all over to celebrate with the Vietnamese. So you might also.

After the dancing dragon's show and the inevitable speeches, children receive gifts. Then merrymakers move to the buffet table, which is a melange of Far Eastern and Middle Eastern food.

Robert Burns Supper

About the same time as the Vietnamese New Year, the Scottish are remembering Robert Burns. These tartan wearers and hearty singers of "Loch Lomond" and "Charlie is My Darling" aren't leftovers from British Mandate days. They are Jewish Israelis from Scotland.

They have their sentimental fling over their country of origin at the annual kosher Robert Burns Supper. It is held in the middle of February in that partying town down the road, Tel Aviv, or its neighbor, Herzliya, and is sponsored by the British Olim Society.

What is a Scottish feast without haggis, sometimes considered the Scottish national dish? The dish generates reverence and repugnance because of its contents of minced heart, liver, and lung of a sheep, mixed with oatmeal, onions, suet, and spices and boiled in the animal's stomach.

Well, Scottish Israelis believe it's the thought that counts. They have learned to improvise and make a kosher haggis that's eaten with as much gusto as the genuine article. After all, it is a culinary relation to the Jewish Eastern European dish *derma,* cooked in a steer's intestines. The cockaleekie soup and tatties (potatoes), also integral to the Scottish meal, are authentic.

For this party honoring poet Burns, who immortalized the evening's main dish with his "Ode to a Haggis," a piper is a must. Whoever he is, he's a trouper, for not only does he play traditional Scottish songs but he is also expected to deliver a bagpipe rendition of "Heveinu Shalom Aleichem."

Having Scottish ancestry is no prerequisite to attending the Robert Burns Supper (but saying "Scottish" and not "Scotch" might be). Actually, all a person has to do to be accepted into the fold is to sing "Auld Lang Syne" along with everyone else at the end of the evening. Call the British Olim Society in Jerusalem for further information, (02) 563-4822.

Another Burns Supper, as it is called in Scotland, happens now and then (even as early as January), in Jerusalem at St. Andrew's Scots Memorial Church (The Church of Scotland), near the train station. Yes, they serve haggis, neeps (turnips), and tatties. The church's chef makes the haggis from his own secret recipe. Since Scottish turnips are yellow, the chef adds a little carrot to color the white Israeli turnips. St. Andrew's haggis isn't made in a skin, but in a bowl and then turned into a tray. The desert is Scots Trifle. Whiskey polishes off the meal. Occasionally, staff members who might be in Scotland at the appropriate time bring a genuine haggis back to Jerusalem. The evening isn't complete without dancing led by the Scottish Country Dance Group, which meets at the church every Tuesday morning. Call St. Andrew's early in January to book reservations, (02) 673-2401. Only some 50 people can be accommodated.

Purim

Purim, in mid-Adar in late winter, offers the treats of Halloween without the tricks. And lots more: costumes for adults as well as children, special foods, a carnival spirit (dowdy Jerusalem style), silliness, and too much wine.

Purim celebrates the deliverance of the Jews of ancient Persia from wicked Haman through the intercession of Queen Esther. Esther was not only beautiful but also secretly Jewish. Despite danger to her life, she dared to reveal that fact to her husband, King Ahasuerus, in hopes of saving her people. Her bravery succeeded. In the end, it was Haman, plus his sons, who were put to death.

On Purim, schools are closed, banks are closed, and businesses may be open only half a day. In much of Israel, the celebration lasts one day (Adar 14), but in cities that were walled at the time of Joshua—and that includes Jerusalem—the festival is celebrated on Adar 15. This is because in the Purim story, the Jews of Shushan, a walled city, were saved a day later than the rest of the Persian Jews.

Someone who moves fast could run down to Tel Aviv and celebrate with the Adloyada procession on the first day of Purim. The name is an acronym for a commentary on the Book of Esther that says you should drink wine until you don't know the difference between Mordechai, Esther's Uncle, and Haman. Tel Avivians especially go in for Carnival-like activities on Purim, and Adloyada floats often have a sambalike character (yes, samba, as in Brazil). The most outrageous things Tel Avivians can think of—and they know how to be outrageous—will be on the floats.

Then you could head back to Jerusalem (or Safed) for what is called Shushan Purim, beginning while Purim is winding down in Tel Aviv.

In synagogues or gatherings elsewhere on the evening Purim begins, the *megillah* (Biblical Book of Esther) is read. Often, there is a women's megillah reading. Every time evil Haman's name is mentioned, everyone rattles "groggers" or other noisemakers, blows horns or whistles, or simply hoots and stamps their feet. Anything to drown out his name.

At home, there is royal feasting and a tradition of sending two ready-to-eat foods to at least two people. Since the tradition has kept up with the times, even popcorn qualifies. Stores sell pre-made baskets. But the very special culinary treat of Purim is a triangular pastry filled with fruit or poppy seeds. Jews in the Diaspora call these cakes *hamantaschen*—"Haman's pockets"—which for some inexplicable reason look like three-cornered hats. But in Israel, they are *oznei haman*—"Haman's ears" (a difference for anthropologists to ponder). As at other Jewish festivals, Purim is a time to remember the needy with gifts.

Perhaps the most elegant Purim affair in Jerusalem is the grand costume ball for patrons of the Israel Museum. Sometimes Jerusalem also has a Purim procession—nothing close to Tel Aviv's Adloyada, however. Participants will be wearing more clothes, and entertainment, not shock, is the goal.

Purim is a time for laughter. Some pop music radio programs carry more laughter—in cackles, giggles, gales, or torrents—than music. It's all part of the silliness that's Purim.

Even being tipsy is a Purim tradition. But getting knock-down drunk is rare. We're talking about people who generally aren't used to a lot of alcohol—and by and large don't really enjoy it—so a little goes a long way. Those with the biggest problems might be yeshiva boys, at least those on their own for the first time

But then comes the morning after. Perhaps men don't say much, but women complain that between all the baking, company, and parties, they're exhausted. Despite Purim, they never felt like queen for the day—Esther or otherwise.

Passover

"Next year in Jerusalem!" In the Diaspora, every Passover (Pesach) Seder concludes with these words. To be in Jerusalem during Passover is the dream Jews grow up with and harbor all their lives. Three times a year, Jews are to make a pilgrimage to Jerusalem: at Succot, Passover, and Shavuot. Perhaps the most important is Passover. That's why Jesus was in Jerusalem: Like a good Jew, he was making the pilgrimage.

During the Seder (which means "the order of things" in Hebrew), the Haggadah is read aloud to retell the story of the Hebrew people's escape from Egypt and slavery some 3,500 years ago. Jews today not only have responsibility to recite the story again and again but each Jew is meant to feel as if he or she, personally, made the escape.

Passover begins with the full moon on the 15th of Nisan in March or April. In the Diaspora, Passover lasts eight days. The Haggadah is read the first two nights, while family and friends gather around the dinner table laden with symbolic foods.

In Israel, Pesach lasts seven days, and the Haggadah is read the first night only. And no one has to say at the end, "Next year in Jerusalem!" Here the words are, "Next year in the completed Jerusalem."

But no matter where they are, Jews don't eat leavened bread during this time. Instead, they eat matzo, a brittle, flat, quickly baked mixture of flour and water—in memory of the fleeing Hebrews who had no time to wait for their bread to rise. Ashkenazim also avoid certain legumes and rice during Passover, but by some quirk of tradition, these foods are acceptable to Sephardim.

What goes on during this major happy holiday in the magical Jerusalem that Diaspora Jews dream of? Lots of things. Passover is primarily a family occasion, so the major events take place privately at home. Passover doesn't announce itself much outwardly.

Because school is closed during Passover, a third of Jerusalem's population uses that time to head for Eilat or the Sinai, another third flies off to Majorca or London, and the rest, remaining home, grumble over not being able to get away.

Yet streets are thronged, largely because of the influx of Diaspora Jews carried to Jerusalem on those words they first heard in childhood and by Israelis from other parts of the country who make the pilgrimage, even in a secular way. Both groups create a vibrant mood in the city. Added to their numbers are Christians from around the world who come to Jerusalem to celebrate Easter, should the holidays coincide. So an added abundance of energy charges the city, in spite of many residents' exodus.

Jerusalem becomes one huge traffic jam, not only in the center—where certain streets are closed to cars—but also on roads leading in and out of the city. The usual 25-minute drive from Jerusalem to the northern tip of the Dead Sea can take more than an hour. Cars are front to end, like joints of some crawling monster. And that's going downhill. Only Old City residents are allowed to drive into the Old City. Even getting into the parking garage opposite Jaffa Gate can age you.

But on the bright side (literally), color sets the city gloriously aflame. Pink, blue, and white blossoms crown the trees, and spring flowers grow in every possible space. Before the holiday begins, because of Passover dietary prohibitions, every household must be cleaned from top to bottom to make sure no speck of *chumetz* (leaven) remains. Look for small fires at curbsides in residential Jerusalem on the morning Passover will start. Going up in smoke is each household's gathering of crumbs.

At sundown, the siren sounds and the first day of Passover settles on the city. As on Shabbat, businesses will be locked up and buses still.

While Jerusalemites get together in their homes for the Seder and its accompanying grand dinner, hotels have Seders for their guests and any visitors who wish to attend. An invitation to a Seder in an Israeli home could be the nicest thing that could happen to you at Passover, especially (for an Anglo-Saxon) if the invitation comes from a Sephardi family. It could be the only time in your life you won't face a pale hunk of gefilte fish at the start of the meal. Food, songs, and ritual will be different from those of any other Passover you've experienced. Even the matzo that first night will seem strange.

At an Iraqi Seder, for instance, several times during the Haggadah reading everyone at the table will reach forward and grasp one matzo simultaneously as a prayer is said. The pose will remind a Westerner of the school football team with everyone touching the ball, just before charging forth to beat Central High.

Instead of hiding the *afikomen,* a small piece of matzo for children

Before Passover, *chumetz* is burned at curbside.

241

to hunt down later, a family from Baghdad will wrap it in a scarf and tie it beneath the armpit of one of the women. At the end of the evening, everyone gets a piece. You are expected to nibble it down to the size of a button, then put in your pocket, where it is to remain until next Passover.

For a Diaspora Jew in Jerusalem, even though "Next year in Jerusalem" is now, it might seem as if something is missing. Something is: the second Seder.

The eight days of Passover in the Diaspora ensure that, wherever they are in the world, Jews will share the Seder together. According to the rabbis, Diaspora Jews—even if they are in Israel at the time—are to abide by their own tradition and observe Passover for eight days, as they would at home, and attend a second Seder. And the reverse is true. Israelis, including those originally from the Diaspora, when outside Israel go to bed that second night—while their hosts are still trying to get out of Egypt.

The problem is to find a second Seder. Many hotels and private organizations have them. Check with Yakar, the Israel Center, or the Center for Conservative Judaism.

During the holiday week, businesses, if they are open at all, are open only in the morning. Supermarkets and neighborhood food stores hang white sheets over shelves of forbidden foods. Needless to say, bread bins are empty and every little crumb has been cleared out. While this is a

---

Jerusalem Scene

Only in Israel: When it was time to cut the hair of a new contingent of Israeli Defense Forces parachutists, all the young men complied with the required haircut—except one.

It wasn't that the Jerusalem teenager had objections to having his hair cut short. After all, it was the patriotic thing to do. But he did have objections to anyone cutting his hair but his father, a barber.

The young man stood his ground and insisted to his commanding officers, "No one has ever cut my hair except my father, and no one ever will."

So what did the Israeli military do? It let the new parachutist go home to Jerusalem—so his father could cut his hair. Of course.

242

vacation time for most bakers, a few—at least one in Mea She'arim—sell special Passover cakes and cookies.

Passover becomes a major public event on the third morning when the Kohanim, the descendants of Aaron, are blessed at the Western Wall as they were during Succot. Enormous crowds come to the event. To see, people stand precariously on the slope up to the walk to the Temple Mount.

Jews of Kurdistani background again celebrate their Saharana festival somewhere in Israel, as they did during Succot. This get-together lasts for days.

During Passover, the city schedules free walking tours of the Old City, and the Bible Lands Museum has a handicrafts fair. The flurry of events is listed in the *Jerusalem Post*.

On the seventh day, Passover is given a send-off for another year. With the siren ushering in the last day of the holiday, the day is treated like Shabbat.

After the holiday ends, when three stars are seen in the sky, if you ache to sink your teeth into a fluffy hunk of bread after a week of crunching on matzo, take a walk through your neighborhood. Your nose and the lines outside doors will lead you to bakeries already turning out the leavened stuff.

And with Passover ending, immediately Mimouna begins.

Mimouna

Since 1965, the celebration of Mimouna has been the Israeli way of culminating Passover. Mimouna (the meaning of the word is unclear) was brought to Israel by Moroccan and other North African Jews, but it is especially identified with the large Moroccan community. (Moroccans were the largest ethnic group in Israel until the influx from the former Soviet Union.)

Most Jewish communities in Moslem lands share this tradition, with variations and called by other names, such as the Kurds' Saharana. The common feature of the holiday was that the entire community would go into the countryside to celebrate for days at a time. Since the local sheikh or *khan* usually safeguarded their homes while they were away, Jews would begin their festival with tributes to their Moslem protector.

Having gone through that formality, they were on their own. Out of sight of their Moslem neighbors, they could be themselves. Alone in the countryside, Jews would let loose. For a while, they could forget the subtle or not-so-subtle repression under which they lived as *dhimmies*—second-class citizens in Moslem regimes.

They would eat, drink, generally whoop it up, visit back and forth, go courting—especially go courting—revel in freedom, and behave in ways even their own society wouldn't allow back home. This outing acted as a sort of societal safety valve.

In Morocco, Jews ushered in Mimouna the evening before setting out for the countryside by literally opening their doors to guests. There were no formal invitations. A house with its door standing wide open was invitation enough. The guest needed to bring no gift, only to give the traditional greeting *"Tirbachu v'tisadu"* ("May you be worthy to succeed").

Today in Israel, both elements of Mimouna—the opening of doors to neighbors and friends and the expedition to the outdoors—have taken root, but in new forms. As the head of Beyahad (Together), the sponsoring organization of the national celebration, said, "You don't have to be Moroccan to enjoy Mimouna." More than 2 million Israelis participate, either as hosts or guests. Hebrew-language newspapers print lists of host families all over the country who open their doors to the general public. (Picture that in Los Angeles or London.)

Does the prospect of walking into a house where you don't know the hosts and probably won't know any of the other guests (and possibly may not even speak their language) seem intimidating? Take it from me, there's no need to be shy. This was my first Mimouna experience:

In that year, the *Jerusalem Post* printed a list of host families. I chose to visit a family living in Jerusalem's Musrara neighborhood. While Musrara is known for its poverty and as birthplace of the local "Black Panther" organization (an ethnic, not a racial self-determination group), it turned out that the Monsungo family lived in a middle-class enclave.

My French-speaking hostess, dressed in a white floor-length *jalabia,* welcomed me graciously. She found a seat for me between other guests, who were crowded around (but not quite at) the dining-room table, heavy with varieties of Moroccan food. I was the only English-speaker, and my Hebrew was rudimentary. Body language was the common coin.

The food at the table was special for Mimouna. Nothing could be salty, only sweet. Giveret (Mrs.) Monsungo took a fork and twirled it in a large bowl of stiff, sugared egg whites dotted with nuts. With a flourish and a grand smile, she presented me with the fork and its sticky, sweet load. From then on, I was on my own.

Other elaborate dishes were passed. I tasted candied baby eggplants, candied *pomelos* (a cross between oranges and grapefruit), fried *sultanas* (raisins cooked with sugar and nuts and served cold), *marzipan* shaped like cherries, all kinds of nuts, and *moufletas* (hot, thin pancakes wrapped around butter and honey). Freshly picked leaves, sheaths of wheat, a cooked fish, and a pitcher of milk also were on the table—all for symbolic reasons.

I embarrassed myself when I pointed to a food I didn't recognize and instead of asking "What is that?" I asked in Hebrew "Who is that?" Nevertheless, when I left my hostess beamed at me and said in Hebrew, "Again, next year."

The outdoor aspect of Mimouna begins the next morning with the central celebration in Jerusalem's Sacher Park. One part of the park is lined with tents and displays. Adjoining are a picnic area and a large wooden stage for free afternoon entertainment.

Families arrive early in the day to claim their turf. They spread blankets on the grass or set up tents as if to camp. Nearly every gathering of at least two people has a brazier barbecue burning and someone standing over it, fanning the coals with a piece of cardboard. Clearly, these people are comfortably ensconced for a long stay. By noon, the air is thick with the aroma of barbecued *shishlik,* kebabs, steaks, and chops. A black cloud rises over the park, and your eyes begin to sting. Meanwhile, ice cream and drink vendors—and even a digital-watch salesman—hawk their wares between the hot stoves.

Since 1983, the Beyahad organization has turned Mimouna into not only a Moroccan festival but also a celebration of Israel's ethnic diversity. In a separate area, Jewish ethnic groups might use the large tents to set up their own cultural exhibitions.

The formal part of Mimouna begins early in the afternoon when the

Ethiopian Jewish children at Mimouna

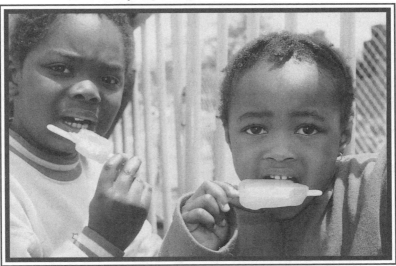

245

president, prime minister, mayor of Jerusalem, and other dignitaries join each other on the stage. Each, mercifully, pledges to speak no more than one minute. Sure.

Then, it's on with the show. Performers range from kibbutz-niks singing contemporary songs to Moroccan Atlas Mountain musicians playing Oriental melo-dies to Tats (a Jewish tribe from the Caucasus) performing athletic dances. The audience loves them all.

Few Israeli celebrations last only a day, and Mimouna is no different. The night after festivities end in Sacher Park, the holiday usually shifts to a Tel Aviv theater to culminate with a performance of North African songs and dances.

Just as everyone is Irish on St. Patrick's Day in the United States, it might soon be that everyone is Moroccan on Mimouna in Israel. The spirit of Mimouna is one of mutual love. As Moroccan Jewry's gift to Israel, it is one of the richest, grandest, sweetest gifts imaginable. One Israeli official of Moroccan background summed it up well: "Too often in the world there is hate for no reason. Mimouna is love for no reason."

For information on open houses, call the Beyahad Movement (Tnuat Beyahad), (02) 625-1263.

Roman Catholic and Protestant Easter

While Jews from all over the world are in Jerusalem to celebrate their ancestors' escape from slavery, Roman Catholics and Protestants from all over the world might also be here to commemorate the crucifixion and resurrection of Jesus. During these often simultaneous Jewish and Christian holy days, with thousands of visiting worshippers, the city is akin to an overripe, juicy, bulging pomegranate, ready to burst and fling its multitudinous seeds far and wide.

Some churches spread Easter events over an 11-day span, from the Friday before Palm Sunday through the Monday after Easter, with daily processions in and out of tortuous, narrow Old City lanes. (This is a time to avoid the souk.) The Franciscans have such a heavy schedule of processions and masses, most of them in the Holy Sepulchre, that observance can be a full-time, totally immersing activity.

On Palm Sunday, several thousand Christians, locals and pilgrims alike, form a double line for the 90-minute procession from the Franciscan monastery at Bethpage on the eastern side of the Mount of Olives, down the slope into the valley, up the other side, and to St. Anne's Church, just inside the Old City at Lion's (St. Stephen's) Gate.

Elsewhere in the city, the Lutheran Church of the Redeemer in the Old City has both an Arabic and an English service. The Baptist Chapel has a Palm Sunday walk beginning at 5:30 a.m.

The rites observed with the widest variation during Holy Week are the Washing of the Feet ceremony on Holy Thursday and the Blessing of the Fire on Holy Saturday. In the first, a senior clergyman washing the feet of 12 members of his congregation re-enacts Jesus washing his disciples' feet.

At St. George's Anglican Church, the ceremony begins with 6 p.m. communion. A vigil until midnight follows. In the Holy Sepulchre, the washing is at 2 p.m. with a Tenebrae Mass afterward. But watch out: Holy Sepulchre doors are locked for a time on Holy Thursday, with no exit or entrance for many hours. Plan accordingly.

In Good Friday's main event, Franciscan friars repeat the walk they make throughout the year at 3 p.m. on Friday. In their somber brown robes, they lead a crowd of people on the Way of the Cross procession, inching along the Via Dolorosa. They follow the route Jesus is said to have taken from the place where he was condemned to Golgotha, the traditional site of the crucifixion, over which the Church of the Holy Sepulchre was built. As the large and solemn international crowd slowly makes its way from station to station carrying an enormous wooden cross, the mood becomes increasingly tense and introspective.

Holy Saturday is the day of the Giving of the Fire, symbolizing the gift of new life. In the Holy Sepulchre, a Latin service at 6:30 a.m. includes the lighting of the Paschal candle and the Blessing of the Fire. Other churches have their own elaborate ceremonies. At St. George's Cathedral in eastern Jerusalem, where the altar was stripped of its decorative objects on Maundy Thursday, a small taper is lit at the back of the darkened Anglican church. An enormous unlit Paschal candle is brought from the altar and lit by the taper. The large candle is then the only light in the church.

It is placed on a stand, and while the congregation sings Psalm 139, "Whither Shall I Go?," acolytes slowly spread light from the Paschal candle throughout the church by passing the flame to the unlit candle held by each worshipper. Gradually, the dark church is illuminated by brilliant light.

Late Saturday night, Roman Catholic churches begin their services to celebrate Easter. They have regular masses on Easter day itself.

Among Protestants, Easter Sunday may begin with a 5 a.m. service at St. Andrew's Church, with its sweeping view of the Hinnom and Kidron Valleys. Another popular place for an early start is the Garden Tomb, which Protestants consider to be Jesus' burial place. There, a series of services begins at 5 a.m. in German and continues at intervals in English, Danish, Finnish, and Dutch.

All of these services are open to the public. The Christian Information

Center and the Municipal Tourist Office have schedules for events that take place during this Holy Week and the one that follows, when Easter comes to the Orthodox churches.

April Fool's Day

Surprising as it may seem, April 1, April Fool's Day, is a big deal in Israel. Recognition of the day goes far beyond someone suddenly screaming, "There's a spider in your hair! Hee, hee. April Fool!"

No, expect nothing benign like that. Instead, you might pick up a newspaper and read that a new tax has been levied, which—Israelis know only too well—is within the realm of possibility. Or you might turn on the radio and hear that, henceforth, women must sit at the back of movie theaters. To all this, you might be sputtering, "Things have gone too far! This is too much!"

But no, don't blame the government or the ultra-Orthodox. It's the nation's news media gone a bit wacky. Let's hope nothing of genuine importance ever happens on April 1. No one in Israel would believe it.

Samaritan Passover

Among those myriad ethnic groups that add spice and surprise to Israel are the Samaritans. Yes, Samaritans, as in the Good Samaritans of Christian Bible fame.

Between the Samaritans who live amid the Arabs of Nablus (Shchem) in the mountains of Samaria and those in the Jewish city of Holon near Tel Aviv, the population numbers some 560 persons. Though they are called "the smallest ethnic minority in the modern world," their current number is a marked increase from the 146 that remained in 1917 after 1,500 years of war, religious persecution, intermarriage, and forced conversion to Christianity and Islam.

Samaritans welcome guests to their Passover celebration, which, according to their calendar, can fall either before, after, or on the normative Jewish Passover. Instead of reading from the Haggadah as do normative Jews, Samaritans read Exodus, chapters 12 to 15. Between passages, they sing a Samaritan hymn from the fifth century. Afterward, they expand the observance by conducting a rite that mainstream Judaism abandoned long ago—the sacrificial slaughter of perfect lambs.

The sacrifice, which is the only part of the Samaritan Passover guests are invited to see, takes place on Mount Gerizim near Nablus, 40 miles north of Jerusalem. Not exactly the suburbs, but the trip is doable, thanks to Egged's bus to Bracha, south of Mount Gerizim. You'll have to hike the rest of the way up the hill, unless you can land a ride.

The Samaritans' origins are lost in the haze of history. They claim descent from the tribes of Ephraim and Menasha and say that when the Assyrians carried off the Ten Tribes of Israel they were overlooked. On the other hand, some historians suggest that instead they are descendants of people imported by the Assyrians to fill the void left by deported Jews. At any rate, Samaritans resemble pale Ashkenazi Jews more than the darker Sephardim. When they intermarry with normative Jews, the Jew in the marriage joins the Samaritans.

Their religion recognizes only the Five Books of Moses. They diverge from normative Jews in other ways: Samaritans maintain that Mount Gerizim, not Jerusalem's Temple Mount, is where Abraham brought Isaac for his intended sacrifice. The slab atop Mount Gerizim is pointed out to visitors as the site where it would have taken place.

And to Samaritans, Mount Gerizim, not Jerusalem, is "the navel of the world." It is there the Samaritan holy sites were built. (In 413 B.C.E., John Hyrcanus, the Hasmonean king, destroyed the holy places and the Samaritan city of Luza.)

It is to this Mount Gerizim that Samaritans must make a pilgrimage three times a year or be excommunicated. During the Passover celebration, houses at the mountaintop are open to visitors and guests.

The drive from Jerusalem to Mount Gerizim is over a winding road and offers views into green chasms and up cultivated terraces cut like steps into the slopes. Above the farmland, the mountains rise rocky and treeless, rolling away to the horizon.

Arab villages here, unlike those in the desert below Jerusalem, have an ordered, prosperous appearance. Even in what still are called refugee camps, handsome, large new houses stand. These Arab villages of delicate and interesting stone buildings make one wonder why Jews often construct—using stones cut by Arabs—dull, ponderous edifices. The Jewish community of Bracha, dating from 1983, is a rugged, windswept, lonely looking place.

At the site of the Samaritan celebration on top of the mountain, bleachers line either side of what looks like a small athletic field. It is here that the sacrifice will take place. On the fence-enclosed field, men and boys wholeheartedly sing traditional songs of narrow melodic range. The dusty scene is reminiscent of a Native American powwow.

The Samaritan high priest sings into a microphone, while around him men and boys exultantly shout melodies in their ancient language, Samaritan-Aramaic. The musical lines run in parallel fifths and often scoop upward in pitch at the end.

The women, who don't take part in the sacrifice, wear their best Western-style clothes. The men dress in white, their loose cotton shirts fluttering over billowing harem pants. Their headdresses tell a cultural story. Elderly priests wear white turbans (they wear red on secular days). Others sport fezes. Younger men wear what has come to be the traditional Samaritan head covering, a white cap that looks like a navy gob's. Also seen are caps that resemble French berets. Yet another common cap seems to cry for the words "John Deere." Protruding here and there out of crowd of singing men are the woolly backsides of tightly held lambs, about to go to their deaths.

The mood of the music changes. Anticipation grows. With a shout from some of the Samaritans in the central areas, men and women holler, laugh, and clap their hands over their heads to the chanted words while some men do a simple dance. And then the lambs, usually one for each family, are sacrificially slaughtered according to the law set down in Exodus, chapter 12.

With so many men and boys participating in the slaughter, it's unlikely that a visitor in the bleachers will actually see the killings through the crowd. But the bloody knives are raised high as each lamb is sacrificed. The warm carcasses are laid on benches directly in front of the bleachers. There, young boys energetically pull off the lambs' skins with their bare hands. The squeamish should be warned.

As part of the ritual, men dab blood on their foreheads. It recalls the Hebrews who put a mark on their doors in Egypt so the Angel of Death

---

Jerusalem Scene

Six-year-old, Israeli-born Taliya and her American-born rabbi father (*abba*) held hands as they walked from Rehov Hess to Rehov Agron. To their left was a high wall enclosing one of the larger Roman Catholic institutions in Jerusalem

Taliya and her father were speaking English. He thought it was important for Taliya to be as fluent in English as she was in Hebrew. The conversation lapsed for a moment, and Taliya looked around her and to the top of the wall. The lofty dome high on the other side drew her eyes up and up to something straight and gleaming topping it. At first she couldn't make out what it was, but then she recognized it.

She turned to her father and asked, "Abba, why is there a 'T' at the top of that building?"

would pass over them before the Exodus began. The men who participate in the ceremony kiss each other on both cheeks or shoulders, carefully keeping their bloody hands off each other's white clothes.

The rite is thousands of years old, but this is the electronic era and television cameras might be here. In that case, cameramen aggressively jostle each other for position. Samaritans, like people everywhere, bloom when the glaring camera lights hit them. At one end of the sacrifice area, a group of Samaritan men, in a brilliantly lit space, lustily sing and clap on cue.

During all this, the near-monotone chanting continues, led most strongly by a white-bearded high priest holding a large, bright blue prayer book. Beyond the slaughter area, visitors will see a glowing full moon rising.

Now the Samaritans prepare to roast the lambs. A long pole of green wood is run through each skinned and cleaned lamb, which then is placed in a roaring fire pit to cook for three or four hours.

It won't be until midnight that the lambs are ready to eat—all the lamb must be consumed before night's end. But at this point, visitors should leave. The festive meal is a private affair.

Back down Mount Gerizim, Bracha sits on its windswept perch under lights that turn night into day, as if perpetually under the eye of a TV camera. Traveling south to Jerusalem, under the full moon, you'll see the rock-ribbed mountains and fertile farmland dance under a silvery glow.

For information on attending a Samaritan Passover, contact Benyamim Tsadaka at (03) 556-7229, by e-mail at tsadakab@netvision.net.il, or on the Net at http://members.tripod.com/ ~ tsedaka/index.htm.

Orthodox Easter
The memory of Latin/Protestant Easter has faded away. Pilgrims have gone home. Jerusalem has done without a celebration or commemoration for perhaps a week. Nervousness begins to pervade the air. Something seems to be missing. But before withdrawal symptoms set in, Eastern and Oriental Orthodox Easter arrives.

Fewer pilgrims descend on the city for Orthodox Easter, but more local residents participate. Greeks, Armenians, Syrians, Copts, Ethiopians, and Russians who adhere to the Orthodox calendar are integral to the Jerusalem community. So Orthodox Easter seems more like a hometown celebration than does its Latin/Protestant predecessor. Of all the pilgrims who do come from foreign countries, most are black-garbed Greeks or Cypriots, who walk the streets carrying olive branches.

Most of the Orthodox denominations have their assigned times and space in the Church of the Holy Sepulchre during Holy Week. The exceptions are the Russians, who conduct services in their church, St. Mary Magdalene on the Mount of Olives; and the Ethiopians, who have their services in Dier es-Sultan, their religious warren on the roof of the Church of the Holy Sepulchre.

Copts and Ethiopians still battle over turf. Time was, Good Friday wasn't complete without priests of these two denominations stoning each other. Because each church jealously guards its rights in and on the Church of the Holy Sepulchre, a special unit of non-Christian guards stands by during Orthodox Easter to make sure that the celebration of the resurrection of the Prince of Peace remains peaceful.

Processions take place in the Holy Sepulchre every day between Lazarus Saturday, the day before Palm Sunday, and Easter Sunday. But the Ethiopians stay put and conduct their processions on their rooftop space.

Of all the events this week, including the washing of feet on a raised platform outside the sepulchre, the most spectacular and literally brilliant is the Ceremony of the Holy Fire (the Giving of the Fire) at 1 p.m. the day before Easter. All the Orthodox denominations—except the Ethiopians, who don't dare leave the roof for fear the Copts will take over—gather in the sepulchre rotunda for this event. Each denomination has a designated place to stand.

Because the Greek Orthodox are the wealthiest and most numerous, they dominate the gathering. Excited, expectant worshippers, carrying fagots of 32 braided, skinny, unlit white candles, squeeze into the church and fill its many nooks as they face the edicule, the covering to what they believe was Jesus' tomb, the sepulchre itself.

The church is so tightly packed it is quite safe to faint—as is one's wont in the heat and crush—without the slightest possibility of hitting the floor. Eight to twelve thousand people will keep you upright.

Teenage boys climb the wooden edicule, stand on narrow ledges, and hang onto any protrusion they can find. Their informality with the nineteenth-century, onion-domed structure comes as a surprise in view of the usual solemnity within this building.

The boys on the edicule are self-appointed cheerleaders for the enormous crowd. It is they who catch the first glimpse of the Greek patriarch in his white satin gown and golden crown as he leads the Greek Orthodox clergy into the church. The Armenian patriarch and his entourage follow. Behind them, in clearly defined pecking order, are the leaders and clergy of other Orthodox denominations, all in resplendent gowns and robes.

With the first sight of the highest representative of the Greek Orthodox Church in Jerusalem, the boys let out a grand roar that resounds through the stone rotunda. Responding, the crowd presses forward, excitedly.

Worshippers hold their candles aloft to keep them from melting, not from fire, which is nowhere yet in the rotunda, but from the heat generated by the assembly.

Up on their perches, the boys defy gravity and clap their hands in rhythm as they sing. The melody sounds strangely like the happy Jewish song heard at a bar mitzvah or wedding, "Simon Tov, oo-Mazel Tov."

The crowd makes room for the Greek patriarch and his followers to march around the edicule, while the congregation joins in singing a stately melody. When the procession comes around to the front of the edicule and its entrance to Jesus' tomb, the rotunda lights are turned off (in the bleakness of the rotunda, it comes as a surprise to realize that lights were on at all), and the church, gloomy on the best of days, falls into twilight in the early afternoon. Only the dome, finished after many years, lets in light.

Ecumenically, the Greek and Armenian patriarchs duck their heads and enter the edicule, while the now-hushed congregation expectantly watches two tiny windows on the structure's sides.

Suddenly, a jubilant cry rings from the crowd. A tongue of fire, said to appear in the tomb through a miracle, is glimpsed from the windows. The patriarchs emerge carrying flaming brands, and worshippers surge forward, almost in a frenzy, to transfer the miraculous fire onto their woven candles. Adding to the excitement, church bells ring wildly.

One after another, throughout the rotunda, candles spring to glowing life. Then, just when the sight becomes a bedazzling sea of burning candles, the crowd suddenly turns to rush out the church's only open door, following the patriarch's procession through the Old City's narrow streets.

Watch out. This is "be careful not to be trampled" time. Whichever way the crowd goes, go too. Be a lemming. Fighting the current is useless and well could be dangerous. Even going with the crowd has its hazards. Few people escape the sting of hot wax dripped on their hands and arms as the human tidal wave sweeps them along. Worshippers everywhere carry the benediction of white streaks of dried wax on their shoulders and hair, an unintentional decoration.

It seems impossible to hope that when the Ceremony of the Holy Fire is over, only the candles will have burned. To protect yourself, don't wear flimsy clothing. The carrier of 32 flaming wicks behind you could be only as tall as your shoulder blade. And where is that person's candle going to be if not close to your back? To offer some reassurance, security people are sprinkled through the crowd. They carry fire extinguishers that shoot water a great distance.

Outside the church, for at least an hour, the Old City is as jammed tight as a wine bottle with no corkscrew. However, by the time the Arab scout troops with their bagpipes, drums, and flags have passed, it begins to be possible to choose your own direction to walk.

The Greek Orthodox have a liturgy service at 1 a.m. before the edicule on Easter morning and a grand procession into the Church of the Holy Sepulchre at noon. The Armenians have mass at 1:30 a.m. in the Holy Sepulchre.

If staying up that late isn't in your plan, the Procession Service of the Armenians, 3 p.m. Easter in the Cathedral of St. James, is a colorful alternative. The service begins in the fairy tale–like cathedral, with its ornate blue tiles and stalactitic forest of innumerable hanging lanterns. The patriarch wears a red and gold-beaded cape, so heavy that men at either side of him help support its weight. Behind him, priests follow in bejeweled crowns and gold-and-wine embroidered gowns. Even the altar boys are richly dressed for the occasion.

The ceremony soon moves outdoors into the Armenian Quarter Compound plaza. There, men arrange themselves in a rectangle and sing chants antiphonally. A choreography emerges as the men cross from one side of the rectangle to the other. Finally, they move into the cathedral courtyard and later back into the cathedral for the service's conclusion.

For Armenians and Syrians, the holiday has one more day of observance. They celebrate a last Easter mass on Monday. For the second day of Easter, the 360 oil lamps and candelabras at St. James' Cathedral are lit—a process that takes three hours. The service lasts from 5:30 to 11 a.m. and is strikingly beautiful in sight and sound. As with Latin/Protestant Easter, complete schedules of events are available at the Christian Information Center.

Holocaust Martyrs and Heroes Remembrance Day

On the 27th of Sivan, less than a week after the tumult of Passover, Mimouna, and Latin/Protestant Easter, comes Holocaust Martyrs and Heroes Remembrance Day, when Israel, like a family, remembers the 6 million Jews murdered by the Nazis during World War II. It is a day that can tear your heart out. Restaurants, movie theaters, and other places of entertainment acknowledge the solemnity of the day by closing.

The central ceremonies in Israel take place at Yad Vashem in Jerusalem. In the evening, Holocaust survivors, soldiers, new immigrants, high government officials, and others gather at the Holocaust memorial for a quiet observance. Admission is by invitation.

At 10 the next morning, sirens sound for two minutes. During that time, the country comes to a halt. Cars and buses stop where they are. Bus passengers who can do so slide out of their seats and stand. Jerusalemites at home step out onto their balconies as a way of sharing the memory with the community. The siren, its sound rising and falling, is an eerie cry.

Later in the day, Yad Vashem hosts another ceremony. Dozens of wreaths are laid, and the Righteous of the Nations, non-Jews who risked their lives to aid Jewish victims of the Nazis, are honored.

It's possible on Remembrance Day to avoid reading a description of how a young child spent two years squeezed between floorboards under a schoolroom floor. There, he could see outside through a crack in the wall and watch sheep—but not Jewish children—wander freely. It's possible to turn off the English radio broadcast to avoid hearing a woman relate in a strained, choked voice how her terrified, screaming three-year-old daughter was pulled from her arms forever by German soldiers. But don't avoid these or other such stories. These people were survivors in the most excruciating sense of the word. They had to use their wits and make the most of every smidgen of sheer luck to survive. To avoid sharing in their experiences is to miss a major part of what Israel is about.

While the Allies were rebuilding a defeated post-war Germany, the British locked Holocaust survivors—trying to get to Israel and with no homes to return to—into detention camps surrounded by guard towers. Many died, some were killed by the British. Others weren't allowed to leave Cyprus for Israel until 1949, a year after Israel's independence.

When these people finally arrived in their new home, they didn't look for sympathy. There was no "trauma control" treatment available to them. They had only their determination to go forward. One survivor was asked if Israelis were interested in hearing his experiences when he arrived. He answered, "I didn't have time to tell them. I needed to get on with my life." He eventually became the head of surgery at Hadassah Hospital.

Jews are a people of hope. Along with their painful memories, which can never disappear, from deep within themselves Holocaust survivors found the hope and courage to rebuild their ravaged lives, to build Israel, and to contribute good to the world.

Independence Day

Israel's Independence Day (Yom Ha'atzma'oot) celebration has a prologue—Remembrance Day, for soldiers who died defending Israel. Remembrance Day begins at sunset, 24 hours before Independence Day starts on the fifth of Iyar (in late April or early May).

Israelis don't say their soldiers have died. Instead, they use the term *fallen*. Despite the reality of modern warfare, the word conjures an almost romantic image of a young warrior stopped in his tracks by the enemy with not a messy bomb or bullet that leaves his entrails on the ground but with something neater—perhaps a spear, as in ancient times.

On this day, places of entertainment and restaurants close at sunset. At 8 p.m., a mournful one-minute siren ushers in a brief state ceremony at the Western Wall for bereaved families. The usually bustling plaza is now subdued. Elsewhere, movement has stopped. Cars and buses are at a standstill. People stop where they are. With the siren, the nations' flags are lowered to half-staff and the president lights a memorial candle at the wall. A few comments by officials follow, and the commemoration comes to an end with Kaddish, the Jewish praise to God said over the dead. The ceremony is especially poignant because of its simplicity and brevity—like so many of the lives it memorializes. A recent innovation is that victims of terrorism also are remembered this day, with a memorial at Mount Herzl.

At 11 the next morning, another two-minute siren brings traffic and all movement to a halt as it did the night before and on Holocaust Remembrance Day. The radio plays only subdued music and television is programmed appropriately. Buses follow their usual schedules, but in the early afternoon stores close and remain closed through Independence Day, which follows.

Ceremonies at military cemeteries for the men and women who died in Israel's many wars, including Druse and Bedouin soldiers in the Israeli army, take place throughout the country. The culmination is the central ceremony just before sunset atop Mount Herzl. In it, a representative group of people of all backgrounds and ages who have made outstanding contributions to Israel light 12 torches representing the 12 Tribes of Israel. This event is by invitation only, but it is televised.

Both remembrance days—for Holocaust victims and for fallen soldiers—provide a useful outlet for mourners. They speak of their pain on television, radio, and at various programs. They show photographs of their loved ones. They read poems and other writings that they or the deceased wrote. In this way their loss is shared. They don't have to mourn alone.

Then an abrupt change of mood happens on Mount Herzl. The quiet, somber observance concludes with a burst of fireworks. Suddenly, the solemnity and sorrow of the previous 24 hours is replaced by an explosion of exultation that is Independence Day. Thus Remembrance Day and Independence Day are linked, carrying out the Jewish tradition of remembering joy in sadness and sadness in joy. It's a swift transition, often a heavy strain on the bereaved. But they say that the celebration gives purpose to their loss.

With Yom Ha'atzma'oot festivities in full swing, a strange sound of clicking is heard in the land. No, giant crickets haven't invaded. The sound comes from plastic hammers. Kids and a lot of adults use them to bop your head. If you have the misfortune of being tall and blond or bald, you offer a challenge kids (and some adults) can't resist. You could have an enormous headache by the time the night is over. But no matter who you are, what your age or appearance, you're fair game. I carry a hammer this night in self-defense, although I am neither tall, blond, nor bald. But if you try to get me, I'm gonna get you first.

Actually, the hammer game isn't as sadistic as it seems. On impact, the hammer compacts and clicks. The sound is far louder than the hammer is heavy. And no one uses much force. It's the "Gotcha!" triumph that these hammer-wielders aim for, but they are noticeably gentler when they bop the heads of toddlers in strollers.

So there you have it: Your first impression of Israelis celebrating their nation's re-birthday could be the sight of swarms of people playfully bopping each other on the head. The sound of the accumulated clicks conjures a movie scene of an old-fashioned Teletype office at crisis time.

Another sight, one less benign, is that of kids wielding spray cans of yucky plastic string, which gets caught up in long hair. Worse, but actually illegal, is sprayed plastic snow.

More remains to be seen besides head hitting and plastic spraying: buildings and streets strung with lights, musicians playing and singing in the heart of Jerusalem, concerts at the Jerusalem Theater, and exuberant, lighthearted crowds filling the streets and dancing. This is also the night for private festivities, the closest Israeli equivalent to the West's New Year's Eve parties.

But the most joyous way to spend the evening is by dancing in the streets. Rehov King George is set aside for dancing. Bands perform in Independence Park, at the plaza in front of HaMashbir, and at Kikar Zion. Dancing goes on in Safra Square in front of the Municipal Building until the buses, which stopped for the night around midnight, start rolling again with the dawn. Don't worry about having a partner. Israeli dancing is done in a circle, drawing steps from Israel's many cultural influences, including Yemenite, Arabic, and Eastern European. If you stand on the sidelines it's by your own choice.

Several circles fill the street. People move in and out of them, strangers holding hands, celebrating together. Kids, the elderly, and all ages in between are out there kicking up their heels. And as exuberant as they are, the high spirits come from the heart, not from booze. Wholesomeness and innocence pervade the atmosphere.

Hotels and major buildings, even main streets, are festooned with colorful lights. Young people on the street are a match. Some wear antennas that light up or show the Israeli flag. Others have multihued, glowing rings around their necks.

You might encounter groups in blue parkas. The logo on the parkas indicates that these people were among Jews from all over the world who took part in the March of the Living. They have come from the death camps of Auschwitz and Berkenau in Poland to celebrate Israel's birthday—another poignant note in the revelries.

Late in the evening, fireworks blaze against the sky from numerous places in the city—the Western Wall, Mount Zion, and the roof of the Sheraton Plaza Hotel among them. The audience is enraptured, and "ooohs" and "aaahs" fill the air with each colorful shower of lights. Midnight celebrations might take place atop the Mount of Olives or Mount Scopus.

The next day, many people go picnicking, and a black cloud from hundreds of smoking barbecues rises over Jerusalem. A string of events is scheduled: government-sponsored outings; an international Bible Quiz competition with youngsters from such disparate countries as Finland, Australia, and Peru; and free admission to certain museums.

Usually late in the morning, the air force presents a flyover of the president's house with F-something-or-others, soaring through the air and leaving behind white and blue trails, the colors of the Israeli flag. About an hour later, planes and helicopters in various formations fly over Independence Park while picnickers turn their stinging eyes away from smoking barbecues to wave and cheer.

The show is quite spectacular. But then, these pilots are descendants of men who streaked across at least two enemy Arab countries and left a destroyed nuclear reactor behind in Iraq in 1981—an astounding military aviation feat that left the world gaping. So their show this day darn well should be good.

By the time the morning after the morning after dawns, you can feel Jerusalem shifting out of party gear and into its business-as-usual gear once again. The party's over for now.

Armenian Remembrance Day

On April 24, virtually the entire Armenian community in Jerusalem takes part in a slow, solemn procession led by black-robed priests from St. James Cathedral in the Old City to their nearby cemetery on Mount Zion.

Armenians, too, carry the memory of a mass annihilation. On April 24, 1915, Turks arrested Armenian intellectual leaders in Istanbul and later executed them. Afterward, the Turks commenced mass deportations and systematic murder of people whom they saw as siding with their enemies, the British and the Russians.

How much of the genocide had to do with the fact that Turks are Moslem and Armenians are Christian has been debated. But Armenians point to the murder of some 1.5 million, including thousands of children—many of them thrown into the sea. Descendants of survivors who escaped to Jerusalem, and many of the survivors themselves, are among the two thousand marchers in the procession.

Graffiti appears on Armenian Quarter walls close to this date. It is young Armenians' way of explaining the purpose of the procession, which isn't only to remember the dead but is also to remind the world, Turkey in particular, of the killings. Armenians still strive for an acknowledgment by Turkey that the massacre took place.

At the cemetery, marchers lay wreathes at the cenotaph memorializing Armenian soldiers who lost their lives fighting with the British against the Turks during the First World War.

Lag B'Omer

The big show in Israel on Lag B'Omer takes place on Mount Meron near Safed on the 18th of Iyar, usually in May. On the evening that Lag B'Omer begins, pilgrims gather at the graves of Shimon Bar-Yochai, reputed author of the basic book of Jewish mysticism, the Zohar, and his son, Elazar. Many of the pilgrims have marched in the procession from Safed. Since 1833, a sefer Torah has been carried in this procession from the Abu family's home to Meron. But if distance and jostling with a crowd of 150,000 to 200,000 madly celebrating people puts you off, Jerusalem offers other ways to enjoy the day.

Lag B'Omer largely is considered to be a 25-hour interlude in the midst of a 49-day period of semi-mourning. In temple times, a measure of barley (an omer) was counted for 49 days, beginning on the second night of Passover and ending 50 days later with the holiday Shavuot.

The counting joined an agricultural festival with temple rites. It was a way of setting the date of two events: the ripening of the wheat crop at the end of the 49 days and the anniversary of the day on which Jews believe God gave them the Torah.

After the destruction of the Second Temple, the 49 days became a period of semi-mourning, in which weddings and haircuts were forbidden. Many explanations have been offered. One benign explanation says that people were needed in the fields and couldn't take time out to go to wedding parties.

But Judaism is known for being considerate of human frailties. The people needed a reprieve from mourning, so Lag B'Omer, a time-out, emerged on the 33rd day of counting. The reasons for this particular date are obscure. One explanation is that Lag B'Omer marks the end of a plague almost two thousand years ago that killed many students of the illustrious Rabbi Akiva.

Ashkenazim view Lag B'Omer as a one-day hiatus for weddings and haircuts. Sephardim look on Lag B'Omer as the first day after Passover on which weddings and haircuts resume. Whichever way it is marked and whatever its origins, Lag B'Omer is a big wedding day. Watch for cars chauffeuring newlyweds. The cars aren't hard to spot, not because of blaring horns and trailing tin cans (since these aren't traditional here) but because they are bedecked with balloons, ribbons, and flowers.

After dark on Lag B'Omer, the Jerusalem sky takes on a red glow and the odor of burning wood seeps into flats. Bonfires have been set in gardens, empty lots, and parks. Instead of people dancing, flames dance. The slope below the Jerusalem Theater is dotted with fires—a dazzling sight. Around some of these fires, whole families gather, strum guitars, celebrate marriage engagements and birthdays, beat drums, and have cookouts.

The tradition of sitting around a fire came from Rabbi Shimon Bar Yochai's idea of reflecting on "the light." Perhaps in mystical Safed people are reflecting, but you don't see much of it in Jerusalem.

One of the biggest fires is in Mea She'arim, the ultra- Orthodox neighborhood. There, residents build a huge, grotesque tower of kindling. If you are nearby before the tower begins to burn briskly, you will find Israeli flags going up in smoke. This can be a shocking sight. It is the work of a small but vociferous group of Jews who believe that since modern Israel wasn't created by God (and they don't see God's hand in newborn Israel's defeat of five Arab armies) it has no reason to exist. Bonfire watchers with Zionist inclinations might want to skip this particular fire.

Lag B'Omer—a three-year-old boy receives his first haircut.

The next morning, Orthodox Jews gather before the Tomb of Simon the Just, off Nablus Road in eastern Jerusalem, for the ceremony in which three-year-old boys receive their first haircuts. Calling them "haircuts" is a bit formal. Actually, each family asks an admired rabbi to take the first snip from the young son's hair. Then a favorite relative takes the next snip and so on. While each lock of hair is returned to the parents, perhaps to be saved, the three-year-old often cries with despair. Sephardi women get the honor of snipping hair along with the men. Among Ashkenazim, as with so much else, it's men only.

If you go into the human-made cave known as Simon's Tomb, you will find it jammed with people praying or milling about. Simon the Just, Ha'-Tzadik in Hebrew, is a revered figure. His best-known words were, "The world stands on three things—Torah, divine service, and charity."

Over the heads of the people in the cave, many of whom are stuffing notes to God in crevices between the rocks, an assortment of anachronistic chandeliers hangs from the stone ceiling. One looks as if it were meant to be an eternal flame.

Outside, after most of the three-year-old boys have had their hair haphazardly trimmed, the celebration continues. Sephardim throw confetti. Food appears everywhere, as if miraculously. Cakes, schnapps, candy, bourekas, and boiled potatoes are some of the goodies passed around. Foods reflect each family's ethnic background.

Fathers lift their children, especially the now-smiling and newly trimmed boys, and carry them in their arms or on their shoulders for a traditional circle dance—"the Yeshiva Two-Step." With their tears gone, along with a lot of their hair, the little boys feel grown up. Traditionally, they now are ready to begin their religious studies.

Jerusalem Day

If your dancing shoes haven't yet been worn out in the Golden City, Jerusalem Day (Yom Yerushalayim), which celebrates the reunification of the city by the Six-Day War, surely should do it. Landing on the 28th of Iyar, less than two weeks after Lag B'Omer, this festivity includes so many events that you need to carry a program to keep track of where you'd like to be and when.

The events vary from year to year. Typically, a major feature is dancing away the night at Safra Square or some other place (since you had all that practice on Independence Day, you now know the Israeli dance-step basics, a "Yemenite right" from a "Yemenite left"). Other activities could include a relay race into the city by ten thousand schoolkids, a midnight march by yeshiva students to the Western Wall, a memorial service on Ammunition Hill where the stiffest fighting against the Jordanians took place, a memorial service for Ethiopian Jews who died on their way to Israel, free walking tours of the city and the municipality complex, and free admission to the Israel and Rockefeller Museums.

But the biggest single event, the one that pulls Jerusalemites and visitors to the city streets, is the annual Jerusalem Day March from Rehov Yafo to Sachar Park. Twenty thousand marchers from schools, businesses, the telephone company, the electric company, the army, the navy, veterans groups, and more take part. They sing as they walk, they wave, they holler greetings, and the young soldiers and sailors reveal (don't tell Israel's enemies) that many don't know their left from their right—or else they simply ain't got rhythm. Parade watchers applaud the marchers, sing, holler "Left, right, left, right," call out greetings, put candy in soldiers' pockets, cross the street in front of an onslaught of marchers, and generally have a great old time.

Meanwhile, the mother of all traffic jams takes place around the city center. Not only can you not get in but it's also difficult to get out. If you're driving, expect to go circuitous miles out of your way to get where you're going. Better yet, walk or take the bus, which will also be traveling circuitous miles, but the driver will be the one sweating.

Again, Jerusalem is bedecked for this day—its very own day—with flags and bright lights. But stores are open, buses roll (where they can), and the dancing continues.

Shavuot

Remember all-night "teach-ins," the phenomenon of the 1960s and 1970s that usually dealt with the Vietnam War? Well, they weren't a new idea. Jews have been having them, perhaps for thousands of years.

Shavuot, on the sixth of Sivan in late May or early June, is the time of Jewish teach-ins. Some say the custom started in the Sinai, with the Hebrew people waiting all night for Moses to come down from the mountain with the Torah. Others say Ashkenazi Jews started the tradition in the twelfth or thirteenth centuries C.E.

The main aspect of Shavuot is to celebrate the giving of the Torah to Moses on Mount Sinai. Orthodox Jews maintain that by implication, Moses brought not only the Ten Commandments down from Mount Sinai but also the entire body of Jewish teaching.

In memory of the night-long wait for Moses, Jews gather to study and discuss the Torah all night. Sessions end with a sunrise service at the Western Wall. In the morning, the Book of Ruth is read, probably because main aspects of the story take place during the spring harvest and also tell of her loyalty to her adopted religion.

All-night study sessions abound all over Jerusalem. Many are conducted in English, including the "Learn-A-Thon" at the Israel Center and the "Study Marathon" at the Center for Conservative Judaism. Several sessions take place in the Jewish Quarter of the Old City.

Because of the study sessions, the first night of Shavuot is alive with movement. People—whole families with children and strollers—are out in the night and early morning as they make their way to learn. Before dawn, the streets are rivers of people heading for the Western Wall.

Shavuot is also significant as one of three agricultural festivals that were once observed with a pilgrimage to Jerusalem. Shavuot celebrates the "first fruits" of the harvest. The day before Shavuot, schoolchildren, looking like sprites, may be seen on city streets with garlands of flowers around their hair.

Traditional Shavuot food consists of dairy dishes. Legend has it that after their long wait for Moses, the Hebrews discovered that the milk in their camp had gone bad, so they made cheese from it. Another explanation is that the Torah is as nourishing as mother's milk. So today, cheesecake and blintzes are a must.

Shavuot is like Shabbat: The siren announces its beginning, no buses run, and stores and schools are closed. Since it takes place in early summer, hotels and beaches are packed.

Canada Day and the Fourth of July

There's always a way of getting in touch with your North American roots in Jerusalem, perhaps more of a way, what with McDonald's and Kentucky Fried Chicken, than we would like. But the official time for commemorating your North American heritage is in July, when the Association of Americans and Canadians in Israel sponsors a celebration in Sacher Park.

True to the organization's name, the celebration falls between Canada Day (July 1) and U.S. Independence Day (July 4). All ethnic groups are welcome to join in. And the mayor always shows up to give his greetings—votes are votes. So dig out your baseball cap and your red, white, and blue clothes. A baseball game, relays, a sing-along, and a barbershop quartet are some of the events. You can buy hot dogs and hamburgers, not that they taste like the ones back home, but it's the nostalgia that counts. The only thing missing is the fireworks.

Tisha B'Av

The dog days of summer are bereft of major holidays, Jewish or Christian. (The constantly whirling Moslem calendar, however, could offer a surprise in the midst of Israel's sun-baked season.) Perhaps the patriarchs were too busy farming to concentrate on religion, or maybe they simply were too hot to think holy thoughts. For two months, there is a drought in religious activity that parallels the absence of rain.

Then Tisha B'Av arrives, usually in early August. It isn't a major holiday, but it does offer a change of pace from the long, sunny days.

263

Tisha B'Av, which means simply "the ninth of the month of Av," is intensely solemn. This is a day of out-and-out mourning over the tragedies in Jewish history. It is the darkest day on the Jewish calendar. It is said that on this day Nebuchadnezzar destroyed the First Temple in 568 B.C.E.; Titus destroyed the Second Temple in 70 C.E..; the Bar Kochba revolt against the Romans collapsed and Hadrian plowed Jerusalem under in 135 C.E.; and, in 1492, King Ferdinand and Queen Isabella expelled all Jews from Spain.

Tisha B'Av concludes a three-week semi-mourning period. During these three weeks, the Orthodox avoid meat and wine and neither wear new clothes, get their hair cut, nor get married. Customarily, when the ninth of Av arrives, leather isn't worn. So out come the sneakers as a substitute.

The Western Wall is the focal point of the Tisha B'Av observance, for the wall is the last original remnant of the temple area. On this day, thousands of Jews converge here. Many sit on mats on the ground or on low benches. The readings are dirges and the Book of Lamentations.

Inside the synagogues, the Ark and all decorations are draped with black cloth. Even the Torah scroll may have black cloth covering its metal breastplate. The only light is from the "eternal flame," which always burns in synagogues. Places of entertainment close down, but work continues. Radio and television broadcasts reflect the theme of mourning.

Traditionally during Tisha B'Av, Jews walk around the periphery of the Old City. Lately, the walk takes place in the evening, after Tisha B'Av begins and after the first reading of Lamentations. It is a stirring event. Marchers walk quietly, especially through the Arab neighborhood, for this is not an "in your face" act. To walk along the western outer periphery of the Old City in the dark, with the lighted Kidron Valley to your left and the lighted Mount of Olives beyond, is thrilling. It is a tradition that many think should be revived as a standard demonstration of love of Jerusalem.

✦ ✦ ✦

Weeks later, the spiky squill plant's tiny white flowers blossom, announcing that summer is almost over. The intense heat of the past months, with its dry desert wind, called *hamsin* in Arabic, *sherav* in Hebrew, wanes.

Jerusalemites' energy picks up. Suddenly (it always seems to happen that way), the High Holidays are approaching. The sound of men practicing the shofar is heard. "Already?" people ask each other, just as they did last year and will again next year. Preparations must be made. All sorts of things to do. Got to get busy. And thus Jerusalem's cycle of holy days, celebrations, and memorials begins again.

16
SETTLING IN

T he dictionary defines a *sojourner* as a person who "stays for a time, resides temporarily." These last chapters are for those of you who are able to become sojourners in the city of Jerusalem. But they are also for those who dream of staying longer or who simply dream of knowing what it's like to live in the Golden City.

Often, sojourners fall through the crack between tourists and immigrants. They have to figure out a lot about the city on their own. This chapter and the six that follow give shortcuts—from how to rent an apartment to where to buy books, make new friends, and watch movies—so the process of savoring Jerusalem can begin as quickly as possible.

Youth Has Its Day

If your extended stay means bringing children to Jerusalem, they are your first consideration. You might wonder, how will they fit in? The following should provide some insight.

I was lingering over coffee in a Rehov Rivlin restaurant during off-hours, irresistibly watching a scene being played out in front of me. A lithe young man, perhaps still in his twenties, was sitting in a chair against a wall holding his baby in his arms. Another man about the same age, tall and broad-shouldered, entered. He saw the father and his baby and approached them. Smiling, he reached out and carefully took the gurgling infant into his arms.

Bedouin boys in Wadi Qelt

After giving the baby a hug, he held her at arm's length so the two could conduct a baby talk conversation. Then a third young man, only slightly less burly than the second, entered, and he, too, stopped to entertain the baby. He jingled his keys and then leaned over to nibble her ear.

After several minutes of this play, the broad-shouldered man pressed the baby against his chest again and then gently returned her to her father. With that, he and the man beside him continued on their way. Apparently they didn't even know the father.

I never had witnessed a scene like this before. I had never

seen men play with a baby, unless they were related or had some other close connection. I told my friend Aaron about the scene, adding, "That was the most beautiful thing I've seen here." He smiled, shrugged, and said, "That's Israel."

Indeed. Israel is a veritable kiddieland, where children truly are treasured. It isn't a matter of mere talk about the importance of children. In Israel, outside the home, every child becomes everyone's child. Strangers give children adoring looks and simultaneously check on their safety. Not only does every child have an anonymous Big Brother watching over him or her but also a Big Sister and substitute Mom and Dad. The only time I heard a child in Israel hollered and nagged at, it turned out his parents were North Americans.

Children are accepted here (some say, "pampered") in many ways they aren't in Western countries. On a business day on which elementary schools are closed, some children simply accompany their parents to work. A bus driver's son stands beside him and punches passengers' tickets. In a bank, a manager is busy talking with a client. When his phone rings, his seven-year-old daughter answers it. You can be sure the caller isn't affronted, and he probably praises her telephone manners.

All this is by way of assuaging those of you who might be concerned about taking your children out of their familiar environment to live in Jerusalem for a while. Kids would be lucky to have such an opportunity!

What American kids find in Israel, perhaps for the first time, is freedom. Not the "freedom" that comes from being indulged or ignored, but the freedom of physical movement that doesn't need to be circumscribed. Other than concerns over traffic, generally speaking, it is safe for children to be out on the streets, even alone. On holiday nights, such as Independence Day, children are out there enjoying the fun often only with other children. It isn't that no creeps exist in Israel; it's that they haven't taken over. The streets still belong to the people, not the perverts. American parents, who worry more and more over their children's safety at home, can relax here.

The most important thing about bringing children to Israel is to plan for them far in advance. When the idea of a stay in Israel first flickers in your mind, you should begin hunting for information.

A good source of information on schools and day camps is the Association of Americans and Canadians in Israel. Note: The AACI cautions prospective immigrants about making such a major move with teenagers. Teenagers are the hardest to uproot, the least adjustable. Eleventh and twelfth grades are especially problematic here, for reasons explained below.

Nevertheless, parents can rest assured that their children will learn

Hebrew and make the cultural adjustment far faster than they will. I have seen children, even teenagers, blend in with their classmates and help steer their parents through the complexities of Israeli life.

The School System

To a non-Israeli, the school system, for all its entanglements, seems like a bowl of spaghetti. It also might be one of the most democratic, yet divisive, systems anywhere, for it reflects the divisions in Israeli society.

Within the state public schools are two parallel systems, secular and religious. In the secular system, religion is taught as cultural heritage. In the religious system, the curriculum is supplemented by religious studies. And when I refer to "religion," I'm talking about the Jewish religion.

In addition, independent, strictly Orthodox Jewish schools, largely maintained by Agudath Israel, are supported by the state. The state recognizes other independent schools that follow an obligatory curriculum, whether they are secular or religious. Another group of schools is unofficial. These are run by various religious groups and don't follow the basic state curricula. So picking a school for your children in Israel can become an existentialist challenge.

Almost all schools teach in Hebrew. Younger children can often swim in this environment, but older ones without a good language background could sink like cement. The municipality recognizes the problem and runs a Hebrew *ulpan* (language school) for seventh through twelfth graders from September to June at Rehov Kav Tet B'November 10. The ulpan is free and lasts two to three months.

Deborah Millgrim, an education counselor for the AACI, has been immersed professionally in the Israeli education system since the 1970s. She suggests that unless your children have a good grounding in Hebrew, you shouldn't expect great academic accomplishments during a sojourn in Jerusalem, especially from teenagers. Nor should you worry about it. She believes the prime goal should be for kids to enjoy themselves and have a positive experience.

Not all schools are right for visiting kids, Millgrim notes. At some, temporary students are left to drift. Others are more supportive. Two schools with good support systems she cited are Frankel in French Hill and Rene Cassin in Ramat Eshkol.

For advice on schools, it's pointless to ask Israelis. Their children don't have the same problems as yours. You have to speak with other parents in your situation who have "been there" already.

Millgrim says that except for high school, you should first find the school you want your children to attend, then rent a flat in its area. Most high schools are private. They decide which students they will accept—

Jerusalem Scene

Canadian-born Richard was living in Kiryat HaYovel in the thick of a community of Georgian Jews. The ways of the Gruzinim, as they are called here, were far different from his. Richard suffered housewives throwing their scrubwater and garbage out the window and onto on his clean laundry. He heard loud talk and music day and night. He was particularly fed up with an elderly Gruzini—a Georgian man who usually sat outside his building. The old man spent his day sipping mint tea and acting as the self-appointed monitor of everyone who entered or exited.

Then Richard had to join his military unit and go to war. Weeks later, he returned home. Exhausted and dirty, he struggled to reach his building and his own four walls. He was eager, finally, to wash away the war and get some sleep.

As he approached his building, he cringed as he heard the usual noise that emanated from it at every hour. There, sitting as usual, placidly drinking his mint tea and watching everyone's coming and going, was the elderly Gruzini.

Richard gave a perfunctory wave to the old man as he headed for his mailbox to collect the letters that had accumulated while he was fighting the enemy. He was eager for contact with normal life—words from far-away loved ones, even bills.

But when he reached his mailbox, he was thunderstruck. It was smeared over by brazen brush strokes of red paint. Richard was furious. He had risked his life for these people, and they had vandalized his mailbox. Did they know nothing about common decency?

Richard turned and angrily stalked toward the self-appointed guard. "Who vandalized my mailbox?" he shouted.

The Gruzini looked at Richard with astonishment. "But nobody hurt your mailbox."

"No?" Richard frantically pointed. "What do you call that red paint?"

"That?" The old man was taken aback. In a quiet voice, he said, "We painted over your mailbox so while you were at war, the Angel of Death wouldn't be able to find you."

That episode, Richard says, was the turning point of his acceptance of life in Israel. He realized that it wasn't only a matter of his neighbors learning his ways but of him learning theirs.

And he still lives in Kiryat HaYovel.

but the government pays the bill. The particular problem with 11th and 12th grades here, Millgrim maintains, is that these grades are devoted to preparation for the national matriculation exams, which could be compared to the New York State Regents Exams. In these grades, visiting students might not get enough attention, even in the best schools.

You might consider a private school in which English is the language of instruction, but there aren't many such schools. Most of them are run by Christian institutions. Although they are open to all, these schools include instruction in the Christian religion. The Anglican Church School is the most highly regarded.

The situation is much better for preschoolers. They have many options, since the percentage of Israeli youngsters placed in some sort of day care is among the highest in the Western world. A few nursery schools are bilingual (Hebrew-English). Some are exclusively English-speaking.

Registration for elementary school takes place at the municipality offices, Building 3 at Safra Square. Registration for secular junior high school is also at the municipality. Apply directly to the desired high school for admission. High school registration takes place as early as January.

Millgrim suggests that for starters, parents get the AACI booklet on education (which she wrote). She will also talk to anyone who needs help.

"I don't want people to make decisions on the basis of ignorance," Millgrim says. "A lot of places aren't friendly to visitors. You want your children to go to a place where they'll be accepted and supported and can get a good feeling about country." She's a gift to baffled parents.

Extracurricular and Summer Activities

Most schools have a six-day week, with classes starting at 8 a.m. and finishing between noon and 2:45, depending on the grade. Perhaps the most important thing to remember about the Israeli school day is that the 10 a.m. snack is sacred. Children all the way through high school arrive with snacks in hand.

Because of such short days, extracurricular activities, especially for younger children, abound. There are art classes at the Israel Museum, music lessons at the Rubin Academy, classes in a variety of arts at the International Cultural Center for Youth, outdoor activities with the Society for the Protection of Nature, storytelling programs, and a potpourri of offerings at Beit HaNo'ar and the YMCA. Youth centers and community centers offer children various other activities, including sports. The AACI is involved with Jerusalem Youth Baseball.

English-language story hours take place regularly in certain libraries and community centers for children ages 3 to 10. The schedule appears in AACI's bimonthly publication, *Jerusalem Voice.*

Teenagers can chat with other teenagers on the Internet. Two addresses are www.geocities.com/EnchantedForest/Dell/3239 and TEEN-TO-TEEN, a virtual magazine, at www.ttt.org.il. The site lists recreational spots and hangouts for teens in Israel.

In summer, day camps abound. Activities range from lanyard-making to sports to computers. Institutions like the Israel Museum and the Natural History Museum run day camps. The Ein Yael Living Museum near Malha Canyon runs what it calls a "traditional arts and crafts day camp." Some camps are for English-speaking children specifically. The bad news is that registration often closes at the end of May. Worse news is that day camps last only two or three weeks and they might not meet daily.

There are some sleep-away camps for English-speaking children. For horse lovers, the King David Riding School at the Moshav Neve Ilan Ranch has both a day camp and a sleep-away camp. Most day camps and sleep-away camps advertise in a *Jerusalem Post* supplement at the end of May.

While You're in the Neighborhood

Jerusalem is the sum of its parts. Not only are its parts many, but new parts keep springing up. Jerusalem is a jumble of neighborhoods, some as small as a city block, others massive groups of residential buildings that make up small cities in themselves. It's important to get a handle on neighborhood names so you can find your way around, understand references to them, and to decide where you would like to stay during your time in Jerusalem.

The Old City, Rehavia, and Mea She'arim are the neighborhoods people seem to learn most quickly. It can seem as if all the others are called "Moshe Something." I know the problem, for many neighborhoods do have the name Moshe in them—all named for Sir Moses Montefiore. To get the lay of the land and pin down the major areas, open your trusty city map, and we'll check brief descriptions against some of the names.

The **Old City** (Jewish Quarter): Called the Rova, it is picturesque, full of tourists, and doesn't easily connect with the rest of the city. Living there could meet spiritual, historical, and aesthetic needs.

Rehavia: Old Ashkenazi Jerusalem, in the south-central part of the city, is becoming more and more mixed. Everyone who was anyone in Israel's establishment once lived here, and some still do. It was the city's first "garden suburb," founded in 1921. It has a snooty reputation, less and less deserved. Its location is central and thus terrific.

Talbia: Just south of Rehavia, it's a bit newer and richer than Rehavia. Former Arab homes add grace to the neighborhood. Martin Buber lived here at Rehov Hovevei Zion 3. Don't confuse Talbia with Talpiot. Some maps and street signs call it Komemiyut, but if you do, no one will know what you're talking about. As in several other neighborhoods, the Arab name persists, despite civic efforts to replace it.

Kiryat Shmuel: East of Talbia, south of Rehavia, "It would like to be Rehavia," is a snippy comment often made about it. The truth is, anyone who wants to sell or rent property here tries to up its status by telling prospects, "This is Rehavia." It was founded in 1928 and named for Rabbi Shmuel Salant. It has a great location between the city center and the Jerusalem Theater, but few people are familiar with its name.

Yemin Moshe: East and south of the King David Hotel, this is one of Jerusalem's most picturesque neighborhoods and has glorious views of the Old City. Before the Six-Day War, it was home to poor Sephardim, then to artists, and now to the well-to-do and upward. It is an affluent island, up and down a steep hill from the rest of the city and without even a *mako-let* (grocery store) to sell you a loaf of bread.

Old Katamon: The other side of Rehov HaPalmach from Kiryat Shmuel, it was a wealthy Christian Arab neighborhood at one time. Several foreign consulates have their homes here. Natan Sharansky is one of the most famous residents of this in-demand neighborhood, living on a tiny street no one can find. Jerusalem mayor Ehud Olmert lives on Rehov Kaf Tet b'November.

Katamonim: Below Old Katamon, this is a neighborhood of big, unattractive developments thrown up quickly for low-income families. Also known as Gonen, it has come to symbolize the poor and petty criminals. But with the influx of Russian immigrants, some of them world-renowned scientists, the image might change.

Neve Granot: South of the Israel Museum, this is a choice neighborhood with a lot of academics among its residents. It has newer buildings and is close to Hebrew University's Givat Ram campus.

Neve Sha'anamin: Sandwiched between the Israel Museum and the university, this is another pleasant neighborhood of many academics.

Nahlaot: This collection of small neighborhoods, east of Sacher Park and on both sides of Rehov Bezalal, was once a poor Sephardi area. Many of the original residents still live here, but gentrification is proceeding apace. With the area's central location, real estate prices have shot up.

Sha'are Hessed: South of Nahlaot, between Rehov Narkiss and Rehov Keren Kayemet, this was once a poor Ashkenazi neighborhood. Now the hovels are being bought up and turned into four-story houses. But unlike Nahlaot, this is a neighborhood of strictly observant Jews. Most of it is closed to automobile traffic during Shabbat.

German Colony: To the east of Old Katamon and on both sides of Rehov Emek Refaim, this neighborhood is the latest yuppie heaven. It was founded in 1880 by German Templars (whom the British deported during

World War II), the people often said to be largely responsible for Jerusalem's red-tiled roofs and green shutters. New restaurants and shops constantly spring up on Rehov Emek Refaim.

Greek Colony: Where it and the German Colony divide is arguable, but it shares access to the Emek Refaim neighborhood and excellent bus transportation. Lovely old houses still stand here, some with exotic decoration.

Baka: Literally across the railroad tracks from the German Colony, it had the economic stigma of that location for many years. Today it is a mix of lower and upper-middle class families and is another choice location. Derech Bet Lehem is its main street. The British Council Library is on Rehov Shimshon, in a beautifully renovated building with a peaceful park in front. Baka's "other name" on the map is G'ulim. Don't bother trying to remember it.

Abu Tor: East of Baka, with Derech Hevron as its main street, sits this mixed Arab and Jewish neighborhood. Like other such neighborhoods, when it was divided between Israel and Jordan only poor Jews lived on the Israeli side. Now wealthier people have moved into new and old buildings to relish the neighborhood's splendid view of the Old City, a view constantly threatened by developers. Friction between Jews and Arabs erupts here every so often. Even famed Jewish resident Meron Benveniste, a longtime Palestinian supporter, has had his car torched.

Wash day in Nahlaot

Beit HaKerem: On the south side of Shderot Herzl sits this green, quiet, and attractive neighborhood, established in 1922. It is losing its open spaces to mass development.

Beit VeGan: South of Beit HaKerem, the area has physical similarities to its northern neighbor but its population largely is religiously observant. Its name means "house and garden," and that is exactly what its founders intended when they constructed it in the early 1920s.

Old Talpiot: South of Abu Tor, it is another "garden city" built in the 1920s. Like the others from that date, it shows its age primarily through its greenery. The home of Nobel Prize–winning author S. Y. Agnon, at Rehov Klausner 16, is now a museum.

Arnona: This is the somewhat newer continuation south of Old Talpiot and leading to Ramat Rahel and its excellent swimming pool. If you get lost in this neighborhood, the sudden striking flash of gold from the Dome of the Rock will orient you. I don't know how residents deal with living in a neighborhood with the same name as the much-hated property tax.

Malha: Once an Arab village at the top of a hill, a hefty distance west of Rehavia, it became Jewish with the unplanned exchange of populations after the War of Independence. It was largely poor, but occasionally artsy. Now a huge new development has emerged down its back slope. Besides the views, Malha's claims to fame—or the bane of its existence—are industrial development and proximity to the Jerusalem Canyon (for a while the largest mall in the Middle East), the zoo, and Teddy Stadium with its traffic and noisy soccer games. The neighborhood's "other" name is Manahat. The main road that passes old Malha is Golumb.

Kiryat HaYovel: Down the road from Malha is this large newer development that is blessed with a local swimming pool.

Ge'ula: Northwest of Mea She'arim, Ge'ula is ultra-Orthodox, but not quite as ultra-Orthodox as its older neighbor and slightly better off economically. Its main street is Rehov Malchai Yisrael, with many stores to tempt the olfactory senses.

Ramat Eshkol: North of Shderot Eshkol, this is a post-1967, middle-class neighborhood with its share of "villas" (as private homes are called here, even if they aren't palatial). The homes used to have a stunning view across a valley, until that site turned into the overpowering new development Kiryat Shlomo.

French Hill: Farther northeast of Ramat Eshkol, it originated about the same time. It is the closest residential area to the Hebrew University and Hadassah-University Hospital on Mount Scopus. Because of its hilltop location, it might be Jerusalem's coolest neighborhood in summer and coldest in winter. French Hill's official name is Givat Shapira.

Givat Shaul: Like the Talpiots, more than one Givat Shaul is a cause of confusion. It is the name of both a residential neighborhood in the northwestern part of the city and an industrial and business area. The industrial and business area is newer than Talpiot, and from Talpiot its builders learned how to build havoc. The fact that streets are wider here and more parking space is provided could be looked on as an improvement over the older model, but not enough of an improvement.

Har Nof: Past the industrial section of Givat Shaul is a newer neighborhood surrounded, except by a corridor linking it with the rest of the city, by the Jerusalem Forest. Despite its bucolic location, it is a mountain of stone. The largely Orthodox population, including Ovadia Yosef, former chief Sephardi rabbi, and Knesset member Aryeh Deri, spends a lot of time fighting city hall, which wants to nibble away at the forest. Jerusalem city fathers apparently agree with Ronald Reagan's statement about redwoods, "If you've seen one, you've seen 'em all."

Ein Kerem: West of the city and separated from it by a long, infrequent bus ride and hills and valleys, it retains its original village character—so far. But again, residents are fighting city hall to preserve that character; a developer wants to build 1,000 residences at Ein Kerem's entrance. (Sad to say, instead of being the protectors of Jerusalem, city hall and the mayor have been the willing tool of developers and thus have been the city's exploiters, even its destroyer.)

East Talpiot, east of Old Talpiot and below the Sherover-Haas Promenades (the Tayelet); **Gilo**, south of the main population area and close to Bethlehem; **Neve Ya'acov**, north of the city; and **Ramot**, west of the city, are among newer development areas. They are virtually cities unto themselves, built on the heights. Foreign journalists often write of their fortresslike appearance. But building on the heights is traditional in a part of the world that has seen constant invasions; a valley location was like announcing, "Conquer me."

These enormous hunks of stone often have charming private homes and flats inside. All were built after 1967, but Neve Ya'acov was Jewish-owned before the Six-Day War. Even newer neighborhoods are **Pisgat Ze'ev**, next to Neve Ya'acov; **Kiryat Shlomo**, on a ridge beyond Ramat Eshkol; and, perhaps by the time you read this, **Har Homa** to the south, not far from Gilo.

Not to be confused with Old Talpiot or East Talpiot (or Talbia) is yet another **Talpiot**—the industrial area, located along and east of Rehov Pierre Koenig. This is a shopping area with a local Ace Hardware affiliate, a big electric-goods shop, marble cutters, automobile repair places, and others. It's a total mess. It is chaos. You have to hunt for the sidewalks: They're under the parked cars.

A Room with a View—Maybe

All right, you know some basics about Jerusalem—the transportation system, store hours, nightlife, and the best place for falafel. Now you must find a place to live.

First, some terms that need defining: *Flat* is the local name for an apartment. In Israel, most people own their own flats. You probably will rent from a flat owner, not from a management company.

275

You will undoubtedly look for a furnished flat. The degree to which it is furnished will depend on your needs and what you will be lucky enough to land. Unless you are simply house-sitting for vacationing owners, you probably won't find amenities like sheets, blankets, pots, pans, and dishes. For a flat that includes these, your rent will be far higher. Your alternative is to bring or send supplies on ahead of you, or buy them here and sell them before you leave.

Rental Costs

How much you can expect to pay for a roof over your head depends on a lot of things: supply, demand, and other variables beyond your control. Add to the equation your budget—another matter over which you might not have control—and the style of living you are willing to accept. Unless you are Rockefeller, if not Rothschild, prepare to gear down your living standards.

Of course, the shorter your stay, the higher the rent. When discussing facilities, bathrooms and kitchens aren't counted as rooms. A flat listed as two rooms has two rooms, plus a bathroom and kitchen.

Property is expensive and rents are high in Jerusalem, especially in relation to salaries. Friends and I were in the Hebron Hills visiting the ruins of the ancient village of Sussia. We entered living quarters and stood in one room partially submerged underground and with a minimum of light. Quipped my friend, "Move this to Jerusalem, and the owner could get $300,000 for it." It was a slight exaggeration, but you get the drift.

Ballpark rental figures for basic furnished flats are minimally $400 for one room, $500 for two rooms, and $600 for three rooms. A pleasant, fully furnished, centrally located two-room flat can cost $1,500 a month or more.

Although inflation isn't a problem, landlords continue to give rental figures in dollars. If you have to convert your money to shekels, you will actually pay more than the given dollar figure. Your landlord will want shekels according to the representative exchange rate, while the bank will give you shekels for dollars at the lower purchasing rate. If your landlord has a dollar account and will accept an American check, you'll be better off.

Early fall, before the university opens, is the height of flat-hunting season. Rental prices tend to drop a bit after the crush and during winter.

On the Trail

If you plan on a long stay and have no friends or relatives who can put you up while you go flat hunting, find a temporary place to stay through the options listed in Chapter 5: "A Place to Lay Your Head." With that accomplished, you can scour the town for a flat. There are several ways of tracking one down.

Very good Jerusalem friends or relatives might look for a place for you in advance. It's a time-consuming and taxing task. If you know people who will do this for you, kiss their feet. Take them to dinner at Darna.

If you are flat hunting from long distance, you can check out the ads in the *International Jerusalem Post* or contact an agency like Habitat, P.O. Box 7310, Jerusalem 91-042, (02) 561-1222, e-mail: portico@net-vision.net.il, fax: (02) 561-1176. Try to have an on-site inspection before closing the deal.

Going to an agency won't cost you money, unless you conclude a deal. Then, both you and the landlord will pay a fee on each month's rent. Your share might be between 2 and 5 percent.

For a fee, you can see She'al's rental lists, organized by neighborhood, price, and number of rooms. For the equivalent of $17, you get a one-time look. For $40, the lists will be faxed to you for a month, but not overseas. For $54, you can pick up the lists at the office. (All prices are approximate.) Contact She'al by phone at (02) 625-4456 or on the Web at www.malin.co.il.

Check ads in the Friday *Jerusalem Post*. Also check the bulletin board at the AACI (Rehov Mane 9) and the Israel Center (Rehov Strauss 10). For a small fee, you can put up your own notice at either place. You can also place your own ad in the *Jerusalem Post.*

Tell everyone you know that you are looking for a flat. Tell people you climb over on the bus, people who offer assistance when they see you stopped on the sidewalk studying your map, and taxi drivers, especially. Everybody. Almost everyone in Jerusalem knows someone who knows someone with a place to rent. Don't be shy.

Deborah, a young Canadian, can be your role model. Knowing not one word of Hebrew, she stationed herself for days on a choice residential street and asked passersby if they knew of a flat for rent. She finally found what she was looking for.

If you're alone, not to be overlooked is the possibility of sharing a flat. In Israel, strangers, even of the opposite sex, often split a rental between two or more people. But there are ticklish business details and personal matters to be agreed upon. And your own room might be the only place where you can entertain friends.

If you want to live in an Arab neighborhood, you face a whole different set of problems, for no rental agencies exist there. Everything is accomplished by word of mouth. Customarily, rather than renting an entire flat, in Arab neighborhoods you rent a room with a family.

Ask at neighborhood churches. Staff members often have personal connections with families in their congregations renting out rooms. Ask restaurant owners. Everyone in eastern Jerusalem, it seems, has a cousin who can solve all problems. If you let people know what kind of work or study you are pursuing, someone with similar interests might materialize to help you.

Note that life in Arab neighborhoods is conservative. A guest will live under constraints there not experienced in western Jerusalem. For instance, in Moslem families, alcoholic beverages are forbidden. With Christians or Moslems, social life with the opposite sex might be limited.

When you learn of a flat that interests you, leap to see it immediately. Even at night. Otherwise you could arrive at your appointment and time and again hear, "It's already taken." You must be the early bird.

What You See and What You Will Get

What can you expect to find when you go to see rentals? Usually a few pieces of old furniture dragged up from Aunt Esther's storage room. You will get a bed, perhaps no wider than an army cot, a free-standing closet, a table, and a chair or two. If there's anything more than that, consider yourself lucky. Looking down from the ceiling on your few sticks of furniture will be a naked light bulb. That is the hallmark of Jerusalem rentals.

Typically, the kitchen will be devoid of even a can-opener. But it should have a refrigerator and stove of some sort. The latter could be a two-burner tabletop model. If there is an oven, your friends will oooh and aaah over your good fortune.

Before you say, "I'll take it," pin down exactly what furniture will be left in the flat. You can't assume that what you see will be what you'll get. If old tenants still live there, you have to check exactly what belongs to them or you could get a shock.

Find out how the place will be heated, how you will get hot water, and what the telephone arrangement will be. Also, check out security, especially if this is a ground-floor flat. Are security bars on the windows?

The matter of heat may not seem like a concern if you are renting in sunny September. Besides, this is the desert, isn't it?

Just wait. Despite palm trees in Jerusalem, winters can be wet and miserable, even snowy. Many flats have no heat. Will your landlord supply a heat source? You will probably have to buy your own electric or kerosene heater to inspire yourself to get out from under the covers on a cold morning.

Some flats have an outlet for a plug-in gas heater (hopefully on the premises), for which you will have to buy cylinders (*balomin*—from "balloon") of butane gas. Your flat might be small enough and the heater strong enough to do a reasonable job.

You might strike a flat in a building with central heating. Don't jump for joy, although that's a big step forward in comfort. You will pay a steep price for probably no more than four hours of heat in the evening, maybe a couple of hours in the morning. It's up to the building committee, called the Vad, how much heat you'll get. If you'll be in your flat a lot during the day, with no heat until say 5 p.m., you might begin to see your breath as it hits the frigid air. Inevitably you will buy your own heater, so you will end up paying two heating bills. Keep that in mind.

Getting hot water isn't as troublesome as keeping warm. A lot of buildings have solar water-heating, which saves on the high cost of electricity, at least during summer and when the sun is bright in winter. You might encounter confusion over the word *solar*. In Hebrew, it refers to oil heating fuel and isn't connected with the sun. In any event, every flat has its own water tank, which you can heat whenever you flick the switch.

The telephone will normally remain in the landlord's name. You will pay the bills, but Information will not know from you. Bezek, the local telephone monopoly, one day discovered this gap in renters' lives. Now, if you bring a copy of your rental contract and written permission from your landlord you can have a listing in your own name, although the line will continue to belong to your landlord. Or you could rent or buy a cellular phone and walk down the street and talk into the air like everyone else.

Back to security matters: Bars at windows are a fact of life here. Centuries of invaders have made such bars socially acceptable, as well as a necessity. They don't have the stigma that they do in the United States. At the same time, even with bars, keep purses, wallets, and other valuables out of reach of open windows.

Most windows have outside shutters that roll up and down with the sound of a shovel scraped along the sidewalk. They are no substitute for bars on lower floors. They keep out light, keep pelting rain off windows, and are some help keeping out the cold, but they don't keep out burglars.

It's a good idea to check the flat's exterior door locks. If they are flimsy and the landlord won't replace them, pop for a deadbolt. The landlord will surely agree to this, and for you it's a worthwhile investment.

Rent Is Only the Beginning

With the cost of rent in mind, remember you could also have to pay the costs of heat, water (your flat probably will have its own meter—not that you'll be able to figure out how to read it), electricity (your flat will have its own meter), telephone, municipal property taxes, and *vad ha'beit* (the monthly fee each building resident pays to keep hallways clean, the garden green, and the flats warm if there is central heating).

You'll also need butane cylinders (balonim) to supply fuel to that little stove of yours and to a gas heater, if you have one. Balonim are kept in pairs. When one becomes empty, order a new one from the company that supplies your flat. Get the telephone number and customer number from your landlord. You probably will have to go to the office and pay in advance. Perhaps you can use your Visa card. And while we're on the subject of the stove, local advice is that the valve to your stove or gas heater should be turned off when not in use.

All these items and services can drive your housing costs up, up, up. Be thankful that you know about them before you make a commitment, so you can avoid future shock. But now that you have checked on all these details and have decided on the flat you want, a new set of agonies begins: contract negotiations.

Signing on the Dotted Line

Don't rush to see how your signature looks on the contract. Remember what Israelis say: Everything is negotiable. And that includes rent.

Israelis rightly maintain that foreigners are at a huge disadvantage negotiating a rental contract because often they don't understand the system. Some veteran tenants insist that foreigners shouldn't stumble through negotiations alone, that they should have a tough-minded Israeli along from the start. You should be so lucky.

Go over every detail of the contract. Make sure you understand it all.

The first time I went through a rental contract, I was in an utter daze as expense after expense fell to me. I couldn't keep track of all the additional costs over the rent. Shkalim seemed to fly past my eyes and out the window. Having to pay the municipal tax *(arnona)* seemed to be the final indignity. Maybe, just maybe, you can convince the landlord to split it, but it's doubtful.

And then there are strange twists and turns that the landlord can come up with during negotiations. You could be so unlucky as to get a landlord like the one I had on my very first contract. His last name translated into the name of a precious gem, but I will call him Mr. Selah. That means "rock"—like his head.

Mr. Selah owned the entire building, which was my rotten luck. He insisted that fuel (oil, in this case) for his centrally heated building be paid for in advance in the fall. He argued that he wanted to buy it before the price went up. There was logic to that, but then I never knew how much he actually used and what it really cost to heat my flat, since there were no separate meters. At the time, I didn't know anything about meters. It occurred to me later that what I paid was keeping him and everyone else in the building toasty. It certainly didn't do much for me.

The only defense against a Mr. Selah is to ask as many people as possible in the building what they are paying for heat. My big handicap was that I was desperate for a flat. Because Mr. Selah owned the building, there was no building committee. Mr. Selah was a law unto himself.

All things being equal, if you have a choice between a building run by its owner or a resident committee, choose the one run by the committee. A committee should have no qualms about letting you see its bills—but just try asking the owner to show you his actual fuel bill.

After the monthly rent, given in a dollar figure, and those additionals have been agreed on (or swallowed), the next shock is to settle the matter of how many months' rent you will pay in advance. Landlords often ask for, and get, rents in advance for up to a year. You will lose both the use of your money during the months ahead as well as the interest it might have earned you. So what will you get in return? Israelis suggest you ask for a 10 to 15 percent discount on the total rent.

One renter I know readily agrees to paying his rent a year in advance. But then he turns his baby blues on his prospective landlord and says, "Of course, I know you aren't trying to make money off me, so you'll pay me the interest my money will earn this coming year, won't you?" My friend swears the demand for rent a year in advance is dropped like a slippery, wet fish every time.

On my last rental contract, I paid four months' rent on signing—the first two and the last two. Every two months, I paid another two months' rent. This meant that my landlady always had from two to four months of my rent money in her hands and plenty of notice, should I have wanted to leave.

Then there's the matter of security for the landlord. After all, you're a stranger from another country, to which you will be returning. Friends coming here on a short-term rental were asked for a telephone deposit of $1,000 cash in American money. I was acting on their behalf, and I raised a rumpus over the demand. My English-born lawyer calmed me. He told me of the kid from Bolivia who called home every night and then left the country. Unfair things happen in both directions.

In all probability, your landlord will ask for an up-front damage deposit. Fight like crazy to leave the deposit in escrow with a lawyer and not in the landlord's hands. He or she will also want a local resident who knows and trusts you to sign a legal document as your guarantor. With this, if you skip out on those phone calls to Bolivia, your now ex-friend will have to pay your bill.

Something to get into the contract specifically for your benefit is a statement that you can sublet the flat. Who knows the future? Something could require you to move out early, and you shouldn't have to walk away from all that money you plunked down.

There is a standard legal form for tenants and landlords. Even with that, details can be altered by mutual consent, as long as they aren't forbidden by law. But don't be surprised if you run into a Mr. Selah, who laboriously writes out every contract by hand.

After all the haggling, unless you have gone through an agent who often deals with foreigners, you will find every detail of the contract spelled out in Hebrew. At least the numbers will be recognizable.

But even if the contract is in English, still keep that ballpoint pen hidden until you have shown the document to a lawyer. Find out in advance what he or she charges. By this time, you don't need any more surprises.

After all my words about Mr. Selah, let me tell you about another one of my landlords, Haggai Lev of Ramat Eshkol. And that's his real name. His last name means "heart," and he truly had one. When I casually mentioned to him that water from the solar water heater was tepid, he immediately installed auxiliary water heaters in my flat. When a health emergency forced me to move out, he let me break my contract instantly, without my having to hunt for someone to take it over, and he returned my money down to the last cent. So you see, there are all kinds, but not enough Haggai Levs.

Watching Out for Number One

All the nit-picking details are agreed upon, the contract has been signed, and you have relieved yourself of all that money weighing you down. Now, on moving in, itemize the contents of the flat and prepare a damage list. And watch for your landlord's nervous reaction to the list if it is in English.

Immediately, read your electric meter and call Bezek (199) for the telephone meter reading, called a *kriyat monay* (yes, telephones are also on meters), so you'll know where you're starting from. Check the numbers against your first bill. You will take readings again when you leave.

Good news and bad news: Should you have a serious problem with your landlord after you move in, Israeli law favors the tenant. Normally, it almost takes an act of God to oust a tenant. But most landlords will require you to sign away that protection in your contract.

Even if you still have that right, it's the landlord who knows how to shut off the water, telephone, and electricity to your place—all of which Mr. Selah did to me. Never mind that such action isn't legal or that you're in the right. What counts is how long you can live without a flushing toilet and if that is longer than it takes to get legal action going.

Making It Seem Like Home

Now you are settled in your Jerusalem abode, but it might resemble a prison cell. To turn it into a home, you'll need to use your ingenuity and pocketbook.

A naked bulb can be made decent with an inexpensive paper shade imported from the Far East. You can find them at The Happening, Rehov Ben Yehuda 3, and Home Design Center, a highfalutin name for a discount home-furnishing store at Rehov Yad Harutzim 11.

For furniture and appliances, you might see used items advertised on the bulletin board at the AACI, in Friday and Wednesday Bargain Basement ads in the *Jerusalem Post*, or in secondhand stores.

Most second-hand stores are concentrated in the Mea She'arim-Geula area. Shmontses is at Rehov Yehezkiel 6, and Yahad HaShniya is at Rehov Shivtei Yisrael 38. For rugs, check the Arab souk in the Old City. For new kitchen supplies and clothes hangers, blankets, and linens, scour Mahane Yehuda. If you aren't ready to buy on the spot, make a note of where you saw what or you might never be able to find your way back there again. Also check out Big Deal at the Bell Tower, Rehov King George 3.

Do buy a *sirpella*—known in English by its literal translation, "Wonder Pot." And it is. It looks like an angel food cake ring, but is actually a stove-top oven. Even if your kitchen has an oven, it often is a simpler undertaking to use the sirpella. They are sold in the shouk at Mahane Yehuda or in the souk of the Arab Quarter in the Old City. Make sure you have all three parts, its lid, and the metal piece to sit on the flame. The sirpella works amazingly well for baked potatoes, stuffed peppers, casseroles, kugels, even cakes. Just keep the flame low.

If your flat has no television, you can buy a used one through the *Jerusalem Post*'s "Bargain Basement" column for $100 and less. You can sell it before you leave.

For locating stores, the *Jerusalem Post* distributes English-language phone books. Call the paper to track one down. The book is limited, however. It isn't an equivalent of the Hebrew yellow pages, but it's a start.

With a few posters on your walls, either from the Israel Museum, the Museum of Islamic Art, or a commercial store like The Happening on Rehov Ben Yehuda, you might discover that your flat, which seemed user-unfriendly at first, is welcoming you. You will have made a home in Jerusalem.

Laundry

Maybe you will be blessed with a washing machine in your flat. If so, you were born under a lucky star. Otherwise, except for the use of another wonderful, reliable washing machine known as your very own hands, it is expensive maintaining clean clothes and linens in Israel.

Laundromats in the middle-class neighborhoods are shockingly expensive. You'll do better to scout out Laundromats in less affluent areas—but forget putting a quarter in the machine. The Laundry Place at Rehov Shamai 12, one of the least expensive laundromats in town, charges about $3 for a load of up to 7 kilos, which is more than 15 pounds. Thirty minutes of drying costs about $1. Detergent costs about 70 cents, but you can bring your own.

If you don't have the leisure to watch your clothes get clean, an attendant will take your laundry or dry cleaning through its paces for an additional charge. At Superclean, Rehov HaPalmach 16, where attendants look after the wash, the charge is upward of $10 a load. One sheet costs the same as a whole load.

Between the time and money involved, it seems that most people resort to hand-washing a good portion of their clothing. That explains why an Israeli detergent is made expressly for hand-washing.

A Winter's Tale

The biggest shock about living in Jerusalem is the discovery that you could freeze to death (or so you'll think) in winter. You will wonder, "Is this the hot desert I envisioned?" It certainly isn't.

At the beginning of November, you'll see a window display in HaMashbir with kiddie-sized dummies modeling new snowsuits and fixed to look as if they are romping in a pile of white stuff. You can take that as a hint as to what's ahead.

Blame it on Jerusalem's altitude. The city ranges from an elevation of 2,230 feet at Ein Kerem to 2,700 feet on Mount Scopus. Remember, people go "up" to Jerusalem, literally as well as spiritually. Tel Aviv can be 10 degrees Fahrenheit warmer than Jerusalem. During winter, Jerusalemites going to Tel Aviv for the day have to plan their wardrobe carefully.

There can be months of cold, heavy rain. Snow normally falls twice annually. But one year I stopped counting after 12 snowfalls—most of them annoying mush. I've also seen more than a foot of crunchy snow on the Golden City.

Sizeable snowfalls shut the city down. Nothing moves. Buses don't run, and drivers are urged to stay off the streets. Schools close, courts close, doctors' appointments are cancelled. Banks and post offices might not open until the afternoon, if at all. The highway to Tel Aviv closes, tree branches collapse, electric wires might fall, power outages might ensue.

Why such an impact? Primarily because the wet snow is heavy and treacherous for driving and walking. Besides, no one owns a snow shovel in Jerusalem. By and large, unless you're the victim of a power outage, heavy snowfall means a holiday. One winter, the city shut down four times.

Jerusalem's beautiful stone buildings that reflect light so gloriously also keep the heat out in summer and the cold in in winter. Unheated or minimally heated buildings add to the bitter, damp chill. Even my big strapping Canadian friends have been reduced to crybabies by Jerusalem winters, whimpering that they've never been so cold in their lives.

It isn't that the temperature drops so low—it rarely goes below freezing. It's that when the weather gets cold, especially cold and rainy or snowy, it's nearly impossible to keep your flat warm. Those mean days can be just the time for a trip to Eilat, Tiveria, the Dead Sea, or any place, like Haifa, at sea level.

But there you are, stuck in Jerusalem. What to do? To keep comfortably warm in a centrally "heated" flat, you will have to remain in perpetual motion. If your flat is equipped with a gas heater attached to a balloon of butane gas, the room with the heater might be quite pleasant. But what happens when you go to the bathroom?

The goal is to be in charge of your goosebumps. To do that, you will have to buy or borrow a means of keeping warm that you can control where and when you want. The choices are electric or kerosene heaters. Their initial cost is about the same, depending on the sophistication of

Snowfall takes many visitors and new residents by surprise.

the model. But the cost of operation might be quite different. Usually, kerosene is cheaper to run and it makes a nice, even heat. But you'll have to have a way of hauling the kerosene (*neft* in Hebrew) home from the gas station.

Kerosene also requires several safety precautions. The heater must be lit and extinguished outdoors. When it's in operation, you must keep a window open. It might seem that with all the cracks around doors and windows in your flat, there is already more than enough ventilation. Don't take a chance. It's a matter of your life. Open that window a little.

It isn't only your little kerosene stove you need to be concerned about. Heating systems other than electric require fresh air. Even the elegant gas Junker system, which also provides hot water and often is found in newer flats, must have ventilation. Double-check this matter with your landlord. He wants you to remain healthy as much as you do.

Electricity is probably the more expensive, but it's wonderfully simple to operate. The cheapest electric heaters are little radiant heaters. They do a good job of putting your feet in the toaster while the rest of you is in the fridge.

You'll have to dress warmer than you are used to doing in an overheated American house or office. Many women in Israel wear silk underwear—not something out of Victoria's Secret but silk undershirts with sleeves that go to their wrists. Extra blankets or a sleeping bag will help keep you warm in bed at night.

So if you expect to be in Jerusalem in winter, don't think Middle East, think Siberia. It's really disconcerting to be in Jerusalem and see weather reports that it's warmer in New York, Zurich—even Helsinki.

However, it might be your luck to hit a mild Jerusalem winter and wonder what I've been talking about. Look at it this way: Expect the worst. If the worst doesn't happen, you won't be disappointed.

17
TO HEALTH

The thought of needing a doctor thousands of miles from home is enough to make a grown person reach for a security blanket. Feel comforted that Israel is an international leader in medicine, but it does have its medical peculiarities. Being forewarned isn't as good as being vaccinated, but it should help.

These days, the city doesn't present any particular health problem other than its increasing air pollution. That, in itself, can be a health problem to many.

The Israeli medical profession is well equipped to handle any major medical problem and can be excellent. But that isn't what gets most of us. It's the minor, annoying things like tummy aches, colds that won't go away, and fingers caught in a door. What to do about them?

Israeli Health Care

First, understand Israel's health setup. All citizens and permanent residents pay monthly fees into one health fund. Then they can join the health delivery system of their choice out of several available. All offer certain variations on required basic services. You, as a tourist, are out of the loop.

Jerusalem Scene

Jay Shapiro, an American-born physicist who has written a book on immigrating to Israel, tells what happened when he joined the Israeli army.

He was excited about the prospect of becoming a soldier, for he felt that would make him a true Israeli. But he had one worry: When he was called up for the American army years before, he was rejected because of nearsightedness.

Not to worry. He passed the Israeli exam with flying colors. How did he accomplish that, he wanted to know. He asked the doctor. "Look, how come Israel accepts me as a soldier when the United States didn't? And now yet! I'm 20 years fatter, slower, and older. I'm more nearsighted than ever."

The doctor's face took on a serious expression. In a thoughtful tone he answered, "Both America and Israel have enemies. The difference is, America's enemies are far away. Israel's are close."

Private practice exists side by side with the delivery systems. The same doctor can work in both—seeing clinic patients part of the day and private patients later. For private treatment, patients pay out of their own pockets and, possibly, through supplementary insurance. Doctors with private office hours are available to you, even if they also work at a hospital, like Hadassah. Seeing a doctor privately is expensive (more than $125 for the visit), and there is no waiting room with magazines to help you pass the time, only a few hard benches.

Before you leave home, check with your health-care provider to find out what costs will be covered overseas and get a packet of insurance forms, just in case. If you have to pay cash in Israel, be sure to get a receipt and have the doctor translate the diagnosis and treatment into English (good luck). Have the total figure, if it was paid in shkalim, converted into dollars.

Several insurance companies offer special insurance for overseas travel, should you need it. Your travel agent should be able to give you information.

If you have no other options, you can buy health insurance in Israel. One company that specializes in it is Shiloah-Harel Insurance in the City Tower next to HaMashbir, (02) 530-0400. The payments could be high, but one trip to the hospital costs a lot more.

The Association of Americans and Canadians in Israel remains a source of help in dealing with medical and dental needs. Do become a member. You will benefit in many ways.

Yes, one encounters physicians here who don't speak English. Besides Hebrew, you can hear from them in Spanish, French, Italian, and lots of Russian. Don't ask Israelis which doctors speak English. They often haven't a clue. My dear landlord, Haggai Lev, took me to my health plan's emergency care facility one evening. The duty doctor spoke Russian and rudimentary Hebrew. In the crisis of the moment, I was capable of speaking zilch. Lev solved the problem. He spoke Russian fluently, having learned it in a British prison with other future Israelis in Kenya for four years during and after the Mandate years.

If you have no other sources for care of that smashed finger or the cold that won't go away, the Wolfson Medical Center virtually is an English-speaking island at Rehov Diskin 9A, (02) 563-6265. A dental clinic also is in the building.

If needed, Magen David Adom (the Israeli equivalent of Red Cross) gives emergency treatment (tel. 101), or you can go to a hospital emergency room. Have your insurance documents handy.

Lest the thought of dealing with the Israeli health delivery system seem too discouraging, listen to Rahel's story. Moving from South Africa more than five years earlier, she had made, at best, a mixed-bag adjustment to Israel. When she faced a major surgical procedure, she not only was fearful and depressed by the prospect but also overwhelmed by having to go through the surgery in Israel and not in the orderly South Africa environment she knew.

The outcome was a happy one. Rahel's hospitalization became the pivot. She said the kindness, attention, and warmth she received were beyond all expectation. They touched her heart so deeply, she felt, at long last, that Israel was home.

Other Health Tips

The drinking water in Israeli towns and cities is fine. Caution elsewhere is worthwhile. Bottled water is available everywhere. Note that Israeli's water, with its heavy salts and minerals, can bring on diarrhea in people here for a month or so. It doesn't happen often, but be prepared.

Don't underestimate the sun and heat. Wear a hat in the sun, even if Israelis don't. Drink lots of water when the temperature goes up. Drink it

---

Jerusalem Scene

An elderly woman, perhaps in her eighties, shabbily dressed and with two empty plastic sacks in her hands, shuffled into Shaare Zedek Hospital's emergency room on Shabbat morning.

She was looking for a specific doctor, she said. The two duty nurses, busily distributing breakfast trays, matter-of-factly told her the doctor wasn't in yet; she should sit and wait.

So she sat and waited. And waited. Her patience was impressive. The nurses went by collecting the breakfast trays. Still, apparently, there was no sign of the doctor the old woman wanted.

The nurses returned. This time, they carried sacks of their own. From them, they pulled hard-boiled eggs, croissants, yogurt, and other food, which they carefully transferred to the old woman's sacks. Clearly these were unused portions of food from the breakfast menu.

Then they announced, "The doctor won't be in today. Come back next Shabbat to see him."

---

even before you feel a need. You can buy a water-bottle carrier to sling over your shoulder.

Wash fresh produce with a small amount of dish detergent and lots of water to remove animal and human waste and, hopefully, some of the insecticides.

If you spend any time in the Jordan Valley, be aware of leishmaniasis, a skin infection caused by a parasite carried by sand flies. Locally, the infection is called the Rose of Jericho, after the scar it can leave. The disease was dying out until Israelis moved into the Jordan Valley after the Six-Day War and provided a link in the parasite's life cycle. If you have an insect bite that won't heal, get medical attention as soon as possible. Treatment has improved greatly in recent years.

Finally, check with your doctor before leaving home about the advisability of getting a vaccination against infectious hepatitis.

18
MONEY TALK

A mong Anglo-Saxons, at least on their home turf, it is considered bad manners to talk about money. But in Israel no one blushes to ask other people, even strangers, how much they earn, how much they paid for their flat, how much a shirt cost, and so forth. So we'll do as Israelis do and talk money.

Upon Arrival

You should arrive with traveler's checks and at least two credit cards that allow withdrawals from automatic teller machines. Find out in advance what your credit-card providers charge when you withdraw shekels from an Israeli ATM.

Before you leave home, or as soon as possible afterward, ask your credit-card companies to send bills to your overseas address. You can always rent a post office box if you're not sure where you'll be living.

With your credit card, you will be able to charge many purchases, even in supermarkets and gas stations. Charging might save you the expense of converting dollars to shkalim. On the other hand, most credit-card companies take a 1 percent commission, and you have to be compulsive to track down their exchange rate on the day you made your purchase.

Where a business accepts credit cards, Visa works fine. For an inexplicable reason, MasterCard won't approve my purchases here, nor will my gas station even accept MasterCard. About traveler's checks: Cashing them at an Israeli bank is expensive. At Bank Leumi, there is a basic $6 fee for the transaction and another $2.50 charge on each check. If you cash a $20 check, don't spend the nickel you'll walk away with all at once.

Instead of a bank, go to a foreign currency exchange to get shkalim from traveler's checks or cash. They don't charge a commission, but their rate of exchange isn't tops either. Still, balanced against the bank's charges, you could be way ahead. At some exchanges, showing your AACI membership card brings you a better rate. An alternative for traveler's checks or cash is the post office, which also doesn't charge a commission. At neither place is a personal check accepted.

Banking

To be financially functioning during an extended stay, you will need to open two accounts with a Jerusalem bank. One will be a foreign currency savings account, into which you will put your checks from home. The other will be a checking account in shkalim. Israeli banks love tourists and foreigners who open accounts, and you might be given some special breaks. AACI members also get breaks, which differ from bank to bank. With your checking account, you will receive a plastic bank card and secret code to use for withdrawals from an ATM. The card will also enable you to get a printout of your shekel and foreign-currency accounts.

Your foreign-currency checks, once deposited, will have to "ripen" before you can change your money to shkalim—one of the little ways banks make money on us. Different banks have different ripening times. Bank Leumi currently requires 14 days, to which you must add Saturdays, Sundays, and religious holidays, so figure 20 days. Your deposit receipt will show the date on which you can move the money to your shekel account without additional charges added to the slew that already exist.

In a financial emergency, you can move your money sooner, even directly, into your shekel account, but you'll pay a fine for that privilege. Because of service charges, avoid depositing foreign checks or moving them to the checking account in amounts smaller than $1,000.

When you deposit a foreign check and when you move money into your checking account, you will receive a receipt. Keep your receipts to check against any printouts you receive.

Don't expect to receive bank statements in the mail. Every so often I receive a statement about my dollar account, but I never know what inspires its arrival. You'll get your shekel-account statement from a machine in the bank by running your Israeli ATM card through it. The statement will include a variety of small, baffling charges. When I asked my favorite bank teller what they were, he said, "Never mind. It's too complicated to find out."

Using Checks

It will take about 10 days for your Israeli bank checks to be printed with your name, address, and telephone number. Your checks will be good almost everywhere, except at some supermarkets if they are less than a certain amount. If you can't write names or numbers in Hebrew, go ahead and write them in English.

Writing the date on checks is a precise matter here and any variation throws Israelis into panic. (In fact, any number or letter that has been written over creates a crisis. You will have to write your whole name next to the over-stroke to prove that it was you and not a thief who did it, or write out a whole new check.) Dates are written: day, dot, month, dot, year. So October 7, 2003, would be 7.10.03. To remember, think of moving from the smallest specific unit, the day, to the larger ones.

When you write a check, particularly if you mail it, put two parallel vertical lines above the name of the payee and cross out the word *lifku-dot*. Write instead *bilvad* (in Hebrew letters) or "only" in English. This means that the check can't be transferred to anyone else and must go into the payee's bank account.

Most of us, in our native lands, are conscientious about not bouncing checks. Israeli banks, for an interest charge, allow their clients to write checks up to a certain amount over their balances. Living on overdraft is the Israeli way of life. But that's the privilege of Israeli citizenship. You, as a tourist, don't get to enjoy paying now and thinking about it later. That's the law.

You won't get cancelled checks from your bank. Should you ask for them, the bank teller will faint. Instead, keep track of your account status through the bank's printout machine. Save important receipts and make copies of them. Should you need cancelled checks for the American IRS, tell the IRS to go argue with an Israeli bank. However, if you do need a copy of a check for some legal matter, for a fee, you can get it.

More Banking Tips

Banking hours are different from one day to the next. Just get there in the mornings and you'll be all right. If you are going to move money to your shekel account, don't do it on Sunday. The new exchange rates aren't in, and you will pay a hefty fine.

There are limits on the amount of cash you can withdraw from an ATM on your overseas ATM card. However, if you need to receive a larger amount, the live teller inside the bank will call your credit-card company for approval.

Bank employees here will appear far more informal in style than in banks back home. Don't look for a suit and tie on the bank manager. But do expect to see a glass of coffee or tea in front of the tellers. At least they no longer blow cigarette smoke in your face.

If school is out, bank employees may even have their children with them. That makes for another contribution to the homey scene. And so do the dogs standing in line with their owners.

If all this informality seems unprofessional in an institution dealing with high finances and your money, relax. An American-born top Israeli bank official, who has worked at his bank's branches in two American cities, advised me not to be fooled by appearances. "These people here are brighter, more responsive, and have more initiative than either of my staffs in the States." His very words.

19
COMMUNICATION

J erusalemites devour books with the gusto of Texans downing chili. Bookstores abound in Jerusalem. They range from the brightly lit Steimatsky stores, where never a speck of dust is to be found, to the dark, cluttered Stein Bookstore near Hechal Shlomo, which Saul Bellow wrote about adoringly in *To Jerusalem and Back*. These stores carry books in an array of languages. But the problem with English-language books is that, even in paperback, their high price tags can make you think you no longer can read numbers.

I've never stopped missing a public library or a good bookstore where almost all the books I ever wanted could be found or ordered. But, eventually, I found some make-do alternatives.

Among them are the semiprivate British and American libraries, where all the employees are English speakers. In fact, all except the top brass at the American Library are English or English-Commonwealth born. There's a reason: The economy-minded American State Department saves money on Social Security payments by not hiring Americans.

A drawback at both places is that tourist-visa holders aren't allowed to take out books unless they are students on a year's program or can wrangle a letter from an impressive institution vouching for their serious purpose amid the stacks. Even if joining is impossible, both libraries have amenities available nowhere else in town, and the collections of both may be used on the premises.

At the British Council Library, Rehov Shimshon 5 near Derech Beit Lehem, (02) 673-6733, everything is written by British authors. If you qualify, you can check out books, records, tapes, and videos. The extensive collection of British periodicals is available for browsing.

Like the British Council Library, the American Cultural Center Library, Rehov Keren HaYesod 8, (02) 625-5755, has one of the most comfortable reading rooms in Jerusalem. Enter at ground level. The lobby and stairwell might include a powerhouse display of splashy art, perhaps of brilliantly colored Andy Warhol posters. While the policy toward tourist-visa holders is the same as at the British Council Library, here you can read *Rolling Stone, Consumer Reports,* the *New York Times,* and other American publications and use computers to browse the Internet.

The newest library in town is sponsored by the women's organization Amit, at its building at Rehov Alkalai 8 in Talbia, (02) 561-9222. The building itself is worth a visit, for it is a classic of Arab design. The library is composed of whatever books have been donated, so nationality of the author isn't a consideration. Amit charges a slight fee for the privilege of checking out books.

To buy books at the most reasonable prices, check out stores selling used paperbacks and hardcovers. Sefer v'Sefel is the most popular; climb the stairs at Rehov Yavetz 4, behind the Bell Tower. The selection here is wide. You can sell your paperbacks back to the store, which will help on the price for your next books. Reselling hardcovers is practically impossible here, however. Another used-book seller is the Book Mark, Rehov Esther HaMalka 1 off Derech Bet Lehem, a particularly congenial place.

The *Jerusalem Post* has a book sale every so often. There you can find some bargains, particularly on reprints of classics.

Last of all, take advantage of informal book swaps between English-readers. Don't be shy about asking a friend for books. It happens all the time. We're all a little book-starved.

None of this, of course, will come close to your local Borders or Barnes & Noble. Nevertheless, Jerusalem might be in the Middle East, but intellectually it isn't in a desert.

Ulpanization (Learning Hebrew)

Non-Israelis usually insist that everyone knows English in Israel. It can sound that way, as long as you stick to Rehov King George in Jerusalem. But inevitably, the moment you stray or face a crisis, you can't find anyone who can say more than "America good" and the Anglo-Saxon four-letter words they learned from TV. I remember my anguish in Rosh Pina when I had to change buses to Safed, and I didn't know on which side of the road I should wait. Shabbat was descending, and buses would disappear well before the day's light. Could anyone understand my urgent question? I might as well have arrived from Jupiter.

Crises or not, if a person is going to do more than simply pass through a foreign country, he or she ought to know as much as possible of that country's language. Fortunately, there is a marvelous way for even abject beginners to get a handle on Hebrew and for those who have familiarity with the language to improve their skills. It is through that almost miraculous institution, the ulpan. An *ulpan* is a program of intensive Hebrew study. (The word actually means "studio.")

The Israeli ulpan pioneered the method of teaching a language *in* that language. Hebrew only is allowed in the classroom (although students who share another language find ways of getting around that rule, especially when the teacher's back is turned).

To the uninitiated, little in the world can sound more like gobbledygook than Hebrew. Guttural gobbledygook, at that. And trying to learn the language can seem like memorizing gibberish. Few Hebrew words relate to any language Westerners know.

The method of teaching brings to mind what the Italians of Parma shouted to a particular tenor. The audience kept calling him out on stage for what seemed like encore after encore. Finally, he bowed, thanked the audience, and apologized that he was exhausted. The Parmans hollered, "You'll sing it until you learn it." In ulpan, through drill, drill, and more drill, you'll do it until you learn it.

Intensive Hebrew classes meet five mornings a week, usually from 8 a.m. to 12:30 p.m. Less-intensive classes meet fewer hours per session and two or three times a week, mornings, afternoons, or evenings.

There are classes all over Jerusalem. They begin in late summer and fall, depending on the institution, and again in January or February. But as long as there is space it is possible to join at any time and, at many places, for as short a time as a month. Fees range from more than $150 a month for intensive Hebrew to $25 for sessions twice a week. Not included are texts and optional, but choice, outings organized by the school.

Enrollment offers tremendous fringe benefits. The fact is, attending ulpan is the very best way to meet people in Jerusalem. New immigrants, old immigrants who want to improve their Hebrew, temporary residents, and Arabs share the same space for months on end. Your class could be a mixture of Moslems, Christians, Jews, perhaps a few stalwart atheists, and, especially in intensive Hebrew, missionaries.

One intensive ulpan I was enrolled in included a Syrian Orthodox priest from Iraq, a young Christian woman from Ethiopia, many young Arabs from the Jerusalem area, a Dutch gynecologist of Christian background who insisted she hated all religions, and Jews from Switzerland, the Netherlands, Australia, Mexico, France, Tunisia, Canada, and the United States. Among the latter was a man of Syrian background who startled the Arabs by speaking to them in Arabic. Among the Tunisians was a convert to Judaism. Just picture us all taking part in the class Chanukah program.

The Association of Americans and Canadians in Israel, ads in the *Jerusalem Post*, and the ulpan office at Beit Ha'Am, Rehov Bezalel 11, are the best sources of information about classes. The ulpan office is open mornings, Sunday through Thursday.

Bells Are Ringing

My future home was being built. "Order your telephone," the contractor told me in July. "You'll be in by September." But—and it's an old joke here—he didn't tell me which September.

In August, I ordered my phone. By September 15, the new flat's walls weren't finished, there was no electricity and no telephone outlets, and, since I innocently believed my contractor, I had no place to live.

But thanks to Bezek, the local telephone company, despite everything I didn't have, I did have voice mail. Wherever I was in the world, I could call my new telephone number and collect my messages.

Bezek's high-tech certainly is miraculous. It's the low-tech that's a problem. (That might be said about everything in Israel.) Because in my homeless state I had trouble keeping track of life's business matters, the next April I wanted Bezek to give me copies of my first four phone bills. I couldn't order them over the telephone. I had to go to the main office, take a number, read the newspaper through twice while I waited for my number to come up, then meet with a representative.

No copies of my bills arrived. In June I repeated the ordeal. Still nothing. In September I went back and demanded to meet with the supervisor. In October I received an itemized account of every phone call I had made in the past four months, not simple statements of my first four bills.

I sent a letter to Bezek's chairman of the board, whose name I happened to come across in the newspaper. An employee called me back and asked who he was. Later, I found the name of the company president. I was ready to write to him when, lo and behold, statements of my first four bills arrived, nine months after my initial request.

Now you get the picture of Israel's telephone system. Once that telephone is in your hands, it does wonderful things: transfer your calls to another number, wake you up at your designated time, and irritate you during phone conversations by signaling that another call is on the line. This last feature is called (by telephone users, not by Bezek) the "nudnik" feature. It comes automatically with your telephone number, but it can be removed on request.

When you rent a flat, the telephone will remain in the owner's name.

Glossary of "Engbrew," "Hebrish," and Slang

apchew: what a sneeze sounds like in Hebrew
bek exil: back axle
front bek exil: front axle
oof me poh: scram (literally, fly from here)
shvitz: show off; a transformation of the Yiddish word for sweat
shvitzer: a show-off
tchik-tchak: fast (slang)
veenker: blinker (as on a car)
visher: windshield wiper

Don't bother arguing. In the past, renters' friends had to scrupulously keep their phone numbers, because Information wouldn't know from them. But Bezek reached the twentieth century shortly before the arrival of the twenty-first century, and the company made it possible for renters to at least obtain a listing with Information.

Should you have a friend who isn't listed and you have lost that person's phone number, Information can look up telephone numbers by address. Your challenge will be to figure out which of the names the operator gives you is your friend's landlord. Just hope your friend lives in a small building.

Even without your name attached to your landlord's phone, you will have to pay for all calls and the monthly service charge. Remember that phone calls are metered in Israel. There's a charge for each call and a tie-in not only with distance but also length of the call and time of day. While a lot of space falls into the 02 calling area, not all charges in 02 are the same. Calling outside Jerusalem is more expensive than inside Jerusalem. Bezek's rates are a maze; only mathematical geniuses can keep track of them. And just when you think you have a grip on them, they change. Keep all your telephone and other utility bills for your final settlement with your landlord.

As an alternative to a phone in the flat, you can rent a cellular phone. Then you can walk around as if you're talking to God, just like everyone else. But be considerate and talk to God in your own space.

To use public phones, you can buy a phone card at the post office. Directions are given in pictures. Occasionally, just when you must place an immediate call, you will find a public phone that takes only money and you're out of change.

The rates of international calls from Israel have plummeted. No longer do we have the excuse that exorbitant charges keep us from making those

---

Fractured English
(seen on store signs and menus):

Toest	I.D.F. Spoke
Welco	Sman
Ich Cream	Has moved.
Coketails	

calls. But avoid Sprint, MCI, and AT&T if you will be here for any length of time. Why? A friend in Finland and I found that his calls to Israel on Sprint cost $2 a minute. Mine to Finland via one of the local independent companies cost 30 cents a minute.

Another glorious change is that the international rates are now the same 24 hours a day. No more setting the alarm for 3 a.m. to reach someone nine or ten time zones away when the rates are cheapest. Still, the logistics of figuring out when either side of the world is sleeping can be baffling. All your calculations will be thrown off during fall and spring, when Israel goes off or on Daylight Savings Time (called here Summer Time) and the rest of the world doesn't.

You can use Bezek's regular international service or, better yet, register at no charge with one of three companies, Bezek International, Barak, or Golden Lines. Your bill can go on your Visa card. Compare the companies' rates before you register; you can choose only one. There is no minimum length of service, but be sure to cancel it before you leave—or the next person using the phone in your flat will have even less costly international phone calls than you.

Anytime you call Bezek, you may request an English-speaking operator. But if you must do business at the Bezek office, don't count on finding an English-speaking employee there. Russian, perhaps, but not English. And bring something to read while you wait.

Telephone repair is another surprisingly efficient service in Israel, as long as the telephone is rented from Bezek or is within a year of purchase from Bezek. If something disastrous happens to your Bezek telephone, take heart. While I was carrying on a lengthy conversation, the base of my phone sat on the floor between me and my electric heater. Oh, panic! The phone melted! It simply caved in, as if it had been in the soup too long. But someone told me about Bezek's repair service.

In exchange for my pathetic, lopsided phone, I received a bright new one. What it cost—if anything—I never figured out from looking at my next few bills, but at least I never had to explain the damage to my landlord, the infamous Mr. Selah.

Call Bezek at 166 to report problems on your telephone line or to inquire about a Bezek phone that needs repair. If you own a non-Bezek phone and you call for someone to fix it, the phone won't be repaired and you, nevertheless, will be charged a service call.

From my first days here, I looked on finding a name in the Hebrew telephone book as a challenge I could overcome. That's known as chutzpah. Some transliterations are impossible to figure out. I lost hair over looking for the name of the American author Miriam Chaikin. (I finally found it, as if pronounced in Hebrew "Hi-kin.") Then there are the names of institutions. How are we supposed to know that Hebrew University is listed as HaUniversita HaIvrit—*The* Hebrew University? It took me 10 years to find national government listings. Of course, in a pinch, you can call Information, 144, and be charged four meter units for this single act of desperation.

Speaking of desperation, here are some important numbers:

• Police......100
• Emergency Medical Assistance (Magen David Adom)....101
• Fire.........102
• Operator-assisted overseas calls...188 (For overseas information, you will be connected with AT&T and charged approximately $2.50.)

For a collect or international credit-card call to the United States, dial ICC at 177-100-6063 or AT&T at 800/940-2727. To Canada, dial AT&T at 800/940-2727.

The free little English-language telephone book has no private names listed, just businesses. Although it might seem as if most of what you are looking for is in Azariya or Ma'ale Adumim, you can unearth some useful information in this book—and also some wrong numbers.

Playing Post Office

Israeli mail service has a whimsical side. Mail usually arrives, but occasionally it seems to take the alternate route to the moon. I've sent mail from Jerusalem to other Israeli cities that neither reached its destination nor was returned to me. Letters sent to me from Jerusalem never arrived in Jerusalem. Early in my stay, one letter sent to me from the United States went to Ireland. Another went to Ho Chi Min City.

On the other hand, I did get a letter from Cairo addressed only with my name, Jerusalem, and the wrong zip code. I forever marvel how it reached me—unless the fact that the return address read American Embassy had some influence on the efficiency of delivery.

Actually, I'm convinced that Israeli mail carriers, most of them barely more than kids and wearing whatever they happen to own, are geniuses. Walk into a building and look at the mailboxes. Every name is written in a different style, names are crossed out and written over. Some are illegible. How these mail kids figure all this out is beyond me. They have to have excellent memories, imagination, and language abilities. Whether it looks that way or not, mail is delivered every day, or so a post office official insisted.

The matter of Israeli's equivalent of a zip code can be a problem with mail from the United States. Since Israeli code numbers (*mikud*) consist of five digits, they can be confused with American zip codes. That means that mail for Jerusalem, which has 9 as the first number, can wander along the American West Coast before some alert postal worker looks at the envelope and realizes, "Oh, Jerusalem. Israel. Oh, yeah." The last place I lived, my address's alter ego was Homeland, California.

This is how you solve the problem: Make sure the mikud follows or precedes the word *Jerusalem*. That's not all. Insert a hyphen. I usually put it after the second digit. That way, the American post office scanner is baffled. With these precautions, I rarely have a problem. To learn your mikud, ask a neighbor or at the post office.

Mailboxes here are red or yellow and can be located almost anywhere—stuck into walls along a sidewalk, for instance. The yellow boxes are for Jerusalem mail only. Everything else, including mail to other Israeli locations, goes into red boxes.

Packages, even small ones, aren't delivered. Instead the mail kid will leave a note in your letter box telling which post office has the package. You might have to bring identification to claim it. Packages from overseas valued under $35 (this allowance might increase) are duty-free, even if they contain something electronic. Over the allotted amount, the duty varies with the item.

The Central Post Office, Rehov Yafo 23, is open from 7:30 a.m. to 7 p.m. weekdays and until 3 p.m. Friday. It is closed on Shabbat. Other major post offices are open from 8 a.m. until 5, 6, or 7 p.m. weekdays, depending on the branch. These include post offices in Rehavia, the Clal Center, the Bell Tower, and on Rehov Shamai. Smaller post offices or postal agencies break from 12:30 p.m. to 3:30 p.m. and then are open until 6 p.m. On Wednesday or Tuesday, depending on the location, they close at 1 p.m. for the day. During August, many post offices close by 2 or 3:30 p.m.

Israeli post offices aren't only for buying stamps and telephone cards or even sending express mail overseas. You can pay all your utility bills

Hebrew: God's Native Tongue

There once was a 87-year-old Boston dowager who began studying Hebrew. Her friends asked why in the world, at her ripe age, she would begin the study of a language. She answered, "Because if, after my death, I should be able to meet God, I want to speak to him in his native tongue." (Or did she say, "I want to speak to her?")

and arnona property tax there. For air mail, ask the clerk to give you a string of air-mail stickers, which are blue and feature a drawing of a gazelle. Israelis joke that it's really a turtle.

Postage rates change without warning. It's a big nuisance to buy several overseas stamps and then find the price has gone up, and now you will have to stand in line for a 20-agorot stamp. It pays to buy a book of local stamps or air letters in bulk. The cost doesn't appear on them.

Every trip to the post office, where your business is everybody else's, can be interesting. On one of my errands to the Rehavia post office, where the line often resembles a dog show with all the people who bring Fido to keep them company as they wait, I asked for 10 air letters. The clerk counted them out, then told me to count them too. So I did. I got to "six, seven, eight ..." when a man at my elbow behind me suddenly bellowed to the clerk, "Nine! Only nine!" Well, what else did my neighbor in line have to do except watch the dogs and look out for my interests? Now, he, the clerk, I, and anybody else who could crane his or her neck to see, counted the air letters again. They still totaled nine, and the clerk dutifully handed me another one.

The post office line, like all lines, is constantly challenged by line crashers. My mercy is limited to women either heavy with child or with a babe in one arm and a squalling two-year-old in the other. That's it.

Be sure to bring stamps from home for the many times you can locate "courier service." Shoving letters into the hands of anyone going to the Old Country is a common practice. They drop your letters in a mailbox after arrival (you hope), which speeds delivery and saves on postage.

When word gets around that you are returning home, you'll be amazed at the people you hardly know who ask when your flight will be. Don't be touched by their interest. It isn't personal, it's purely pragmatic. Their next question will be, "Will you have room for a letter or two?"

There's always room for a letter or two—or more.

Does It Compute?

With a laptop computer that's smart enough to know what kind of electricity it's using, you're in business. Mine needed only an adapter plug. I used a dot-matrix printer and an external modem on a transformer for years with no problem.

But the situation can be hair-raising if your computer needs service and you can't locate a local representative for your make. I've been there. While writing this book, the A-drive on my antiquated laptop died. And I was facing a deadline. While I sought a solution, I lost count of the number of computer techies who looked at my equipment, clucked their tongues, and said, "That's a very old computer."

As if that was news to me. As if I wouldn't have replaced it years earlier if I could have.

Some of the solutions offered would have meant losing an unknown amount of information on my hard drive, and it was impossible for me to copy any of it beforehand. From call after call—even one to a techie doing his army duty, who might have been sitting on a hill in Lebanon for all I knew—I located a company, actually within walking distance, that dealt with my brand of computer. I had found no hint of its existence in the telephone book or even from Computerland. The message is: If you can't find official technical support for your computer, don't take the first solution you hear. Keep asking. Something will come up.

If official technical support is in Tel Aviv, it's worth the schlepp. Jerusalemites were ready to perform not a mere circumcision on my first laptop, but castration to get it to accept Israeli electricity. The official techie in Tel Aviv, who looked about 14, simply sold me a new cord for a cost of about $5.

If you declare your laptop when you arrive in the country you will be charged a customs fee, which will be returned to you when you leave. But you don't have to carry a wad of money for this—only your credit card. When you leave Israel, you will find a customs representative at a desk upstairs at Ben-Gurion Airport. Show him that you are taking your computer with you, and your credit slip will be destroyed.

If you would rather buy a computer here and sell it before you leave, note that laptops are very expensive. Desktops are almost reasonable. Nor are printers a major financial outlay. Office Depot has outlets in the Tel Aviv area but, at this writing, not in Jerusalem. If you need a printer and someone wants to sell you a used dot matrix, beware. Dot-matrix paper and ribbons virtually are extinct.

You will treasure each sheet of computer paper. Five hundred sheets of borderless paper costs almost $8. Floppies and ink cartridges cost in the ballpark of those back home.

The AACI has a computer club that meets monthly. There you can make connections, discuss your computer problems, and, perhaps, find solutions.

20
STOCKING UP

The activity that might be scariest for anyone in a foreign country is shopping, especially for food. You're hungry. You need to buy provisions. But all those foreign words on the products tell you nothing. You feel helpless—as if you don't even know how to tie your own shoes. Eventually, you will get the hang of it. Of course it helps that more and more American and English products find their way onto grocery shelves here. They might be three times the price back home, but it can be comforting to buy a jar of Skippy Peanut Butter.

This chapter is aimed at providing some shortcuts. Specialty shops include greengrocers with fresh fruits and vegetables; the grocery (*mako-let*—remember that word, for it's basic to your life) with emphasis on non-perishables, dairy products, and bread; butcher shops; fishmongers; natural-food stores; bakeries (which abound more frequently than is good for one's dimensions); shops selling nuts and sweets; and shops selling Middle Eastern salads and olives. The shouk at Mahane Yehuda and the Arab souk in the Old City are a gathering of specialty shops.

Grocery Shopping

The best way to get your bearings and learn what Israeli food stores offer is to explore the supermarkets. You can take as much time as you want to wander through the aisles and ogle. You are most likely to find English-speaking shoppers to help solve stumpers at Super-Sol on Rehov Agron and the Co-op Supermarkets in the basement of HaMashbir, in the Wolfson Building on Rehov Dis-kin, and on Rehov HaPalmach. As in the United States, supermarkets here carry a lot besides food, like household cleaning supplies, candles, matches, and toiletries, even pots, pans, and brooms.

Watermelons for sale in Mahane Yahude

You'll find Captain Crunch, Paul Newman salad dressings, and Tabasco sauce. Often, there are Israeli equivalents to American products (although not to those just mentioned), which can be a taste come-down or, occasionally, superior.

Supermarkets have delicatessen counters with hummus, tahini, hot carrots, Turkish salad, baba ghanouj, and barrels of different kinds of olives. You can taste the various salads before you buy. Super-Sol also has a counter of ready-cooked food with chicken dishes and meatballs.

Although, for a fee, your supermarket purchases will be delivered, you will do your own sacking. Do your "ecological thing": Save plastic bags and bring them back next time rather than taking new ones on each visit. This is a small country, and used plastic has no place to go.

The dairy department is possibly the most baffling in a supermarket because of its variety. The Super-Sol manager walked the length of the dairy counter with me one day and identified some of the products. He noted that cheeses are divided by their color. Yellow are hard cheeses, usually with a high fat content, which can be from 20 to 45 percent. Most white cheeses are soft and go from 0 to 16 percent fat. You can buy packages of yellow cheese pre-sliced or have it sliced at the cheese counter. The white is sold pre-packaged or in bulk, also at the cheese counter.

These are the Israeli names of yellow cheeses and their internationally known equivalents:

- **emek**—Dutch edam, made of cow's milk
- **gush halav**—Dutch edam, but more expensive than emek
- **gilboa**—a less fatty relative of emek and gush halav
- **tal HaEmek**—Emmenthal Swiss cheese
- **bashan**—smoked provolone
- **gad**—Danish danbo
- **Ein Gedi**—Camembert
- **galil**—Roquefort
- **gilead**—Balkan *kashkaval* (smoked), sheep's milk

Brie, Camembert, cheddar, Parmesan, provolone, and feta also are available. Specialty yellow cheeses, usually processed and smoked or sharp, come in sausagelike shapes.

White cheese is Bulgarian style, which means salty. In increasing amounts of fat, brand names of some salty white cheeses are Gamad, Betit, and Kafrit (which can be substituted for feta). Hermon is a heavy white cheese with 16 percent fat. A white spreadable cheese (with the consistency of thick sour cream) comes in round cartons or rectangular tubs and with varying fat content, up to 9 percent.

Other cheeses are Shanit and Symphony, which are similar to cream cheese, while genuine Philadelphia Cream Cheese is available. The local versions can have additions, like olives, so look carefully before you buy. Also, there is Shumit, like Boursin, but with garlic and herbs; and Pilpelit, also like Boursin but with black pepper and spices; as well as the original French Boursin and Fromez, made from goat's milk. Popular Labane

311

is a classic Middle Eastern member of the dairy family and is a runny combination of white cheese and yogurt.

Cottage cheese, called here *co-tege*, comes in small round tubs. It could be the most delicious cottage cheese you have ever tasted, especially in its 9 percent-fat form.

Yogurt-related products seem to be endless. The unflavored variety starts (by the lowest fat content) with Gil and its equivalents. Gil is thin enough that grocery shoppers often take a container from the display case, shake it up, and slurp it down right then and there. Next comes Eshel, with red letters, and its equivalents by other dairies. Then there's Shemenet, which is like sour cream; and genuine sour cream, which has the name written in English.

New names of plain, flavored, or dessert-type yogurts change as fast as dairy companies' marketing departments can dream them up. Some have pieces of fruit or are fruit-flavored. You can find pineapple, peaches, apricots, cherries, strawberries, bananas, and blueberries in yogurt. Lemon or orange yogurt are seen, but rarely. At the moment, there's a nut yogurt and yogurt with coconut, as well as pear yogurt.

I used to serve a heavenly mango yogurt to bedazzled foreign guests. Suddenly it disappeared, never to be seen again. (Never say "never"?) Yogurts here are as trendy as obstetrics. It seems there's a new line on the market all the time, while the lip-smacking one you dote on suddenly disappears.

Jerusalem Scene

Malkah, Russian-born, British-raised, and very proper, walked into a bakery to treat herself to a cake one summer day. But she was mortified at the sight of masses of flies crawling over the baked goods. Enraged, she turned on her heels and stormed out the door, even before the proprietor could ask for her order.

Startled, he ran down the sidewalk after her. "Giveret!" (Madame) Giveret!" he shouted. "Why are you leaving?"

She hollered over her shoulder, "Because of the flies on the food. It's disgusting."

"Giveret," the man said in a helpless tone, "but this is the Middle East."

You can buy coffee yogurt as well as butterscotch, caramel, mocha, and many kinds of chocolate puddings. Some of these puddings, like Milki, come with a whipped-cream topping. Milki is an Israeli institution, like the presidency. But the presidency could disappear before Milki does.

Buying milk can be confusing, because of the different kinds of containers. The standard is a one-liter plastic bag, for which you must make the one-time purchase of a plastic holder to set it in. You can buy the same milk in a carton for about 20 percent more. Halav Amid is "long-life" milk. It comes in cartons and requires no refrigeration, until opened. I've never seen powdered milk or powdered coffee whitener here.

Buttermilk lovers can find it in half-liter cartons, with "buttermilk" written in English. It comes in various flavors. Fat content is 2 percent. Coffee Rich, written in English, is a coffee creamer. Whipping cream comes in one-quarter liter cartons. Sugarless *parve* cream whip (suitable to serve with meat meals) is available.

The last knot to unravel in the dairy case is the one that pertains to margarine and butter. Margarine is simply margarine back in the United States. Here, the local product is specialized. There are several types of Blue Band margarine—for frying, for baking, or including milk. You can find that information written in English. A product known as Margarina is made of sunflower oil and tastes similar to butter, some people say. Calorina margarine is a dietetic brand. Another member of the family, Afical, wrapped in blue and silver paper, is used for making pastry dough. Standard butter, European-type, is wrapped in silver paper (no salt) or gold paper (salted). Another type, known as Dutch or American butter, is salty and deeper yellow. Only Tnuva's blocks of butter say in English if they have salt or not. You can find a small rectangular tub that contains butter with half the normal fat.

Another item not to be overlooked in the dairy case is an individual serving of chocolate mousse. You also can find tofu. One kind is labeled Jerusalem Tofu, which sounds like as much of a cultural clash as Beijing Bourekas.

Now that all the above information is being digested (perhaps along with a chocolate Milki), we'll deal with other food-shopping matters. Eggs aren't refrigerated; they simply sit on a shelf. The Super-Sol manager gave me an amazed expression when I asked if it wasn't bad for eggs to be left unrefrigerated. He explained that the customer's protection is the sales date on each box. Carefully pick up each egg before you buy to make sure it hasn't already drooled into the cardboard.

The basic Israeli bread is sold unwrapped. (But as I write this, the prospect of wrapping basic bread and challah is being investigated, in which case there could be a major revolution in shopping habits here.)

Long loaves of what are called white and black bread, but really are "whitish" and "a little-less whitish" and to me look just about the same from both inside and outside, are put onto shelves or left in the cardboard containers in which they arrived. The "black" loaf is a bit shorter than the "white."

If you're seized with the urge to squeeze a loaf for freshness (which really isn't necessary), the polite way to do it is to first slip your hand into a plastic bag and then fondle the loaf. (You'll wish everyone did this, but Israelis are cavalier about their bread and blithely plunk unbagged loaves onto yucky counters to pay for them.)

Israeli bread has a crunchy crust and often is still warm from the oven when you buy it. It's tempting to start gobbling it immediately. Stores and Mahane Yehduda sell all sorts of bread, from French-style baguettes to wide, flat Iraqi bread. In the shouk, breads simply sit on a counter or a street stand. Not only can you buy some breads sliced, at least in the supermarkets, but certain supermarkets also have do-it-yourself bread slicers.

Wandering around the supermarkets, you might miss items from back home. On the other hand, because this is the Middle East and because Israel buys from European countries, the choice and variety might be wider. For instance, you can buy frozen *malawah*, delicious, flaky Yemenite bread (just put it in a dry frying pan and brown both sides) or Swedish ginger biscuits.

Unless you are fluent in Hebrew, it's simplest to buy fresh fish from a store like Daglicatess (a play on the words *dag*, Hebrew for fish, and *delicatessen*) at Rehov Rahel Imenu 1 off Rehov Emek Refaim, (02) 561-1488, where the staff is used to people like us. The supermarkets also have fresh-fish counters. Again, Super-Sol on Rehov Agron, being the international crossroads of supermarkets, probably has employees most versed in dealing with foreigners' needs and absence of Hebrew. There are many fish markets at Mahane Yehuda, where the fish might still be flapping, but cleaning can be minimal and service grudging, if at all.

Frozen-food cases have fish patties with recognizable pictures on the package and other fish products. Don't waste your time looking for shrimp or lobster in supermarkets. They can be found only in non-kosher specialty shops.

Frozen chicken might be cheaper than fresh chicken, which must have a date of slaughter on its cellophane wrapping. The Ministry of Health requires fresh chicken to be sold within three days of slaughter. Don't be surprised by the pinfeathers, and don't believe anyone who tells you their survival has to do with kashrut. A well-known rabbi said nonsense to that—their presence is simply due to inefficient cleaning processes.

One company, Landau, advertises "No pinfeathers" (more expensive, but worth it?).

Meat cuts aren't the same as in the United States. You'll need to explain to the butcher how you want to prepare a piece of meat, and he will probably know what to sell you. Some cuts you might be used to aren't kosher: They won't be in the supermarkets or Mahane Yehuda.

Schnitzel is ubiquitous on the Israeli dinner table. Frozen schnitzel is cooked like traditional veal schnitzel, but usually it is made of chicken or turkey. And there's a variety of vegetarian schnitzels.

The selection in fresh produce is wide: strawberries starting in the fall and going on and on, football-sized mangoes, huge heads of Romaine lettuce, kiwis, fennel, artichokes, and umpteen sizes and shapes of citrus fruit. But don't look for blueberries or raspberries. You might see some puny blueberries for a minute at a price that will make you think you are buying pearls. You have a better chance of finding mulberries, especially in the shouk, which are pale, fat, and taste like subtle strawberries.

Persimmons are part of the Israeli winter scene. They are bright-colored and sweet, and you eat them like apples. But beware, they can be hazardous to your digestive system. It is advisable not to eat too many at once and to eat them only when they are very soft. Otherwise, you could find yourself making a sudden trip to the hospital.

Fresh chicken: Beware of pinfeathers.

A drink you might want to try is Nesher Malt, a non-alcoholic black beer. Advertisements claim that it promotes muscle development—after consumers work off the added girth Nesher will give them, no doubt.

Pastry shops, whether Jewish or Arab, are totally seductive. Arab shops specialize in sticky, sweet, pistachio-filled goodies. Jewish shops often reflect the baker's ethnic origin. Around the Mahane Yehuda shouk, you can buy varieties of bourekas, along with cookies and pastries.

If you are in the Old City and want to treat yourself to something less heavenly and rich, but tasty in its own way, try a *beigele*, the soft, doughnut-shaped, sesame-seed covered bread sold by Arab vendors. It may or may not be an ancestor of today's bagel. For a more flavorful taste, ask for *zaytar*, which comes wrapped in a piece of newspaper. It is a wild spice from the mountains, akin to a blend of oregano and marjoram. Dip your beigele into it as you eat. Some vendors will sell you more salt than zaytar. You can always buy your own zaytar in the supermarket.

To get the best food prices, like anything else, you have to shop around. The shouk at Mahane Yehuda is often, but not always, the cheapest place. However, one study reported that pasta, beans, and lentils not only were cheaper at some supermarkets but also had fewer stones in them.

At Mahane Yehuda, prices on fresh produce go down on Friday afternoon, before everything closes for Shabbat. But the scene can become wild, with people elbowing each other to reach the tomatoes. And by then, the fight could be over the dregs. At any rate, the *Into the Heart of Jerusalem* principle on shopping in Mahane Yehuda is: Whatever bargain price you pay for your purchase, a moment later you will find it even cheaper.

The most complete natural-food shop is Nitzat HaDuvdevan (The Cherry Blossom) at Rehov Agrippas 99, (02) 623-4859. The aisles usually are jammed. Another shop is Kol HaTeva at Rehov Aza 29, (02) 563-2270. *The Key to Cooking in Israel*, by Amit Women, has charts with meat cuts and their names in Hebrew, Hebrew names for herbs and spices, temperature equivalents in Celsius, metric measurements, and other useful information, besides a lot of recipes. It is somewhat outdated, but still useful. The book costs about $12. Amit Women's address is Rehov Alkalai 8.

Toothpaste, Toilet Paper, and Diapers
All those favorite brand names from home—Colgate, Ponds, Dove, Clairol, Flex, Johnson & Johnson, Pampers, Nivea, Vaseline, Tampax, and many more—are available in Israel, but at prices resembling grand larceny.

Israeli-made products don't necessarily cost less, but they're worth checking out (though the local toothpaste demands some getting used to). In the city, try Alba Pharmacy at Rehov Yafo 42 and Ben Yehuda 7, as well as Super-Pharm on Rehov HaHistadrut near King George, which often has flyers just inside the entrance advertising current sales.

An Israeli product is Ahava cream from the Dead Sea. A friend gave me Ahava hand cream at a time when even Godzilla would have winced shaking hands with me. Suddenly my hands turned to silk. The cream costs almost $8 a tube at Alba, but is cheaper at the airport duty-free shop. Ahava also sells foot cream for the same price. Perhaps with that you'll have no excuse not to bring your feet into bed with you.

Look for Big Deal, a store run by Americans at Rehov Luntz 3 off Ben Yehuda. It sells a jumble of items, from children's games to household goods and cooking supplies, at good prices. The stock always keeps changing.

Both campuses of the Hebrew University have two Acadamon stores each. One is a bookstore. The other sells toiletries, various gadgets you'll need in your flat, notebooks, computer paper, and ribbons, usually at good prices. On Mount Scopus, Acadamon is in a passageway off the main administration building, which you reach via escalators from the bus stop. At Ramat Gan, Acadamon is in the first building to your right after the campus entrance, and you don't have to go crazy looking for it.

In the supermarket's household-cleaning department, you will see some familiar products. Fantastik and Sano products get a lot of recommendations. Precious little information in English might be on the containers, but ask fellow shoppers for help.

Let's talk about a delicate subject. Because of Jerusalem's crusty water, cleaning toilet bowls is a major occupation here. Be sure to buy a brush and a toilet-cleaning product. In general, you'll have to scrub relentlessly. And while we're on the subject, I was next in line to pay for my granola at a little shop on Agrippas when a 20-something fellow in front of me asked the clerk in English for a bag for his purchase—a package of 24 rolls of toilet paper. The clerk's jaw dropped. I realized the clerk didn't have the words to explain the problem, so I jumped into the gap. "There's no bag in Israel big enough," I said. "You just have to walk through the streets of Jerusalem carrying your package of 24 rolls of toilet paper like everyone else." Twenty-something blanched. Then he meekly said "Oh," and tried to smile.

You can buy discreet packages of four rolls of toilet paper, but Israel is a small country, and its toilet-paper rolls are in proportion. You'll end up running to the store for more about as often as you buy bread. So you just say what the hey and buy a package of 24 or even 32 rolls and march up Rehov King George with your head high. The packages come with handles.

Tip: Sunday is a bad time for Mahane Yehuda shopping. Many foods, lettuce in particular, don't arrive that day, since Sunday follows Shabbat, the day of rest.

Shopping Free-for-All

Clothes, other than those hanging outside stores on Rehov Yafo or Agrippas, are expensive. But at least Israel finally discovered the true meaning of the word *sale*. Time was, a 10 percent reduction was touted as a sale or *mivtza*. You and I know that's hardly worth getting out of bed for. Now I see signs advertising reductions of 50 percent and far more. But prices at the better shops start ridiculously high for the product, so 50 percent off might put them in reasonable range.

Some places advertise good prices all year round. Mahson, at Rehov HaLamed Hey 15 in Katamon, sells American name brands of casual clothes for men, women, and children and claims the goods are less expensive than in the United States. It carries Talbot's and Geoffrey Beene, among others, for they are made in Israel. The best choices are children's clothes.

Y. Schwartz, in the center of town at Rehov HaHavatzelet 2 and 4, is a dreary place, but with attractive prices on men's and women's clothes, especially winter jackets. Schwartz also has an outlet in Canyon Yisrael, at Rehov Yad Haruztim in the Talpiot industrial area.

Tania's Shop, at Rehov HaHagana 21 in French Hill, is a well-known secondhand establishment. Another is Alexandra, the first store you come to going down the steps on Rehov Ma'alot Nahalot, at the entrance to Nahalat Shiva from Rehov Yafo.

At any rate, male or female, you don't have to give much thought to clothes here. Jerusalem is the poorest large city in Israel, and what you see on the streets reflects that. But at any economic level, tradition rules. Israeli men consider the simple act of putting on a white shirt to be dressing up. Women, from the age of 13, think that wearing black stamps them as sophisticated. They even wear black to bar mitzvahs.

21
LAND OF
RECREATION

Coming to Jerusalem alone, I had two major concerns: Was it safe and would I have a social life?

Answers I found to the first question appear in the section on safety in Chapter 2: "Facts of Jerusalem Life." The freedom of movement I enjoy here day and night sometimes makes me feel like a carefree kid. Not completely, however. I know that purse snatchers and wallet lifters prowl certain hotel areas and the shouk and souk, and it's always wise to stay alert to my surroundings. But the general violence that haunts women's lives in a country such as the United States doesn't exist here. For that reason, Israel can be a glorious, free, liberating experience for a woman.

Gender Relations

I thought that as a single woman living in Jerusalem, a male-female social life would be zero. Too many wars I concluded. There can't be available men. I was wrong. Israeli men make themselves available. Sometimes more than you wish they would. But how many other places in the world can a Jewish woman run to the store for a loaf of bread and be followed home by not only a Frenchman but also a Jewish Frenchman who invites her to coffee?

As a woman goes about her business on bustling Jerusalem streets, she frequently finds herself approached by men in a casual, friendly way. Israeli men's standard opening line is "Do you know what time it is?" or "Do you know where Rehov X is?" Now, they actually could want to know what time it is or where to find Rehov X. Few people in the city seem to own a watch or to have figured out the jumbled streets. But, usually, another purpose to the question exists.

One man's variation on the standard opener was "Don't you come from Philadelphia?" He approached me twice, months apart, with the same line. And, oh yes, I have been asked, "What's your sign?"

If finding out the time or where to find a certain street was merely an opening gambit, expect to hear next "Where are you from?"; "Do you live alone?" (Watch out for that one); and then an invitation "to drink the coffee." What to answer? Most women can size up a creep before he's uttered a complete sentence or asked if she's from Philadelphia. Otherwise, drinking coffee with a stranger can be totally harmless and interesting, even if the man isn't Mr. Right.

Ami invited me to drink not coffee but cinnamon tea after we got into a telephone conversation. He had called about an ad I placed to sublet my flat so I could escape from Mr. Selah. Ami was a bright graduate student in political science. I learned things from him about the experience of Jewish Moroccan immigrants in Israel that I might otherwise not have known.

320

But for such encounters to remain pleasant, the woman has to retain control. If I accept an invitation to "drink the coffee" or tea, I pay for what I order. As a wonderful American jazz singer advised, "Girl, pay the cost and be the boss."

After a few missteps, my answer to "Do you live alone?" became "I live with my aunt and uncle and their five children." The choice was between honesty and self-preservation. Never underestimate the persistence of Israeli men, married or not. I figured I always could "'fess up" later, if that seemed to be the thing to do. Meanwhile, the answer dampened the enthusiasm of pesky pursuers.

I tell no male over the age of five my address, unless I don't mind him dropping by whenever the spirit moves him. Unannounced visits are a custom in Israel, but some are inopportune, not to mention unwanted.

Culture Clash
While dealing with Jewish men is relatively simple, dealing with Arab men can border an international incident. So let's talk frankly.

When my former husband read what I had written on the subject in the first edition of this book, he called me a racist. I, who had stormed the barricades during the Civil Rights struggle and lived in an integrated neighborhood!

I answered that I was not racist—I had simply learned to be careful based on constant repetition of events. And when the first edition was written, I hadn't yet had a teenager pinch my cheek—hard—when I stopped my car in an Arab neighborhood and did nothing more provocative than ask for directions.

Invitations to drink coffee or sweet mint tea are an integral part of Arab courtesy. It could seem inhospitable for a Western woman to refuse such an invitation. But by accepting, she inadvertently could be sending messages that she is agreeable to more than coffee or tea. The sight of Western women with their freedom to come and go as they please, their independence, and their reputation—deserved or not—for sexual availability, makes most Arab men's hormones light up like a pinball machine.

If a woman wants to accept coffee or tea and chat with an Arab man for awhile, fine. But as with Jewish men, she should stay in control of the situation. She should in no way feel she has to submit or even tolerate advances that could begin with arm patting and suddenly escalate to a man pressing his body against hers.

These incidents don't even need the courtesy of coffee or tea to occur. They can happen when a woman merely steps into a shop to look around. While she is checking on the merchandise, the shopkeeper could be checking vigorously on her.

When Jordan occupied Jerusalem, shopkeepers who played feelies with their female customers were subject to stiff penalties by the police. But with the delicate international situation between Arabs and Israelis, a woman has only herself for protection, unless things really get rough. When I tell a Jewish man on the street to buzz off, we part with a handshake, a smile, and good wishes. There is a lightheartedness about the Jewish approach, as if we both know it's a game.

But a woman handing a firm "no" to an Arab man probably will hear in return, at the very least, an outraged cry that she doesn't honor "friendship." The parting could include a string of obscenities shouted in public. The experience can be distressing and humiliating.

I was a slow learner about all this, but learn I did. One day, finally knowledgeable, I looked for a sherut near Damascus Gate to take me to an Arab village some miles from Jerusalem. An Arab driver assured me his car was a sherut. Bargaining settled the fare at several dollars. Because a couple was already in the back seat, I had to take the seat next to the driver. The couple got out a mile or so later, and I stayed put. It would be rude if I got into the back seat, I thought. He'd think I didn't trust him. Still in the city, he suddenly put his hand on my thigh. I pushed him away and demanded, "Keep your hands off me." Then I added, "You know that if someone did this to your sister, you'd kill him." The last line was bravado on my part, but he sheepishly nodded in agreement.

I was about to order him to stop the car and let me out, when he turned the car around and drove back almost to where we started—but not quite. Instead of taking me to Damascus Gate, he took me to a place where there were genuine sherut loading stands. His car wasn't a sherut at all, but a private taxi. He pointed out the sherut I should take to my destination. And this man who had wanted several dollars for the trip told me, "Don't pay more than 50 cents."

This episode had a peaceful outcome, and I even saved money. But problems like this one don't arise only between Western women and Arab men who are strangers. Problems can arise even after a lengthy acquaintance. Ibrahim was a shopkeeper I'd met through a mutual friend. For years, I had enjoyed drinking tea with him in his store and listening to his poetry recitals and talk of his family. Then he decided our relationship should become cozier. I refused. He angrily shook his fist at me and shouted, "I won't open the shop tomorrow. You'll see."

I never went by to check on it.

"Na-Eem May-Od"

"Na-eem may-od" is the Hebrew equivalent of "Pleased to meet you." But Israel being a somewhat disorganized country, formal introductions are few. So how do you meet people in Jerusalem? That was what I wondered when I arrived knowing no one. But, as I wrote earlier, out of my taxi ride from Ben-Gurion Airport to the city came a treasured friendship with Aaron, the driver, his wife, and their five children.

One week later, I stopped at the Jewish Agency to track down information on ulpanim. The receptionist sent me down the hall to talk with Morty Dolinsky. An American-born longtime Israeli, Morty swept me into his office, asked what I'd like to drink (coffee, tea, or juice—the standard Israeli fare), and plied me with questions about who I was, why I was there, and so on.

Before that day had ended, two visiting American men and I had gone with Morty to a wedding in Herodion—Herod's ruined fortress southeast of Bethlehem—had danced and feasted at the wedding party in the village of Tekoa, and had been shaken up in Morty's ancient auto as it bounced up and down the hills of the Judean Desert. When we returned to Jerusalem, Morty took us to the Mount of Olives and Mount Scopus to see one gorgeous view after another of Jerusalem, still golden under its lights at night.

Later, when I wearily climbed out of the car well past midnight, Morty asked, "Say, why did you come to my office this morning?" I struggled to remember. "To find out about ulpans," I finally recalled. With a tone of amazement, he said, "But I don't know a damn thing about ulpans." And so started another friendship.

I met my darling friend Malkah, a feisty septuagenarian journalist, when she and I shared snippy comments over the uncooperative behavior of a woman ahead of us in the supermarket check-out line. Friday afternoon tea in Malkah's tiny Arab house became a ritual.

I've gotten to know both men and women as I walked down the street. Jerusalemites are curious, talkative, generous-hearted, unpredictable, and spontaneous. Thanks to them, being a stranger in Jerusalem is but a transitory stage. Granted, women should recognize that some of the red-carpet treatment they receive has sexual overtones. But suffice it to say that anyone in Jerusalem—male or female—who has a sense of adventure and humor will make friends rapidly. Anyone who is timid should pretend not to be, and the results will be the same as for a gregarious soul.

Serendipity works beautifully in Jerusalem, but there's no need to trust only luck. You can take matters into your own hands. You can initiate conversation with a stranger. You're not on the New York subway. No one in Jerusalem will look at you peculiarly for doing so, since everybody does it.

A newcomer to the city can join interest groups and clubs, enroll in ulpan, take classes, attend lectures, and call Jerusalemites whom friends back home said you had to get in touch with. Don't expect all of them to respond. But those who don't, you won't miss.

Organizations

The first order of business for anyone in Jerusalem for any length of time at all should be to join the Association of Americans and Canadians in Israel, located at Rehov Mane 6 in Talbia, (02) 561-7151. A year's membership costs only a few dollars and entitles you to parties and a slew of activities, some according to age group, marital status, or specific interests—like the Computer Club. AACI also has counselors with free advice for members on almost any problem they might have.

Yakar, Rehov HaLamed Hey 10, is an Orthodox Jewish study center. In this case, that covers a lot of territory. It sponsors many events that bring people together: musical performances, discussions of social concerns, or peeks into how a play evolves. One program was subtitled "Kicking the guts out of traditional poetry." For the New Moon, a Saturday night program is entitled Dancing with the Moon. Contact Yakar at (02) 561-2310, yakar@actcom.co.il, or www.cyberscribe.com/yakar.

The women's organization Hadassah sponsors Merkaz HaMagshimim specifically for people 19 to 35 years old. Among activities at the center, at Rehov Dor V'Dorshav 7a (continue into the backyard a long way from the street) near Rehov Emek Refaim, (02) 561-9233, are an Independence Day barbecue, a pub tour, and theater performances.

A person who still has unfilled time or needs can find almost any special interest group you can imagine: Overeaters Anonymous, bridge, yoga, aerobic dancing, folk dancing, Singles 30-Plus, Rotary Club, Scrabble, and Al-Anon. The Friday *Jerusalem Post*'s "In Jerusalem" section has listings for most of these.

Lectures

Ashkenazi immigrants from Central Europe brought with them not only their love of Brahms and Mozart but also their devotion to lectures and discussion groups. Should you desire, you could be lectured to almost day and night (and that's in English, even). Talks could be on Israeli politics, the economy, Israeli politics, Arab propaganda, Israeli politics, Judaism, and Israeli politics. You could hear from a member of Knesset, the mayor of Jerusalem, a former Christian missionary, or a Hebrew University professor.

On one Tuesday evening, the events calendar listed the following lectures in English: "Do the Prophets Speak of Jesus?," "Women in the Yishuv (pre-state Israel) and the Early State," "The History of Emotions," "Tort Liability of Statutory Authorities," "Great Hasidic Masters," "Character in

Literature and Criticism," "To the Tombs of the Righteous: Pilgrimage in Contemporary Israel," and "Is a Vegetarian Diet Healthy?" Among organizations that regularly sponsor talks in English are the Center for Conservative Judaism, Rehov Agron 2, which holds lectures at 8 p.m. Monday; and the Israel Center, Rehov Strauss 10, which holds lectures at various times all week, except Shabbat.

Friends of Friends

About picking up the telephone and calling those names mutual friends have given you: It can seem a little scary at first. But it goes on all the time, sometimes getting out of hand for Jerusalemites. After all, this is the crossroads of the world.

Margo, originally from New York, won't let anyone except her immediate relatives west of the Atlantic have her telephone number—and then only with the strictest warning that if they pass it on to anyone coming to Jerusalem, she will call them collect every week. Margo isn't a grouch by nature, but circumstances turned her into one on this matter. She found that heretofore-unmet American after American invited himself, family, and friends over for dinner. When some of these self-invited guests used her place as a crash pad for weeks at a time, enough was enough.

If mutual friends want you to deliver a message to Jerusalemites, by all means do so. But don't force anything. If you'd like to meet the person, you can issue the first invitation. Invite the Jerusalemite to your place or a café (the treat's on you) for coffee and cake.

I had names and names of mutual friends to call when I was here for my leave-of-absence, and some of them I did call. Their courtesy was beyond expectation. Considering that I planned to be here only for a year and never to return, I didn't think my friends' friends would be willing to make any sort of investment of emotions or time in our relationship. I was totally wrong.

Hanging out in Jerusalem

Hanging out in Jerusalem is more than a means of seeing and being seen. It is first and foremost a way of being involved in conversation. Yes, there is a lot of prayer in Jerusalem, but talk comes first: talk about politics, the latest jokes, the weather—and religion. A constant hum fills the air as people earnestly, often emotionally, engage in their favorite social activity. And since talking is more comfortable when participants sit down, drink some coffee, and maybe eat a cake or two—why not?

Keep in mind that an order of tea brings you a tea bag in a glass, with mint or a piece of cinnamon—pronounced "kinnamon." If you order coffee, you usually get instant coffee, generally referred to as *nes*. If you order black coffee you get Turkish coffee. A slang term for it is *botz*, which translates as mud, but that's only in appearance, not taste. My favorite coffee is *hafooch*, which means "reversed." It's a cross between capuccino and a café au lait. It comes topped with creamy foam.

Jerusalem's focal point of talk (after the Knesset, of course) is the **Ben-Yehuda Mall** and its cafés. Not far behind are those on Rehov Yoel Salomon and Rehov Rivlin. Rehov Emek Refaim in the German Colony is another gathering place. **Caffit** at number 35 and **Kapulsky's** down the street are places to be. The **Coffee Mill** at number 23 is a cozy hangout in which you can sip coffee from a variety of places—from Indonesia to Costa Rica.

The area around the Russian Compound is more noted for nightspots but is also the location of the **Strudel Internet Bar** at Rehov Monbaz 11. It's not a place to scatter strudel crumbs between computer keys. The name comes from the fact that the "@" in an e-mail address is known locally as a "strudel." (Israeli officers' shoulder stars are called "falafels." What can I say? Israelis like food.) The clientele is largely native English-speakers, for whom Strudel is a home away from home.

The coffee shops and restaurants at the Jerusalem (Malha) Canyon are a distant possibility, not only geographically from the center of town but also because the noise is so excruciatingly loud there that it's a struggle to carry on a conversation.

Almost any café on the Ben-Yehuda Mall is good for relaxing, but the **Cafe Atara** is special. Its original location was down the street, where Burger King now resides—a sacrilege to most Jerusalemites. There, until the doors closed, it looked pretty much as it did in when it was the center of Jerusalem's cultural and intellectual life from the 1930s to the 1960s. Its peak, perhaps, was the Mandate years. The people who hung out there then talk about how the Atara deliberately had no liquor license during the Mandate—to discourage British soldiers from patronizing the place and discovering members of the Jewish underground army, the Hagana, holding meetings in its back rooms. Or they can tell you how an enormous bomb blast on the street in 1948 severely damaged the café, which somehow managed to keep going.

In 1996 those venerable doors shut for a last time. Later, the café reopened up the street, smaller and having to establish new memories. Even today, the best Atara drink isn't alcoholic but a cup of hot chocolate—rich and under a mountain of whipped cream. There is even an Atara in the "suburbs"—at the edge of Rehavia at Rehov Aza 29.

Fink's, at Rehov HaHistadrut 2, dates to 1932 and is Israel's best-known social institution. During the Mandate period, only Fink's and the King David Hotel were recommended for patronage by officers of the rank of captain and above. What they didn't know was that the Hagana kept an arms cache next to the wine cellar. When owner Moshe Fink, in his native Hungarian, ordered goulash with chocolate sauce, it was a warning to Hagana members to beat it—British officers were arriving.

Fink's is tiny (six tables and an 11-stool bar), resembles something out of London's Fleet Street, and usually is jammed. In 1982 the establishment was named by *Newsweek* magazine and Ballantine Scotch as among the 52 greatest bars in the world. Fink's fans have decorated the walls with contributions of humorous bar signs, drinking glasses, and mugs from just about anyplace you can think of. Fink's attracts the glitterati, visiting international movie stars, and the ubiquitous press. But Shmuel Azrieli, who runs the place, isn't impressed. He refused entrance to Henry Kissinger when Kissinger insisted on taking over the whole bar. "Mooli" wasn't about to chase out his regular customers for anybody. He told me he wasn't interested "in the nouveau riche or big shots." The place is open only in the evening, but not Friday. Don't go to dinner without a reservation, (02) 623-4523. Goulash is a specialty; escargots also are served. Needless to say, Fink's isn't kosher.

HaTsarif, at Rehov Harkenos 5, is romantic at night. A floodlight illuminates greenery outside a glass wall, and on winter nights a roaring fire blazes in the fireplace. But the place has a drawback. Usually crowded and with all the talk that goes on, the room achieves a noise level that ties with a jet takeoff. Also, Hatzarif isn't kosher and thus is off-limits for a lot of people. Still, it can be a place for lingering over mint tea.

With its connection to the Cinematheque movie theater, the **Cinematheque Restaurant** off Derech Hevron has become chichi for its intellectual aura, good food, glorious view, and dancing on Thursday night. Besides these, the Old City explodes during July and August with young tourists hanging out in cafés, particularly in the Arab sector. The tourists often stay in the Old City's many church hostels to absorb the area's color, sounds, and aromas.

Also in summer, street musicians from other countries perform day and night in the middle of the Ben-Yehuda Mall. By sitting on the edge of the brick planters in the mall, you can take it all in and surely find people with whom to carry on a conversation, even without the price of coffee, tea, or cake.

For those occasional times when you'd rather see than be seen, there is the coffee shop at the **King David Hotel**. You can sit on the terrace and peacefully observe the play of light on the walls of the Old City. Sure, there are newer hotels in Jerusalem, but at the King David, along with your coffee comes a hefty serving of history.

Digging for Roots

Jewish genealogy is well documented in the Bible. Jews don't refer to themselves as "members of the tribe" without good reason. But what happened between ancient Biblical days and now? Wouldn't we all like to know? People descended from Spanish Jews, who often kept track of their family histories, or those whose ancestors lived in a nation of compulsive record keepers, like Germany or Austria, have the best chance at uncovering some of those mysteries.

But Jews whose background stems from what became the Soviet Union (most North American Jews) or from North Africa (most Israelis, until the latest mass Russian influx) realistically shouldn't expect to learn more about their families after a dig in the limited Jewish archives than they have learned already from elderly Aunt Sarah. But if dig one must while in Jerusalem (and who can resist?), the city's archival collections might offer some insight into one's ancestral area.

Before starting out, people seeking their roots should resign themselves to looking on the venture as a test of their frustration level. The first stumbling block is that people who work in geneological archives speak a language most of us don't—and I don't mean Serbo-Croation. Their language is the terms of their trade. When they refer to *genealogy,* they mean specifically birth, marriage, and death records—and these weren't kept for the Jews of Eastern Europe. The rest of the information the archivists deal with is called *communal*—referring to places and communal life. So if your ancestor was a member of, say, a community board, tidbits about that person might be uncovered. And just because no one kept genealogical records in pre-Soviet Berezno on the Shlutz River where

---

Word of Warning

Local common courtesy is to offer guests and others who arrive at your door, such as workmen, something to drink. In Israel, that doesn't mean something alcoholic. Cold water is especially welcome on a hot day.

But if a stranger knocks on your door and asks for water, especially if you know he isn't renovating the empty flat below you, use your common sense. It's fine to pass a glass of water through your doorway, but don't let a stranger into your home.

Grandpa came from, discovering a communal record from Berezno—such as a local lumberman's receipt book—can provide its own thrill.

The *Guide to the Archives in Israel* tells in English what information is located where. It is available at the Jewish National and University Library Archives. It isn't easy for a novice to use, however. Below are places in Jerusalem where you can try to unearth the hidden past. Keep in mind that financial support for these archives is low on Israel's priority list and that helping the public isn't the employees' main job.

The **Central Archives for the History of the Jewish People,** crammed into a few tiny rooms on the Hebrew University Givat Ram campus, probably has the most extensive collection of documents concerning Diaspora Jews. The largest amount is from Germany and Italy, with a good deal from Poland and Russia.

Because people searching for information about their backgrounds seem to know that the Central Archives has an item from the twelfth century, they often have hopes that the archives will be able to trace their ancestors halfway back to Rabbi Akiva. As a staff person commented, "We don't keep papyrus and stone tablets here." The fact is, most of the documentation here goes back only to the seventeenth century. And most of the material is communal.

Something to remember before attempting to look through records in this or any similar institution is that, much to the surprise of many roots-diggers, English wasn't the language in which these records were kept. The Central Archives offers a little help by listing place names in its catalogs in Latin characters. Specialists in various languages work on different days. They may be able to spare some time to offer a translation, but there are no promises.

The Sprinzak Building, which houses the Central Archives is in a string of buildings to the right after entering the Hebrew University gates. Go downstairs and look for room 13. The facilities are available to anyone. Contact the archives by phone (02) 563-5716 or on the Web at http://sites.huji.ac.il/archives.

Next door to the Central Archives is the **Library Center for Research and Documentation of East-European Jewry**. For anyone with roots in Eastern Europe, it would seem that this is the place for information. But stop. The name on the door is misleading. What these facilities contain are books on post–World War II Eastern Europe. "Go next door," advises an employee to any roots seeker.

The **Department of Manuscripts and Archives** in the **Jewish National University Library** might be the best place for genealogical information, but people who aren't academics have no access. Should you have some clout, read on. The archives, below the library's entrance level, has *pinkassim* (registers) of births and deaths from a wide range of communities, including those in North Africa and the former Soviet Union. But there aren't a lot of them. The Russian pinkassim, for example, come from only 17 towns and villages.

This is a convenient place to look through the *Guide to the Archives in Israel*. If you find a listing of a document you would like to see, you must fill out an order slip and deposit it in the library's main room. Then you wait for the requested material to surface. The archives are for serious researchers (in the academic meaning of serious), and access is allowed only by a letter of recommendation. The Jewish National and University Library is the large building at the end of the walk that continues past the Sprinzak Building. The phone number is (02) 658-5055.

For tracking down information from Ottoman or British-Mandated Palestine, the **Archives of the Sephardi Community** at Rehov HaHavatzelet 12a is rich in communal material, I am told, but again poor in genealogy. When I was there, people in the office sent me next door to the Burial Society, where I was sent back to the Sephardi Archives.

The place to dig really isn't in Jerusalem but in Tel Aviv. You can use a computer to search family roots at **Beth Hatefutsoth (Diaspora Museum)** on the Tel Aviv University campus. Even if you don't give a hoot about digging, this museum is not to be missed. If you do care, this place is exciting for its possibilities.

For approximately $2 per 15-minute session, the facilities at the museum's **Douglas E. Goldman Jewish Genealogy Center** can be yours. You can access the database of Jewish family trees, receive information on yours, create a family tree, and register in the database. The center can also connect you with other resources for Jewish genealogy. You can connect with the center by e-mail: bhgnlgy@post.tau.ac.il, by Web site: www.bh.org.il, by fax: (03) 646-2134, or by mail: P.O. Box 39359, Tel Aviv 61-392, Israel. The center's telephone is (03) 646-2061 or (03) 646-2062. Dan buses 24, 25, 27, 45, and 49 can get you there.

Be a Sport

Moshe, a Jerusalemite born in ultra-Orthodox B'nai Brak, is an Orthodox rabbi. You might pigeonhole him as such on first sight, with his chest-long graying beard, his black suit, and black homburg precariously perched on his head. But one thing about him—out of the ordinary in most any circle—is that he is six feet, four inches tall. It turns out, this Orthodox rabbi is a dedicated swimmer and an expert scuba diver. Now there's a picture to demolish a stereotype—a six-foot-four bearded rabbi wearing a snorkel.

A generality seems to be that Jewish men are myopic, 120-pound weaklings who never leave the library. That generality doesn't stand up to facts. Israelis love sports. And they love the outdoors. They combine the two loves whenever they can. Those aren't tourists toe-to-toe on the Tel Aviv beaches. Israelis participate in sports and they adore watching them.

Soccer

The most consuming sports activity in Israel is soccer. Israelis, from the time they are kids, play soccer, watch soccer, talk soccer, scream soccer. Soccer (called football) is the national passion. Professional soccer lasts from October to May. During that time, the country is in a soccer frenzy. Soccer fans don't believe in repressing a single emotion that the game arouses in them—and the game arouses plenty of emotions.

All this used to take place in the heart of the city, when the only place for professional soccer was the YMCA soccer field across from the King David Hotel. In those days, people living in flats overlooking the field had every relative they never knew and friends of those relatives visiting them to watch the games free from their balconies. But Jerusalem keeps getting more sophisticated. Now the games take place in the big, professional Teddy Stadium (named for former mayor Teddy Kollek) in Malha, near the Jerusalem Canyon and the zoo.

Other Team Sports

Basketball is the next-favorite sport, both to watch and to play. The most prominent place for a pickup game is Liberty Bell Park, behind the Laromme Hotel. The Amateur Basketball League has teams with names like Menora Financial, Cafe Rimon, and Village Green—for their sponsors.

Baseball and softball leagues with the same or similar sponsors are at bat. The AACI has a team, as do Ziontours, Eyeworld, Archaeological Seminars, and Alexander's Insurance, among others, which makes for newspaper headlines such as "Mamma Mia Beats Dave's Hair."

A Little League has connection to the AACI. It's always looking for coaches and umpires. And there's also a women's league, at least in Ma'ale Adumim, if not in Jerusalem.

The British brought cricket to Israel, and immigrants from England, South Africa, and India keep it alive. At the moment, matches aren't played in Jerusalem. They take place, primarily, in the center of the country, and Jerusalemites join in. To track down the matches, check the Internet at www.cricket.org, and search for cricket in Israel.

331

Tennis

Tennis is booming in the Holy Land. Two reasons explain why: It's an inexpensive way of getting kids from poor neighborhoods off the streets, and it's a way for Israel to develop competitors for international athletic meets.

Jerusalem's **Israel Tennis Center**, for a brief time, was the largest tennis center in Israel when it debuted in 1983 with 18 all-weather courts. Newer locations near Tel Aviv have passed it by since then. The center is open seven days a week. Children under 16 play free from 2 to 4 and may borrow equipment. For information on hours and costs, contact the center, Rehov Elmaliach 5, (02) 679-2726.

Moadon HaOleh, at Rehov Alkalai 9, has a tennis court—but even the staff admits it doesn't have a good surface. It costs about $1.50 an hour. Make a reservation between 8 and 8 at (02) 563-3718.

Swimming

We've all seen posters touting the glories of Israeli beaches. But the truth is, for anyone living in Jerusalem, going for a swim—even in a pool, let alone a beach—is a pain. Nearby pools are expensive and often crowded. Getting to the Mediterranean beaches is a shlepp. Beaches really aren't so far away, but once you're ensconced in Jerusalem, it's amazing how quickly you pick up a landlocked mentality and how your concept of distance shrinks to Israeli size.

Tel Aviv beaches are the easiest to get to, what with the city only an hour away by bus and buses running one right after the other. But those beaches can be crowded and the water dirty. A black flag on the beach tells you if water is unfit for swimming. What's more, thieves love Tel Aviv beaches for their "easy pickin's." These aren't ordinary thieves but specialists—some at spiriting away your belongings on the sand, others at breaking into swimmers' cars. They might even have a union that prevents one specialist from encroaching on the area of another. Don't assume there aren't thieves at beaches. It's better to assume there are, so you take proper precautions.

A less-convenient beach, but worth exploring as a Tel Aviv alternative, is at **Ashkelon**, where the sand is great and the surf is gentle. By bus, the trip could last two hours.

As for swimming pools, we all know that Jerusalem is at the edge of the desert, that having enough water is a constant worry, and that water is expensive. But it seems as if some pools are filled with champagne for the high cost charged for dunking in them.

While some pools allow single-day admission on weekdays, most pools, private and some public, require memberships, which can be for a month or more. Several private pools are out of town, but accessible by bus. Some have tennis courts, separate children's pools, and times reserved for men or women only. The major hotels have pools that are also open to the public on a membership basis. The King David Hotel has a pool in an idyllic setting, but it is open only in summer.

Another particularly attractive pool is at the **Mount Zion Hotel**, Derech Hevron 17, (02) 567-9555. With a view of Old City Walls and the Hinnom Valley, who can swim? Again, this pool is open only in the summer. You can buy a membership for as few as ten entrances. The price comes to approximately $11.50 a day.

Year-round facilities operate at the **Renaissance Jerusalem Hotel** at Shderot Herzl and the Ruppin Bridge, (02) 659-9999. The hotel has a health club at no extra charge. Other pools are at the **Laromme Hotel**, Rehov Jabotinsky 3, (02) 675-6666, and the **Dan Pearl Hotel** at the foot of Rehov Yafo opposite the Old City, (02) 622-6600.

Less fancy, but available on a daily basis and open all year is the **Jerusalem Pool** with its Olympic-sized pool, on Rehov Emek Refaim 43, German Colony, (02) 563-2092. A pool popular with dedicated swimmers is at **Mitzpa Ramat Rahel**, (02) 670-2920, at the southern end of the Bus 7 run. Here is a good place to reminisce about history, for Ramat Rahel was the famous kibbutz that protected the city against Arab forces during the 1948 War of Independence.

Horseback Riding

For horseback riding across the desert or through the mountains, there are several options. I'm listing three, one east of the city, one west, and one in the city.

The **Arabian Horse Riding Club** is in the Kiryat Moshe neighborhood, (02) 651-3585. Instructor and owner Yehudah Alfi, who describes himself as "a son of Jerusalem," gave me instructions to reach his place: On Rehov Beit Hadfus, you turn left at the gas station and go down the road for about 300 meters. Bus 11 has the closest stop. The cost is less than $20 an hour. Trails are through the Jerusalem Forest to Beit Zeit. Alfi specializes in teaching riding to those who are blind, autistic, or have various physical problems.

The **Judean Desert Farm**, Kfar Adumim, (02) 535-4769 or 052-381-815, offers the romantic idea of horseback riding through the desert. The price for riding is approximately less than $14 for 50 minutes. Kfar Adumim, a lovely village overlooking Wadi Qelt and the Judean Desert, is worth a visit in itself. A problem is that bus service to Kfar Adumim is infrequent. To get to Jerusalem, car-less locals stand by the exit gate and tremp. But use your good judgment in assessing offers.

333

King David Ranch and School at Moshav Neve Ilan, (02) 534-0535 or 050-571-681, is 12 minutes west of the city by car. Bus transportation is easier here than to Kfar Adumim. The school, named for King David because he was a horse aficionado, offers lessons and trail rides that last from an hour to a full day. The manager says his profession is in his genes. He describes his Russian grandfather as a horse-riding bandit against the marauding Cossacks. An hour of riding here costs about $24.

Hiking

Thanks to the Society for the Protection of Nature in Israel, Jerusalem and all Israel is a hiker's paradise. Check the society's English brochure or call (02) 625-7682. Some SPNI walks last only a few hours, some for days. The SPNI brochure indicates difficulty level and which hikes have English-speaking guides. The SPNI also has a clutch of walking trips in Jerusalem itself. Some examples: A walk through the Rehavia neighborhood guided by famed architect-photographer David Kroyanker; a walk through the Musrara neighborhood or Talbia.

The Mosaic Hiking Club hikes around Jerusalem and also far afield. Again, check it out in the JP. New hiking groups constantly spring up.

Fitness Clubs

There is no need for falafel to make more of you. You can eat and laugh, even in Israel, because health clubs and gyms are at every corner, almost. Membership at hotel swimming pools usually gives you access to their health clubs and even the advice of their trainers.

A few other health clubs are the **Women's Club**, Rehov HaUman 9, Talpiot Industrial Area, (02) 679-5318; the **Health and Fitness Center**, Clal Building, Rehov Agrippas 42, (02) 623-3377, www.jump.co.il; **Great Shape/YMCA Exercise Studio**, which advertises such enticements as African funk, at Rehov King David 26, (02) 623-8436; and **Bodyline** (for women), Lev Yerushalayim Hotel, Rehov King George 18, (02) 623-2763.

Rappelling

If rappelling (called "snappeling" in Israel), which could be described as going down a mountain backward, is your sport, contact **Metzukei Dragot, the International Center for Adventure**, (02) 994-4342. The center offers group rappelling expeditions at Qumran, as well as rappelling lessons. While at Qumran, you always could imagine that yet another clay pot of scrolls is waiting to be discovered, perhaps by you.

Just because a genuine cliff isn't handy doesn't mean there isn't rappelling in Jerusalem. Occasionally you can see intrepid souls rappelling against Suleiman's Walls of the Old City between Jaffa Gate and the walk up to Mount Zion. **Tipusim** is a center for equipment and information for hikes and climbers. Contact the center by phone, (03) 602-2902, fax, (03) 602-2901, or e-mail, tipusim@outdoors.co.il.

Folk Dancing

Chapter 8: "Is There Life After Dark in Jerusalem" gives information on folk dancing at the International Cultural Center for Youth (ICCY) on Tuesday and at Hebrew Union College on Sunday night in summer. A few other dance locations and times are **Beit Ha'Am**, Rehov Bezalel 11, beginning 7 p.m. Sunday, and **Tel Or**, corner of Rehov HaHistadrut and King George, beginning 8 p.m. Monday. Almost every community center also has folk dancing. You can find a place to dance every night of the week, should you wish, except Friday.

Running

For a while I regularly hiked to the Western Wall on Saturday morning beginning around 5:30 a.m. Out there in the tingling air and glorious stillness, I felt that I owned Jerusalem. And just as I was reveling in my self-proclaimed status, along would come a jogger. The jogger probably was thinking the very same thing—wondering why I was intruding on his or her turf. Frankly, I don't understand the difference between running and jogging, except that jogging sounds as if it should be slower. At any rate, strenuous souls do one or the other, even in the Holy City.

Now and then the **Israeli Trail Blazers Running Club** gets together. When it does, members don their running shoes at 2 p.m. Friday in Sacher Park, near the underpass below Rehov Ruppin. Runs are four kilometers and more, and even people to whom four kilometers might as well be 40 are welcome to join in. The reward is peanut-butter sandwiches.

If you can't find Trail Blazers but would like to connect with them or any other sports activity, put a free notice in the Friday "In Jerusalem" section of the *Jerusalem Post* so like-minded people can contact you. If you find all that physical exercise exhausting, and you'd rather exercise your brain, read on.

Board and Card Games

Jerusalem Scrabble Club members get access to tables and competition with either English or Hebrew Scrabble boards. The Jerusalem Scrabble Club is one of the largest and most active anywhere. And I know of at least one marriage that came out of the game. For variations on mental gymnastics, bridge, backgammon, chess, poker, and a myriad of other such groups abound. Check with the AACI and "In Jerusalem."

Reel Life in Jerusalem

Movie theaters in Jerusalem have gone the way of the West: Most are multiplexes in shopping malls. The Jerusalem Canyon has six theaters, and Rav Chen has seven.

The Gil theaters in the Jerusalem Canyon are accessible by bus. Rav Chen in the Rav-Mecher Building, Rehov HaUman 19 in the Talpiot industrial zone, is a nightmare to reach, however. Even traveling by car, you need a bloodhound to lead the way. The building is behind buildings that front the street. By bus—oh, agony—from the 14 bus stop, you must hike along Rehov HaUman, a street built without the slightest thought to pedestrians or water drainage. And the worst part is that Rav Chen has better movies than the Gil.

Another commercial movie house is Smadar at Rehov Lloyd George 5, German Colony, which shows offbeat and intelligent American and English movies that don't attract the teen crowd. The Jerusalem Theater shows choice foreign movies, usually with English subtitles, but not always. The Cinematheque off Derch Hevron shows a constant string of revivals, some barely out of commercial movie theaters. The Israel Museum frequently shows movies as well.

In most Jerusalem theaters, you will be blasted by screaming commercials for 10 minutes before the movie starts. Then, when you are deeply engrossed in the action, wham, the movie stops. "Hafsakah" ("Break") flashes on the screen and the house lights pop on. You can run out for more popcorn. You can run to the lavatory. On both counts, you'll probably be late returning and have to stumble over people to get to your seat. Or you can just sit there and twiddle your thumbs while you wait.

When the movie ends, you might see the credits. But the house lights will have gone up, so the words will scroll by dimly, and the usher will stand impatiently trying to get you to leave.

In the canyons, you can't leave the theater the way you entered. You have to go out the door marked "Exit" in Hebrew. Then you'll find yourself in back halls with no hint of how to get back into the mall. You could wander around in the maze of corridors forever. Following other moviegoers doesn't always help, for they might be going to the parking lot. Film critic Pauline Kael's book of reviews was called *I Lost It at the Movies*. In Jerusalem, you can get lost at the movies.

22
LEAVING
JERUSALEM

L eave-taking can be a painful unwinding of all the connections formed during your time in the Golden City. They can bind your heart with velvet chains of love. But in the midst of what may be a confluence of emotions, practical matters must be attended to.

For those who have settled in, a good bit of activity will center on your flat. To get your last phone bill, you must call the phone company and ask for a *kriyat monay,* a meter reading. Verify the cost of each telephone unit, so if you make an additional call after you receive the reading, such as to Nesher, you can add it to the final count for your landlord. Cancel your international telephone service. Read your electric meter and calculate it against your last bill, figuring in, once again, the cost of each unit. In any event, the landlord probably will hold your deposit until the last bills have arrived. This could take a month or so, since billing is bimonthly. For clothes or other items you don't want to haul back home, remember such organizations as WIZO-Women's International Zionist Organization, at Rehov Hillel 11.

Don't forget to confirm your departure flight reservation at least 72 hours in advance and to set aside the cost of the trip to the airport. For about $3.50, should you choose, you can check your luggage the day before and receive a boarding pass at Rehov Kanfei Nesharim 8. Entrance is in the rear. If you drive, you'll have to pay for parking, although at a reduced rate for airport business. Finally, don't forget to call Nesher the day before your flight to set a time for your pickup.

You might wonder: Is leaving less painful if you take a flight in the early morning, so that you will struggle all night with your departure, then drive out of the city before it is awake? Or is it better to have one more day to feel close to Jerusalem and then depart for the airport at twilight, just as the sky takes on a glow? I've done both and I've also been on planes that took off at hours in between. I have no answer. I only know, at any time, leaving Jerusalem is a lonely matter.

Almost everyone who has spent time in Jerusalem has his or her own itinerary of places to see, even to touch, one last time. You could write a desperately held wish on a scrap of paper and wedge it into a crack, side by side with other notes of desperately held wishes, between the huge stones of the Western Wall. You could choose to adopt the practice of the Hasids when they or someone they know departs on a trip: Before you leave, give money to charity—perhaps to a street beggar or an organization that helps those in need.

And now, you might want to cling to the kaleidoscope that is Jerusalem. It fills your senses. Your eyes have caught the sight of flowers everywhere, cats as ubiquitous as flowers, dogs snoozing in quiet streets, pomegranate trees drooping with ripe fruit, preschool children carrying

338

tiny black violin cases, torches flickering from a nighttime Mount of Olives during a funeral, a camel on city streets, purple bougainvillea falling from balconies like waterfalls, sunsets.

Your ears have heard the sounds of Hebrew chanting from synagogues, the muezzin's amplified call during the middle of the night, the sudden scrape of shutters being pulled up or let down, sonic booms that rattle windows and bones, a flutist practicing at home, the Shabbat siren, the six beeps before radio news begins, church bells, "Ah-lo, ah-lo" before someone pushing a loaded cart almost runs you down, a crowing rooster. You have heard the thunderous silence on Yom Kippur and as the city comes to a halt to remember the 6 million and the men and women who fell so there could be an Israel.

Jerusalem's aromas, too, will be part of your memory: the perfumed air in spring; cumin and cardamom from mizrachi restaurants; the brittle smell during a *hamsin*—the hot, dry wind in the rainless summer; the musty odor of old buildings during the cold, rainy winter; the combination of hashish, urine, and spices in the narrow lanes of the Old City; rosemary when it blossoms in the fall.

Your taste buds, too, have stored their memories—of crispy falafel balls, stinging hot harreen, crunchy still-warm bread, tangy olives, and peppery Jerusalem kugel. So my parting gift to you is a recipe for Jerusalem kugel, your Jerusalem "madeleine" to taste and set you dreaming:

- 8 to 12 ounces of fine egg noodles or very thin spaghetti
- $1/2$ cup cooking oil
- $1/2$ cup sugar
- $1^1/2$ teaspoons black pepper
- 3 eggs, beaten

Cook noodles until al dente. Drain well. Heat oil and sugar in saucepan. Stir constantly until sugar becomes almost black. Add noodles, pepper, and eggs. Stir well. Taste. If not peppery enough, add more. Pour into greased casserole dish. Bake uncovered $1^1/2$ hours in oven at 350 degrees. (The kugel cooks beautifully on top of stove in a sirpella.) When firm, remove pan from oven, turn upside down and unmold. *B'tayavon*—Good appetite.

As you leave, remember: In Hebrew, there is no such word as "goodbye." You never can say goodbye to Jerusalem. Say instead "Shalom, Yerushalayim"—"Peace to Jerusalem." Jerusalem always will be with you.

Appendix

Taxi Companies
Gilo Taxis, (02) 676-5888
HaPalmach Taxis, (02) 679-3333
Malha Taxis, (02) 679-4111
Smadar Taxis, (02) 566-1235
Talpiot Taxis, (02) 671-1111
Zion Taxis, (02) 588-6398

Other Transportation
Egged, (02) 530-4704; outside Jerusalem, (03) 694-8888
Nesher, (02) 625-7227
Railway Station, Kikar Remez, Derech Hevron, (02) 673-3764

Tourist Information
Christian Information Center, Jaffa Gate, (02) 627-2692
Government Tourist Information Office, Ben-Gurion Airport and the corner of Rehov King George and Shatz
Israel Government Tourist Office, 800 Second Ave., New York, NY 10017, (800) 596-1199
Jerusalem Municipal Tourist Office, Building 3, Safra Square, Rehov Yafo, (02) 625-8844, Hotline: 106, 531-4600-4
Keren Kayemet (Jewish National Fund) forests, toll free: (177) 022-3484
Tourist Police, (02) 539-1254, (02) 539-1263.
Visa Department, Ministry of the Interior, Rehov Shlomzion HaMalka 1

Tours and Guides
Archaeological Seminars, Rehov Habad 34, (02) 627-3515; fax (02) 627-2660
Association of Guides, (03) 751-1132
Egged-Tlalim, Rehov Shlmozion HaMalcha 8, (02) 622-3399
Society for the Protection of Nature in Israel, Rehov Helena HaMalka 13, (02) 625-7682
United Tours, Rehov King David 23, (02) 625-2187
Zion Walking Tours, inside Jaffa Gate beside Bank Leumi, (02) 628-7866

341

Cultural and Community Associations
American Cultural Center, Rehov Keren HaYesod 9, (02) 625-5755
Association of Americans and Canadians in Israel, Jerusalem Region,
Rehov Mane 6 (or Rehov Pinsker 11), (02) 561-7151
British Council Library, Rehov Shimshon 3, (02) 673-6733
British Olim Society, Rehov Ben-Maimon 13, (02) 563-4822
Center for Conservative Judaism, Beit Knesset Moreshet Yisrael, Rehov
Agron 4, (02) 625-3539
International Cultural Center for Youth, Rehov Emek Refaim 12a,
(02) 563-3869
Israel Center, Rehov Strauss 10, (02) 538-4206

Tenant and Consumer Services
Habitat, Rehov Diskin 9A, (02) 561-1222; fax (02) 561-1176;
e-mail portico@netvision.net.il
Israel Consumer Council, Rehov Yafo 210, (02) 537-5466
She'al Rental Agency, Rehov King George 19,
(02) 625-4456; www.malin.co.il

Health Care Services
Magen David Adom (emergency health care), phone: 101
Shiloah-Harel Insurance, City Tower, Rehov Ben Yehuda 34, (02) 530-0400
Wolfson Medical Center, Rehov Diskin 9a, (02) 563-6265

Ulpanim
Beit HaAm, Rehov Bezalel 11, (02) 625-4156 or (02) 625-4157
Mitchell, Rehov Sokolow 15, (02) 563-7505 or (02) 563-3378
Mo'adon Ha'oleh, Rehov Alkalai 9, (02) 561-8235 or (02) 563-3718
YMHA (Beit HaNo'ar), Rehov Herzog 105, (02) 678-0513 or (02) 678-0442

Web Sites
www.city.net/countries/israel (geared to tourists)
www.huji.ac.il/jeru/jerusalem/html (features the Old City)
www./jpost.co.il *(Jerusalem Post)*

Celebrating 2000
Millennium Events and Tours

While the year 2000 arrives 3,760 years after the Jewish calendar's year 2000, Israel marks the millennium as the calendar milestone that it is and recognizes its religious significance to Christians. Israel's Celebrating 2000 events will be both secular and religious.

Selected Millennium Events

- **Israeli Chamber Orchestra.** In conjunction with the Upper Galilee Choir and the Mormonic Choir, the orchestra will perform Handel's "Messiah" at a variety of locations throughout the year. For more information contact the Israeli Chamber Orchestra, tel. (02) 696-1167.
- **Israel Museum.** Millennium events will include tours of the museum, dinner featuring the Feast of the Patriarchs, and live performances of liturgical music on Sunday evenings. Exhibits will focus on the Crusades, ancient maps of the Holy Land, Christian archaeology, and other topics. For further information contact Israel Museum Events Department, tel. (02) 670-8985; e-mail sarits@jmj.org.il.
- **Productions 2000.** The group will present plays designed to capture the essence of biblical feasts and seasons. For more information contact Conventions and Special Events, tel. (03) 566-6166; e-mail comtec@netvision.net.il.
- **Society for the Protection of Nature in Israel.** Events will include Jubillenium Marches and In the Footsteps of Jesus walking tours. For more information contact the Society for the Protection of Nature in Israel, tel. (03) 638-8672; e-mail tourism@spni.org.il.
- **Tower of David.** Millennium events will include a sound and light show telling the story of Jerusalem and *Chihuly: In the Light of Jerusalem*, an exhibit by American glass artist Dale Chihuly. For more information contact the Tower of David, tel. (02) 626-5333.

General Year 2000 Information
- **Bethlehem 2000**: tel. (02) 274-2224, fax (02) 274-2227; www.bethlehem2000.org
- **Israel Information Center**: 800/596-1199 (in the United States); www.goisrael.com
- **Israel 2000**: www.israel-2000.co.il
- **Jerusalem Tourist Information Centers**: tel. (02) 625-8844 (Safra Square), (02) 628-0382 (Jaffa Gate), or 106 (24-hour hotline); www.jerusalem.muni.il

Selected Tour Operators
- **Egged Tlalim**: Prearranged tours for individuals, including tours to Bethlehem. Tel. (02) 622-1999, fax (02) 622-1717; www.eggedtlalim.co.il
- **Net Tours**: Tours for Christian religious groups to all parts of Israel, plus Bethlehem and other areas under Palestinian control. Tel. (02) 628-2515, fax (02) 628-2415; www.netours.com
- **Peltours**: Prearranged tours, plus tailor-made tours for groups and individuals. Tel. (03) 517-0871, fax (03) 516-0060, e-mail pel@ peltours.co.il
- **Trans-Global Tours**: "Jesus 2000" group tours to Bethlehem, Jericho, and surrounding areas. Tel. (02) 570-0777, fax (02) 570-0786, e-mail tgt@netvision.net.il
- **United Tours**: Prearranged tours for individuals, including tours of Bethlehem. Tel. (02) 625-2187/8, fax (02) 625-5013; www .unitedtours.co.il

Glossary of Terms

afikomen: a small piece of matzo that is hidden by adults and hunted by children at the Passover seder

agarot: the smallest unit of Israeli money; 100 agarot equal one shekel

ahlan: Arabic; hello

Anglo-Saxim: plural of Anglo-Saxon

Anglo-Saxon: designation for those whose native language is English

Ashkenazim: Jews with roots in Northern and Eastern Europe

bab: Arabic; gate

baba ghanoug: eggplant with tahini

bar mitzvah: ceremony that ushers a Jewish boy into adult religious responsibilities

bas mitzvah: ceremony that ushers a Jewish girl into adult religious responsibilities

B.C.E.: Before the Common Era

beit knesset: a synagogue

bima: the raised platform in a synagogue from which services are conducted

bourekas: flaky pastry with cheese or spinach filling

brit milah: ritual circumcision, performed on eight-day-old baby boys

b'vaka-sha: please

canyon: a large covered shopping mall

C.E.: the Common Era

challah: braided Shabbat bread

chanukiah: a candelabra lit during Chanukah

cholent: a dish that usually includes beans, potatoes, other vegetables, and beef or chicken

chumetz: leaven, leavened bread

chuppah: the canopy over a couple taking marriage vows

etrog: a sort of overgrown lemon, used during Succot ceremonies

falash: stranger; a disparaging name for Ethiopian Jews in their homeland
fashla: Arabic; a bungle, a screw-up

garinei chamnia, garinim: sunflower seeds
givah: hill
gregar: a twirling noisemaker, used during Purim

hamantaschen: triangular pastry filled with fruit or poppy seeds and
served during Purim
hareef: hot sauce
Hasidim: members of observant Jewish sects, descendants of alternative Jewish groups that sprang up in Eastern Europe in the 1700s
hora: traditional Israeli circle dance

Kaddish: a prayer to glorify God, often said as part of graveside services
kashrut: dietary regulations that prohibit mixing meat and dairy products and eating pork and shellfish
katayif: Arabic; a special treat at the holiday of Ramadan; a pancake,
filled with almonds and fruit or honey and fried
kef: Arabic; fun
keffiyeh: Arabic; scarf worn on the head
kessim: Ethiopian Jewish priest
ketubah: marriage contract
kfar: village
khachkar: stone cross
kiddush: the blessing recited over wine before Jewish festive meals
kikar: open area or square
kippah: the round, closely fitting skull cap worn by observant Jewish
men
kippot: plural of kippah
kiryah: town or center
Kohanim: the Jewish priestly class
kubbeh: Kurdi dish of meat wrapped in bulgur or cracked wheat

latkes: potato pancakes
lavash: large, floppy bread often called Iraqi bread

makolet: grocery store
matzo: unleavened bread
me'moola'im: stuffed vegetables filled with spices and meat or rice
megillah: the Biblical Book of Esther

346

menorah: a candelabra with seven branches; a symbol of Israel

mezuzah: rectangular containers of Biblical verse, affixed to doorposts of homes in accordance with religious law

mezze: a tableful of hors d'oeuvres, salads, and appetizers

Midrash: a Jewish allegory of scripture

mikud: Israeli equivalent of an American postal code

mikvot: Jewish ritual baths

minyan: the quorum of 10 adult Jews required for communal worship

mitzvot: the 613 Hebrew commandments

mivtza: sale

mizrachi: eastern

mohel: the expert who performs Jewish ritual circumcisions

moufleta: a hot, thin pancake wrapped around butter and honey; a Moroccan Mimouna treat

muezzin: the Moslem crier who calls the hour of daily prayers

mushabek: a pastry eaten on the Moslem holiday of Awwal Muharram

nes: instant coffee

nudnik: from Yiddish; something or someone that annoys

parve: food suitable for either dairy or meat meals; fish is parve

payot: the side locks of hair worn by Jewish boys and men

ramah: a height

rayguh: "Hold it!"

rehov: street

sabra: native-born Israeli

sambusak: chickpea-filled pastry, an Iraqi-Kurdi specialty

Sephardi: Originally, Spanish Jews and their descendants after expulsion from Spain in 1492; currently, Jews from Moslem countries who also trace their families back to Spain. Also called Oriental or Afro-Asian Jews.

Shabbat: the Jewish Sabbath; sunset Friday through Saturday night (when three stars can be seen in the sky)

shammash: the "servant candle," used to light the others on the chanukiah during Chanukah

shderot: boulevard

shekel: basic unit of Israeli money; one shekel equals 100 agarot

sherut: a shared taxi or minivan for public transportation between cities

shishlik: grilled meats

shiva: the traditional seven days of mourning after a death

shkalim: plural of shekel
Shoah: the Hebrew word for the Holocaust
shofar: ram's horn, blown during religious services; an important part of High Holiday observance
shouk: the Jewish marketplace
shwarma: thin slices of grilled meat eaten in a pita
simha: a happy occasion, such as marriage
sirpella: a stove-top oven
slee-cha: "Excuse me"
slichot: special prayers for forgiveness, said during the period of introspection before Rosh HaShana and Yom Kippur
souk: shopping area in Jerusalem's Arab section
succah: A temporary dwelling, used during Succot, with sides of wood or canvas. The roof is a covering of palm branches.
sufganiot: sugar-dusted jelly doughnuts; a Chanukah treat

ta'am: taste, flavor
tahini: sesame seed sauce
tallit: a man's prayer shawl
tallitot: plural of tallit
Talmud: the summary of Jewish oral law
Tanach: an acronym for the Hebrew names of the Hebrew Bible, the Prophets, and the Writings, including Psalms and the Books of Ruth, Esther, and Daniel
tayelet: promenade
tfillin: phylacteries; two small leather boxes containing parchment inscribed with Hebrew scripture. Observant Jewish men strap one box to the forehead and the other to the left arm during morning prayers.
todah: "Thanks"
Torah: the five books of the Hebrew Bible from Genesis through Deuteronomy; also meaning everything in the Tanach
tremping: hitchhiking
tzedaka: charity
tzitzit: the fringed undergarments worn by observant Jewish men

ulpan: Hebrew language school
ulpanim: plural of ulpan

yeshiva: Jewish religious school
yeshivot: plural of yeshiva

Index

About the Author

Before moving to Jerusalem, Arlynn Nellhaus was a feature arts writer and jazz critic at the *Denver Post*. Her articles also appeared in the *New York Times*, *Playboy* magazine, and other publications. After her first visit to Israel, Nellhaus became the *Post*'s representative at an international meeting there of women journalists. She later resigned from the *Post* to move to Jerusalem.

Nellhaus now lives in a little house on a roof in central Jerusalem. From her home, she can see fireworks displayed from every corner of the city.